Science Fiction Story Index

second edition
1950-1979

Marilyn P. Fletcher

American Library Association
Chicago 1981

Library of Congress Cataloging in Publication Data

Fletcher, Marilyn P   1940–
    Science fiction story index, 1950–1979.

    "An expanded and updated version of the Science
fiction story index, 1950–1968 by Frederick Siemon."
    Bibliography: p.
    1. Science fiction––Bibliography. I. Siemon,
Frederick, 1935–   . Science fiction story index,
1950–1968. II. Title.
Z5917.S36S5 1979 [PN3433.5] 016.823'0876 80–28685
ISBN 0-8389-0320-7

Printed in the United States of America

Contents

The present work, *Science Fiction Story Index 1950-1979,* is an expanded and updated version of the *Science Fiction Story Index 1950-1968* by Frederick Siemon. Other anthologies published during the years 1950-1968 were located and indexed. Corrections to the original edition have been made in the cases of obvious errors, but not all of the original data was verified for this edition.

In the years since the first index was published, science fiction as a literary medium has come into a new era. College courses are now being offered in science fiction. Crossovers into other intellectual media have begun to emerge, as evidenced by anthologies linking science fiction with psychology, government, religion, history, and even sex. New authors and anthologers are contributing more and more to the literature.

Although the years covered by this index include only works published from 1950 through 1979, the actual time span for many of the stories is much greater. Many anthologies published in earlier years have been reprinted and thus were eligible for inclusion. Additionally, works listing the "best of" individual authors may include stories originally published before 1950. Anthologers are now reaching back for science fiction tales from such authors as Plato, Voltaire, Hawthorne, and Poe. Finally, some anthologies published recently are collections of stories from past years.

This index attempts to list, by title and author, the science fiction stories found in anthologies published from 1950 through 1979. Single and multiple author anthologies are included, as well as anthologies containing novellas. Some poems are indexed, if they appeared in anthologies along with stories. Prefaces, introductions, and other material not considered a "story" have not been included in this work. Those which did appear in the original edition have been omitted.

Joint editors of anthologies and joint authors of stories are indexed. Anthology titles may be found in the title index and under editor or compiler in the author index. Anthology in brackets follows the anthology titles. This was done to distinguish between collections which may often have the same title as one of the stories in the collection.

Pseudonyms are used in the index. The author's name is indexed as it appeared on the story (different forms of an author's name are standardized whenever possible). The author's real name follows the pseudonym in brackets so that the user may check under both names.

In the present edition, the only symbol used in the anthology listing is an asterisk (*), which indicates that the contents were indexed from sources other than the book itself. The primary source used for this purpose was the OCLC library system. Over 2000 libraries across the country, including the Library of Congress, contribute bibliographic information to the OCLC system. An author search was performed for most anthologers, enabling the editor to see listings of all works by the author. OCLC was helpful in the identification of anthologies to be indexed and, when contents notes appeared on the record, they were used for indexing purposes.

Indications of whether or not an anthology appears in *Books in Print* and various library catalogs have not been included in this edition. It was felt that information of such a nature becomes too quickly obsolete.

No index of this kind, which covers a large undefined universe of material, can ever be complete. Present plans are to issue supplements on a regular basis until the next cumulative edition. The supplements will include new anthologies, older anthologies located and indexed, and corrections to the index.

Special thanks to the following persons and their institutions for their assistance: Herb Bloom, Senior Editor, American Library Association; Claire Bensinger, University of New Mexico General Library; Faye Backie, Interlibrary Loan Librarian, University of Southwestern Louisiana Library; Bayouland Library System (Carla Keller, Director); Sam Bullard, Systems Analyst, University of Southwestern Louisiana Computing Center; student assistants, Lisa Pierce, Cindy Robertson, Carol Tingle, for indexing; George Hirezi and Eglee Zambrano-Rincon, for entering the data. Special thanks to my husband, Tom, and my daughters, Elizabeth and Catherine, for their help and patience during this project.

Acknowledgments

Sources

Sources Used to Identify Anthologies

Books in Print, 1976-1979.
Contento, William. *Index to Science Fiction Anthologies and Collections.* Boston: G.K. Hall, 1978.
Cumulative Book Index, 1950-1979.
Library Journal, 1976-1979.
Library of Congress, *Books: Subject,* 1968-1975.
New England Science Fiction Association, *NESFA* Index, 1973-1975.
Publishers' Weekly, 1976-1979.
Short Story Index, 1970-1977.

Sources Used for Pseudonyms

Ash, Brian. *Who's Who in Science Fiction.* New York: Taplinger, 1976.
Siemon, Frederick. *Science Fiction Story Index 1950-1968.* Chicago: American Library Association, 1971.

General Information Sources

Barron, Neil. *Anatomy of Wonder: Science Fiction.* New York: Bowker, 1976.

Science Fiction Story Index 1950-1979 is divided into three parts: a list of anthologies indexed, title index, and author index. Part 1 should be consulted for complete bibliographic information: author, editor, or compiler; title; place of publication; publisher; and date of publication. Part 2 anaylzes by title and Part 3 by author the stories in the anthologies.

The list of anthologies is alphabetically arranged, with each item identified by code number. The first two characters of the code are alphabetic; the remaining four are numeric. To locate the anthology in which a particular story appears, find the story in either the title or author index. This entry will be followed by a six-character code, which refers to the alphabetical list supplied in Part 1.

Symbols Used

Anthology section —	*	Indicates that the contents were taken from a source other than the book itself, usually the OCLC data base.
Title index and author index	[anthology]	Indicates that the title is an anthology
Author index —	[pseud. of ...]	The author's real name is found in the brackets.

Initial articles (a, an, and the) were omitted from titles to aid in computer sorting.

AC0200   Ackerman, Forrest J., ed. Best science fiction for 1973. New York, Ace Books, 1973.

AL0300   Aldiss, Brian W. The airs of earth. London, Faber and Faber, 1965.

AL0310   Aldiss, Brian W. All about Venus. Ed. by Brian W. Aldiss. Assisted by Harry Harrison. New York, Dell, 1968.

AL0360   Aldiss, Brian W. Best fantasy stories. London, Faber and Faber, 1962.

AL0365   Aldiss, Brian W. Best science fiction stories of Brian W. Aldiss. Rev. ed. London, Faber and Faber, 1971

AL0375   ★   Aldiss, Brian W. The book of Brian Aldiss. New York, DAW Books, 1972.

AL0390   Aldiss, Brian W. Brian Aldiss Omnibus 2. London, Sidgwick and Jackson, 1971.

AL0400   ★   Aldiss, Brian W. Decade, the 1940's. Ed. by Brian W. Aldiss and Harry Harrison, London, MacMillan, 1975.

AL0401   ★   Aldiss, Brian W. Decade, the 1950's. Ed. by Brian W. Aldiss and Harry Harrison, St. Martin's, 1978.

AL0402   ★   Aldiss, Brian W. Decade, the 1960's. Ed. by Brian W. Aldiss and Harry Harrison, London, MacMillan, 1977.

AL0405   Aldiss, Brian W. Evil earths. London, Weidenfeld and Nicolson, 1975.

AL0410   Aldiss, Brian W. Galactic empires, Vol. 1. Ed. by Brian W. Aldiss. New York, St. Martin's, 1976.

AL0411   Aldiss, Brian W. Galactic empires, Vol. 2. Ed. by Brian W. Aldiss. New York, St. Martin's, 1976.

AL0418   ★   Aldiss, Brian W. Intangibles Inc. London, Corgi, 1975.

AL0420   Aldiss, Brian W. Introducing science fiction. London, Faber, 1964.

AL0425   ★   Aldiss, Brian W. Introducing science fiction. London, Faber, 1964.

AL0435   Aldiss, Brian W. Last orders. London, Cape, 1977.

AL0437   ★   Aldiss, Brian W. Neanderthal planet. New York, Avon, 1969.

AL0440   ★   Aldiss, Brian W. New arrivals, old encounters. New York, Harper, 1979.

AL0450   Aldiss, Brian W. The Penguin science fiction omnibus. Middlesex, England, Penguin 1974.

AL0480   ★   Aldiss, Brian W. Space odysseys. Ed. by Brian W. Aldiss. Garden City, N.Y., Doubleday, 1976.

AL0510   Aldiss, Brian W. Space opera. Garden City, New York, Doubleday, 1975.

AL0540   Aldiss, Brian W. Who can replace man? New York, Harcourt, Brace, 1965.

AL0650		Allen, Dick. Looking Ahead. Ed. by Dick Allen and Lori Allen. New York, Hartcourt, Brace, 1975.
AL0665		Allen, Dick. Science fiction. New York, Harcourt, Brace, 1971.
AM0510		Amis, Kingsley, ed. Spectrum 1. Ed. by Kingsley Amis and Robert Conquest. New York, Harcourt, Brace, 1961
AM0511		Amis, Kingsley, ed. Spectrum 2. Ed. by Kingsley Amis and Robert Conquest. New York, Harcourt, Brace, 1962
AM0512		Amis, Kingsley, ed. Spectrum 3. Ed. by Kingsley Amis and Robert Conquest. New York, Harcourt, Brace, 1963
AM0513		Amis, Kingsley, ed. Spectrum 4. Ed. by Kingsley Amis and Robert Conquest. New York, Harcourt, Brace, 1965
AM0514		Amis, Kingsley, ed. Spectrum 5. Ed. by Kingsley Amis and Robert Conquest. New York, Harcourt, Brace, 1966
AN0101		Analog 1. Ed. by John W. Campbell. Garden City, N.Y., Doubleday, 1963
AN0102		Analog 2. Ed. by John W. Campbell. Garden City, N.Y., Doubleday, 1964
AN0103		Analog 3. Ed. by John W. Campbell. Garden City, N.Y., Doubleday, 1965
AN0104		Analog 4. Ed. by John W. Campbell. Garden City, N.Y., Doubleday, 1966
AN0105		Analog 5. Ed. by John W. Campbell. Garden City, N.Y., Doubleday, 1967
AN0106		Analog 6. Ed. by John W. Campbell. Garden City, N.Y., Doubleday, 1968
AN0107		Analog 7. Ed. by John W. Campbell. Garden City, N.Y., Doubleday, 1969
AN0108		Analog 8. Ed. by John W. Campbell. Garden City, N.Y., Doubleday, 1971
AN0109		Analog 9. Ed. by Ben Bova. Garden City, N. Y., Doubleday, 1973.
AN0140	★	Analog. Best of Analog. Ed. by Ben Bova. New York, Baronet, 1978.
AN0150	★	Prologue to Analog. Ed. by John W. Campbell. Garden City, N.Y., Doubleday, 1963
AN0160	★	Anderson, Poul. The best of Poul Anderson. New York, Pocket Books, 1976.
AN0165		Anderson, Poul. Beyond the beyond. London, Hodder, 1973.
AN0180	★	Anderson, Poul. The book of Poul Anderson. New York, DAW, 1975.
AN0190	★	Anderson, Poul. The day the sun stood still. Nashville, Nelson, 1972
AN0200		Anderson, Poul. Earthman's burden. New York, Gnome Press, 1957

AN0230		Anderson, Poul. Flandry of Terra. New York, Chilton, 1965.
AN0250		Anderson, Poul. Homeward and beyond. Garden City, N.Y., Doubleday, 1975.
AN0260		Anderson, Poul. The horn of time. New York, New American Library, 1968.
AN0280		Anderson, Poul. The many worlds of Poul Anderson. Edited by Roger Elwood. Radnor, Pa. Chilton, 1974.
AN0295	★	Anderson, Poul. The night face. Boston, Gregg, 1978.
AN0305	★	Anderson, Poul. The queen of air and darkness. Boston, Gregg, 1978.
AN0315		Anderson, Poul. Seven conquests. New York, Macmillan, 1969.
AN0325	★	Anderson, Poul. Strangers from earth. New York, Ballantine, 1961.
AN0335		Anderson, Poul. Time and stars. Garden City, N.Y., Doubleday, 1964.
AN0340		Anderson, Poul. Trader to the stars. New York, Doubleday, 1964.
AN0370		Anderson, Poul. Trouble twisters. Garden City, N.Y., Doubleday, 1966.
AN0400	★	Anderson, Poul. The war of two worlds. Boston, Gregg, 1978.
AS0070		Ashley, Mike. Souls in metal. New York, St. Martin's, 1977.
AS0170	★	Asimov, Isaac. Before the golden age. Garden City, N.Y., Doubleday, 1974.
AS0172		Asimov, Isaac. Asimov's choice: astronauts & androids. New York, Davis, 1977.
AS0173	★	Asimov, Isaac. Asimov's choice: black holes & bug-eyed monsters. New York, Davis, 1977.
AS0175		Asimov, Isaac. Asimov's choice: comets & computers. New York, Dale, 1978.
AS0180		Asimov, Isaac. Asimov's choice: dark stars & dragons. New York, Dale, 1978.
AS0200	★	Asimov, Isaac. The best of Isaac Asimov. Garden City, N.Y., Doubleday, 1974.
AS0230	★	Asimov, Isaac. The bicentennial man. Garden City, N.Y., Doubleday, 1976.
AS0250		Asimov, Isaac. Buy Jupiter. Garden City, N.Y., Doubleday, 1975.
AS0280		Asimov, Isaac. The early Asimov. Garden City, N.Y., Doubleday, 1972.
AS0310		Asimov, Isaac. Earth is room enough. New York, Doubleday, 1957.
AS0335	★	Asimov, Isaac. The far ends of time and earth. Garden City, N.Y., Doubleday, 1979.
AS0340		Asimov, Isaac. Fifty short science fiction tales. New York, Collier, 1963.

AS0370		Asimov, Isaac. The Hugo winners, vol. 1. Garden City, N.Y., Doubleday, 1962.
AS0400		Asimov, Isaac. The Hugo winners, vol. 2. Garden City, N.Y., Doubleday, 1971.
AS0401		Asimov, Isaac. The Hugo winners, vol. 3. Garden City, N.Y., Doubleday, 1977.
AS0430		Asimov, Isaac. I, Robot. Garden City, N.Y., Doubleday, 1950.
AS0440		Asimov, Isaac. Isaac Asimov's masters of science fiction. Ed. by George Scithers. New York, Davis, 1978.
AS0450	*	Asimov, Isaac. Isaac Asimov presents the great science fiction stories, v.1, 1939. Co-ed. by Martin H. Greenberg. New York, DAW, 1979.
AS0451	*	Asimov, Isaac. Isaac Asimov presents the great science fiction stories, v. 2, 1940. New York, DAW, 1979.
AS0452		Asimov, Isaac. Isaac Asimov presents the great sciencee fiction stories, v.3, 1941. Co-ed. by Martin H. Greenberg. New York, DAW, 1979.
AS0470		Asimov, Isaac. The Martian way. Garden City, N.Y., Doubleday, 1955.
AS0500		Asimov, Isaac. Nightfall. Garden City, N.Y., Doubleday, 1969.
AS0530		Asimov, Isaac. Nine tomorrows. Garden City, N.Y., Doubleday, 1959.
AS0555		Asimov, Isaac, ed. 100 great science fiction stories. Joint eds. Martin Harry Greenberg and Joseph D. Olander. Garden City, N.Y., Doubleday, 1978.
AS0558		Asimov, Isaac. Prisoners of the the stars, v.2. Garden City, N.Y., Doubleday, 1979.
AS0560		Asimov, Isaac. The rest of the robots. Garden City, N.Y., Doubleday, 1964.
AS0575	*	Asimov, Isaac, ed. The science fictional solar system. Co-ed. by Martin H. Greenberg and Charles G. Waugh. New York, Harper, 1979.
AS0585	*	Asimov, Isaac. The thirteen crimes of science fiction. Garden City, N.Y., Doubleday, 1979.
AS0590		Asimov, Isaac. Tomorrow's children. Garden City, N.Y., Doubleday, 1966.
AS0620		Asimov, Isaac. Triangle. Garden City, N.Y., Doubleday, 1965.
AS0645	*	Asimov, Isaac. Where do we go from here? Greenwich, Conn., Fawcett, 1971.
AS0650		Astounding-Analog reader, vol. 1. Ed. by Harry Harrison and Brian W. Aldiss. Garden City, N.Y., Doubleday, 1972.
AS0651		Astounding-Analog reader, vol. 2. Ed. by Harry Harrison and Brian W. Aldiss. Garden City, N.Y., Doubleday, 1973.

ASO700		Astounding science fiction anthology. Selected by John W. Campbell. New York, Simon & Schuster, 1951.
ASO750	*	Astounding; John W. Campbell memorial anthology. Ed. by Harry Harrison. New York, Random House, 1973.
BAO120		Ballard, J.G. The best short stories of J. G. Ballard. New York, Holt, 1978.
BAO150	*	Ballard, J.G. Chronopolis. New York, Putnam, 1971.
BAO185		Ballard, J.G. The drowned world and the wind from nowhere. Garden City, N.Y., Doubleday, 1965.
BAO205	*	Ballard, J.G. Low-flying aircraft. London, Cape, 1976.
BAO210	*	Ballard, J.G. Passport to eternity. New York, Berkley, 1976.
BAO215		Ballard, J.G. Terminal beach. New York, Berkley, 1964.
BAO235		Baxter, John. The Pacific book of science fiction. Sydney, Angus & Robertson, 1969.
BAO240	*	Baxter, John. The second Pacific book of science fiction. Sydney, Angus & Robertson, 1971.
BEO020		Bearne, C.G., ed. Vortex. London, MacGibbon & Kee, 1970.
BEO200		Best science fiction stories 1950. Ed. by Everett F. Bleiler and T.E. Dikty. New York, Fell, 1950.
BEO201		Best science fiction stories 1951. Ed. by Everett F. Bleiler and T.E. Dikty. New York, Fell, 1951.
BEO202		Best science fiction stories 1952. Ed. by Everett F. Bleiler and T.E. Dikty. New York, Fell, 1952.
BEO203		Best science fiction stories 1953. Ed. by Everett F. Bleiler and T.E. Dikty. New York, Fell, 1953.
BEO205		Best science fiction stories 1955. Ed. by T.E. Dikty. New York, Fell, 1955.
BEO206		Best science fiction stories 1956. Ed. by T.E. Dikty. New York, Fell, 1956.
BEO208		Best science fiction stories 1958. Ed. by T.E. Dikty. Chicago, Advent, 1958.
BEO290		Best science fiction stories of the year (1972). Ed. by Lester DelRey. New York, Dutton, 1972.
BEO291		Best science fiction stories of the year, second annual collection. Ed. by Lester DelRey. New York, Dutton, 1973.
BEO299		Best science fiction stories of the year, third annual collection. Ed. by Lester DelRey. New York, Dutton, 1974.
BEO300		Best science fiction stories of the year, fourth annual collection. Ed. by Lester DelRey. New York, Dutton, 1975.
BEO301		Best science fiction stories of the year, fifth annual collection. Ed. by Lester DelRey. New York, Dutton, 1976.

BE0302	Best science fiction stories of the year, sixth annual collection. Ed. by Gardner Dozois. New York, Dutton, 1977.
BE0303	Best science fiction stories of the year, seventh annual collection. Ed. by Gardner Dozois. New York, Dutton, 1978.
BE0400	Bester, Alfred. The light fantastic, v.1. New York, Berkley, 1976.
BE0500	Beyond this horizon: an anthology of science fact and fiction. Sunderland, Coelfrith, 1973.
BI0100 ★	Biggle, Lloyd. A galaxy of strangers. Garden City, N.Y., Doubleday, 1976.
BI0150 ★	Biggle, Lloyd. The metallic muse. Garden City, N.Y., Doubleday, 1972.
BI0200 ★	Biggle, Lloyd. The rule of the door. New York, Modern Literary Editions, 1967.
BL0100	Bleiler, Everett F., ed. Imagination unlimited. Ed. by Everett F. Bleiler and T.E. Dikty. New York, Strauss, 1952.
BL0120	Bleiler, Everett F., ed. Science fiction omnibus. Ed. by Everett F. Bleiler and T.E. Dikty. Garden City, N.Y., Garden City Books, 1952.
BL0125 ★	Blish, James. Anywhen. Garden City, N.Y., Doubleday, 1970.
BL0180 ★	Blish, James. Best science fiction stories 1973. London, Faber, 1973.
BL0190 ★	Blish, James. Cities in flight. Garden City, N.Y., Doubleday, 1970.
BL0200	Blish, James. Galactic cluster. New York, New American Library, 1959.
BL0210	Blish, James, ed. New dreams this morning. New York, Ballantine, 1966.
BL0240 ★	Bloch, Robert. The best of Robert Bloch. New York, Ballantine, 1977.
BL0250 ★	Bloch, Robert. Cold chills. Garden City, N.Y., Doubleday, 1977.
BO0100	Boardman, Tom V. Connoisseur's science fiction. Baltimore, Penguin, 1964.
BO0120	Boucher, Anthony. The compleat werewolf. New York, Simon & Schuster, 1969.
BO0150	Boucher, Anthony. A treasury of great science fiction, vol. 1. Garden City, N.Y., Doubleday, 1959.
BO0151	Boucher, Anthony. A treasury of great science fiction, vol. 2. Garden City, N.Y., Doubleday, 1959.
BO0200	Boulle, Pierre. Time out of mind. New York, Vanguard, 1966.
BO0210 ★	Bova, Ben. Aliens. New York, St. Martin's, 1978.
BO0240	Bova, Ben, ed. The Analog annual. New York, Pyramid, 1976.
BO0245 ★	Bova, Ben. Exiles. New York, St. Martin's, 1978.

B00250	*	Bova, Ben. Forward in time. New York, Walker, 1973.
B00260	*	Bova, Ben, ed. The many worlds of science fiction. New York, Dutton, 1971.
B00300		Boy's Life book of outer space stories. New York, Random House, 1969.
BR0070	*	Brackett, Leigh. The best of Leigh Brackett. New York, Doubleday, 1977.
BR0080		Brackett, Leigh. The best of Planet stories no. 1. New York, Ballantine, 1975.
BR0090		Brackett, Leigh. The book of Skaith. Garden City. N.Y., Doubleday, 1976.
BR0095		Brackett, Leigh. The halfling. New York, Ace, 1973.
BR0100		Bradbury, Ray. The day it rained forever. London, Hart-Davis, 1962.
BR0130		Bradbury, Ray. The golden apples of the sun. Garden City, N.Y., Doubleday, 1953.
BR0170		Bradbury, Ray. The illustrated man. New York, Doubleday, 1958.
BR0200		Bradbury, Ray. The machineries of joy. New York, Simon & Schuster, 1964.
BR0230		Bradbury, Ray. The Martian chronicles. Garden City, N.Y., Doubleday, 1958.
BR0270		Bradbury, Ray. A medicine for melancholy. Garden City, N.Y., Doubleday, 1958.
BR0280		Bradbury, Ray. The October country. New York, Ballantine, 1964.
BR0300		Bradbury, Ray. R is for rocket. New York, Bantam, 1966.
BR0330		Bradbury, Ray. S is for space. Garden City, N.Y., Doubleday, 1966.
BR0360	*	Bradbury, Ray. The small assassin. London, New English Library, 1970.
BR0380		Bradbury, Ray. Timeless stories for today and tomorrow. New York, Bantam, 1961.
BR0400		Bradbury, Ray. Twice twenty-two. Garden City, N.Y., Doubleday, 1966.
BR0415		Bradbury, Ray. The Vintage Bradbury. New York, Vintage, 1965.
BR0430		Brown, Frederic. Angels and spaceships. New York, Dutton, 1954.
BR0435		Brown, Fredric. The best of Fredric Brown. Ed. by Robert Bloch. New York, Ballantine, 1977.
BR0460		Brown, Frederic, ed. Science fiction carnival. Ed. by Frederic Brown and Mack Reynolds. Chicago, Shasta, 1953.
BR0490		Brown, Frederic. Space on my hands. Chicago, Shasta, 1951.
BR0520		Brown, J.G. From Frankenstein to Andromeda. London, Macmillan, 1966.

BRC550		Brunner, John. No future in it. Garden City, N.Y., Doubleday, 1964.
BU0070	*	Bulychev, Kirill. Half a life. New York, Macmillan, 1977.
BU0100		Burroughs, Edgar. At the earth's core. New York, Dover, 1963.
BU0120		Burroughs, Edgar. The land that time forgot. New York, Dover, 1963.
BU0140		Burroughs, Edgar. Pirates of Venus and Lost on Venus. New York, Dover, 1963.
BU0160		Burroughs, Edgar. A princess of Mars and A fighting man of Mars. New York, Dover, 1964.
BU0180		Burroughs, Edgar. Tales of three planets. New York, Canaveral Press, 1964.
BU0200		Burroughs, Edgar. Three Martian novels. New York, Dover, 1962.
CA0100		Campbell, John W., ed. Analog anthology. London, Dobson, 1965.
CA0105		Campbell, John W., ed. Astounding tales of space and time. New York, Berkley, 1969.
CA0110	*	Campbell, John W. The best of John W. Campbell. London, Sidgwick & Jackson, 1973.
CA0115		Campbell, John W. The black star passes. Reading, Pa., Fantasy Press, 1953.
CA0130		Campbell, John W. Cloak of Aesir. Westport, Conn., Hyperion, 1976.
CA0140		Campbell, John W. John W. Campbell anthology. Garden City, N.Y., Doubleday, 1973.
CA0150		Campbell, John W. The space beyond. New York, Pyramid, 1976.
CA0160		Campbell, John W. Who goes there? Chicago, Shasta, 1976.
CA0170	*	Carnell, John. Gateway to the stars. London, Museum Press, 1954.
CA0200	*	Carnell, John. Gateway to tomorrow. London, Museum Press, 1954.
CA0210	*	Carnell, John. Lambda I. Harmondsworth, Eng., Penguin, 1965.
CA0230		Carnell, John. No place like earth. London, Boardman, 1952.
CA0231		Carr, Terry, ed. The best science fiction of the year no. 1. New York, Ballantine, 1972.
CA0234	*	Carr, Terry, ed. The best science fiction of the year no. 4. New York, Ballantine, 1975.
CA0235		Carr, Terry, ed. The best science fiction of the year no. 5. New York, Ballantine, 1976.
CA0236		Carr, Terry, ed. The best science fiction of the year no. 6. New York, Holt, 1977.
CA0237		Carr, Terry, ed. The best science fiction of the year no. 7. New York, Ballantine, 1978.
CA0238	*	Carr, Terry, ed. The best science fiction of the year no. 8. New York, Ballantine, 1979.

CA0241		Carr, Terry, ed. The best science fiction novellas of the year no. 1. New York, Ballantine, 1979.
CA0255		Carr, Terry, ed. Classic science fiction. New York, Harper & Row, 1978.
CA0260	★	Carr, Terry, ed. Creatures from beyond. Nashville, Nelson, 1975.
CA0265	★	Carr, Terry, ed. Fellowship cf the stars. New York, Simon & Schuster, 1974.
CA0275	★	Carr, Terry, ed. The ides cf tomorrow. Boston, Little, Brown, 1976.
CA0277	★	Carr, Terry, ed. The infinite arena. Nashville, Nelson, 1977.
CA0280		Carr, Terry, ec. Into the unknown. Nashville, T. Nelson, 1973.
CA0310		Carr, Terry, ed. No mind of man. Ed. by Terry Carr, Richard A. Lupoff and Robert Silverberg. New York, Hawthorne, 1973.
CAC320	★	Carr, Terry, ed. Planets of wonder. Nashville, Nelson, 1976.
CA0340		Carr, Terry, ed. Science fiction for people who hate science ficticn. Garden City, N.Y., Doubleday, 1966.
CA0360	★	Carr, Terry, ed. This side cf infinity. New York. Ace, 1972.
CA0368		Carr, Terry. Universe 1. New York, Ace, 1971.
CA0370		Carr, Terry. Universe 3. New York, Random House, 1973.
CA0371		Carr, Terry. Universe 4. New York, Random House, 1974.
CA0372	★	Carr, Terry. Universe 5. New York, Random House, 1974.
CA0373	★	Carr, Terry. Universe 6. New York, Random House, 1976.
CA0374	★	Carr, Terry. Universe 7. Garden City, N.Y., Doubleday, 1977.
CA0375	★	Carr, Terry. Universe 8. Garden City, N.Y., Doubleday, 1978.
CA0376	★	Carr, Terry. Universe 9. Garden City, N.Y., Doubleday, 1979.
CAC420	★	Carr, Terry, comp. Worlds near and far. Nashville, Nelson, 1974.
CE0100		Cerf, Christopher, ed. The Vintage anthology of science fantasy. New York, Vintage, 1966.
CH0100	★	Cheetham, Anthony, comp. Bug-eyed monsters. London, Sidgwick & Jackson, 1972.
CL0100		Clareson, Thomas D. A spectrum of worlds. Garden City, N.Y., Dcubleday, 1972.
CL0110		Clarion II. Ed. by Robin Scott Wilson. New York, New American Library, 1972.
CL0130		Clarke, Arthur C. Across the sea of stars. New York, Harcourt, Brace, 1959.

CL0160   Clarke, Arthur C. An Arthur C. Clarke omnibus.
                London, Sidgwick & Jackson, 1965.
CL0190   Clarke, Arthus C. An Arthur C. Clarke second
                omnibus. London, Sidgwick & Jackson, 1968.
CL0200   *   Clarke, Arthur C. The best of Arthur C. Clarke.
                Ed. by Angus Wells. London, Sidgwick &
                Jackson, 1973.
CL0220   Clarke, Arthur C. Childhood's end. New York,
                Ballantine, 1953.
CL0250   Clarke, Arthur C. Expedition to earth. New York,
                Ballantine, 1965.
CL0280   Clarke, Arthur C. From the ocean, from the stars.
                New York, Harcourt, Brace, 1953.
CL0310   Clarke, Arthur C. The nine billion names of God.
                New York, Harcourt, Brace, 1967.
CL0340   Clarke, Arthur C. The other side of the sky.
                New York, Harcourt, Brace, 1967.
CL0370   Clarke, Arthur C. Prelude to Mars. New York,
                Harcourt, Brace, 1965.
CL0400   Clarke, Arthur C. Reach for tomorrow. New York,
                Ballantine, 1956.
CL0430   Clarke, Arthur C. Tales from the White Hart.
                New York, Harcourt, Brace, 1970.
CL0470   Clarke, Arthur C. Tales of ten worlds. New York,
                Harcourt, Brace, 1962.
CL0500   Clarke, Arthur C. Time probe. New York, Delacorte,
                1966.
CL0530   *   Clarke, Arthur C. The wind from the sun. London,
                Gollancz, 1972.
CL0590   Clem, Ralph, ed. The city: 2000 A.D. Ed. by Ralph
                Clem, Martin Harry Greenberg and Joseph Olander.
                Greenwich, Conn., Fawcett, 1976.
C00100   Conklin, Groff, ed. Another part of the galaxy.
                Greenwich, Conn., Fawcett, 1966.
C00130   Conklin, Groff, ed. Big book of science fiction.
                New York, Crown, 1950.
C00140   *   Conklin, Groff, ed. Elsewhere and elsewhen.
                New York, Berkley, 1968.
C00150   Conklin, Groff, ed. 5 unearthly visions. Green-
                wich, Conn., Fawcett, 1965.
C00160   Conklin, Groff, ed. Giants unleashed. New York,
                Grosset & Dunlap, 1965.
C00190   Conklin, Groff, ed. Great science fiction about
                doctors. Ed. by Groff Conklin and Noah D.
                Fabricant. New York, Collier, 1963.
C00220   Conklin, Groff, ed. Great stories of space travel.
                New York, Grosset & Dunlap, 1963.
C00250   Conklin, Groff, ed. Invaders of earth. New York,
                Vanguard, 1952.
C00280   Conklin, Groff, ed. Omnibus of science fiction.
                New York, Crown, 1952.

C00310	*	Conklin, Groff, ed. Operation future. New York, Permabooks, 1955.
C00340	*	Conklin, Groff, ed. Possible worlds of science fiction. New York, Vanguard, 1951.
C00370		Conklin, Groff, ed. Science fiction adventures in dimension. New York, Vanguard, 1951.
C00400		Conklin, Groff, ed. Science fiction adventures in mutation. New York, Vanguard, 1955.
C00430		Conklin, Groff, ed. Science fiction by scientists. New York, Collier, 1962.
C00460	*	Conklin, Groff, ed. Science fiction galaxy. New York, Permabooks, 1950.
C00490		Conklin, Groff, ed. Science fiction oddities. New York, Berkley, 1966.
C00520		Conklin, Groff, ed. Science fiction terror tales. New York, Gnome, 1955.
C00550		Conklin, Groff, ed. Science fiction thinking machines. New York, Vanguard, 1954.
C00560		Conklin, Groff, ed. Selections from science fiction thinking machines. New York, Bantam, 1964.
C00580		Conklin, Groff, ed. Seven come infinity. Greenwich, Conn., Fawcett, 1966.
C00610		Conklin, Groff, ed. Seven trips through time and space. Greenwich, Conn., Fawcett, 1968.
C00640	*	Conklin, Groff, ed. 17 x infinity. New York, Dell, 1963.
C00670	*	Conklin, Groff, ed. 6 great short novels of science fiction. New York, Dell, 1960.
C00700	*	Conklin, Groff, ed. Six great short science fiction novels. New York, Dell, 1960.
C00720		Conklin, Groff, ed. 13 above the night. New York, Dell, 1965.
C00730		Conklin, Groff, ed. A treasury of science fiction. New York, Berkley, 1965.
C00760		Conklin, Groff, ed. Twelve great classics of science fiction. Greenwich, Conn., Fawcett, 1963.
CR0100		Crispin, Edmund, ed. Best SF science fiction stories. London, Faber, 1962.
CR0101		Crispin, Edmund, ed. Best SF 2, science fiction stories. London, Faber, 1956.
CR0102		Crispin, Edmund, ed. Best SF 3, science fiction stories. London, Faber, 1958.
CR0103		Crispin, Edmund, ed. Best SF 4, science fiction stories. London, Faber, 1961.
CR0104		Crispin, Edmund, ed. Best SF 5, science fiction stories. London, Faber, 1963.
CR0170		Crispin, Edmund, ed. The stars and under. London, Faber, 1968.
CR0200		Crossen, Kendall F., ed. Adventures in tomorrow. New York, Greenberg, 1951.

CR0230   Crossen, Kendall F., ed. Future tense. New York, Greenberg, 1952.

CR0250   The crystal ship. Ed. by Robert Silverberg. Nashville, Nelson, 1976.

CU0070   Curtis, Richard, ed. Future tense. New York, Dell, 1968.

DA0140   Dann, Jack, ed. Faster than light. Ed. by Jack Dann and George Zebrowski. New York, Harper & Row, 1976.

DA0170   Dann, Jack, ed. Future power. Ed. by Jack Dann and Gardner Dozois. New York, Random House, 1976.

DA0180   Dann, Jack, ed. Immortal. New York, Harper & Row, 1978.

DA0200   Dann, Jack, ed. Wandering stars. New York, Harper & Row, 1974.

DA0230   Davenport, Basil, ed. Invisible men. New York, Ballantine, 1966.

DA0235   Davidson, Avram. The best of Avram Davidson. Ed. by Michael Kurland. Garden City, N.Y., Doubleday, 1979.

DA0238   Davidson, Avram. The Redward Edward papers. Garden City, N.Y., Doubleday, 1978.

DA0240   *   Davidson, Avram. Strange seas and shores. Garden City, N.Y., Doubleday, 1971.

DA0270   *   Davis, Richard, comp. Space 1. London, Abelard-Schuman, 1973.

DA0271   *   Davis, Richard, ed. Space 2. London, Abelard-Schuman, 1974.

DA0272   *   Davis, Richard, comp. Space 3. London, Abelard-Schuman, 1976.

DA0273   *   Davis, Richard, ed. Space 4. London, Abelard-Schuman, 1977.

DE0070   *   DeCamp, Lyon Sprague. The best of L. Sprague DeCamp. Garden City, N.Y., Doubleday, 1978.

DE0100   DeCamp, Lyon Sprague. Continent makers. New York, Twayne, 1953.

DE0130   DeCamp, Lyon Sprague. A gun for dinosaur. Garden City, N.Y., Doubleday, 1963.

DE0160   DeCamp, Lyon Sprague. Tales beyond time. Comp. by L. Sprague DeCamp and Catherine Crook DeCamp. New York, Lothrop, 1973.

DE0190   DeCamp, Lyon Sprague. 3000 years of fantasy and science fiction. New York, Lothrop, 1972.

DE0210   *   DeFord, Miriam Allen. Elsewhere, elsewhen, elsehow. New York, Walker, 1971.

DE0220   DeFord, Miriam Allen, ed. Space, time, and crime. New York, Paperback Library, 1968.

DE0250   DeGraeff, Allen, ed. Human and other beings. New York, Collier, 1963.

DE0255   Delany, Samuel R. Driftglass. Boston, Gregg, 1977.

DE0265	*	DelRey, Judy-Lynn, ed. Stellar 1. New York, Ballantine, 1974.
DE0267	*	DelRey, Judy-Lynn, ed. Stellar 3. New York, Ballantine, 1977.
DE0268		DelRey, Judy-Lynn, ed. Stellar 4. New York, Ballantine, 1978.
DE0275	*	DelRey, Judy-Lynn, ed. Stellar science fiction stories. New York, Ballantine, 1978.
DE0280	*	DelRey, Judy-Lynn, ed. Stellar short novels. New York, Ballantine, 1976.
DE0310		DelRey, Lester. The year after tomorrow. Philadelphia, Winston, 1954.
DE0340		Derleth, August, ed. Beachheads in space. London, Weidenfeld & Nicolson, 1952.
DE0370		Derleth, August, ed. Beyond time and space. New York, Pellegrini & Cudahy, 1950.
DE0400		Derleth, August, ed. Far boundaries. New York, Pellegrini & Cudahy, 1951.
DE0430	*	Derleth, August. Harrigan's file. Sauk City, Wisc., Arkham House, 1975.
DE0470		Derleth, August, ed. The outer reaches. New York, Pellegrini & Cudahy, 1951.
DE0500		Derleth, August, ed. Portals of tomorrow. New York, Rinehart, 1954.
DE0530		Derleth, August, ed. Time to come. New York, Farrar, 1954.
DE0560		Derleth, August, ed. Travelers by night. Sauk City, Wisc., Arkham House, 1967.
DE0590		Derleth, August, ed. Worlds of tomorrow. New York, Pellegrini & Cudahy, 1953.
DI0070	*	Dick, Philip K. The best of Philip K. Dick. Ed. by John Brunner. New York, Ballantine, 1977.
DI0075		Dick, Philip K. The book of Philip K. Dick. New York, DAW, 1973.
DI0078	*	Dick, Philip K. A Philip K. Dick omnibus. London, Sidgwick & Jackson, 1973.
DI0083	*	Dick, Philip K. The preserving machine. London, Gollancz, 1971.
DI0085		Dick, Philip K. The variable man. New York, Ace Books, 1957.
DI0100	*	Dickson, Gordon R. Ancient, my enemy. Garden City, N.Y., Doubleday, 1974.
DI0110	*	Dickson, Gordon R. Combat SF. Garden City, N.Y., Doubleday, 1975.
DI0115		Dickson, Gordon R. Gordon R. Dickson's sf best. Ed. by James R. Frenkel. New York, Dell, 1978.
DI0125		Dickson, Gordon R. The star road. Garden City, N.Y., Doubleday, 1973.
DI0130		Dikty, T.E. Every boy's book of outer space stories. New York, Fell, 1960.
DI0160		Dikty, T.E. Five tales from tomorrow. Greenwich, Conn., Fawcett, 1957.

DIO190		Dikty, T.E. Great science fiction stories about Mars. New York, Fell, 1966.
DIO210	*	Disch, Thomas M. The early science fiction stories of Thomas M. Disch. Boston, Gregg, 1977.
DIO215	*	Disch, Thomas M. Getting into death. New York, Knopf, 1976.
DIO220		Dikty, T.E. Great science fiction stories about the moon. New York, Fell, 1967.
DIO230		Disch, Thomas M. New constellations. New York, Harper, 1976.
DIO240		Disch, Thomas M., ed. The new improved sun. New York, Harper & Row, 1975.
DIO250		Disch, Thomas M., ed. The ruins of earth. New York, G.P. Putnam's, 1971.
DIO260	*	Disch, Thomas M. Strangeness. Co-ed. by Charles Naylor. New York, Scribner, 1977.
DIO280		Dixon, Richard, ed. Destination: Amaltheia. Moscow, n.d.
DO0100		Doherty, G.D., ed. Aspects of science fiction. London, Murray, 1959.
DO0130		Doherty, G.D., ed. Second orbit. London, Murray, 1965.
DO0160		Doyle, Arthur Conan. The poison belt. New York, Macmillan, 1964.
DO0165		Dozois, Gardner R., ed. Another world. Chicago, Follett, 1977.
DO0170	*	Dozois, Gardner R., comp. A day in the life. New York, Harper & Row, 1971.
DO0230		Dozois, Gardner R. The visible man. New York, Berkley, 1977.
DU0100		Dutt, Violet L. Soviet science fiction. New York, Collier, 1962.
EA0100	*	Earley, George W., comp. Encounters with aliens. Los Angeles, Sherbourne, 1968.
ED0150		Edelstein, Scott, ed. Future pastimes. Nashville, Aurora, 1977.
EF0150	*	Effinger, George Alec. Chains of the sea. Nashville, Nelson, 1973.
EF0180	*	Effinger, George Alec. Dirty tricks. Garden City, N.Y., Doubleday, 1978.
EF0210	*	Effinger, George Alec. Irrational numbers. Garden City, N.Y., Doubleday, 1976.
EF0240	*	Effinger, George Alec. Mixed feelings. New York, Harper, 1974.
EL0120		Elam, Richard M. Science fiction stories. New York, Pocket Books, 1964.
EL0140		Elam, Richard M., Jr. Teen-age science fiction stories. New York, Lantern, 1952.
EL0160		Elam, Richard M., Jr. Teen-age super science stories. New York, Lantern, 1957.

ELO180		Elder, Joseph, ed. Eros in orbit. New York, Trident, 1973.
ELO200		Elder, Joseph, ed. The farthest reaches. New York, Trident, 1968.
ELO220		Ellison, Harlan, ed. Again, dangerous visions. Garden City, N.Y., Doubleday, 1972.
ELO240	*	Ellison, Harlan. Alone against tomorrow. New York, MacMillan, 1971.
ELO260		Ellison, Harlan. Approaching oblivion. New York, New American Library, 1976.
ELO280		Ellison, Harlan. The beast that shouted love at the heart of the world. Bergenfield, N.J., New American Library, 1969.
ELO300		Ellison, Harlan, ed. Dangerous visions. Garden City, N.J., Doubleday, 1967.
ELO320	*	Ellison, Harlan. Deathbird stories. New York, Harper, 1975.
ELO340		Ellison, Harlan. Ellison wonderland. New York, New American Library, 1974.
ELO360		Ellison, Harlan. From the land of fear. New York, Belmont, 1967.
ELO380		Ellison, Harlan. I have no mouth and I must scream. New York, Pyramid, 1967.
ELO400	*	Ellison, Harlan. Love ain't nothing but sex misspelled. New York, Trident, 1968.
ELO420	*	Ellison, Harlan. Paingod and other delusions. New York, Pyramid, 1975.
ELO440	*	Ellison, Harlan. Partners in wonder. New York, Walker, 1971.
ELO460		Elwood, Roger, ed. Adrift in space. Minneapolis, Lerner, 1974.
ELO480	*	Ellison, Harlan. Alien earth. New York, Macfadden-Bartell, 1969.
ELO500		Elwood, Roger, ed. And walk now gently through the fire. Philadelphia, Chilton, 1972.
ELO520		Elwood, Roger, ed. Androids, time machines and blue giraffes. Comp. by Roger Elwood and Vic Ghidalia. Chicago, Follett, 1973.
ELO540		Elwood, Roger, ed. Children of infinity. New York, F. Watts, 1973.
ELO560		Elwood, Roger, ed. Chronicles of a comer. Atlanta, John Knox, 1974.
ELO580		Elwood, Roger, ed. Continuum 1. New York, Putnam's, 1974.
ELO581		Elwood, Roger, ed. Continuum 2. New York, Berkley, 1974.
ELO582		Elwood, Roger, ed. Continuum 3. New York, Berkley, 1974.
ELO640	*	Elwood, Roger, ed. Crisis. Nashville, Nelson, 1974.
ELO660		Elwood, Roger, ed. Dystopian visions. Englewood Cliffs, N.J., Prentice-Hall, 1975.

ELC680	*	Elwood, Roger, comp. The far side of time. New York, Dodd, Mead, 1974.
ELO700	*	Elwood, Roger, comp. Flame tree planet. St. Louis, Concordia, 1973.
ELO720		Elwood, Roger, ed. Future city. New York, Trident, 1973.
ELO740	*	Elwood, Roger, comp. Future kin. Garden City, N.Y., Doubleday, 1974.
ELO760	*	Elwood, Roger, ed. The gifts of Asti. Chicago, Follett, 1975.
ELO780		Elwood, Roger, ed. The graduated robot. Minneapolis, Lerner, 1974.
ELO800		Elwood, Roger, ed. Journey to another star. Minneapolis, Lerner, 1974.
ELO820		Elwood, Roger, ed. The killer plants. Minneapolis, Lerner, 1974.
ELO840	*	Elwood, Roger, ed. The learning maze. New York, J. Messner, 1974.
ELO860	*	Elwood, Roger, ec. Long night of waiting. Nashville, Aurora, 1974.
ELO880		Elwood, Roger, ed. The mind angel. Minneapolis, Lerner, 1974.
ELO900		Elwood, Roger, ed. The missing world. Minneapolis, Lerner, 1974.
ELO920	*	Elwood, Roger, comp. More science fiction tales. Chicago, Rand McNally, 1974.
ELO940		Elwood, Roger. The new minc. New York, Macmillan, 1973.
ELO960		Elwood, Roger. Night of the sphinx. Minneapolis, Lerner, 1974.
ELO980	*	Elwood, Roger, comp. Omega. New York, Walker, 1973.
EL1000	*	Elwood, Roger, ed. The other side of tomorrow. New York, Random House, 1973.
EL1020	*	Elwood, Roger, ed. Saving worlds. Ed. by Roger Elwood and Virginia Kidd. Garden City, N.Y., Doubleday, 1973.
EL1040	*	Elwood, Roger, ed. Science fiction tales. Chicago, Rand McNally, 1973.
EL1060		Elwood, Roger, ed. Showcase. New York, Harper & Row, 1973.
EL1080	*	Elwood, Roger, comp. Signs and wonders. Old Tappan, N.J., Revell, 1972.
EL1100	*	Elwood, Roger, ed. Six science fiction plays. New York, Washington Square, 1976.
EL1120		Elwood, Roger, ed. Strange gods. New York, Pocket Books, 1974.
EL1140	*	Elwood, Roger, comp. Survival from infinity. New York, Watts, 1974.
EL1160		Elwood, Roger, ed. Ten tomorrows. Greenwich, Conn., Fawcett, 1973.

EL1180	*	Elwood, Roger, ed. Tomorrow. New York, M. Evans, 1975.
EL1200		Elwood, Roger, ed. Tomorrow's alternatives. New York, Macmillan, 1973.
EL1220		Elwood, Roger, ed. The tunnel. Minneapolis, Lerner, 1974.
EL1240		Elwood, Roger, ed. Visions of tomorrow. New York, Pocket Books, 1976.
EN0070	*	Engdahl, Sylvia, ed. Anywhere, anywhen. New York, Atheneum, 1976.
EN0100	*	Engdahl, Sylvia. Universe ahead. Ed. by Sylvia Engdahl and Rick Roberson. New York, Atheneum, 1975.
EV0100		Evans, I.O., ed. Science fiction through the ages 1. London, Panther, 1966.
FA0215		Fantastic Universe omnibus. Ed. by Hans Stefan Santesson. Englewood Cliffs, N.J., Prentice-Hall, 1960.
FA0240		Farmer, Philip Jose. The books of Philip Jose Farmer. New York, DAW, 1973.
FA0245	*	Farmer, Philip Jose. Down in the black gang. Garden City, N.Y., Doubleday, 1971.
FA0270		Fast, Howard. Time and the riddle. Pasadena, Ward Ritchie, 1975.
FA0300		Fast, Howard. A touch of infinity. New York, Morrow, 1973.
FE0110		Ferman, Edward L., ed. The best from fantasy and science fiction. Garden City, N.Y., Doubleday, 1974.
FE0170		Ferman, Edward L., ed. Final stage. New York, Charterhouse, 1974.
FE0200		Ferman, Edward L., ed. Once and future tales. Delphi, 1968.
FE0230		Ferman, Edward L., ed. Twenty years of the Magazine of Fantasy and science fiction. Ed. by Edward L. Ferman and Robert P. Mills. New York, Putnam's, 1970.
FE0260		Ferman, Joseph, ed. No limits. New York, Ballantine, 1964.
FI0070		Finney, Jack. The third level. New York, Rinehart, 1957.
FI0090	*	Fitzgerald, Gregory, ed. The late great future. Ed. by Gregory Fitzgerald and John Dillon. Greenwich, Conn., Fawcett, 1976.
FI0095	*	Fitzgerald, Gregory, ed. Neutron stars. Greenwich, Conn., Fawcett, 1977.
FI0100		Five fates. Garden City, N.Y., Doubleday, 1970.
FO0100	*	Ford, G. Science and sorcery. Los Angeles, Fantasy, 1953.
FO0130	*	Four futures. New York, Hawthorn, 1971.
FR0070		Franklin, H. Bruce. Future perfect. Rev. ed. New York, Oxford Univ. Press, 1978.

CODE		ANTHOLOGY

FR0100   The frozen planet. New York, Macfadden-Bartell, 1966.

FU0100   Furman, A.L., ed. Teen-age outer space stories. New York, Lantern, 1962.

FU0130   Furman, A.L., ed. Teen-age space adventures. New York, Lantern, 1972.

FU0160   * Futurelove. New York, Bobbs-Merrill, 1977.

GA0100   Galaxy. The best from Galaxy, vol. 4. New York, Award Books, 1976.

GA0140   Galaxy. The [1st] Galaxy reader of science fiction. Ed. by H.L. Gold. New York, Crown, 1954.

GA0141   Galaxy. The 2nd Galaxy reader of science fiction. Ed. by H.L. Gold. Garden City, N.Y., Doubleday, 1958.

GA0142   Galaxy. The 3rd Galaxy reader of science fiction. Ed. by H.L. Gold. Garden City, N.Y., Doubleday, 1958.

GA0143   Galaxy. The 4th Galaxy reader of science fiction. Ed. by H.L. Gold. Garden City, N.Y., Doubleday, 1959.

GA0144   Galaxy. The 5th Galaxy reader of science fiction. Ed. by H.L. Gold. Garden City, N.Y., Doubleday, 1961.

GA0145   Galaxy. The 6th Galaxy reader of science fiction. Ed. by H.L. Gold. Garden City, N.Y., Doubleday, 1962.

GA0146   Galaxy. The 7th Galaxy reader of science fiction. Ed. by Frederik Pohl. Garden City, N.Y., Doubleday, 1964.

GA0147   Galaxy. The 8th Galaxy reader of science fiction. Ed. by Frederik Pohl. Garcen City, N.Y., Doubleday, 1965.

GA0148   Galaxy. The 9th Galaxy reader of science fiction. Ed. by Frederik Pohl. Garcen City, N.Y., Doubleday, 1966.

GA0149   Galaxy. The 10th Galaxy reader of science fiction. Doubleday, 1967.

GA0190   Galaxy. Bodyguard. Garden City, N.Y., Doubleday, 1960.

GA0220   Galaxy. Five Galaxy short novels. Ed. by H.L. Gold. Garden City, N.Y., Doubleday, 1958.

GA0250   Galaxy. Mind partner. Ed. by H.L. Gold. New York, Pocket Books, 1961.

GA0280   Galaxy. The six fingers of time. New York, Macfadden-Bartell, 1965.

GA0310   Galaxy. Time waits for Winthrop. Ed. by Frederik Pohl. Garden City, N.Y., Doubleday, 1962.

GA0340   Galaxy. The world that couldn't be. Garden City, New York, Doubleday, 1959.

GA0370   * Gallant, Joseph, ed. Stories of scientific imagination. New York, Oxford, 1954.

GE0150		Gerrold, David, ed. Alternities. Assoc. ed., Stephen Goldin. New York, Dell, 1974.
GE0180		Gerrold, David, ed. Science fiction emphasis. Co-ed. by Stephen Goldin. New York, Ballantine, 1974.
GI0100		Ginsburg, Mirra. Last door to Aiya. New York, S.G. Phillips, 1968.
GI0130		Ginsburg, Mirra. The ultimate threshold. New York, Holt, 1970.
G00030		Goldin, Stephen, ed. The alien condition. New York, Ballantine, 1973.
G00070	★	Goulart, Ron. Broke down engine. New York, Macmillan, 1971.
G00100		Goulart, Ron. Nutzenbolts and more trouble with machines. New York, Macmillan, 1975.
G00130		Goulart, Ron. Odd job 101. New York, Scribner, 1975.
G00150	★	Goulart, Ron. What's become of screwloose. New York, Scribner, 1971.
GR0040	★	Grant, Charles L., ed. Shadows. Garden City, N.Y., Doubleday, 1978.
GR0070		Graven images. Ed. by Edward L. Ferman and Barry N. Malzberg. Nashville, Nelson, 1977.
GR0100		Greenberg, Martin Harry, ed. All about the future. New York, Gnome, 1955.
GR0130		Greenberg, Martin Harry, ed. Coming attractions. New York, Gnome, 1952.
GR0140		Greenberg, Martin Harry. Dawn of time. Co-ed. by Joseph D. Olander and Robert Silverberg. New York, Elsevier, 1979.
GR0160		Greenberg, Martin Harry, ed. Five science fiction novels. New York, Gnome, 1951.
GR0190		Greenberg, Martin Harry, ed. Journey to infinity. New York, Gnome, 1951.
GR0220		Greenberg, Martin Harry, ed. Men against the stars. New York, Gnome, 1950.
GR0250		Greenberg, Martin Harry. Political science fiction. Englewood Cliffs, N.J., Prentice-Hall, 1974.
GR0280		Greenberg, Martin Harry. The robot and the man. New York, Gnome, 1953.
GR0300	★	Greenberg, Martin Harry, ed. Tomorrow, inc. Ed. by Martin Harry Greenberg and Joseph D. Olander. New York, Taplinger, 1976.
GR0310		Greenberg, Martin Harry, ed. Travelers of space. New York, Gnome, 1951.
GU0100	★	Gunn, James, ed. Breaking point. New York, Walker, 1972.
GU0130		Gunn, James, ed. The road to science fiction. v.1: From Gilgamesh to Wells. New York, New American Library, 1977.
GU0160		Gunn, James. Some dreams are nightmares. New York, Scribner, 1974.

HA0100		Haining, Peter, ed. The future makers. New York, Belmont, 1974.
HA0130	*	Haldeman, Joe W., comp. Cosmic laughter. New York, Holt, 1974.
HA0137		Haldeman, Joe W. Infinite dreams. New York, St. Martin's, 1978.
HA0145		Haldeman, Joe W., ed. Study war no more. New York, St. Martin's, 1977.
HA0155	*	Hamilton, Edmond. The best of Edmond Hamilton. Ed. by Leigh Brackett. New York, Ballantine, 1977.
HA0158		Harding, Lee, ed. The alterec I. New York, Berkley, 1978.
HA0159		Harding, Lee, ed. Rooms of paradise. New York, St. Martin's, 1979.
HA0160		Harrison, Harry, ed. Best SF: 1967. Ed. by Harry Harrison and Brian W. Aldiss. New York, Berkley, 1968.
HA0161		Harrison, Harry, ed. Best SF: 1968. Ed. by Harry Harrison and Brian W. Aldiss. New York, Putnam's, 1969.
HA0162		Harrison, Harry, ed. Best SF: 1969. Ed. by Harry Harrison and Brian W. Aldiss. New York, Putnam's, 1970.
HA0163		Harrison, Harry, ed. Best SF: 1970. Ed. by Harry Harrison and Brian W. Aldiss. New York, Putnam's, 1971.
HA0164		Harrison, Harry, ed. Best SF: 1971. Ed. by Harry Harrison and Brian W. Aldiss. New York, Putnam's, 1972.
HA0165		Harrison, Harry, ed. Best SF: 1972. Ed. by Harry Harrison and Brian W. Aldiss. New York, Putnam's, 1973.
HA0166		Harrison, Harry, ed. Best SF: 1973. Ed. by Harry Harrison and Brian W. Aldiss. New York, Putnam's, 1974.
HA0167		Harrison, Harry, ed. Best SF: 1974. Ed. by Harry Harrison and Brian W. Aldiss. Indianapolis, Bobbs-Merrill, 1975.
HA0168		Harrison, Harry, ed. Best SF 75. Ninth annual. Ed. by Harry Harrison and Brian W. Aldiss. Indianapolis, Bobbs-Merrill, 1976.
HE0170		Healy, Raymond J., ed. Selections from Adventures in time and space. Co-ed. by J. Francis McComas. New York, Bantam, 1966.
HA0200		Harrison, Harry, ed. Four for the future. London, Macdonald, 1969.
HA0210	*	Harrison, Harry, ed. The light fantastic. New York, Scribner, 1971.
HA0220	*	Harrison, Harry. One step from earth. New York, Macmillan, 1970.
HA0232		Harrison, Harry, ed. SF: authors' choice 2. New York, Berkley, 1970.

HA0233	*	Harrison, Harry, ed. SF: authors' choice 3. New York, Putnam's, 1971.
HA0234		Harrison, Harry, ed. SF: authors' choice 4. New York, Putnam's, 1974.
HA0250	*	Harrison, Harry, comp. Science fiction novellas. Ed. by Harry Harrison and Willis E. McNelly. New York, Scribner, 1975.
HA0260		Harrison, Harry, ed. A science fiction reader. Ed. by Harry Harrison and Carol Pugner. New York, Scribner, 1973.
HA0270	*	Harrison, Harry. Two tales and eight tomorrows. New York, Bantam, 1968.
HA0290		Harrison, Harry, ed. Worlds of wonder. New York, Doubleday, 1969.
HA0300		Harrison, Harry, ed. The year 2000. Garden City, N.Y., Doubleday, 1970.
HE0100		Healy, Raymond J., ed. Famous science fiction stories. Ed. by Raymond J. Healy and Francis McComas. New York, Modern Library, 1957.
HE0130		Healy, Raymond J., ed. New tales of space and time. New York, H. Holt, 1951.
HE0160		Healy, Raymond J., ed. 9 tales of space and time. New York, H. Holt, 1954.
HE0190		Heinlein, Robert A. Assignment in eternity. New York, New American Library, 1953.
HE0220		Heinlein, Robert A. The best of Robert Heinlein. London, Sidgwick & Jackson, 1973.
HE0250		Heinlein, Robert A. The green hills of earth. Chicago, Shasta, 1951.
HE0280		Heinlein, Robert A. The man who sold the moon. New York, New American Library, 1963.
HE0310		Heinlein, Robert A. The menace from earth. New York, New American Library, 1959.
HE0340		Heinlein, Robert A. The past through tomorrow. New York, Putnam's, 1967.
HE0350	*	Heinlein, Robert A. The Robert Heinlein omnibus. London, Science Fiction Book Club, 1958.
HE0370		Heinlein, Robert A. Three by Heinlein. Garden City, N.Y., Doubleday, 1965.
HE0400		Heinlein, Robert A. Tomorrow the stars. Garden City, N.Y., Doubleday, 1952.
HE0420	*	Heinlein, Robert A. The unpleasant profession of Jonathan Hoag. Hicksville, N.Y., Gnome, 1959.
HE0430		Heinlein, Robert A. Waldo and Magic, Inc. New York, Pyramid, 1963.
HE0440		Heinlein, Robert A. The worlds of Robert A. Heinlein. New York, Ace, 1966.
HE0460		Henderson, Zenna. The anything box. Garden City, N.Y., Doubleday, 1965.
HE0490		Henderson, Zenna. The people: no different flesh. Garden City, N.Y., Doubleday, 1967.

HE0520		Herbert, Frank. The book of Frank Herbert. New DAW, 1973.
H00100		Hollister, Bernard C. Another tomorrow. Dayton, Pflaum, 1974.
H00110		Hoskins, Robert, ed. The future now: saving tomorrow. Greenwich, Conn., Fawcett, 1977.
H00119		Hoskins, Robert, ed. Wondermakers. New York, Fawcett, 1972.
H00120	*	Hoskins, Robert, comp. Wondermakers 2. Greenwich, Conn., Fawcett, 1974.
H00130		Howard, Ivan, ed. Escape to earth. New York, Belmont, 1963.
H00160		Howard, Robert E. The coming of Conan. New York, Gnome, 1953.
H00190		Howard, Robert E. Conan, the adventurer. By Robert E. Howard and L.S. DeCamp. New York, Lancer, 1966.
H00220		Howard, Robert E. Conan, the warrior. By Robert E. Howard and L.S. DeCamp. New York, Lancer, 1967.
H00250		Howard, Robert E. Tales of Conan. By Robert E. Howard and L.S. DeCamp. New York, Gnome, 1955.
H00280		Howard, Robert E. Wolfshead. Ed. by Glenn Lord. New York, Lancer, 1968.
H00310		Hoyle, Fred. Element 79. New York, New American Library, 1967.
IF0100		If magazine. The If reader of science fiction. Ed. by Frederik Pohl. Garden City, N.Y., Doubleday, 1966.
IF0102		If magazine. Fredrick Pohl's the second If reader of science fiction. by Frederik Pohl. New York, Ace, 1968.
IF0170		If magazine. The best from If, v.2. New York, Award Books, 1974.
IN0100	*	The inner landscape. London, Allison & Busby, 1969.
JA0070		Jakes, John. The best of John Jakes. Ed. by Martin Harry Greenberg and Joseph D. Olander. New York, DAW, 1977.
JA0100		Jameson, Malcolm. Bullard of the space patrol. Ed. by Andre Norton. Cleveland, World, 1951.
JA0130		Janifer, Laurence M., ed. Master's choice. New York, Simon & Schuster, 1966.
J00150		Jones, Langdon, ed. The new S.F. London, Hutchinson, 1969.
KA0070	*	Katz, Harvey A., ed. Introductory psychology through science fiction. Co-eds: Patrica Warwick and Martin Harry Greenberg. Chicago, Rand McNally, 1974.
KE0070	*	Keller, David Henry. The Folsom flint. Sauk City, Wisc., Arkham House, 1969.

KE0100   Kelley, Leo P. Themes in science fiction. New
                York, McGraw-Hill, 1972.

KI0070   *   Kidd, Virginia, ed. Millenial women. New York,
                Delacorte, 1978.

KN0070   *   Knight, Damon. The best of Damon Knight. New
                York, Pocket Books, 1976.

KN0100   Knight, Damon, ed. Best stories from Orbit, vol.
                1-10. New York, Berkley, 1975.

KN0120   Knight, Damon, ed. Beyond tomorrow. New York,
                Harper & Row, 1965.

KN0130   Knight, Damon, ed. A century of great short science
                fiction novels. New York, Delacorte, 1964.

KN0160   Knight, Damon, ed. A century of science fiction.
                New York, Simon & Schuster, 1962.

KN0190   Knight, Damon, ed. Cities of wonder. Garden City,
                N.Y., Doubleday, 1966.

KN0220   Knight, Damon, ed. The dark side. Garden City,
                N.Y., Doubleday, 1965.

KN0250   Knight, Damon, ed. Far out. New York, Simon &
                Schuster, 1961.

KN0280   Knight, Damon, ed. One hundred years of science
                fiction. New York, Simon & Schuster, 1968.

KN0301   Knight, Damon, ed. Orbit 1. New York, Putnam's,
                1966.

KN0302   Knight, Damon, ed. Orbit 2. New York, Putnam's,
                1967.

KN0303   Knight, Damon, ed. Orbit 3. New York, Putnam's,
                1968.

KN0304   Knight, Damon, ed. Orbit 4. New York, Putnam's,
                1968.

KN0305   Knight, Damon, ed. Orbit 5. New York, Putnam's,
                1969.

KN0306   Knight, Damon, ed. Orbit 6. New York, Berkley,
                1970.

KN0307   Knight, Damon, ed. Orbit 7. New York, Putnam's,
                1970.

KN0308   Knight, Damon, ed. Orbit 8. New York, Putnam's,
                1970.

KN0309   Knight, Damon, ed. Orbit 9. New York, Berkley,
                1971.

KN0310   Knight, Damon, ed. Orbit 10. New York, Putnam's,
                1972.

KN0311   *   Knight, Damon, ed. Orbit 11. New York, Putnam's,
                1972.

KN0312   Knight, Damon, ed. Orbit 12. New York, Putnam's,
                1973.

KN0313   Knight, Damon, ed. Orbit 13. New York, Berkley,
                1974.

KN0314   *   Knight, Damon, ed. Orbit 14. New York, Harper &
                Row, 1974.

KN0315   Knight, Damon, ed. Orbit 15. New York, Harper &
                Row, 1974.

CODE		ANTHOLOGY

KNO316		Knight, Damon, ed. Orbit 16. New York, Harper & Row, 1975.
KNO317		Knight, Damon, ed. Orbit 17. New York, Harper & Row, 1975.
KNO318		Knight, Damon, ed. Orbit 18. New York, Harper & Row, 1976.
KNO319		Knight, Damon, ed. Orbit 19. New York, Harper & Row, 1977.
KNO320		Knight, Damon, ed. Orbit 20. New York, Harper & Row, 1978.
KNO450		Knight, Damon, ed. Perchance to dream. Garden City, N.Y., Doubleday, 1972.
KNO460	*	Knight, Damon, ed. A pocketful of stars. Garden City, N.Y., Doubleday, 1971.
KNO470		Knight, Damon, ed. Rule golden. New York, Avon, 1979.
KNO480		Knight, Damon. Science fiction argosy. New York, Simon & Schuster, 1972.
KNO490		Knight, Damon, ed. A shocking thing. New York, Pocket Books, 1974.
KNO510		Knight, Damon. Three novels. Garden City, N.Y., Doubleday, 1967.
KNO540		Knight, Damon, ed. Tomorrow and tomorrow. New York, Simon & Schuster, 1973.
KNO570		Knight, Damon, ed. Tomorrow x 4. Greenwich, Conn., Fawcett, 1964.
KNO580	*	Knight, Damon, ed. Toward infinity. New York, Simon & Schuster, 1968.
KNO600		Knight, Damon. Turning on. Garden City, N.Y., Doubleday, 1966.
KNO630		Knight, Damon. Worlds to come. New York, Harper & Row, 1967.
KO0070	*	Kornbluth, Cyril M. The best of C.M. Kornbluth. New York, Taplinger, 1977.
KO0100		Kornbluth, Cyril M. The explorers. New York, Ballantine, 1963.
KO0130		Kornbluth, Cyril M. A mile beyond the moon. Garden City, N.Y., Doubleday, 1958.
KO0160		Kornbluth, Mary, ed. Science fiction showcase. Garden City, N.Y., Doubleday, 1959.
KU0100		Kuebler, Harold W., ed. The treasury of science fiction classics. Garden City, N.Y., Hanover, 1954.
KU0130		Kuttner, Henry. Ahead of time. New York, Ballantine, 1953.
LA0070	*	Laumer, Keith. Bolo: the annals of the Dinochrome brigade. New York, Berkley, 1976.
LA0100		Laumer, Keith. Galactic diplomat. Garden City, N.Y., Doubleday, 1965.
LA0130	*	Laumer, Keith. Nine by Laumer. Garden City, N.Y., Doubleday, 1967.

LA0160   Laurance, Alice. Cassandra rising. Garden City,
                N.Y., Doubleday, 1978.

LE0100   *   Leiber, Fritz, Jr. The best of Fritz Leiber.
                New York, Ballantine, 1974.

LE0130   Leinster, Murray, ed. Great stories of science
                fiction. New York, Random House, 1951.

LE0160   Leinster, Murray, ed. Sidewise in time. Chicago,
                Shasta, 1950.

LE0200   *   Lem, Stanislaw. Mortal engines. New York,
                Seabury, 1977.

LE0220   Lesser, Milton, ed. Looking forward. New York,
                Beechhurst, 1953.

LO0050   *   London, Jack. Selected science fiction & fantasy
                stories. Lakemont, Ga., Fictioneer Books,
                1978.

LO0080   Long, Frank Belknap. Night fear. New York,
                Zebra, 1979.

LO0100   Loughlin, Richard L. Journeys in science fiction.
                Ed. by Richard L. Loughlin and Lilian M. Popp.
                New York, Globe, 1961.

MA0191   Magazine of Fantasy and Science Fiction. Best
                from Fantasy and Science Fiction, 1st series.
                Ed. by Anthony Boucher and J. Francis McComas.
                Boston, Little Brown, 1952.

MA0192   Magazine of Fantasy and Science Fiction. Best
                from Fantasy and Science Fiction, 2d series.
                Ed. by Anthony Boucher and J. Francis McComas.
                Boston, Little Brown, 1953.

MA0193   Magazine of Fantasy and Science Fiction. Best
                from Fantasy and Science Fiction, 3d series.
                Ed. by Anthony Boucher and J. Francis McComas.
                Garden City, N.Y., Doubleday, 1954.

MA0194   Magazine of Fantasy and Science Fiction. Best
                from Fantasy and Science Fiction, 4th series.
                Ed. by Anthony Boucher. Garden City, N.Y.,
                Doubleday, 1955.

MA0195   Magazine of Fantasy and Science Fiction. Best
                from Fantasy and Science Fiction, 5th series.
                Ed. by Anthony Boucher. Garden City, N.Y.,
                Doubleday, 1956.

MA0196   Magazine of Fantasy and Science Fiction. Best
                from Fantasy and Science Fiction, 6th series.
                Ed. by Anthony Boucher. Garden City, N.Y.,
                Doubleday, 1957.

MA0197   Magazine of Fantasy and Science Fiction. Best
                from Fantasy and Science Fiction, 7th series.
                Ed. by Anthony Boucher. Garden City, N.Y.,
                Doubleday, 1958.

MA0198   Magazine of Fantasy and Science Fiction. Best
                from Fantasy and Science Fiction, 8th series.
                Ed. by Anthony Boucher. Garden City, N.Y.,
                Doubleday, 1959.

CODE	ANTHOLOGY
MA0199	Magazine of Fantasy and Science Fiction. Best from Fantasy and Science Fiction, 9th series. Ed. by Robert P. Mills. Garden City, N.Y., Doubleday, 1960.
MA0200	Magazine of Fantasy and Science Fiction. Best from Fantasy and Science Fiction, 10th series. Ed. by Robert P. Mills. Garden City, N.Y., Doubleday, 1961.
MA0201	Magazine of Fantasy and Science Fiction. Best from Fantasy and Science Fiction, 11th series. Ed. by Robert P. Mills. Garden City, N.Y., Doubleday, 1962.
MA0202	Magazine of Fantasy and Science Fiction. Best from Fantasy and Science Fiction, 12th series. Ed. by Avram Davidson. Garden City, N.Y., Doubleday, 1963.
MA0203	Magazine of Fantasy and Science Fiction. Best from Fantasy and Science Fiction, 13th series. Ed. by Avram Davidson. Garden City, N.Y., Doubleday, 1964.
MA0204	Magazine of Fantasy and Science Fiction. Best from Fantasy and Science Fiction, 14th series. Ed. by Avram Davidson. Garden City, N.Y., Doubleday, 1965.
MA0205	Magazine of Fantasy and Science Fiction. Best from Fantasy and Science Fiction, 15th series. Ed. by Edward L. Ferman. Garden City, N.Y., Doubleday, 1966.
MA0206	Magazine of Fantasy and Science Fiction. Best from Fantasy and Science Fiction, 16th series. Ed. by Edward L. Ferman. Garden City, N.Y., Doubleday, 1967.
MA0208	Magazine of Fantasy and Science Fiction. Best from Fantasy and Science Fiction, 18th series. Ed. by Edward L. Ferman. New York, Ace, 1972.
MA0210	Magazine of Fantasy and Science Fiction. Best from Fantasy and Science Fiction, 20th series. Ed. by Edward L. Ferman. Garden City, N.Y., Doubleday, 1973.
MA0330	Magazine of Fantasy and Science Fiction. A decade of Fantasy and Science Fiction. Ed. by Robert P. Mills. Garden City, N.Y., Doubleday, 1958.
MA0360	Magidoff, Robert, comp. Russian science fiction. New York, New York Univ. Press, 1964.
MA0390	Magidoff, Robert, comp. Russian science fiction, 1968. New York, New York Univ. Press, 1968.
MA0420	Magidoff, Robert, ed. Russian science fiction 1969. New York, New York Univ. Press, 1969.
MA0450	Malec, Alexander. Extrapolation. Garden City, N.Y., Doubleday, 1967.

MA0455   Malzberg, Barry N. Down here in the dream
                    quarter. Garden City, N.Y., Doubleday, 1976.
MA0460   Malzberg, Barry N. The many worlds of Barry
                    Malzberg. New York, Popular Library, 1975.
MA0465   *   Malzberg, Barry N., ed. Neglected visions. Co-ed.
                    by Martin Harry Greenberg and Joseph D. Olancer.
                    Garden City, N.Y., Doubleday, 1979.
MA0470   Mansfield, Roger. The starlit corridor. New York,
                    Pergamon, 1967.
MA0475   Margulies, Leo, ed. Get out of my sky. Greenwich,
                    Conn., Fawcett, 1960.
MA0480   Margulies, Leo, ed. The giant anthology of science
                    fiction. New York, Merlin, 1954.
MA0485   Margulies, Leo, ed. Three times infinity.
                    Greenwich, Conn., Fawcett, 1958.
MA0490   Margulies, Leo, ed. The unexpected. New York,
                    Pyramid, 1961.
MA0520   *   Martin, George R.R., ed. New voices in science
                    fiction. New York, Macmillan, 1977.
MA0521   *   Martin, George R.R., ed. New voices 2. New York,
                    Jove, 1979.
MA0540   Martin, George R.R. Songs of stars and shadows.
                    New York, Pocket Books, 1977.
MA0550   *   Mason, Carol, ed. Anthropology through science
                    fiction. Ed. by Carol Mason, Martin Harry
                    Greenberg, and Patricia Warrick. New York,
                    St. Martin's, 1974.
MA0600   Maurois, Andre. The weighers of souls and The
                    earth dwellers. New York, Macmillan, 1963.
MC0150   McCaffrey, Anne, comp. Alchemy and academe.
                    Garden City, N.Y., Doubleday, 1970.
MC0165   McCaffrey, Anne. Get off the unicorn. New York,
                    Ballantine, 1977.
MC0180   McComas, J. Francis, ed. Special wonder. New York,
                    Random House, 1970.
MC0280   *   McHargue, Georgess, comp. Hot & cold running
                    cities. New York, Holt, 1974.
MC0285   *   McIntyre, Vonda N. Fireflood. Boston, Houghton-
                    Mifflin, 1979.
MC0300   *   McKenna, Richard. Casey Agonistes. New York,
                    Harper & Row, 1973.
MC0400   McNelly, Willis E. Above the human landscape.
                    Ed. by Willis E. McNelly and Leon E. Stover.
                    Pacific Palisades, Calif., Goodyear, 1972.
ME0150   *   Menville, Douglas, comp. Ancestral voices. Ed.
                    by Douglas Menville and R. Reginald. New York,
                    Arno, 1975.
ME0170   Merril, Judith. The best of Judith Merril.
                    New York, Warner, 1976.
ME0201   Merril, Judith, ed. SF, the best of the best,
                    part 2. London, Mayflower, 1970.

ME0230		Merril, Judith, ed. Beyond human ken. New York, Random House, 1952.
ME0260		Merril, Judith. Beyond the barriers of space and time. New York, Random House, 1954.
ME0290		Merril, Judith, ed. England swings SF. Garden City, N.Y., Doublecay, 1968.
ME0310		Merril, Judith, ed. Human? New York, Lion Books, 1954.
ME0356		Merril, Judith, ed. S-F 56. New York, Gnome, 1956.
ME0357		Merril, Judith, ed. S-F 57. New York, Gnome, 1957.
ME0358		Merril, Judith, ed. S-F 58. New York, Gnome, 1958.
ME0359		Merril, Judith, ed. S-F 59. New York, Gnome, 1959.
ME0360		Merril, Judith, ed. The 5th annual of the year's best S-F. New York, Simon & Schuster, 1960.
ME0361		Merril, Judith, ed. The 6th annual of the year's best S-F. New York, Simon & Schuster, 1961.
ME0362		Merril, Judith, ed. The 7th annual of the year's best S-F. New York, Simon & Schuster, 1962.
ME0363		Merril, Judith, ed. The 8th annual of the year's best S-F. New York, Simon & Schuster, 1963.
ME0364		Merril, Judith, ed. The 9th annual of the year's best S-F. New York, Simon & Schuster, 1964.
ME0365		Merril, Judith, ed. The 10th annual of the year's best S-F. New York, Delacorte, 1965.
ME0366		Merril, Judith, ed. The 11th annual of the year's best S-F. New York, Delacorte, 1966.
ME0367		Merril, Judith, ed. SF 12. New York, Delacorte, 1968.
MI0150		Mills, Robert P., ed. The worlds of science fiction. New York, Dial, 1963.
MI0180		Milstead, John W., ed. Sociology through science fiction. New York, St. Martin's, 1974.
MI0250		Mitchell, Edward Page. The crystal man. Ed. by Sam Moskowitz. Garden City, N.Y., Doubleday, 1973.
MO0100	*	Mohs, Mayo, comp. Other worlds, other gods. Garden City, N.Y., Doubleday, 1971.
MO0150		The molecular cafe. Translated from the Russian. Moscow, MIR, 1968.
MO0155	*	Monteleone, Thomas F., ed. The arts and beyond. Garden City, N.Y., Doubleday, 1977.
MO0162		Moorcock, Michael, ed. The best sf stories from New Worlds 2. New York, Berkley, 1968.
MO0163		Moorcock, Michael, ed. The best sf stories from New Worlds 3. New York, Berkley, 1970.
MO0164		Moorcock, Michael, ed. The best sf stories from New Worlds 4. New York, Berkley, 1971.

MO0165		Moorcock, Michael, ed. The best sf stories from New Worlds 5. New York, Berkley, 1971.
MO0166		Moorcock, Michael, ed. The best sf stories from New Worlds 6. New York, Berkley, 1970.
MO0170		Moore, C.L. The best of C.L. Moore. Ed. by Lester delRey. Garden City, N.Y., Doubleday, 1975.
MO0200		Moskowitz, Sam, ed. The coming of the robots. New York, Collier, 1963.
MO0230		Moskowitz, Sam, ed. Doorway into time. New York, Macfadden & Bartell, 1965.
MO0260		Moskowitz, Sam, ed. Editors choice in science fiction. New York, McBride, 1954.
MO0290		Moskowitz, Sam, ed. Exploring other worlds. New York, Collier, 1963.
MO0320		Moskowitz, Sam, ed. Masterpieces of science fiction. New York, World, 1966.
MO0350		Moskowitz, Sam, ed. Modern masterpieces of science fiction. New York, World, 1965.
MO0365		Moskowitz, Sam, ed. Science fiction by gaslight. Westport, Conn., Hyperion, 1974.
MO0370		Moskowitz, Sam. A sense of wonder. London, Sidgwick & Jackson, 1967.
MO0380		Moskowitz, Sam, ed. Strange signposts. Ed. by Sam Moskowitz and Roger Elwood. New York, Holt, 1966.
MOC400	★	Moskowitz, Sam, comp. Under the moons of Mars. New York, Holt, 1970.
MO0410	★	Moskowitz, Sam, ed. When women rule. New York, Walker, 1972.
MU0100	★	Murry, Colin. The custodian. London, Gollancz, 1976.
NE0151		Nebula award stories 1. Ed. by Damon Knight. Garden City, N.Y., Doubleday, 1966.
NE0152		Nebula award stories 2. Ed. by Brian W. Aldiss and Harry Harrison. Garden City, N.Y., Doubleday, 1967.
NE0153		Nebula award stories 3. Ed. by Roger Zelazny. Garden City, N.Y., Doubleday, 1968.
NE0154		Nebula award stories 4. Ed. by Poul Anderson. Garden City, N.Y., Doubleday, 1969.
NE0155		Nebula award stories 5. Ed. by James Blish. Garden City, N.Y., Doubleday, 1970.
NE0156		Nebula award stories 6. Ed. by Clifford D. Simak. Garden City, N.Y., Doubleday, 1971.
NE0157		Nebula award stories 7. Ed. by Lloyd Biggle, Jr. New York, Harper & Row, 1972.
NE0158		Nebula award stories 8. Ed. by Isaac Asimov. New York, Harper & Row, 1973.
NE0159		Nebula award stories 9. Ed. by Kate Wilhelm. New York, Harper & Row, 1974.
NE0160		Nebula award stories 10. Ed. by James Gunn. New York, Harper & Row, 1975.

NE0161   Nebula award stories 11. Ed. by Ursula K. LeGuin.
            New York, Harper & Row, 1977.
NE0162   Nebula winners 12. Ec, by Gorcon R. Dickson.
            New York, Harper & Row, 1978.
NE0200   The best of New dimensions. Ed. by Robert
            Silverberg. New York, Pocket Books, 1979.
NE0201   New dimensions 1. Ed. by Robert Silverberg.
            Garden City, N.Y., Doubleday, 1971.
NE0202   New dimensions 2. Ed. by Robert Silverberg.
            Garden City, N.Y., Doubleday, 1972.
NE0203   New dimensicns 3. Ed. by Robert Silverberg.
            Garden City, N.Y., Doubleday, 1973.
NE0204   New dimensions 4. Ed. by Robert Silverberg.
            New York, New American Library, 1974.
NE0205   New dimensicns 5. Ed. by Robert Silverberg.
            New York, Harper & Row, 1975.
NE0207   New dimensicns 7. Ed. by Robert Silverberg.
            New York, Harper & Row, 1977.
NE0208   New dimensions 8. Ea. by Robert Silverberg.
            New York, Harper & Row, 1978.
NE0209   New dimensions 9. Ed. by Robert Silverberg.
            New York, Harper, 1979.
NE0280   * New Soviet science fiction. Translated by
            Helen Saltz Jacobscn. New York, Collier, 1979.
NE0301   New writings in SF-1. Ed. by John Carnell.
            London, Dobson, 1964.
NE0302   New writings in SF-2. Ed. by John Carnell. New
            York, Bantam, 1966.
NE0303   New writings in SF-3. Ed. by John Carnell.
            London, Dobson, 1965.
NE0304   New writings in SF-4. Ed. by John Carnell.
            New York, Bantam, 1968.
NE0305   New writings in SF-5. Ed. by John Carnell.
            London, Dobson, 1965.
NE0306   New writings in SF-6. Ed. by John Carnell.
            London, Dobson, 1965.
NE0307   New writings in SF-7. Ed. by John Carnell. New
            York, Bantam, 1971.
NE0308   New writings in SF-8. Ed. by John Carnell.
            London, Dobson, 1966.
NE0309   New writings in SF-9. Ed. by John Carnell.
            London, Dobson, 1966.
NE0319   New writings in SF-19. Ed. by John Carnell.
            n.p., Corgi, 1971.
NE0326   New writings in SF-26. Ed. by Kenneth Bulmer.
            London, Sidgwick & Jackson, 1975.
NI0120   Niven, Larry. Ccnvergent series. New York,
            Ballantine, 1979.
NI0150   Niven, Larry. Tales of known space. New York,
            Ballantine, 1975.
NO0150   Nolan, William F., ed. The future is now.
            Los Angeles, Sherbourne, 1970.

N00180		Nolan, William F., ed. The human equation. Los Angeles, Sherbourne, 1971.
N00200		Nolan, William F. Men against tomorrow. New York, Avon, 1965.
N00210		Nolan, William F. The pseudo-people. Los Angeles, Sherbourne, 1965.
N00230	*	Nolan, William F. A wilderness of stars. Los Angeles, Sherbourne, 1969.
N00240		Norton, Andre. Gates to tomorrow. Ed. by Andre Norton and Errestine Donaldy. New York, Atheneum, 1973.
N00250		Norton, Andre. The many worlds of Andre Norton. Ed. by Roger Elwood. Radnor, Pa., Chilton, 1974.
N00270		Norton, Andre. Space pioneers. New York, World, 1954.
N00300		Norton, Andre. Space police. New York, World, 1956.
N00330		Norton, Andre. Space service. Cleveland, World, 1953.
N00360		Nourse, Alan E., M.D. The counterfeit man. New York, McKay, 1952.
N00390		Nourse, Alan E., M.D. Tiger by the tail. New York, McKay, 1961.
N00401		Nova 1. Ed. by Harry Harrison. New York, Dell, 1971.
N00402		Nova 2. Ed. by Harry Harrison. New York, Walker, 1972.
N00403	*	Nova 3. Ed. by Harry Harrison. New York, Walker, 1973.
N00404		Nova 4. Ed. by Harry Harrison. New York, Walker, 1974.
OB0140		The Observer [London] AD2500. London, Heineman, 1955.
OL0150		Olander, Joseph D., ed. American government through science fiction. Ed. by Joseph D. Olander, Martin H. Greenberg, and Patricia Warrick. Chicago, Rand McNally, 1974.
OL0165		Olander, Joseph D., ed. School and society through science fiction. Ed. by Joseph D. Olander, Martin Harry Greenberg, and Patricia Warrick. Chicago, Rand McNally, 1974.
OL0170	*	Olander, Joseph D., ed. Time of passage. Ed. by Joseph D. Olander and Martin Harry Greenberg. New York, Taplinger, 1978.
OL0180		Olney, Ross R., ed. Tales of time and space. Racine, Wisc., Western, 1969.
PA0150		Padgett, Lewis. A gnome there was. New York, Simon & Schuster, 1950.
PA0180		Padgett, Lewis. Robots have no tails. New York, Gnome, 1952.
PA0210		Path into the unknown. New York, Delacorte, 1968.

PE0150		The petrified planet. New York, Twayne, 1952.
PL0150		Playboy. The Playboy book of science fiction and fantasy. Chicago, Playboy Press, 1966.
PL0155	*	Playboy. The fiend. Chicago, Playboy Press, 1971.
P00100	*	Poe, Edgar Allan. The science fiction of Edgar Allan Poe. Ed. by Harold Beaver. New York, Penguin, 1976.
P00120	*	Pohl, Carol, comp. Science fiction: the great years. Ed. by Carol and Frederik Pohl. London, Gollancz 1974.
P00150		Pohl, Frederik. Assignment in tomorrow. Garden City, N.Y., Hanover, 1954.
P00180	*	Pohl, Frederik. The best of Frederik Pohl. Garden City, N.Y., Doubleday, 1975.
P00190		Pohl, Frederik, ec. Beyond the end of time. Garden City, N.Y., Permabooks, 1952.
P00210		Pohl, Frederik. Digits and dastards. New York, Ballantine, 1966.
P00240		Pohl, Frederik. The expert dreamers. Garden City, N.Y., Doubleday, 1962.
P00260		Pohl, Frederik. The Frederik Pohl omnibus. London, Panther, 1973.
P00290		Pohl, Frederik, ec. Science fiction discoveries. Ed. by Frederik and Carol Pohl. New York, Bantam, 1976.
P00293	*	Pohl, Frederik, ed. Science fiction of the forties. Co-ed. by Martin Harry Greenberg and Joseph D. Olander. New York, Avon, 1978.
P00295		Pohl, Frederik, ed. Science fiction: the great years, v. 2. Co-ed. by Carol Pohl. New York, Ace, 1976.
P00300		Pohl, Frederik. Star of stars. Garden City, N.Y., Doubleday, 1960.
P00330		Pohl, Fredrik. Star fourteen. London, Ronald Whiting & Wheaton, 1960.
P00371		Pohl, Frederik, ed. Star science fiction stories. New York, Ballantine, 1953.
P00372		Pohl, Frederik, ed. Star science fiction stories 2. New York, Ballantine, 1953.
P00373		Pohl, Frederik, ed. Star science fiction stories 3. New York, Ballantine, 1954.
P00374		Pohl, Frederik, ed. Star science fiction stories no. 4. New York, Ballantine, 1958.
P00376		Pohl, Frederik, ed. Star science fiction stories no. 6. New York, Ballantine, 1959.
P00400		Pohl, Frederik, ed. Star short novels. New York, Ballantine, 1954.
P00430		Pournelle, Jerry, ed. The endless frontier. New York, Ace, 1979.

P00450		Pournelle, Jerry, ed. 20 20 vision. New York, Avon, 1974
PR0150		Pratt, Fletcher, ed. World of wonder. New York, Twayne, 1951.
PR0160	★	Priest, Christopher, ed. Anticipations. London, Faber, 1978.
PR0170	★	Priest, Christopher. An infinite summer. New York, Scribner, 1979.
PR0180		Prokofieva, R. More soviet science fiction. New York, Collier, 1962.
PR0210		Pronzini, Bill, ed. Shared tomorrows. Co-ed. by Barry N. Malzberg. New York, St. Martin's, 1979.
R00150		Roberts, Keith. Machines and men. London, Hutchinson, 1973.
R00180		Roselle, Daniel, ed. Transformations. Greenwich, Conn., Fawcett, 1973.
R00210	★	Roselle, Daniel, ed. Understanding American history through science fiction. Greenwich, Conn., Fawcett, 1974.
R00240		Ross, Joseph, ed. Best of Amazing. Garden City, N.Y., Doubleday, 1967.
R00270		Rottensteiner, Franz. View from another shore. New York, Seabury, 1973.
RU0070		Russell, Eric Frank. The best of Eric Frank Russell. New York, Ballantine, 1978.
RY0100	★	Ryan, Charles C., ed. Starry messenger, the best of Galileo. New York, St. Martin's, 1979.
SA0080		Sallis, James, ed. The shores beneath. New York, Avon, 1971.
SA0100	★	Sallis, James, comp. The war book. London, Hart-Davis, 1969.
SA0120	★	Salmonson, Jessica Amanda, ed. Amazons! New York, DAW, 1979.
SA0150		Sanders, Thomas E. Speculations. New York, Glencoe, 1973.
SA0180		Santesson, Hans Stefan. Crime prevention in the 30th century. New York, Walker, 1969.
SA0210		Santesson, Hans Stefan, ed. The days after tomorrow. Boston, Little Brown, 1971.
SA0220	★	Sargent, Pamela, ed. More women of wonder. New York, Vintage, 1976.
SA0230	★	Sargent, Pamela, ed. The new women of wonder. New York, Vintage, 1978.
SA0240	★	Sargent, Pamela, comp. Women of wonder. New York, Vintage, 1975.
SA0270		Saturday Evening Post. The Post reader of fantasy and science fiction. Garden City, N.Y., Doubleday, 1964.
SA0300		Sauer, Rob. Voyages. New York, Ballantine, 1971.

Code		
SC0150		Schmitz, James H. Agent of Vega. Hicksville, N.Y., Gnome, 1960.
SC0180		Schmitz, James H. A nice day for screaming. New York, Chilton, 1965.
SC0190	*	Schmitz, James H. A pride of monsters. New York, Macmillan, 1970.
SC0210		The science fiction hall of fame, vol. 1. Ed. by Robert Silverberg. Garden City, N.Y., Doublecay, 1970.
SC0211		The science fiction hall of fame, vol. 2A. Ed. by Ben Bova. Garden City, N.Y., Doubleday, 1973.
SC0212		The science fiction hall of fame, vol. 2B. Ed. by Ben Bova. Garden City, N.Y., Doubleday, 1973.
SC0250	*	A science fiction omnibus on pollution. London, Sidgwick & Jackson, 1971.
SC0300		The science fiction roll of honor. Ed. by Frederik Pohl. New York, Random House, 1975.
SC0400		The science fictional Sherlock Holmes. Denver, Council of Four, 1960.
SC0450		Scortia, Thomas N. Strange bedfellows. New York, Random House, 1972.
SC0460		Scortia, Thomas N. Two views of wonder. Ed. by Thomas N. Scortia and Chelsea Quinn Yarbro. New York, Ballantine, 1973.
SE0150		Serling, Rod. New stories from The twilight zone. New York, Bantam, 1962.
SE0180		Serling, Rod. Rod Serling's The twilight zone. New York, Grosset & Dunlap, 1963.
SH0150		Sharkovsky, Arthur. Everything but love. Moscow, MIR, 1973.
SH0160	*	Shaw, Bob. Cosmic kaleidoscope. Garden City, N.Y., Doubleday, 1977.
SH0180	*	Sheckley, Robert. The Robert Sheckley omnibus. London, Gollancz, 1973.
SH0210		Sheckley, Robert. The wonderful world of Robert Sheckley. New York, Bantam, 1979.
SI0100	*	Silverberg, Robert, ed. The aliens. Nashville, Nelson, 1976.
SI0120	*	Silverberg, Robert, ed. Alpha 1. New York, Ballantine, 1970.
SI0121		Silverberg, Robert, ed. Alpha 2. New York, Ballantine, 1971.
SI0123	*	Silverberg, Robert, ed. Alpha 4. New York, Ballantine, 1973.
SI0124	*	Silverberg, Robert, ed. Alpha 5. New York, Ballantine, 1974.
SI0125	*	Silverberg, Robert, ed. Alpha 6. New York, Berkley, 1976.
SI0126	*	Silverberg, Robert, ed. Alpha 7. New York, Ballantine, 1977.
SI0127	*	Silverberg, Robert, ed. Alpha 8. New York, Berkley, 1977.

SI0128   Silverberg, Robert, ed. Alpha 9. New York,
                    Berkley, 1978.
SI0280   *   Silverberg, Robert. The best of Robert Silverberg.
                    New York, Pocket Books, 1976.
SI0300   *   Silverbert, Robert. Beyond control. Nashville,
                    Nelson, 1972.
SI0320   Silverberg, Robert. Born with the dead. New
                    York, Random House, 1974.
SI0340   *   Silverberg, Robert. The calibrated alligator.
                    New York, Holt, 1969.
SI0360   *   Silverberg, Robert. The cube root of uncertainty.
                    New York, Macmillan, 1970.
SI0380   Silverberg, Robert, ed. Dark stars. New York,
                    Ballantine, 1969.
SI0400   *   Silverberg, Robert, ed. Deep space. Nashville,
                    Nelson, 1973.
SI0420   *   Silverberg, Robert, ed. Earth is the strangest
                    planet. Nashville, Nelson, 1977.
SI0440   Silverberg, Robert. Earthmen and strangers.
                    New York, Duell, Sloan and Pearce, 1966.
SI0460   Silverberg, Robert, ed. The ends of time. New
                    York, Hawthorne, 1970.
SI0480   Silverberg, Robert, ed. Epoch. Ed. by Robert
                    Silverberg and Roger Elwood. New York, Berkley,
                    1975.
SI0500   *   Silverberg, Robert. An exaltation of stars. Ed.
                    by Terry Carr. New York, Simon & Schuster,
                    1973.
SI0520   *   Silverberg, Robert, comp. Explorers of space.
                    Nashville, Nelson, 1975.
SI0540   *   Silverberg, Robert. The feast of St. Dionysus.
                    New York, Scribner, 1975.
SI0560   *   Silverberg, Robert, ed. Galactic dreamers. New
                    York, Random House, 1977.
SI0580   *   Silverberg, Robert, ed. Infinite jests. Radnor,
                    Pa., Chilton 1974.
SI0600   *   Silverberg, Robert, comp. Invaders from space.
                    New York, Hawthorn, 1972.
SI0620   Silverberg, Robert, ed. Lost worlds, unknown
                    horizons. New York, Nelson, 1978.
SI0640   *   Silverberg, Robert, comp. Men and machines. New
                    York, Meredith, 1968.
SI0660   Silverberg, Robert, comp. Mind to mind.
                    Nashville, Nelson, 1971.
SI0680   *   Silverberg, Robert, comp. The mirror of infinity.
                    New York, Harper & Row, 1970.
SI0700   *   Silverberg, Robert, comp. Mutants. Nashville,
                    Nelson, 1974.
SI0720   *   Silverberg, Robert, ed. The new Atlantis. New
                    York, Hawthorn, 1975.
SI0740   Silverberg, Robert, ed. Other dimensions. New
                    York, Hawthorn, 1973.

SI0760   *   Silverberg, Robert. Parsecs and parables. Garden
             City, N.Y., Doubleday, 1970.

SI0780   Silverberg, Robert, ed. The science fiction
             bestiary. Nashville, Nelson, 1971.

SI0800   *   Silverberg, Robert. The shores of tomorrow.
             Nashville, Nelson, 1976.

SI0820   Silverberg, Robert. Strange gifts. Nashville,
             Nelson, 1975.

SI0840   *   Silverberg, Robert. Sundance. Nashville,
             Nelson, 1974.

SI0860   *   Silverberg, Robert. Sunrise on Mercury.
             Nashville, Nelson, 1975.

SI0880   *   Silverberg, Robert, comp. Threads of time.
             Nelson, 1974.

SI0900   Silverberg, Robert, comp. To the stars. New
             York, Hawthorn, 1971.

SI0920   Silverberg, Robert. To worlds beyond. New York,
             Chilton, 1965.

SI0940   Silverberg, Robert, comp. Tomorrow's worlds.
             New York, Meredith, 1969.

SI0960   *   Silverberg, Robert, ed. Trips in time.
             Nashville, Nelson, 1977.

SI0980   Silverberg, Robert, ed. Unfamiliar territory.
             New York, Scribner, 1973.

SI1000   Silverberg, Robert, ed. Voyagers in time. New
             York, Meredith, 1967.

SI1020   *   Silverberg, Robert, ed. Windows into tomorrow.
             New York, Hawthorn, 1974.

SI1040   *   Silverberg, Robert, ed. Worlds of maybe. Camden,
             N.J., T. Nelson, 1970.

SI1060   Simak, Clifford D. All the traps of earth.
             Garden City, N.Y., Doubleday, 1962.

SI1080   Simak, Clifford D. Best science fiction stories
             of Clifford D. Simak. Garden City, N.Y.,
             Doubleday, 1971.

SI1100   Simak, Clifford D. City. New York, Gnome,
             1952.

SI1120   *   Simak, Clifford D. Skirmish. New York, Putnam's,
             1977.

SI1140   Simak, Clifford D. So bright the vision. New
             York, Ace, 1968.

SI1160   Simak, Clifford D. Strangers in the universe.
             New York, Simon & Schuster, 1966.

SI1180   Simak, Clifford D. The worlds of Clifford Simak.
             New York, Simon & Schuster, 1960.

SL0150   Sloane, William Milligan. The rim of morning.
             New York, Dodd, Mead, 1964.

SL0180   Sloane, William Milligan, ed. Space, space, space.
             New York, Grosset & Dunlap, 1953.

SL0210   Sloane, William Milligan, ed. Stories for
             tomorrow. New York, Funk & Wagnalls, 1954.

SM0150		Smith, Clark Ashton. Tales of science and sorcery. Sauk City, Wisc., Arkham House, 1964.
SM0180		Smith, Cordwainer. The best of Cordwainer Smith. New York, Ballantire, 1975.
ST0150		Stapledon, Olaf. To the end of time. New York, Funk & Wagnall, 1953.
ST0161	★	The Star Trek reader 1. Adapted by James Blish. New York, Dutton, 1976.
ST0162	★	The Star Trek reader 2. Adapted by James Blish. New York, Dutton, 1977.
ST0163	★	The Star Trek reader 3. Adapted by James Blish. New York, Dutton, 1977.
ST0164	★	The Star Trek reader 4. Adapted by James Blish. New York, Dutton, 1978.
ST0180		Startling stories. The best from Startling stories. Comp. by Samuel Mines. New York, Holt, 1953.
ST0210		Stover, Leon E., ed. Aceman, spaceman. Ed. by Leon E. Stover annd Harry Harrison. Garcen City, N.Y., Doubleday, 1968.
ST0220	★	Strick, Philip, ec. Antigrav. New York, Taplinger, 1976.
ST0230	★	Stubbs, Harry C., comp. First flights to the moon. Ed. by Hal Clement. Garden City, N.Y., Doubleday, 1970.
ST0240		Sturgeon, Theodore. Case and the dreamer. Garden City, N.Y., Doublecay, 1974.
ST0270		Sturgeon, Theodore. E Pluribus unicorn. New York, Abelard, 1953.
ST0300		Sturgeon, Theodore. More than human. New York, Ballantine, 1953.
ST0320		Sturgeon, Theodore. Starshine. New York, Pyramid, 1966.
ST0325		Sturgeon, Theocore. Sturgeon in orbit. New York, Jove, 1978.
ST0330		Sturgeon, Theodore. A touch of strange. Garden City, N.Y., Doubleday, 1958.
ST0360		Sturgeon, Theodore. A way home. New York, Funk & Wagnalls, 1955.
SU0150		Sullivan, Charles William. As tomorrow becomes today. Englewood Cliffs, N.J., Prentice-Hall, 1974.
SU0180		Suvin, Darko, ed. Other worlds, other seas. New York, Random House, 1970.
SZ0150		Szilard, Leo. The voice of the dolphins. New York, Simon & Schuster, 1961.
TE0150		Tenn, William, ed. Children of wonder. New York, Simon & Schuster, 1953.
TE0180		Tenn, William. Of all possible worlds. New York, Ballantine, 1955.
TH0210		Three trips in time and space. New York, Hawthorn, 1973.

TU0150		Tucker, A.W., ed. Science fiction subtreasury. New York, Rinehart, 1954.
VA0140	*	VanVogt, A.E. The best of A.E. Van Vogt. New York, Pocket Books, 1976.
VA0150		VanVogt, A.E. The book of Van Vogt. New York, DAW, 1972.
VA0180		VanVogt, A.E. Destination: universe. New York, Pellegrini & Cudahy, 1952.
VA0205		VanVogt, A.E. The sea thing. London, Sidgwick & Jackson, 1970.
VA0210		VanVogt, A.E. Triad. New York, Simon & Schuster, 1951.
VA0220		Vance, Jack. The best of Jack Vance. New York, Pocket Books, 1976.
VA0250		Vance, Jack. Eight fantasms and magics. New York, Macmillan, 1969.
VA0280	*	Varley, John. Persistence of vision. New York, Dial, 1978.
VI0070		Vinge, Joan D. Eyes of amber. New York, New American Library, 1979.
WA0100	*	Warrick, Patricia, ed. The new awareness. Ed. by Patricia Warrick and Martin Harry Greenberg. New York, Delacorte, 1975.
WA0130		Warrick, Patricia, ed. Science fiction: contemporary mythology. Joint eds: Martin Harry Greenberg and Joseph Olander. New York, Harper & Row, 1976.
WA0160		Waugh, Charles G., ed. Mysterious visions. Co-ed. by Martin Harry Greenberg and Joseph Olander. New York, St. Martin's, 1979.
WE0150	*	Weinbaum, Stanley G. The best of Stanley G. Weinbaum. New York, Ballantine, 1974.
WE0158		Weinbaum, Stanley G. A Martian odyssey. Westport, Conn., Hyperion, 1974.
WE0200		Wells, H.G. Best science fiction stories. New York, Dover, 1966.
WE0210		Wells, H.G. The complete short stories of H.G. Wells. London, Benn, 1965.
WE0220		Wells, H.G. Seven science fiction novels of H.G. Wells. New York, Dover, 1950.
WE0230		Wells, H.G. Three prophetic novels. New York, Dover, 1960.
WE0240		Wells, H.G. The time machine and The war of the worlds. New York, Heritage, 1964.
WE0250		Wells, H.G. 28 science fiction stories of H.G. Wells. New York, Dover, 1952.
WE0260		Wells, H.G. The war in the air... New York, Dover, 1963.
WE0270		Wells, H.G. The war of the worlds. New York, Platt, 1963.
WE0290		Weston, Peter, ed. Andromeda 1. New York, St. Martin's, 1979.

WH0150		Whaley, Stephen V. Man unwept, by Stephen V. Whaley and Stanley J. Cook. New York, McGraw-Hill, 1974.
WH0160		White, James. Monsters and medics. New York, Ballantine, 1977.
WH0175	*	White, Ted, ed. The best from Amazing. London, Hale, 1976.
WH0180	*	White, Ted, ed. The best from Fantastic. London, Hale, 1976.
WI0150		Wilhelm, Kate. The downstairs room. Garden City, N.Y., Doubleday, 1968.
WI0135		Wilhelm, Kate. Abyss. Garden City, N.Y., Doubleday, 1971.
WI0165		Wilhelm, Kate. The infinity box. New York, Harper, 1975.
WI0180		Wilhelm, Kate. Somerset dreams. New York, Harper, 1973.
WI0201		Williams-Ellis, Amabel, ed. Out of this world 1. Joint ed. Mably Owens. London, Blackie, 1960.
WI0202		Williams-Ellis, Amabel, ed. Out of this world 2. Joint ed. Mably Owens. London, Blackie, 1961.
WI0203		Williams-Ellis, Amabel, ed. Out of this world 3. Joint ed. Mably Owens. London, Blackie, 1961.
WI0204		Williams-Ellis, Amabel, ed. Out of this world 4. Joint ed. Mably Owens. London, Blackie, 1964.
WI0205		Williams-Ellis, Amabel, ed. Out of this world 5. Joint ed. Mably Owens. London, Blackie, 1965.
WI0206		Williams-Ellis, Amabel, ed. Out of this world 6. Joint ed. Mably Owens. London, Blackie, 1967.
WI0210		Williams-Ellis, Amabel, ed. Out of this world 10. Joint ed. Michael Pearson. London, Blackie, 1973.
WI0245	*	Williams-Ellis, Amabel, ed. Strange orbits. Glasgow, Blackie, 1976.
WI0250	*	Williams-Ellis, Amabel, ed. Strange universe. Joint ed. Michael Pearson. Glasgow, Blackie, 1974.
WI0280		Williams-Ellis, Amabel, ed. Worlds apart. Ed. by Amabel Ellis-Williams and Mably Owen. London, Blackie, 1966.
WI0310	*	Williamson, Jack. The early Williamson. Garden City, N.Y., Doubleday, 1975.
W00120	*	Wolfe, Gene. The new Atlantis. Ed. by Robert Silverberg. New York, Hawthorn, 1975.
W00150		Wollheim, Donald A., ed. The best from the rest of the world. Garden City, N.Y., Doubleday, 1976.
W00180		Wollheim, Donald A., ed. The DAW science fiction reader. New York, DAW, 1976.
W00210		Wollheim, Donald A., ed. The end of the world. New York, Ace, 1956.

W00240	Wollheim, Donald A., ed. Everybody's book of science fiction. New York, Fell, 1951.
W00270	Wollheim, Donald A., ed. Flight into space. New York, Fell, 1950.
W00300	Wollheim, Donald A., ed. The hidden planet. New York, Fell, 1959.
W00330	Wollheim, Donald A., ed. The portable novels of science. New York, Viking, 1945.
W00360	Wollheim, Donald A., ed. Swordsmen in the sky. New York, Ace, 1964.
W00390	Wollheim, Donald A., ed. The ultimate invader. New York, Ace, 1954.
W00405	Wollheim, Donald A., ed. World's best science fiction 1965. Joint ed. Terry Carr. New York, Ace, 1965.
W00406	Wollheim, Donald A., ed. World's best science fiction 1966. Joint ed. Terry Carr. New York, Ace, 1966.
W00407	Wollheim, Donald A., ed. World's best science fiction 1967. Joint ed. Terry Carr. New York, Ace, 1967.
W00409	Wollheim, Donald A., ed. World's best science fiction 1969. Joint ed. Terry Carr. New York, Ace, 1969.
W00410	Wollheim, Donald A., ed. World's best science fiction 1970. Joint ed. Terry Carr. New York, Ace, 1970.
W00411	Wollheim, Donald A., ed. World's best science fiction 1971. Joint ed. Terry Carr. New York, Ace, 1971.
W00412	Wollheim, Donald A., ed. The 1972 annual world's best SF. Joint ed. Arthur W. Saha. New York, DAW, 1972.
W00413	Wollheim, Donald A., ed. The 1973 annual world's best SF. New York, DAW, 1972.
W00414	Wollheim, Donald A., ed. The 1974 annual world's best SF. New York, DAW, 1974.
W00415	Wollheim, Donald A., ed. The 1975 annual world's best science fiction. New York, DAW, 1975.
W00416	Wollheim, Donald A., ed. The 1976 annual world's best SF. New York, DAW, 1976.
W00417	Wollheim, Donald A., ed. The 1977 annual world's best SF. New York, DAW, 1977.
W00419	Wollheim, Donald A., ed. The 1979 annual world's best SF. Co-ed. by Arthur W. Saha. New York, DAW, 1979.
WY0150	Wyndham, John. Consider her ways. London, Michael Joseph, 1961.
WY0180	Wyndham, John. The John Wyndham omnibus. New York, Simon & Schuster, 1964.

WY0210		Wyndham, John. The seeds of time. London, Michael Joseph, 1960.
YA0100	*	Yarbro, Chelsea Quinn. Cautionary tales. Garden City, N.Y., Doubleday, 1978.
YE0403		Year's best science fiction novels 1952. Ed. by Everett F. Bleiler and T.E. Dikty. New York, Fell, 1952.
YE0404		Year's best science fiction novels 1953. Ed. by Everett F. Bleiler and T.E. Dikty. New York, Fell, 1953.
YE0405		Year's best science fiction novels 1954. Ed. by Everett F. Bleiler and T.E. Dikty. New York, Fell, 1954.
Y00150		Yolen, Jane, comp. Zoo 2000. New York, Seabury, 1973.
Y00180		Young, Robert F. The worlds of Robert F. Young. New York, Simon & Schuster, 1965.
ZE0150		Zebrowski, George. Tomorrow today. Santa Cruz, Unity, 1975.
ZE0180		Zelazny, Roger. The coors of his face, the lamps of his mouth. Garden City, N.Y., Doubleday, 1971.
ZE0190		Zelazny, Roger. Four for tomorrow. New York, Ace, 1967.

All the last wars at once	Effinger, George Alec	CA0231
All the last wars at once	Effinger, George Alec	CA0234
All the last wars at once	Effinger, George Alec	CA0368
All the last wars at once	Effinger, George Alec	EF0240
All the last wars at once	Effinger, George Alec	KA0070
All the last wars at once	Effinger, George Alec	SI1020
All the last wars at once	Effinger, George Alec	WA0130
All the myriad ways	Niven, Larry	SI1040
All the people	Lafferty, R.A.	SI0820
All the sounds of fear	Ellison, Harlan	EL0340
All the sounds of fear	Ellison, Harlan	EL0400
All the sounds of fear	Ellison, Harlan	ME0363
All the tea in China	Bretnor, Reginald	ME0362
All the time in the world	Clarke, Arthur C.	CL0280
All the time in the world	Clarke, Arthur C.	CL0340
All the time in the world	Clarke, Arthur C.	OL0180
All the traps of earth	Simak, Clifford D.	SI1060
All the traps of earth	Simak, Clifford D.	SI1080
All the traps of earth	Simak, Clifford D.	SI1120
All the traps of earth [anthology]	Simak, Clifford D.	SI1060
All the troubles of the world	Asimov, Isaac	AS0530
All the troubles of the world	Asimov, Isaac	H00110
All the troubles of the world	Asimov, Isaac	WI0206
All the universe in a mason jar	Haldeman, Joe W.	HA0137
All the way back	Shaara, Michael	AL0410
All the world's tears	Aldiss, Brian W.	AL0375
All we have on this planet	VanVogt, A.E.	VA0140
All you can eat	Bilker, Audrey L.	EL0540
All you can eat	Bilker, Harvey L.	EL0540
All you zombies	Heinlein, Robert A.	HE0220
All you zombies	Heinlein, Robert A.	HE0420
All you Zombies	Heinlein, Robert A.	MA0199
All you zombies	Heinlein, Robert A.	MI0150
All you zombies	Heinlein, Robert A.	SI0680
All you zombies	Heinlein, Robert A.	SU0150
Allamagoosa	Russell, Eric Frank	AS0370
Allamagoosa	Russell, Eric Frank	C00220
Allamagoosa	Russell, Eric Frank	D00130
Allamagoosa	Russell, Eric Frank	RU0070
Allegiances	Bishop, Michael	GA0100
Allegiances	Bishop, Michael	W00416
Alley man	Farmer, Philip Jose	FA0240
Allies	Yarbro, Chelsea Quinn	YA0100
Almost empty rooms	Shirley, John	NE0207
Almost the end of the world	Bradbury, Ray	BR0100
Almost the end of the world	Bradbury, Ray	BR0200
Alone against tomorrow [anthology]	Ellison, Harlan	EL0240
Alone in space	Tofte, Arthur	EL1040
Along the scenic route	Ellison, Harlan	EL0280
Along the scenic route	Ellison, Harlan	EL0320
Alpha in Omega	Stones, Jonathan	030140
Alpha 1 [anthology]	Silverberg, Robert	SI0120
Alpha Ralpha Boulevard	Smith, Cordwainer	MA0201
Alpha Ralpha Boulevard	Smith, Cordwainer	SI0460

And name my name	Lafferty, R.A.	KN0313
And now the news	Sturgeon, Theodore	CE0100
And now the news	Sturgeon, Theodore	D00130
And now the news	Sturgeon, Theodore	JA0130
And now the news	Sturgeon, Theodore	KA0070
And now the news	Sturgeon, Theodore	KN0540
And now the news	Sturgeon, Theodore	MA0196
And read the flesh between the lines	Lafferty, R.A.	CA0371
And seven times never kill man	Martin, George R.R.	MA0540
And so died Riabouchinska	Bradbury, Ray	BR0200
And so say all of us	McAllister, Bruce	W00410
And some were savages	Blish, James	BL0125
And someday to Mars	Long, Frank Belknap	M00260
And the moon be still as bright	Bradbury, Ray	BL0120
And the moon be still as bright	Bradbury, Ray	BR0230
And the power	Payes, Rachel Cosgrove	EL0500
And the power...	Payes, Rachel Cosgrove	EL0300
And the rock cried out	Bracbury, Ray	BR0100
And the rock cried out	Bradbury, Ray	BR0415
And the sailor, home from the sea	Bradbury, Ray	BR0200
And the sea like mirrors	Benford, Gregory	EL0220
And the stagnation of the heart	Aldiss, Brian W.	CA0360
And the stagnation of the heart	Aldiss, Brian W.	HA0200
And the walls came tumbling down	Wyncham, John	DE0340
And then she found him	Budrys, Algis	FE0260
And then the dark	Sallis, James	SA0100
And then there were none	Russell, Eric Frank	B00245
And then there were none	Russell, Eric Frank	P00120
And then there were none	Russell, Eric Frank	SC0211
And then there were none	Russell, Eric Frank	SL0210
And then there were none	Russell, Eric Frank	YE0403
And this did Dante do	Bradbury, Ray	N00401
And us, too, I guess	Effinger, George Alec	EF0150
And us, too, I guess	Effinger, George Alec	EF0210
And walk now gently through the fire [anthology]	Elwood, Roger	EL0500
And walk now gently through the fire	Lafferty, R.A.	EL0500
And we sailed the mighty dark	Long, Frank Belknap	L00080
Androids don't cry	Wellen, Edward	BE0299
Androids, time machines, and blue giraffes [anthology]	Elwood, Roger	EL0520
Androids, time machines, and blue giraffes [anthology]	Ghidalia, Vic	EL0520
Andromeda 1 [anthology]	Weston, Peter	WE0290
Angel of the Lord	Post, Melville Davisson	WA0160
Angel of truth	Eklund, Gordon	SI0480
Angel was a yankee	Benet, Stephen Vincent	ME0230
Angel's egg	Pangborn, Edgar	C00250
Angel's egg	Pangborn, Edgar	CR0101
Angel's egg	Pangborn, Edgar	KN0160
Angel's egg	Pangborn, Edgar	SI0123
Angela's satyr	Cleeve, Brian	ME0363
Angelic angleworm	Brown, Frederic	BR0430

Asian shore	Disch, Thomas M.	DI0215
Asian shore	Disch, Thomas M.	HA0163
Asian shore	Disch, Thomas M.	HA0250
Asian shore	Disch, Thomas M.	KN0306
Asian shore	Disch, Thomas M.	SA0080
Asimov's choice: astronauts & androids [anthology]	Asimov, Isaac	AS0172
Asimov's choice: black holes & bug-eyed monsters [anthology]	Asimov, Isaac	AS0173
Asimov's choice: comets & computers [anthology]	Asimov, Isaac	AS0175
Asimov's choice: dark stars & dragons [anthology]	Asimov, Isaac	AS0180
Ask a foolish question	Sheckley, Robert	SH0180
Ask and it may be given	Davis, W.F.	WA0100
Ask me anything	Knight, Damon	GA0140
Asleep in Armageddon	Bradbury, Ray	C00340
Asleep: with still hands	Ellison, Harlan	EL0280
Aspects of science fiction [anthology]	Doherty, G.D.	D00100
Assassin	Hogan, James P.	DE0268
Assassin	Hogan, James P.	DE0275
Assassination of John Fitzgerald Kennedy considered as a downhill motor race	Ballard, J.G.	AL0402
Assassination of John Fitzgerald Kennedy considered as a downhill motor race	Ballard, J.G.	BA0120
Assassination of John Fitzgerald Kennedy considered as a downhill motor race	Ballard, J.G.	HA0160
Assassination of John Fitzgerald Kennedy considered as a downhill motor race	Ballard, J.G.	ME0290
Assassination of John Fitzgerald Kennedy considered as a downhill motor race	Ballard, J.G.	OL0150
Assassins of air	Zebrowski, George	EL0720
Assault on a city	Vance, Jack	CA0371
Assignment in eternity [anthology]	Heinlein, Robert A.	HE0190
Assignment in tomorrow [anthology]	Pohl, Frederik	P00150
Assignment to Alderbaran	Crossen, Kendall F.	YE0405
Assignment: earth	Blish, James	ST0161
Assimilating our culture, that's what they're doing!	Niven, Larry	NI0120
Assisted passage	White, James	CA0170
Asteriod of gold	Simak, Clifford D.	W00240
Asteroid of fear	Gallun, Raymond Z.	N00270
Astoria incident	Roberson, Rick	EN0070
Astouncing [anthology]	Harrison, Harry	AS0750
Astounding analog reader. V.1 [anthology]	Aldiss, Brian W.	AS0650
Astounding analog reader. V.1 [anthology]	Harrison, Harry	AS0650

Best from if, v.2 [anthology]	anonymous	IFO170
Best from Startling stories [anthology]	Startling Stories	STO180
Best from the rest of the world [anthology]	Wollheim, Donald A.	WOO150
Best is yet to be	Chin, M.L.	RYO100
Best of A.E. VanVogt [anthology]	VanVogt, A.E.	VAO140
Best of all possible worlds	Bradbury, Ray	BRO200
Best of amazing [anthology]	Ross, Joseph	ROO240
Best of Analog [anthology]	Bova, Ben	ANO140
Best of Arthur C. Clarke [anthology]	Clarke, Arthur C.	CLO200
Best of Arthur C. Clarke [anthology]	Wells, Angus	CLO200
Best of Avram Davidson [anthology]	Davidson, Avram	DAO235
Best of Avram Davidson [anthology]	Kurland, Michael	DAO235
Best of C.L. Moore [anthology]	DelRey, Lester	MOO170
Best of C.M. Kornbluth	Kornbluth, Cyril M.	KOO070
Best of Cordwainer Smith [anthology]	Pierce, J.J.	SMO180
Best of Damon Knight [anthology]	Knight, Damon	KNOO70
Best of Edmond Hamilton [anthology]	Hamilton, Edmond	HAO155
Best of Eric Frank Russell [anthology]	Russell, Eric Frank	RUOC70
Best of Frederic Brown [anthology]	Bloch, Robert	BRO435
Best of Frederic Brown [anthology]	Brown, Frederic	BRO435
Best of Frederik Pohl [anthology]	Pohl, Frederik	POO180
Best of Fritz Leiber [anthology]	Leiber, Fritz, Jr.	LEO100
Best of Isaac Asimov [anthology]	Asimov, Isaac	ASO200
Best of Jack Vance [anthology]	Vance, Jack	VAO220
Best of John Jakes [anthology]	Greenberg, Martin Harry	JAO070
Best of John Jakes [anthology]	Jakes, John	JAO070
Best of John Jakes [anthology]	Olander, Joseph D.	JAOC70
Best of John W.Campbell [anthology]	Campbell, John W.	CAO110
Best of Judith Merril [anthology]	Merril, Judith	MEO170
Best of L. Sprague de Camp [anthology]	Anderson, Poul	DEO070
Best of L. Sprague de Camp [anthology]	DeCamp, Lyon Sprague	DEOC70
Best of Leigh Brackett [anthology]	Brackett, Leigh	BRO070
Best of New Dimensions [anthology]	New Dimensions	NEO200
Best of New Dimensions [anthology]	Silverberg, Robert	NEO200
Best of Philip K. Dick [anthology]	Dick, Philip K.	DIO075
Best of planet stories no. 1 [anthology]	Brackett, Leigh	BROO80
Best of Poul Anderson [anthology]	Anderson, Poul	ANO160
Best of Robert Bloch [anthology]	Bloch, Robert	BLO240
Best of Robert Heinlein [anthology]	Heinlein, Robert A.	HEO220
Best of Robert Silverberg [anthology]	Silverberg, Robert	SIO280
Best of Stanley G. Weinbaum [anthology]	Weinbaum, Stanley G.	WEO150
Best policy	Garrett, Randall	SIO440
Best science fiction novellas of the year no. 1 [anthology]	Carr, Terry	CAO241
Best science fiction of 1973 [anthology]	Ackerman, Forrest J.	ACO200
Best science fiction of the year no.1 [anthology]	Carr, Terry	CAO231

Best science fiction of the year no.4 [anthology]	Carr, Terry	CA0234
Best science fiction of the year no.5 [anthology]	Carr, Terry	CA0235
Best science fiction of the year no.6 [anthology]	Carr, Terry	CA0236
Best science fiction of the year no.7 [anthology]	Carr, Terry	CA0237
Best science fiction of the year no.8 [anthology]	Carr, Terry	CA0238
Best science fiction stories [anthology]	Blish, James	BL0180
Best science fiction stories [anthology]	Wells, H.G.	WE0200
Best science fiction stories and novels: 1955	Dikty, T.E.	BE0205
Best science fiction stories and novels: 1956	Dikty, T.E.	BE0206
Best science fiction stories of Clifford D. Simak [anthology]	Simak, Clifford D.	SI1080
Best science fiction stories of Brian W. Aldiss [anthology]	Aldiss, Brian W.	AL0365
Best science fiction stories of the year, 1972 [anthology]	DelRey, Lester	BE0290
Best science fiction stories of the year, 2d annual collection [anthology]	DelRey, Lester	BE0291
Best science fiction stories of the year, 3rd annual collection [anthology]	DelRey, Lester	BE0299
Best science fiction stories of the year, fourth annual collection [anthology]	DelRey, Lester	BE0300
Best science fiction stories of the year, fifth annual collection [anthology]	DelRey, Lester	BE0301
Best science fiction stories of the year, 6th annual collection [anthology]	Dozois, Gardner R.	BE0302
Best science fiction stories of the year, 7th annual collection [anthology]	Dozois, Gardner R.	BE0303
Best science fiction stories: 1950	Bleiler, Everett F.	BE0200
Best science fiction stories: 1950	Dikty, T.E.	BE0200
Best science fiction stories: 1951	Bleiler, Everett F.	BE0201
Best science fiction stories: 1951	Dikty, T.E.	BE0201
Best science fiction stories: 1952	Bleiler, Everett F.	BE0202
Best science fiction stories: 1952	Dikty, T.E.	BE0202
Best science fiction stories: 1953	Bleiler, Everett F.	BE0203
Best science fiction stories: 1953	Dikty, T.E.	BE0203
Best science-fiction stories and novels,ninth series	Dikty, T.E.	BE0208
Best SF Five science fiction stories [anthology]	Crispin, Edmund	CR0104

Best SF Four science fiction stories [anthology]	Crispin, Edmund	CRO103
Best SF science fiction stories [anthology]	Crispin, Edmund	CRO100
Best SF stories from New Worlds 2 [anthology]	Moorcock, Michael	MO0162
Best SF stories from New Worlds 3 [anthology]	Moorcock, Michael	MO0163
Best SF stories from New Worlds 4 [anthology]	Moorcock, Michael	MO0164
Best SF stories from New Worlds 5 [anthology]	Moorcock, Michael	MO0165
Best SF stories from New Worlds 6 [anthology]	Moorcock, Michael	MO0166
Best SF stories from New Worlds 2 [anthology]	New Worlds	MO0162
Best SF stories from New Worlds 3 [anthology]	New Worlds	MO0163
Best SF stories from New Worlds 4 [anthology]	New Worlds	MO0164
Best SF stories from New Worlds 5 [anthology]	New Worlds	MO0165
Best SF stories from New Worlds 6 [anthology]	New Worlds	MO0166
Best SF Three science fiction stories [anthology]	Crispin, Edmund	CRO102
Best SF Two science fiction stories [anthology]	Crispin, Edmund	CRO101
Best SF: 1967 [anthology]	Aldiss, Brian W.	HA0160
Best SF: 1967 [anthology]	Harrison, Harry	HA0160
Best SF: 1968 [anthology]	Aldiss, Brian W.	HA0161
Best SF: 1968 [anthology]	Harrison, Harry	HA0161
Best SF: 1969 [anthology]	Aldiss, Brian W.	HA0162
Best SF: 1969 [anthology]	Harrison, Harry	HA0162
Best SF: 1970 [anthology]	Aldiss, Brian W.	HA0163
Best SF: 1970 [anthology]	Harrison, Harry	HA0163
Best SF: 1971 [anthology]	Aldiss, Brian W.	HA0164
Best SF: 1971 [anthology]	Harrison, Harry	HA0164
Best SF: 1972 [anthology]	Aldiss, Brian W.	HA0165
Best SF: 1972 [anthology]	Harrison, Harry	HA0165
Best SF: 1973 [anthology]	Aldiss, Brian W.	HA0166
Best SF: 1973 [anthology]	Harrison, Harry	HA0166
Best SF: 1974 [anthology]	Aldiss, Brian W.	HA0167
Best SF: 1974 [anthology]	Harrison, Harry	HA0167
Best SF: 1975 the ninth annual [anthology]	Aldiss, Brian W.	HA0168
Best SF: 1975 the ninth annual [anthology]	Harrison, Harry	HA0168
Best short stories of J.G. Ballard [anthology]	Ballard, J.G.	BA0120
Best stories from Orbit, v.1-10 [anthology]	Knight, Damon	KN0100
Best stories from Orbit, v.1-10	Orbit	KN0100
Betelgeuse bridge	Tenn, William	GA0140

Big book of science fiction [anthology] Conklin, Groff C00130
Big bounce Tevis, Walter S., Jr. AS0645
Big connection Scott, Robin N00401
Big contest MacDonald, John D. KN0630
Big contest MacDonald, John D. ME0310
Big engine Leiber, Fritz, Jr. GA0147
Big flash Spinrad, Norman KN0100
Big flash Spinrad, Norman KN0305
Big flash Spinrad, Norman SA0300
Big flash Spinrad, Norman WH0150
Big flash Spinrad, Norman W00410
Big front yard Simak, Clifford D. AS0370
Big front yard Simak, Clifford D. B00210
Big front yard Simak, Clifford D. SC0212
Big front yard Simak, Clifford D. SI1120
Big front yard Simak, Clifford D. SI1180
Big game Asimov, Isaac AS0170
Big game hunt Clarke, Arthur C. CL0370
Big game hunt Clarke, Arthur C. CL0430
Big holiday Leiber, Fritz, Jr. LE0100
Big hunger Miller, Walter M., Jr. AL0430
Big man with the girls MacCreigh, James H00130
Big man with the girls Merril, Judith H00130
Big pat boom Knight, Damon GA0146
Big pat boom Knight, Damon KN0070
Big pat boom Knight, Damon KN0600
Big rain Anderson, Poul AL0310
Big Sam Davidson, Avram MC0150
Big Sam was my friend Ellison, Harlan EL0380
Big Sam was my friend Ellison, Harlan EL0380
Big shot Russell, Eric Frank MA0490
Big space fuck Vonnegut, Kurt, Jr. EL0220
Big stink Cogswell, Theodore R. DE0250
Big sword Ash, Paul AM0514
Big sword Ash, Paul C00100
Big trek Leiber, Fritz, Jr. LE0100
Big trek Leiber, Fritz, Jr. MA0197
Big trip up yonder Vonnegut, Kurt, Jr. P00150
Big wheel McMorrow, Fred SA0270
Bigger than worlds Niven, Larry P00430
Billenium Ballard, J.G. BA0120
Billenium Ballard, J.G. BA0150
Billenium Ballard, J.G. CL0590
Billenium Ballard, J.G. CR0170
Billenium Ballard, J.G. CU0070
Billenium Ballard, J.G. KN0190
Billenium Ballard, J.G. SA0300
Billenium Ballard, J.G. SI1020
Billenium Ballard, J.G. WA0130
Billenium Ballard, J.G. WI0204
Billiard ball Asimov, Isaac AS0200
Billiard ball Asimov, Isaac IF0102
Binaries Sallis, James KN0100
Binaries Sallis, James KN0309

Brave new word	McComas, J. Francis	GR0300
Brave new word	McComas, J. Francis	MA0194
Brave new world	Huxley, Aldous	KU0100
Brave newer world	Harrison, Harry	FO0130
Brazen locked room	Asimov, Isaac	MC0180
Bread and circuses	Blish, James	ST0164
Breakdown	Roberts, Keith	RO0150
Breakdown	Williamson, Jack	GR0190
Breakfast at twilight	Dick, Philip K.	DI0075
Breakfast at twilight	Dick, Philip K.	DI0075
Breaking point	Gunn, James E.	GU0100
Breaking point [anthology]	Gunn, James E.	GU0100
Breaking strain	Clarke, Arthur C.	CA0230
Breaking strain	Clarke, Arthur C.	CL0130
Breaking strain	Clarke, Arthur C.	CL0160
Breaking strain	Clarke, Arthur C.	CL0220
Breaking strain	Clarke, Arthur C.	CL0250
Breaking strain	Clarke, Arthur C.	WI0201
Breakout in Ecol 2	Bunch, David R.	NO0403
Breath's a ware that will not keep	Monteleone, Thomas F.	EL0660
Breath's a ware that will not keep	Monteleone, Thomas F.	NE0162
Breckerridge and the continuum	Silverberg, Robert	EL1060
Breckenridge and the continuum	Silverberg, Robert	SI0560
Breeds there a man...?	Asimov, Isaac	AS0500
Breeds there a man...?	Asimov, Isaac	DE0340
Brian Aldiss omnibus (2) [anthology]	Aldiss, Brian W.	AL0390
Brick moon	Hale, Edward Everett	MO0320
Bridge	Blish, James	AM0515
Bridge	Blish, James	AS0575
Bridge	Blish, James	AS0651
Bridge builder	Wolf, G.K.	KN0314
Bridge crossing	Dryfoos, Dave	PO0190
Bridle and saddle	Asimov, Isaac	GR0220
Bright coins in never-ending stream	Lafferty, R.A.	KN0320
Bright eyes	Ellison, Harlan	EL0240
Bright eyes	Ellison, Harlan	EL0420
Bright illusion	Moore, C.L.	JA0130
Bright illusion	Moore, C.L.	MO0170
Brightness falls from the air	Saint Clair, Margaret	MC0180
Brightness falls from the air	Seabright, Idris	AL0410
Brightness falls from the air	Seabright, Idris	BE0202
Brightside crossing	Nourse, Alan E., M.D.	AS0575
Brightside crossing	Nourse, Alan E., M.D.	GA0340
Brightside crossing	Nourse, Alan E., M.D.	KN0120
Brightside crossing	Nourse, Alan E., M.D.	NO0390
Brightside crossing	Nourse, Alan E., M.D.	WA0130
Brilliant curiosity	Piserchia, Doris	KN0316
Brillo	Bova, Ben	EL0440
Brillo	Ellison, Harlan	EL0440
Brimstone bill	Jameson, Malcolm	JA0100
Brink of infinity	Weinbaum, Stanley G.	WE0158
Broke down engine	Goulart, Ron	GO0070
Broke down engine, and other trouble with machines [anthology]	Goulart, Ron	GO0070

Broken pit	Maddern, Pip	HA0158
Brooklyn Project	Tenn, William	CO0640
Brooklyn Project	Tenn, William	SI1000
Broomstick ride	Bloch, Robert	BL0240
Brother Charlie	Dickson, Gordon R.	DI0115
Brother to dragons, a companion of owls	Wilhelm, Kate	KN0314
Brotherhood of keepers	McLaughlin, Dean	ME0361
Brothers	Dance, Clifton, Jr. M.D.	CO0190
Brothers	Dickson, Gordon R.	AS0750
Brothers beyond the void	Fairman, Paul W.	DE0590
Brown Robert	Carr, Terry	SI0125
Brushwood boy	Kipling, Rudyard	KN0450
Budding explorer	Robin, Ralph	MA0192
Budget planet	Sheckley, Robert	HA0161
Bug-eyed monsters [anthology]	Cheetham, Anthony	CH0100
Bug-getter	Bretnor, Reginald	AS0555
Build me a mountain	Bova, Ben	PO0450
Build-up	Ballard, J.G.	BA0150
Build-up	Ballard, J.G.	BO0100
Build-up	Ballard, J.G.	SU0150
Building block	Dorman, Sonya	SA0230
Building on the line	Dickson, Gordon R.	DI0125
Built down logically	Schoenfeld, Howard	AS0340
Built up logically	Schoenfeld, Howard	AL0450
Built up logically	Schoenfeld, Howard	KN0480
Built up logically	Schoenfeld, Howard	MC0180
Built up logically	Schoenfeld, Howard	MA0191
Bulkhead	Sturgeon, Theodore	ST0360
Bullard of the space patrol [anthology]	Jameson, Malcolm	JA0100
Bullard of the space patrol [anthology]	Norton, Andre	JA0100
Bullard reflects	Jameson, Malcolm	BO0151
Bullard reflects	Jameson, Malcolm	CA0277
Bullard reflects	Jameson, Malcolm	JA0100
Bulletin	Jackson, Shirley	MA0194
Bulletin from the trustees	Shore, Wilma	MA0204
Bulletin from the trustees	Shore, Wilma	SI1000
Bumberboom	Davidson, Avram	WO0407
Burden of proof	Shaw, Bob	AN0107
Bureau of slick tricks	Fyfe, H.B.	GR0310
Bureaucrat	Jameson, Malcolm	JA0100
Burger creature	Chapman, Steve	KN0312
Burning	Cogswell, Theodore R.	KN0460
Burning bright	Browning, John S.	GR0280
Burning of the brain	Smith, Cordwainer	SI0121
Burning of the brain	Smith, Cordwainer	SM0180
Burning question	Aldiss, Brian W.	GR0250
Burning spear	Denton, Kit	BA0235
Business as usual, during alterations	Williams, Ralph	AN0150
Business as usual, during alterations	Williams, Ralph	CA0100
Business as usual, during alterations	Williams, Ralph	GR0300
Business as usual, during alterations	Williams, Ralph	KN0280
Business of killing	Leiber, Fritz, Jr.	CO0370

Cage	Chandler, A. Bertram	C00760
Cage	Chandler, A. Bertram	MA0197
Cage	Chandler, A. Bertram	MA0550
Cage of bras	Delany, Samuel R.	DE0255
Cage of sand	Ballard, J.G.	BA0120
Cage of sand	Ballard, J.G.	BA0150
Cage of sand	Ballard, J.G.	BA0210
Cage of sand	Ballard, J.G.	DI0250
Cage of sand	Ballard, J.G.	SI0380
Cairn on the headland	Howard, Robert E.	HO0280
Caliban	Silverberg, Robert	SI0980
Calibrated alligator	Silverberg, Robert	SI0340
Calibrated alligator [anthology]	Silverberg, Robert	SI0340
Calibrations and exercises	Benford, Gregory	NE0200
Calibrations and exercises	Benford, Gregory	NE0209
Call from Kerlyana	Carlson, William	G00030
Call from Kerlyana	Laurance, Alice	G00030
Call him lord	Dickson, Gordon R.	AN0106
Call him lord	Dickson, Gordon R.	DI0115
Call him lord	Dickson, Gordon R.	GR0250
Call him lord	Dickson, Gordon R.	NE0152
Call me Adam	Marks, Winston K.	C00310
Call me Ishtar	Lerman, Rhoda	DI0230
Call me Joe	Anderson, Poul	AM0512
Call me Joe	Anderson, Poul	AS0651
Call me Joe	Anderson, Poul	BE0208
Call me Joe	Anderson, Poul	HA0250
Call me Joe	Anderson, Poul	KN0160
Call me Joe	Anderson, Poul	SC0211
Call me Joe	Anderson, Poul	SI0121
Call of the stars	Clarke, Arthur C.	CL0280
Call of the stars	Clarke, Arthur C.	CL0310
Call of the stars	Clarke, Arthur C.	CL0340
Callahan and the wheelies	Barr, Stephen	C00490
Calling all stars	Szilard, Leo	SZ0150
Calling Dr. Clockwork	Goulart, Ron	EL0520
Calling Dr. Clockwork	Goulart, Ron	G00070
Calling Dr. Clockwork	Goulart, Ron	SU0150
Calling Dr. Clockwork	Goulart, Ron	W00406
Callistan menace	Asimov, Isaac	AS0230
Cambridge, 1:58 a.m.	Benford, Gregory	SI0480
Camera obscura	Monteleone, Thomas F.	M00155
Camouflage	Kuttner, Henry	KU0130
Can of paint	VanVogt, A.E.	VA0180
Can you feel anything when I do this?	Sheckley, Robert	KN0480
Can you feel anything when I do this?	Sheckley, Robert	PL0155
Canal builders	Abernathy, Robert	DI0130
Canis familiaris	Bronson, Donna	ED0150
Canis familiaris	Wallace, Robin E.	ED0150
Canticle for Leibowitz	Miller, Walter M., Jr.	CE0100
Canticle for Leibowitz	Miller, Walter M., Jr.	MA0195
Canticle for Leibowitz	Miller, Walter M., Jr.	WA0100
Canticle for Leibowitz [excerpt]	Miller, Walter M., Jr.	BE0206
Canticle for Leibowitz [excerpt]	Miller, Walter M., Jr.	MI0180

Color out of space	Lovecraft, Howard P.	CO0280
Color out of space	Lovecraft, Howard P.	MO0320
Colors	Disch, Thomas M.	DI0215
Colors of fear	Carr, Terry	NE0204
Colossus	Wandrei, Donald	AS0170
Colossus	Wandrei, Donald	DE0370
Columbus on St. Domenica [poem]	Cotton, John	HA0165
Columbus was a dope	Heinlein, Robert A.	AS0340
Columbus was a dope	Heinlein, Robert A.	HA0100
Columbus was a dope	Heinlein, Robert A.	HE0310
Columbus was a dope	Heinlein, Robert A.	PO0295
Columbus was a dope	Monroe, Lyle	GR0310
Combat SF [anthology]	Dickson, Gordon R.	DI0110
Combat unit	Laumer, Keith	LA0070
Come and go mad	Brown, Frederic	BR0435
Come and go mad	Brown, Frederic	BR0490
Come and go mad	Brown, Frederic	MA0490
Come into my cellar	Bradbury, Ray	BR0330
Come into my cellar	Bradbury, Ray	CO0640
Come into my cellar	Bradbury, Ray	GA0146
Come on, wagon!	Henderson, Zenna	HE0460
Come on, wagon!	Henderson, Zenna	MA0192
Come see the last man cry	Holly, J.H.	EL1180
Come sing the moons of Moravenn	Brackett, Leigh	EL1000
Come take a dip with me in the genetic pool	Payes, Rachel Cosgrove	EL0660
Come to me not in winter's white	Ellison, Harlan	EL0440
Come to me not in winter's white	Zelazny, Roger	EL0440
Come to the party	Busby, F.M.	WO0419
Come to the party	Herbert, Frank	WO0419
Come to Venus melancholy	Disch, Thomas M.	FI0090
Come up and see me	Castell, Daphne	MC0150
Comedian's children	Sturgeon, Theodore	FE0260
Comedian's children	Sturgeon, Theodore	ME0359
Comet, cairn, and capsule	Lunan, D.	AS0575
Comic inferno	Aldiss, Brian W.	AL0375
Coming [poem]	Pouln, A., Jr.	SA0150
Coming attraction	Leiber, Fritz, Jr.	BE0201
Coming attraction	Leiber, Fritz, Jr.	GA0140
Coming attraction	Leiber, Fritz, Jr.	JA0130
Coming attraction	Leiber, Fritz, Jr.	LE0100
Coming attraction	Leiber, Fritz, Jr.	MO0350
Coming attraction	Leiber, Fritz, Jr.	SC0210
Coming attraction	Leiber, Fritz, Jr.	WA0130
Coming attractions	Greenberg, Martin Harry	GR0100
Coming attractions [anthology]	Greenberg, Martin Harry	GR0130
Coming back to Dixieland	Robinson, Kim Stanley	KN0318
Coming of age in Henson's tube	Watkins, William Jon	AS0173
Coming of age in Henson's tube	Watkins, William Jon	PO0430
Coming of Conan [anthology]	Howard, Robert E.	HO0160
Coming of the robots [anthology]	Moskowitz, Samuel	MO0200
Coming of the sun	Jones, Langdon	HA0233

Coming-of-age day	Jorgensson, A.K.	DA0170
Coming-of-age day	Jorgensson, A.K.	MCC400
Coming-of-age day	Jorgensson, A.K.	ME0366
Coming-of-age day	Jorgensson, A.K.	SI0380
Command	DeCamp, Lyon Sprague	DE0070
Command	DeCamp, Lyon Sprague	MO0230
Command	DeCamp, Lyon Sprague	MO0350
Command	Kahn, Bernard I.	N00240
Command	Kahn, Bernard I.	N00330
Command performance	Miller, Walter M., Jr.	AL0450
Command performance	Miller, Walter M., Jr.	BE0203
Command performance	Miller, Walter M., Jr.	GA0141
Commando raid	Harrison, Harry	HA0145
Commencement night	Ashby, Richard	AM0514
Commencement night	Ashby, Richard	C00160
Common denominator	Lewis, D.	AN0140
Common denominator	MacDonald, John D.	GA0140
Common time	Blish, James	AL0450
Common time	Blish, James	BL0180
Common time	Blish, James	BL0200
Common time	Blish, James	D00130
Common time	Blish, James	SI0560
Common time	Blish, James	SI0680
Common time	Blish, James	SI0900
Common time	Blish, James	WA0130
Communicants	Sladek, John T.	J00150
Commuter	Dick, Philip K.	DI0075
Commuter's problem	Ellison, Harlan	EL0340
Company store	Silverberg, Robert	GR0300
Company store	Silverberg, Robert	SI0860
Compass [poem]	Corman, Cid	SA0150
Compassion circuit	Wyndham, John	AM0513
Compassion circuit	Wyndham, John	WY0210
Competition	Hull, E.M.	GR0220
Competitors	Lawson, Jack B.	W00405
Compleat consummators	Nourse, Alan E., M.D.	AS0555
Compleat consummators	Nourse, Alan E., M.D.	MA0204
Compleat werewolf	Boucher, Anthony	B00120
Compleat werewolf	Boucher, Anthony	ME0230
Compleat werewolf [anthology]	Boucher, Anthony	B00120
Complete short stories of H.G. Wells [anthology]	Wells, H.G.	WE0210
Completely automatic	Sturgeon, Theodore	C00340
Compound B	Fink, David Harold, M.D.	C00190
Compound B	Fink, David Harold, M.D.	HE0160
Compounded interest	Reynolds, Mack	ME0357
Computer cops	Hoch, Edward D.	SA0180
Computer that fought a dragon	Lem, Stanislaw	SU0180
Computer's mate	Rackham, John	NE0308
Computers don't argue	Dickson, Gordon R.	AL0402
Computers don't argue	Dickson, Gordon R.	AN0105
Computers don't argue	Dickson, Gordon R.	AS0651

Criminal negligence	McComas, J. Francis	DE0220
Crippled spinner	Grigg, David	HA0158
Crisis	Grendon, Edward	CO0250
Crisis [anthology]	Elwood, Roger	EL0640
Crisis in Utopia	Knight, N.L.	GR0160
Crisis, 1999	Brown, Frederic	DE0220
Critical angle	Chandler, A. Bertram	ST0230
Critical factor	Cleeve, Brian	PO0372
Critical mass	Clarke, Arthur C.	CL0370
Critical mass	Clarke, Arthur C.	CL0430
Critical mass	Kornbluth, Cyril M.	GA0147
Critical mass	Pohl, Frederik	GA0147
Critical path	Coles, David	NE0319
Critique of impure reason	Anderson, Poul	AN0335
Critters	Long, Frank Belknap	DE0470
Croatoan	Ellison, Harlan	CA0235
Crooked man	Beaumont, Charles	PL0150
Cross of centuries	Kuttner, Henry	MO0100
Cross of centuries	Kuttner, Henry	PO0300
Cross of centuries	Kuttner, Henry	PO0330
Cross of centuries	Kuttner, Henry	PO0374
Cross the border, close the gap	Fiedler, Leslie	AL0650
Crossing the wastelands	Hecht, Jeff	NE0209
Crowd	Bradbury, Ray	BR0280
Crowd	Bradbury, Ray	BR0360
Crowd of shadows	Grant, Charles L.	NE0162
Crucible of power	Williamson, Jack	GR0160
Crucifixus Etiam	Miller, Walter M., Jr.	AM0514
Crucifixus Etiam	Miller, Walter M., Jr.	FI0090
Crucifixus Etiam	Miller, Walter M., Jr.	ME0310
Crucifixus Etiam	Miller, Walter M., Jr.	SI0940
Cruel and unusual	Niven, Larry	NI0120
Cruel sky	Clarke, Arthur C.	CL0530
Cruelty	Decles, Jon	MC0180
Crusade	Clarke, Arthur C.	CL0530
Crusade	Clarke, Arthur C.	EL0200
Crying jag	Simak, Clifford D.	SI1060
Crying jag	Simak, Clifford D.	SI1080
Crying Willow	Rager, Edward	AS0555
Crystal egg	Wells, H.G.	DO0100
Crystal egg	Wells, H.G.	EL1240
Crystal egg	Wells, H.G.	KN0160
Crystal egg	Wells, H.G.	WE0200
Crystal egg	Wells, H.G.	WE0210
Crystal egg	Wells, H.G.	WE0250
Crystal egg	Wells, H.G.	WE0270
Crystal man [anthology]	Mitchell, Edward Page	MI0250
Crystal ship	Vinge, Joan D.	CR0250
Crystal ship	Vinge, Joan D.	VI0070
Crystal ship [anthology]	Silverberg, Robert	CR0250
Crystallization of the myth	Barfoot, John	KN0311
Cube root of uncertainty [anthology]	Silverberg, Robert	SI0360
Cues	Wolfe, Gene	EL0680
Culture	Shelton, Jerry	CO0130

Dance band on the Titanic	Chalker, Jack L.	WO0419
Dance of a new world	MacDonald, John D.	GR0190
Dance of the changer and the three	Carr, Terry	CH0100
Dance of the changer and the three	Carr, Terry	EL0200
Dance of the changer and the three	Carr, Terry	NE0154
Dance of the changer and the three	Carr, Terry	SI0400
Dance of the changer and the three	Carr, Terry	WA0130
Dance of the changer and the three	Carr, Terry	WO0409
Dance of the dead	Matheson, Richard	PO0300
Dance of the dead	Matheson, Richard	PO0330
Dance of the dead	Matheson, Richard	PO0373
Dance of the solids [poems]	Updike, John	MC0150
Dancer in the darkness	Monteleone, Thomas F.	MA0521
Dancin Partner	Jerome, Jerome K.	BR0520
Dancing Gerontius	Harding, Lee	BA0240
Dancing girl of Ganymede	Brackett, Leigh	BR0095
Dandelion girl	Young, Robert F.	ME0362
Dandelion girl	Young, Robert F.	YO0180
Dandelion wine	Bradbury, Ray	BR0415
Danger! Child at large	Cottrell, C.L.	PO0376
Danger! human!	Dickson, Gordon R.	SI0820
Danger: religion!	Aldiss, Brian W.	AL0437
Danger: religion!	Aldiss, Brian W.	IN0100
Dangerous flags	Disch, Thomas M.	DI0210
Dangerous invention	Zelikovich, E.	MA0360
Dangerous visions [anthology]	Ellison, Harlan	EL0300
Daniel White for the greater good	Ellison, Harlan	EL0400
Dannold cheque	Purdy, Ken W.	HA0162
Darfsteller	Miller, Walter M., Jr.	AS0370
Dark benediction	Miller, Walter M., Jr.	FI0095
Dark conception	Adams, Louis J.A.	MA0204
Dark door	Nourse, Alan E., M.D.	NO0360
Dark interlude	Brown, Frederic	GA0140
Dark interlude	Brown, Frederic	PR0210
Dark interlude	Reynolds, Mack	BE0202
Dark interlude	Reynolds, Mack	DE0250
Dark interlude	Reynolds, Mack	GA0140
Dark interlude	Reynolds, Mack	PR0210
Dark mission	DelRey, Lester	AS0451
Dark night of the soul	Blish, James	BL0210
Dark nuptial	Locke, Robert Donald	ST0180
Dark of the June	Wolfe, Gene	EL0580
Dark sanctuary	Benford, Gregory	PO0430
Dark side [anthology]	Knight, Damon	KN0220
Dark soul of the night	Aldiss, Brian W.	CA0275
Dark stars [anthology]	Silverberg, Robert	SI0320
Dark they were and golden-eyed	Bradbury, Ray	BR0100
Dark they were and golden-eyed	Bradbury, Ray	BR0270
Dark they were and golden-eyed	Bradbury, Ray	BR0330
Dark they were and golden-eyed	Bradbury, Ray	BR0400
Darkness	Carneiro, Andre	HA0165
Darkness	Carneiro, Andre	NO0402
Darkness and dawn	England, G.A.	MO0400
Darkness of day	Sargent, Pamela	EL0582

Day of the boomer dukes   Pohl, Frederik   P00260
Day of the butterflies   Bradley, Marion Zimmer   W00180
Day of the dove   Blish, James   ST0164
Day of the dragon   Endore, Guy   Y00150
Day of the hunters   Asimov, Isaac   AS0250
Day of the Triffids   Wyndham, John   BR0520
Day of the Triffids   Wyndham, John   WY0180
Day of wrath   Gansovsky, Sever   PA0210
Day on death highway   Elliott, Chandler   GA0147
Day Rembrandt went public   Auerbach, Arnold M.   CU0070
Day Rembrandt went public   Auerbach, Arnold M.   ME0363
Day the flag fell   Elam, Richard M.   EL0120
Day the flag fell   Elam, Richard M.   EL0140
Day the founder died   Silverberg, Robert   EL0640
Day the founder died   Silverberg, Robert   SI0800
Day the icicle works closed   Pohl, Frederik   P00180
Day the icicle works closed   Pohl, Frederik   P00260
Day the Martians came   Pohl, Frederik   P00180
Day the sun stood still [anthology]   Anderson, Poul   AN0190
Day they got Boston   Gold, H.L.   C00640
Day they got Boston   Gold, H.L.   GR0250
Day we celebrate   Bond, Nelson S.   C00340
Day we embarked for Cythera [poem]   Couzyn, Jeni   BE0500
Daybroke   Bloch, Robert   BL0240
Daybroke   Bloch, Robert   P00300
Daybroke   Bloch, Robert   P00330
Daybroke   Bloch, Robert   SC0300
Daymare   Brown, Frederic   BR0490
Days after tomorrow [anthology] Santesson, Hans Stefan   SA0180
Days of grass, days of straw   Lafferty, R.A.   NE0203
Days of Perky Pat   Dick, Philip K.   DI0075
Dazed   Sturgeon, Theodore   WA0100
De profundis   Kuttner, Henry   KU0130
De profundis   Leinster, Murray   DE0400
De profundis   Leinster, Murray   LE0160
Dead alien   Martinsen, M.   DA0273
Dead astronaut   Ballard, J.G.   BA0205
Dead center   Merril, Judith   B00151
Dead center   Merril, Judith   ME0170
Dead end   Hodous, Mike   AN0107
Dead end   MacFarlane, Wallace   C00550
Dead end   MacFarlane, Wallace   C00560
Dead in irons   Yarbro, Chelsea Quinn   DA0140
Dead in irons   Yarbro, Chelsea Quinn   SA0230
Dead in irons   Yarbro, Chelsea Quinn   YA0100
Dead knowledge   Campbell, John W.   CA0160
Dead lady of Clown Town   Smith, Cordwainer   SI0560
Dead lady of Clown Town   Smith, Cordwainer   SM0180
Dead letters   Campbell, Ramsey   GR0040
Dead man   Bradbury, Ray   BR0360
Dead man's chest   Serling, Rod   SE0180
Dead past   Asimov, Isaac   AS0200
Dead past   Asimov, Isaac   AS0310
Dead past   Asimov, Isaac   SI0300

Death cf the sea   Gironella, Jose Maria   CE0100
Death or consequences   Dorman, Sonya   EL1180
Death scene   Simak, Clifford D.   SI1180
Death sentence   Asimov, Isaac   AS0280
Death sentence   Asimov, Isaac   DE0470
Death therapy   Kelly, J.P.   CA0238
Death to the keeper   Malzberg, Barry N.   MA0460
Death's masquerade   Serling, Rod   SE0180
Death-trap   Daulton, G.   MO0365
Deathbird   Ellison, Harlan   AS0401
Deathbird   Ellison, Harlan   EL0320
Deathbird   Ellison, Harlan   MA0210
Deathbird   Ellison, Harlan   NE0159
Deathbird   Ellison, Harlan   WO0414
Deathbird stories [anthology]   Ellison, Harlan   EL0320
Deathlove   Pronzini, Bill   GR0040
Deathrights deferred   Piserchia, Doris   PO0290
Deathsong   VanScyoc, Sydney J.   WO0415
Debut   Emshwiller, Carol   KN0306
Debut   Emshwiller, Carol   SA0230
Decade of Fantasy and science fiction   Mills, Robert P.   MA0330
    [anthology]
Decade, the 1940's [anthology]   Aldiss, Brian W.   AL0400
Decade, the 1940's [anthology]   Harrison, Harry   AL0400
Decade, the 1950's [anthology]   Aldiss, Brian W.   AL0401
Decade, the 1950's [anthology]   Harrison, Harry   AL0401
Decade, the 1960's [anthology]   Aldiss, Brian W.   AL0402
Decade, the 1960's [anthology]   Harrison, Harry   AL0402
Decadence   Gary, Romain   ME0365
December 28th   Thomas, Theodore L.   PL0150
Decision makers   Green, Joseph   SU0150
Deep   Asimov, Isaac   AS0200
Deep   Asimov, Isaac   AS0470
Deep   Asimov, Isaac   AS0558
Deep down dragon   Merril, Judith   CO0720
Deep dcwn dragon   Merril, Judith   GA0146
Deep end   Ballard, J.G.   BA0120
Deep end   Ballard, J.G.   BA0150
Deep range   Clarke, Arthur C.   AS0645
Deep range   Clarke, Arthur C.   BR0520
Deep range   Clarke, Arthur C.   CL0280
Deep range   Clarke, Arthur C.   CO0160
Deep range   Clarke, Arthur C.   KN0120
Deep range   Clarke, Arthur C.   PO0300
Deep range   Clarke, Arthur C.   PO0330
Deep range   Clarke, Arthur C.   PO0373
Deep range   Clarke, Arthur C.   YO0150
Deep space   Abernathy, Robert   DI0160
Deep space [anthology]   Silverberg, Robert   SI0400
Deeper than the darkness   Benford, Gregory   MI0180
Deeper than the darkness   Ellison, Harlan   EL0240
Deeper than the darkness   Ellison, Harlan   EL0420
Deepest blue in the world   Dorman, Sonya   HA0233
Deeps   Roberts, Keith   KN0301

Different drummer	Moore, Raylyn	MA0210
Different drummer	Moore, Raylyn	OL0165
Different purpose	Bennett, Kem	MA0199
Digging the weans	Nathan, Robert	ME0357
Digits and dastards [anthology]	Pohl, Frederik	PO0210
DILOPS are coming	Farley, C.	EN0070
Diminishing draft	Kaempffert, Waldemar	CO0130
Dimple in drace	Latham, Philip	KN0302
Dingbat	Goulart, Ron	GO0100
Dinner at Helen's	Carlson, William	SC0450
Dinochrome	Laumer, Keith	LA0130
Dio	Knight, Damon	CO0150
Dio	Knight, Damon	OL0170
Dio	Knight, Damon	SI0123
Diplomatic coop	Galouye, Daniel F.	HA0232
Dipteroid phenomenon	Anderson, Poul	HAC200
Direction	Platt, Charles	JO0150
Direction of the road	LeGuin, Ursula K.	KN0312
Director	Howard, James	EL1120
Dirty tricks [anthology]	Effinger, George Alec	EF0180
Dirty war	Bunch, David R.	ED0150
Disappearing act	Bester, Alfred	BE0400
Disappearing act	Bester, Alfred	BO0100
Disappearing act	Bester, Alfred	GR0250
Disappearing act	Bester, Alfred	MA0470
Disappearing act	Bester, Alfred	PO0300
Disappearing act	Bester, Alfred	PO0330
Disappearing act	Bester, Alfred	PO0372
Disappearing act	Bester, Alfred	SI0740
Disaster story	Platt, Charles	MO0163
Discarded	Ellison, Harlan	EL0240
Discarded	Ellison, Harlan	EL0420
Discontent contingency	King, Vincent	NE0319
Discontinuity	Jones, Raymond F.	CO0580
Discord markers	Reynolds, Mack	CO0250
Discovery [poem]	Mitchell, Adrian	BEC500
Discovery in the woods	Greene, Graham	SA0150
Disguise	Robinson, Kim Stanley	KN0319
Disguise	Wollheim, Donald A.	SL0210
Disinherited	Anderson, Poul	KN0301
Disintegrating sky	Anderson, Poul	AN0325
Disintegration machine	Doyle, Arthur Conan	HO0119
Disintegration machine	Doyle, Arthur Conan	LO0100
Displaced person	Russell, Eric Frank	CA0420
Displaying the flag	Disch, Thomas M.	DI0215
Disposal	Goulart, Ron	CL0590
Disposal	Goulart, Ron	GO0070
Dissolve	Wolf, Gary K.	KN0311
Distortion	Silverstein, Shel	ME0361
Disturb not my slumbering fair	Yarbro, Chelsea Quinn	YA0100
Diversifal	Rocklynne, Ross	BR0080
Divine madness	Zelazny, Roger	SIC960
Divine madness	Zelazny, Roger	ZE0180
Divvil with the women	Wilde, Niall	MA0200

Django	Ellison, Harlan	RY0100
DNA [poem]	Ackerson, Duane	HA0167
Do androids dream of electric love?	Leibscher, Walt	SC0450
Do it for Mama!	Mundis, Jerrold J.	DI0250
Do not go gentle	O'Donnell, Kevin, Jr.	RY0100
Do you know Dave Wenzel?	Leiber, Fritz, Jr.	CA0265
Do-it-yourself	Ellison, Harlan	EL0340
DOCS	Lewis, Richard O.	OL0165
Doctor	Leinster, Murray	WI0230
Doctor	Slesar, Herry	AS0555
Doctor	Thomas, Theodore L.	GR0140
Doctor	Thomas, Theodore L.	KN0100
Doctor	Thomas, Theodore L.	KN0302
Doctor	Thomas, Theodore L.	SI0120
Doctor Gelabius	Bailey, Hilary	ME0290
Doctor Hanray's second chance	Richter, Conrad	SA0270
Doctor of Death Island	Wolfe, Gene	DA0180
Doctor Schmidt	Shamir, Moshe	SA0300
Doctor Zombie and his furry little friends	Sheckley, Robert	HA0164
Dodger fan	Stanton, Will	MA0197
Dodkin's job	Vance, Jack	SI1020
Does a bee care?	Asimov, Isaac	AS0250
Dog eat dog	Feiffer, Jules	ME0364
Cog in a fisherman's net	Delany, Samuel R.	DE0255
Dog star	Clarke, Arthur C.	CL0310
Dog star	Clarke, Arthur C.	CL0470
Dog star	Clarke, Arthur C.	SC0300
Dogfight	White, James	WH0160
Dogman of Islington	Bailey, Hilary	CA0280
Dogtown tourist agency	Vance, Jack	SI0480
Doing Lennon	Benford, Gregory	CA0235
Doll	Greenhough, Terry	WE0290
Doll-house	Cross, James	EL0300
Dolphin's way	Dickson, Gordon R.	DI0115
Dominant species	Neville, Kris	KN0309
Dominions beyond	Moore, Ward	BE0205
Dominions beyond	Moore, Ward	HO0120
Dominoes	Kornbluth, Cyril M.	K00070
Dominoes	Kornbluth, Cyril M.	P00371
Dominoes	Kornbluth, Cyril M.	SI1000
Don Jones	Anderson, Poul	AN0200
Don Jones	Dickson, Gordon R.	AN0200
Don Slow and his electric girl getter	Brand, Thomas	EL0180
Don't fence me in	Wilson, Richard	AS0555
Don't hold your breath	VanVogt, A.E.	EL1020
Don't hold your breath	VanVogt, A.E.	VA0140
Don't live in the past	Knight, Damon	GA0140
Don't live in the past	Knight, Damon	KN0600
Don't look now	Kuttner, Henry	JA0130
Don't look now	Kuttner, Henry	P00293
Don't wash the carats	Farmer, Philip Jose	FA0240
Don't wash the carats	Farmer, Philip Jose	KN0100
Don't wash the carats	Farmer, Philip Jose	KN0303

Doodad	Bradbury, Ray	EL0480
Doodad	Bradbury, Ray	MO0380
Doom from planet four	Williamson, Jack	WI0310
Doom of London	Barr, R.	MO0365
Doom that came to Sarnath	Lovecraft, Howard P.	SI0620
Doomsday deferred	Jenkins, William F.	BE0200
Doomsday deferred	Jenkins, William F.	BL0120
Doomsday deferred	Jenkins, William F.	SA0270
Doomsday machine	Blish, James	ST0161
Doomsday's color-press	Jones, Raymond F.	HO0130
Doomship	Pohl, Frederik	WO0414
Doomship	Williamson, Jack	WO0414
Door	White, E.B.	HA0210
Door in the wall	Wells, H.G.	WE0210
Door to anywhere	Anderson, Poul	GA0149
Doorbell	Keller, David H., M.D.	CO0280
Doors of his face, the lamps of his mouth	Zelazny, Roger	MA0205
Doors of his face, the lamps of his mouth	Zelazny, Roger	NE0151
Doors of his face, the lamps of his mouth [anthology]	Zelazny, Roger	ZE0180
Doors of his face, the lamps of his mouth	Zelazny, Roger	ZE0180
Doors of his face, the lamps of his mouth	Zelazny, Roger	ZE0190
Doorstep	Bretnor, Reginald	ME0357
Doorstep	Laumer, Keith	LA0130
Doorway into time	Moore, C.L.	MO0230
Doorway into time	Moore, C.L.	MO0350
Doorway into time	Moore, C.L.	PO0293
Doorway into time [anthology]	Moskowitz, Samuel	MO0230
Dorg	Lafferty, R.A.	KN0310
Dormant	VanVogt, A.E.	CR0100
Dormant	VanVogt, A.E.	DO0100
Dormant	VanVogt, A.E.	ST0180
Dormant	VanVogt, A.E.	VA0180
Dot and dash bird	Wolfe, Bernard	PL0150
Double dare	Silverberg, Robert	GA0144
Double dare	Silverberg, Robert	SI0360
Double dare	Silverberg, Robert	SI0920
Double dome	Banks, Raymond E.	DE0250
Double edged rope	Biggle, Lloyd	BI0100
Double meaning	Knight, Damon	KN0470
Double minds	Campbell, John W.	CA0110
Double standard	Brown, Frederic	ME0364
Double standard	Brown, Frederic	PL0155
Double take	Finney, Jack	PL0150
Double take	Marks, Winston K.	AS0340
Double whammy	Bloch, Robert	BL0250
Double, double, toil and trouble	Cantine, Holley	MA0200
Double, double, toil and trouble	Cantine, Holley	ME0361
Double-dyed villains	Anderson, Poul	GR0310
Doucement, s'il vous plait	Sallis, James	KN0311

Fast trip	White, James	WI0206
Fast-friend	Martin, George R.R.	DA0140
Faster than light	Zebrowski, George	DA0140
Faster than light [anthology]	Dann, Jack	DA0140
Fasterfaster affair	Anmar, Frank	NO0210
Fastest gun dead	Grow, Julian F.	ME0362
Fatal fulfillment	Anderson, Poul	AN0160
Fatal fulfillment	Anderson, Poul	FI0100
Fateful first day on Efene	Tofte, Arthur	FU0130
Father of the stars	Pohl, Frederik	IF0100
Father of the stars	Pohl, Frederik	PO0180
Father of the stars	Pohl, Frederik	PO0210
Father's in the basement	Farmer, Philip Jose	FA0240
Father's in the basement	Farmer, Philip Jose	KN0311
Father-thing	Dick, Philip K.	AS0590
Father-thing	Dick, Philip K.	BO0150
Father-thing	Dick, Philip K.	DI0075
Father-thing	Dick, Philip K.	KE0100
Father-thing	Dick, Philip K.	WA0130
Faulty register	Gores, Joe	SC0460
Faun	Anderson, Poul	AN0305
Fear hound	MacLean, Katherine	WO0409
Fear is a business	Sturgeon, Theodore	EA0100
Fear is a business	Sturgeon, Theodore	MA0330
Fear planet	Bloch, Robert	DE0400
Fearsome fable	Elliott, Bruce	MA0191
Feast of demons	Morrison, William	GA0144
Feast of demons	Samachson, Joseph	PO0240
Feast of St. Dionysus	Silverberg, Robert	SI0500
Feast of St. Dionysus	Silverberg, Robert	SI0540
Feast of St. Dionysus [anthology]	Silverberg, Robert	SI0540
Feather tigers	Wolfe, Gene	CA0420
Featherbedders	Herbert, Frank	AN0107
Feathered friend	Clarke, Arthur C.	CL0280
Feathered friend	Clarke, Arthur C.	CL0340
Feathers from the wings of an angel	Disch, Thomas M.	DI0215
Feeding time	Sheckley, Robert	AS0555
Feel of desperation	Wilhelm, Kate	WI0150
Feeling of power	Asimov, Isaac	AM0511
Feeling of power	Asimov, Isaac	AS0530
Feeling of power	Asimov, Isaac	WI0210
Feline	Heinlein, Robert A.	HE0340
Fellini beggar	Yarbro, Chelsea Quinn	YA0100
Fellow who married the Maxill girl	Moore, Ward	MA0200
Fellow who married the Maxill girl	Moore, Ward	ME0361
Fellowship of the stars [anthology]	Carr, Terry	CA0265
Felony	Causey, James	BE0205
Feminine intuition	Asimov, Isaac	AS0230
Feminine intuition	Asimov, Isaac	FE0230
Feminine metamorphosis	Keller, David H., M.D.	MO0410
Fence	Simak, Clifford D.	SI1160
Ferguson's capsules	Derleth, August W.	DE0430
Fessenden's worlds	Hamilton, Edmond	DE0370
Fessenden's worlds	Hamilton, Edmond	HA0155

Flame midget	Long, Frank Belknap	NO0240
Flame tree planet	Smith, George Henry	EL0700
Flame tree planet [anthology]	Elwcod, Roger	EL0700
Flames	Stapledon, Olaf	ST0150
Flaming ducks and giant bread	Lafferty, R.A.	KN0315
Flandry of Terra [anthology]	Anderson, Poul	AN0230
Flash crowd	Niven, Larry	TH0210
Flash point	Dozois, Gardner R.	DO0230
Flask of fine Arcturan	MacApp, C.C.	GA0148
Flatland [two excerpts]	Abbott, Edwin A.	HO0119
Flatlander	Niven, Larry	CO0610
Flauna	Jones, Raymond F.	EL0680
Flaw	MacDonald, John D.	BE0200
Flaw	MacDonald, John D.	BL0120
Flies	Asimov, Isaac	AS0500
Flies	Asimov, Isaac	CO0520
Flies	Silverberg, Robert	EL0300
Flies	Silverberg, Robert	SI0280
Flies	Silverberg, Robert	SI0760
Flight into darkness	Marlowe, Webb	HE0100
Flight into space [anthology]	Wollheim, Donald A.	WO0270
Flight of Apollo [poem]	Kunitz, Stanley	SA0150
Flight of ravens	Bradbury, Ray	BR0200
Flight of the Centaurus	Elam, Richard M.	EL0160
Flight on Titan	Weinbaum, Stanley G.	WE0158
Flight that failed	Hull, E.M.	CO0370
Flight to forever	Anderson, Poul	YE0403
Flirgleflip	Tenn, William	TE0180
Flirtation walk	Rogers, Kay	LA0160
Flower arrangement	Brown, Rosel George	GA0145
Flower that missed the morning	Dann, Jack	EL0820
Flower that missed the morning	Zebrowski, George	EL0820
Flowered thundermug	Bester, Alfred	NO0180
Flowering narcissus	Scortia, Thomas N.	EL0180
Flowering of the strange orchid	Wells, H.G.	WE0210
Flowering season	Kidd, Virginia	HO0110
Flowers for Algernon	Keyes, Daniel	AS0370
Flowers for Algernon	Keyes, Daniel	CR0103
Flowers for Algernon	Keyes, Daniel	FI0090
Flowers for Algernon	Keyes, Daniel	KA0070
Flowers for Algernon	Keyes, Daniel	MA0199
Flowers for Algernon	Keyes, Daniel	ME0360
Flowers for Algernon	Keyes, Daniel	SC0210
Fluffy	Sturgeon, Theodore	ST0270
Flux	Moorcock, Michael	CA0210
Flux	Moorcock, Michael	SI1000
Fly	Langelaan, George	ME0358
Fly	Langelaan, George	PL0150
Fly	Porges, Arthur	AS0340
Fly	Porges, Arthur	BE0203
Fly	Porges, Arthur	ME0230
Flying Dutchman	Moore, Ward	CR0200
Flying flowers	Vasilyev, Mikhail	DI0280
Flying flowers	Vasilyev, Mikhail	MA0360

Free men	Heinlein, Robert A.	HE0440
Free vacation	MacFarlane, Wallace	AN0107
Freedom	Reynolds, Mack	GR0250
Freedom	Reynolds, Mack	ME0362
Freedom of space	Clarke, Arthur C.	CL0280
Freedom of space	Clarke, Arthur C.	CL0340
Freeway	Johnson, George Clayton	N00200
Frehman angle	Pangborn, Edgar	EL1160
Fresh guy	Tubb, E.C.	ME0359
Fresh guy	Tubb, E.C.	SA0150
Friar of Chikala	Shefner, Vadim	NE0280
Frictional losses	Campbell, John W.	CA0160
Friday	Kippax, John	WI0201
Friday's child	Blish, James	ST0161
Friend from the stars	Sargent, Pamela	EL0900
Friend island	Stevens, F.	M00400
Friend of the family	Wilson, Richard	P00372
Friend to Alexander	Thurber, James	KN0450
Friend to man	Ellison, Harlan	EL0360
Friend to man	Kornbluth, Cyril M.	K00070
Friend to man	Kornbluth, Cyril M.	K00100
Friendly demon	Defoe, Daniel	MA0191
Friendly man	Dickson, Gordon R.	DI0100
Frightened tree	Budrys, Algis	P00150
Frog pond	Yarbro, Chelsea Quinn	MA0550
Frog pond	Yarbro, Chelsea Quinn	YA0100
From a private mad-house	Repton, Humphry	DE0400
From all of us	Bauer, Gerard M.	EL0940
From beyond	Lovecraft, Howard P.	DE0590
From fanaticism, or for reward	Harrison, Harry	HA0220
From Frankenstein to Andromeda [anthology]	Brown, J.G.	BR0520
From sea to shining sea	Ela, Jonathan	HA0165
From the "London Times" of 1904	Twain, Mark	FR0070
From the earth to the moon and a trip around it	Verne, Jules	VA0150
From the government printing office	Neville, Kris	EL0300
From the land of fear [anthology]	Ellison, Harlan	EL0360
From the notebook of Doctor Stein	Wolfe, Gene	EL0582
From the ocean, from the stars [anthology]	Clarke, Arthur C.	CL0280
From two universes	Buck, Doris Pitkin	MA0205
Frost and fire	Bradbury, Ray	BR0300
Frost animals	Shaw, Bob	CA0376
Frost-giant's daughter	Howard, Robert E.	H00160
Frozen assets	Wissner, Robert	CL0110
Frozen planet [anthology]	Laumer, Keith	FR0100
Fruit at the bottom of the bowl	Bradbury, Ray	BR0400
Fruit at the bottom of the bowl	Bradbury, Ray	BR0415
Fruit of knowledge	Moore, C.L.	M00170
Fruiting body	Brown, Rosel George	FE0200
FTA	Martin, George R.R.	AS0555
Fuel for the future	Hatcher, Jack	GR0130

Gifts of Asti	Norton, Andre	N00250
Gifts of Asti [anthology]	Elwood, Roger	EL0760
Gifts of the gods	Sellings, Arthur	NE0307
Gifts of the gods	Sellings, Arthur	NE0309
Gigolo	Goulart, Ron	G00100
Gil Braltar	Verne, Jules	MA0198
Gilead	Henderson, Zenna	AS0590
Gimmicks three	Asimov, Isaac	AS0310
Ginger star	Brackett, Leigh	BR0090
Ginny wrapped in the sun	Lafferty, R.A.	SI0700
Girl and robot with flowers	Aldiss, Brian W.	AL0365
Girl from Mars	Williamson, Jack	WI0310
Girl had guts	Sturgeon, Theodore	ST0330
Girl in the golden atom	Cummings, Ray	MA0480
Girl in the golden atom	Cummings, Ray	M00400
Girl who drew the gods	Jacobs, Harvey	ME0366
Girl who made time stop	Young, Robert F.	Y00180
Girl who was plugged in	Tiptree, James, Jr.	AS0401
Girl who was plugged in	Tiptree, James, Jr.	NE0203
Girl with rapid eye movements	Wolfe, Bernard	EL0220
Girl with the hundred proof eyes	Webb, Ron	MA0204
Girls from earth	Robinson, Frank M.	BE0203
Girls from earth	Robinson, Frank M.	SL0210
Girls from earth	Robinson, Frank M.	WI0210
Git along	DeCamp, Lyon Sprague	DE0100
Git along	DeCamp, Lyon Sprague	DE0470
Gladys's Gregory	West, John Anthony	FE0230
Glance ahead; being a christmas tale of A.D. 3568	Bangs, J.K.	ME0150
Glass eye	Cross, John Keir	BR0380
Glass eye	Russell, Eric Frank	ME0230
Cleaners	Simak, Clifford D.	FR0100
Gleeb for Earth	Schafhauser, Charles	GA0141
Gleepsite	Russ, Joanna	KN0100
Gleepsite	Russ, Joanna	KN0309
Gleepsite	Russ, Joanna	W00412
Glimpse of Mary	Gyles, G.A.	EL1080
Glimpses of the moon	West, Wallace	DI0220
Glitch	Blish, James	ST0220
Glow of candles, a unicorn's eye	Grant, Charles L.	GR0070
Gnarly man	DeCamp, Lyon Sprague	DE0070
Gnarly man	DeCamp, Lyon Sprague	GR0140
Gnarly man	DeCamp, Lyon Sprague	ME0310
Gnarly man	DeCamp, Lyon Sprague	AS0450
Gnome there was	Kuttner, Henry	AS0452
Gnome there was	Moore, C.L.	AS0452
Gnome there was	Padgett, Lewis	ME0230
Gnome there was [anthology]	Padgett, Lewis	PA0150
Gnomebody	Ellison, Harlan	EL0340
Gnurrs come from the voodvork out	Bretnor, Reginald	BE0201
Gnurrs come from the voodvork out	Bretnor, Reginald	MC0180
Gnurrs come from the voodvork out	Bretnor, Reginald	SI0780
Go for Baroque	Scott, Jody	MA0201
Go, go, go, said the bird	Dorman, Sonya	EL0300

Goat song	Anderson, Poul	AN0250
Goat song	Anderson, Poul	AS0401
Goat song	Anderson, Poul	NE0158
Goat song	Anderson, Poul	WA0130
Goat song	Anderson, Poul	WO0413
God in the bowl	Howard, Robert E.	HO0160
Goddess in granite	Young, Robert F.	MA0197
Goddess in granite	Young, Robert F.	YO0180
Goddess of wisdom	Bloch, Robert	BL0240
Gods are not mocked	Bloch, Robert	BL0250
Gods themselves throw incense	Harrison, Harry	HA0200
Gogol's wife	Landolfi, Tommaso	ME0367
Going	Silverberg, Robert	FO0130
Going	Silverberg, Robert	SI0320
Going down	Arnason, Eleanor	KN0319
Going down	Malzberg, Barry N.	EL0660
Going down smooth	Silverberg, Robert	KA0070
Going down smooth	Silverberg, Robert	SI0760
Going down smooth	Silverberg, Robert	WO0409
Going to the beach	Wolfe, Gene	EL1060
Going up	Driscoll, Dennis	ME0358
Going west	Bryant, Edward	KN0313
Gold at the starbow's end	Pohl, Frederik	AN0109
Gold at the starbow's end	Pohl, Frederik	WO0413
Gold-makers	Haldane, J.B.S.	CO0430
Golden acres	Reed, Kit	HA0161
Golden acres	Reed, Kit	MC0400
Golden acres	Reed, Kit	SA0300
Golden acres	Reed, Kit	SU0150
Golden age	Clarke, Arthur C.	CL0160
Golden ages gone away	Pohl, Frederik	CL0110
Golden apples of the sun	Bradbury, Ray	BR0130
Golden apples of the sun	Bradbury, Ray	BR0400
Golden apples of the sun [anthology]	Bradbury, Ray	BR0130
Golden brick	Hubbard, P.M.	MA0203
Golden bugs	Simak, Clifford D.	CO0580
Golden bugs	Simak, Clifford D.	SI1140
Golden egg	Sturgeon, Theodore	CO0550
Golden egg	Sturgeon, Theodore	CO0560
Golden helix	Sturgeon, Theodore	MA0485
Golden horn	Pangborn, Edgar	MA0202
Golden key	Keller, David H., M.D.	KE0070
Golden kite, the silver wind	Bradbury, Ray	BR0400
Golden lotus, a legend	Greshnov, M.	GI0100
Golden man	Dick, Philip K.	AL0405
Golden man	Dick, Philip K.	ME0260
Golden man	Dick, Philip K.	SI0820
Golden pyramid	Moskowitz, Samuel	FA0215
Golden the ship was ___ oh! oh! oh!	Smith, Cordwainer	SM0180
Goldfish bowl	Heinlein, Robert A.	HE0310
Goldfish bowl	Heinlein, Robert A.	ST0210
Golem	Davidson, Avram	DA0200
Golem	Davidson, Avram	DA0235
Golem	Davidson, Avram	JA0130

Golem	Davidson, Avram	KN0220
Golem	Davidson, Avram	MA0195
Golem	Davidson, Avram	ME0201
Golem	Davidson, Avram	ME0356
Golub-yavan	Stanyukovich, Kirill	DI0280
Gomez	Kornbluth, Cyril M.	B00150
Gomez	Kornbluth, Cyril M.	KE0100
Gomez	Kornbluth, Cyril M.	KN0540
Gomez	Kornbluth, Cyril M.	K00070
Gomez	Kornbluth, Cyril M.	K00100
Gone are the lupo	Hickey, H.B.	W00411
Gone dogs	Herbert, Frank	HE0520
Gone fishin'	Wilson, Robin Scott	HA0163
Gone to the dogs	DeFord, Miriam Allen	DE0210
Gonna roll the bones	Leiber, Fritz, Jr.	AS0400
Gonna roll the bones	Leiber, Fritz, Jr.	EL0300
Gonna roll the bones	Leiber, Fritz, Jr.	LE0100
Gonna roll the bones	Leiber, Fritz, Jr.	NE0153
Goobers	Davidson, Avram	DA0240
Good Indian	Reynolds, Mack	AN0102
Good Indian	Reynolds, Mack	CA0100
Good life	Thurston, Robert	CL0110
Good new days	Leiber, Fritz, Jr.	LE0100
Good news from the Vatican	Silverberg, Robert	BE0290
Good news from the Vatican	Silverberg, Robert	CA0368
Good news from the Vatican	Silverberg, Robert	NE0157
Good news from the Vatican	Silverberg, Robert	SI0280
Good news from the Vatican	Silverberg, Robert	WA0100
Good night Sophie	Aldani, Lino	R00270
Good night, Mr. James	Simak, Clifford D.	DE0470
Good night, Mr. James	Simak, Clifford D.	GA0140
Good night, Mr. James	Simak, Clifford D.	SI1060
Good night, Mr. James	Simak, Clifford D.	SI1120
Good old days	Dann, Jack	EL0800
Good provider	Gross, Marion	AS0340
Good provider	Gross, Marion	C00370
Good provider	Gross, Marion	KE0100
Good ring	Madsen, Svend Age	R00270
Good taste	Asimov, Isaac	AS0172
Good-bye, Robinson Crusoe	Varley, John	AS0173
Good-bye, Ilha!	Manning, Lawrence	C00160
Good-bye, Ilha!	Manning, Lawrence	ME0230
Good-bye, Robinson Crusoe	Varley, John	AS0440
Goodbye Amanda Jean	Shore, Wilma	SI0121
Goodbye, Henry J. Kostkos, goodbye	Knight, Damon	CL0110
Goodbye, Martian!	Yarov, Romen	M00150
Goodbye, Shelley, Shirley, Charlotte, Charlene	Thurston, Robert	KN0311
Goodlife	Saberhagen, Fred	SI0128
Goodly creatures	Kornbluth, Cyril M.	K00100
Gordon R. Dickson's SF best [anthology]	Dickson, Gordon R.	DI0115
Gorgon's head	Bacon, Gertrude	R00180
Gorilla suit	Shepley, John	MA0198
Gorman	Farber, Jerry	HA0163

Great fire	Bradbury, Ray	BR0400
Great fog	Heard, Henry Fitz-Gerald	C00730
Great God Awto	Smith, Clark Ashton	SM0150
Great intellect boom	Anvil, Christopher	OL0165
Great judge	VanVogt, A.E.	AS0340
Great judge	VanVogt, A.E.	WI0210
Great Keinplatz experiment	Doyle, Arthur Conan	C00190
Great Klandnar race	Garrett, Randall	CA0277
Great Klandnar race	Silverberg, Robert	CA0277
Great Nebraska sea	Danzig, Allan	AM0513
Great Nebraska sea	Danzig, Allan	ME0364
Great radio peril	Russell, Eric Frank	MC0400
Great science fiction about doctors [anthology]	Conklin, Groff	C00190
Great science fiction about doctors [anthology]	Fabricant, Noah D.	C00190
Great science fiction stories about Mars [anthology]	Dikty, T.E.	DI0190
Great science fiction stories about the moon [anthology]	Dikty, T.E.	DI0220
Great slow kings	Zelazny, Roger	ZE0180
Great stories of science fiction [anthology]	Leinster, Murray	LE0130
Great stories of space travel [anthology]	Conklin, Groff	C00220
Great supersonic zeppelin race	Bova, Ben	EL0680
Great wide world over there	Bradbury, Ray	BR0400
Greater than gods	Moore, C.L.	AS0450
Greater than gods	Moore, C.L.	M00170
Greater thing	Godwin, Tom	AL0450
Greatest asset	Asimov, Isaac	AS0250
Greatest asset	Asimov, Isaac	BE0291
Greatest love	McCaffrey, Anne	FU0160
Greatest television show on earth	Ballard, J.G.	BA0205
Greatest tertian	Boucher, Anthony	C00250
Green boy	Louden, Leo	EL0880
Green car	Temple, William F.	AS0585
Green cat	Cartmill, Cleve	DE0470
Green fingers	Clarke, Arthur C.	CL0280
Green fingers	Clarke, Arthur C.	CL0340
Green fingers	Clarke, Arthur C.	SA0210
Green hills of earth	Heinlein, Robert A.	AL0665
Green hills of earth	Heinlein, Robert A.	HE0220
Green hills of earth	Heinlein, Robert A.	HE0250
Green hills of earth	Heinlein, Robert A.	HE0340
Green hills of earth	Heinlein, Robert A.	HE0350
Green hills of earth	Heinlein, Robert A.	SA0150
Green hills of earth	Heinlein, Robert A.	SA0270
Green hills of earth [anthology]	Heinlein, Robert A.	HE0250
Green magic	Vance, Jack	MA0203
Green magic	Vance, Jack	MC0180
Green morning	Bradbury, Ray	BR0230
Green patches	Asimov, Isaac	AS0500

Hail to the chief	Sackett, Sam	OL0150
Halcyon in a mirror at midnight	Bradfield, Scott	ED0150
Half a hoka	Dickson, Gordon R.	SC0400
Half a life	Bulychev, Kirill	BU0070
Half a life and other stories [anthology]	Bulychev, Kirill	BU0070
Half an oaf	Robinson, Spider	B00240
Half life	Payes, Rachel Cosgrove	EL0540
Half pair	Chandler, A. Bertram	AL0450
Half the kingdom	Piserchia, Doris	KN0312
Half-baked publisher's delight	Asimov, Isaac	AS0555
Half-baked publisher's delight	Hudson, Jeffrey S.	AS0555
Half-breed	Asimov, Isaac	AS0280
Half-breed on Venus	Asimov, Isaac	AS0280
Half-past eternity	MacDonald, John P.	N00180
Halfling	Brackett, Leigh	BR0095
Halfling	Brackett, Leigh	P00293
Halfling [anthology]	Brackett, Leigh	BR0095
Halfway house	Silverberg, Robert	SI0360
Hall of machines	Jones, Langdon	ME0290
Hall of mirrors	Brown, Frederic	BR0435
Hall of mirrors	Brown, Frederic	P00150
Hallucination	Boulle, Pierre	B00200
Hallucination orbit	McIntosh, J.T.	GA0141
Hammerpond park burglary	Wells, H.G.	WE0210
Han Schnap's spy glass	Chatrian, Alexander	M00380
Hand	Smitter, Wessel Hyatt	BR0380
Hand with one hundred fingers	Lafferty, R.A.	KN0318
Handful of silver	Counselman, Mary Elizabeth	DE0560
Handler	Bradbury, Ray	BR0360
Handler	Bradbury, Ray	MA0490
Handler	Knight, Damon	H00100
Handler	Knight, Damon	KN0070
Handler	Knight, Damon	MC0400
Handler	Knight, Damon	ME0201
Handler	Knight, Damon	ME0360
Hands	Baxter, John	NE0306
Hands across the deep	Elam, Richard M.	EL0120
Hands across the deep	Elam, Richard M.	EL0140
Hands off	Sheckley, Robert	SH0180
Hang head, vandal!	Clifton, Mark	ME0363
Hanged man	Bryant, Edward	CL0110
Hans Phaall-a tale	Poe, Edgar Allan	M00320
Hans Schnap's spy glass	Erckmann, Emile	M00380
Happening	Roberts, Frank	BA0240
Happiest creature	Williamson, Jack	P00300
Happiest creature	Williamson, Jack	P00330
Happiest creature	Williamson, Jack	P00372
Happiest creature	Williamson, Jack	SI0127
Happiest day of your life	Shaw, Bob	AS0555
Happily ever after	Nolan, William F.	N00230
Happy birthday, dear Jesus	Pohl, Frederik	P00180
Happy breed	Sladek, John T.	EL0300

He walked around horses	Piper, H. Beam	PR0150
He who leaves no trace	Parnov, Jeremy	GI0130
He who leaves no trace	Yemtsev, Mikhail	GI0130
He who shapes	Zelazny, Roger	NE0151
He who shrank	Hasse, Henry	AS0170
He who shrank	Hasse, Henry	HE0100
He will wake in two hundred years	Strugatsky, Arkady	BE0020
He will wake in two hundred years	Strugatsky, Boris	BE0020
Head	Bloch, Robert	CA0275
Head and the hand	Priest, Christopher	HA0165
Head hunters	Williams, Ralph	CO0280
Head hunters	Williams, Ralph	SL0210
Head-rape	Thomas, D.M.	MO0164
Headpiece	Bradbury, Ray	BR0400
Heads Africa tails America	Saxton, Josephine	KN0309
Heal the sick, raise the dead	Peel, Jesse	AS0175
Heal the sick, raise the dead	Peel, Jesse	AS0440
Healing orgy	Gerrand, Rob	HA0158
Heart	Sturgeon, Theodore	ST0325
Heart of blackness	Ray, Robert	WI0206
Heart on the other side	Gamow, George	PO0240
Heartburn	Calisher, Hortense	BR0380
Heartland	Hasford, Gustav	KN0316
Heartstop	Effinger, George Alec	EF0180
Heat death of the universe	Zoline, Pamela	AL0402
Heat death of the universe	Zoline, Pamela	ME0290
Heat death of the universe	Zoline, Pamela	MO0163
Heat death of the universe	Zoline, Pamela	SA0230
Heat death of the universe	Zoline, Pamela	SA0300
Heat death of the universe	Zoline, Pamela	SI0680
Heather god	Zebrowski, George	NE0157
Heavens below	Sladek, John T.	DI0240
Heavy duty	Harrison, Harry	HA0220
Heavy metal	Bischoff, Dave	ED0150
heavy planet	Gregor, Lee	HE0100
Heavy planet	Rothman, Milton A.	AS0450
Heavy planet	Rothman, Milton A.	AS0645
Heavy planet	Rothman, Milton A.	HA0260
Heavy planet	Rothman, Milton A.	HA0290
Heavy planet	Rothman, Milton A.	PO0240
Hedonist	Gunn, James E.	GU0160
Heel & toe to the end [poem]	Williams, William Carlos	SA0150
Heir unapparent	VanVogt, A.E.	HA0232
Heirs apparent	Abernathy, Robert	BE0205
Heirs apparent	Abernathy, Robert	MA0194
Helbent 4	Robinett, Stephen	BE0301
Helbent 4	Robinett, Stephen	GA0100
Helbent 4	Robinett, Stephen	WO0416
Helen O'Loy	DelRey, Lester	AS0070
Helen O'Loy	DelRey, Lester	DE0190
Helen O'Loy	DelRey, Lester	JA0130
Helen O'Loy	DelRey, Lester	ME0230
Helen O'Loy	DelRey, Lester	PO0150

Helen O'Loy	DelRey, Lester	PRO150
Helen O'Loy	DelRey, Lester	SCO210
Helix the cat	Sturgeon, Theodore	ASO750
Hell is forever	Bester, Alfred	BEO400
Hell-bound train	Bloch, Robert	BLO240
Hell-bound train	Bloch, Robert	ASO370
Hell-fire	Asimov, Isaac	ASO310
Hell-planet	Rackham, John	NEO302
Help! I am Dr. Morris Goldpepper	Davidson, Avram	DAO235
Help! I am Dr. Morris Goldpepper	Davidson, Avram	GAO142
Help! I am Dr. Morris Goldpepper	Davidson, Avram	SIO580
Helping hand	Anderson, Poul	COO220
Helping hand	Anderson, Poul	COO340
Helping hand	Anderson, Poul	GRO250
Helping hand	DelRey, Lester	POO374
Hemeac	VonWald, E.G.	SUO150
Hemeac	VonWald, E.G.	WOO409
Hemingway in space	Amis, Kingsley	ALO402
Hemingway in space	Amis, Kingsley	MEO361
Her smoke rose up forever	Tiptree, James, Jr.	FEO170
Her strong enchantments failing	Anderson, Poul	ANO280
Herbert George Morley Robert Wells, Esq.	Clarke, Arthur C.	CLO530
Here is thy sting	Jakes, John	JAO070
Here is thy sting	Jakes, John	KNO303
Here there be tygers	Bradbury, Ray	HEO130
Here, there, and everywhere	Busby, F.M.	CLO110
Hereafter, inc.	DelRey, Lester	ASO452
Heredity	Asimov, Isaac	ASO280
Heredity	Asimov, Isaac	POO190
Heresies of the huge God	Aldiss, Brian W.	ALO405
Heresies of the huge God	Aldiss, Brian W.	GAO149
Heresies of the huge God	Aldiss, Brian W.	SIO330
Heresies of the huge God	Aldiss, Brian W.	SIO580
Heresies of the huge God	Aldiss, Brian W.	SIO600
Heresies of the huge God [poem]	Couzyn, Jeni	BEO500
Heritage	Abernathy, Robert	COO280
Hermit of Saturn's ring	Jones, N.R.	WOO270
Hermit on Bikini	Langdon, John	DEO500
Hero	Haldeman, Joe W.	ANO109
Hero	Haldeman, Joe W.	HAO165
Hero as werwolf	Wolfe, Gene	CAO235
Hero as werwolf	Wolfe, Gene	DIO240
Hero's life	Blish, James	HAO200
Heroic feat	Dneprov, Anatoly	MAO390
Hertford manuscript	Cowper, Richard	WOO417
Hertford manuscript	Murry, Colin	MUO100
Hexamnion	Davis, Chandler	NOO401
Hi diddle diddle	Silverberg, Robert	HAO290
Hi diddle diddle	Silverberg, Robert	SIO860
Hickory, dickory, Kerouac	Gehman, Richard	MEO201
Hickory, dickory, Kerouac	Gehman, Richard	MEO359
Hidden ears	Perkins, Lawrence A.	ANO108
Hidden planet [anthology]	Wollheim, Donald A.	WOO300

History lesson	Clarke, Arthur C.	R00210
History makers	Sallis, James	KN0305
History of Doctor Frost	Hodgins, Roderic C.	MA0205
Hitch-hike to paradise	Whybrow, Geoffrey	OB0140
Hobbies	Simak, Clifford D.	SI1100
Hobbyist	Russell, Eric Frank	AL0400
Hobbyist	Russell, Eric Frank	AS0700
Hobbyist	Russell, Eric Frank	CA0105
Hobbyist	Russell, Eric Frank	CR0103
Hobbyist	Russell, Eric Frank	RU0070
Hobo god	Jameson, Malcolm	GR0100
Hobo jungle	Goulart, Ron	GO0150
Hobson's choice	Bester, Alfred	CR0101
Hobson's choice	Bester, Alfred	KN0540
Hobson's choice	Bester, Alfred	MA0192
Hobson's choice	Bester, Alfred	SI0580
Hog-belly honey	Lafferty, R.A.	MA0205
Hoity-toity	Belayev, Alexander	DU0100
Hold back tomorrow	Neville, Kris	BL0100
Holding your eight hands	Lucie-Smith, Edward	HA0162
Holdout	Sheckley, Robert	DE0250
Holdout	Sheckley, Robert	KE0100
Hole in Jennifer's room	LoMedico, E.T.	EL0920
Hole in the floor	Fast, Howard	FA0270
Hole in the floor	Fast, Howard	FA0300
Hole in the moon	Seabright, Idris	MA0192
Hole in the sky	Cox, Irving, Jr.	DE0530
Hole man	Niven, Larry	AN0140
Hole man	Niven, Larry	AS0401
Hole man	Niven, Larry	WA0130
Hole on the corner	Lafferty, R.A.	KN0100
Hole on the corner	Lafferty, R.A.	KN0302
Holes around Mars	Bixby, Jerome	AL0401
Holes around Mars	Bixby, Jerome	AS0645
Holes around Mars	Bixby, Jerome	CO0220
Holes around Mars	Bixby, Jerome	CO0310
Holiday	Bradbury, Ray	DE0400
Holiday man	Matheson, Richard	FE0230
Holland of the mind	Zoline, Pamela	DI0260
Holland of the mind	Zoline, Pamela	J00150
Hollow man	Tuttle, Lisa	MA0521
Holy grail	Purdom, Tom	P00376
Home	Anderson, Poul	AN0305
Home	Anderson, Poul	H00110
Home from the shore	Dickson, Gordon R.	ME0363
Home is the hangman	Zelazny, Roger	AN0140
Home is the hangman	Zelazny, Roger	NE0161
Home is the hero	Tubb, E.C.	CA0200
Home is the hunter	Kuttner, Henry	KU0130
Home is where the wrec is	Tucker, Wilson	TU0150
Home of the gods	VanVogt, A.E.	VA0140
Home on LaGrange	Gehm, Barry	P00430
Home on LaGrange	Higgins, Bill	P00430
Home sweet geriatric dome	Gotschalk, Felix C.	NE0207

Home team advantage	Haldeman, Jack C.	AS0173
Home team advantage	Haldeman, Jack C.	AS0440
Home there's no returning	Moore, C.L.	ME0356
Home there's no returning	Kuttner, Henry	ME0356
Homecoming	Bradbury, Ray	BR0280
Homeland	Wolf, M.	SL0210
Homer's secret	Poleshchuk, Alexander	GI0100
Homeward and beyond [anthology]	Anderson, Poul	AN0250
Homing instinct of Joe Vargo	Barr, Stephen	AM0510
Homo saps	Russell, Eric Frank	RU0070
Homo sol	Asimov, Isaac	AS0280
Homo sol	Asimov, Isaac	CO0280
Honeymoon	McCaffrey, Anne	MC0165
Honeymoon in space	Griffiths, George	AL0510
Honeymoon in the hell	Brown, Frederic	GA0140
Honor	Wilson, Richard	DE0250
Honorable death	Dickson, Gordon R.	KN0460
Honorable death	Dickson, Gordon R.	SI0125
Honorable opponent	Simak, Clifford D.	GA0142
Honorable opponent	Simak, Clifford D.	SI1180
Hoofer	Miller, Walter M., Jr.	ME0356
Hoop	Fast, Howard	FA0270
Hoop	Fast, Howard	FA0300
Hop-friend	Carr, Terry	AS0575
Hop-friend	Carr, Terry	KN0460
Hop-friend	Carr, Terry	MA0202
Hop-friend	Carr, Terry	SI0100
Hopsoil	Young, Robert F.	YO0130
Horars of war	Wolfe, Gene	DI0110
Horars of war	Wolfe, Gene	KN0460
Horars of war	Wolfe, Gene	NO0401
Horizontal man	Spencer, William	NE0306
Horizontals	Long, Frank Belknap	LO0080
Horla	Maupassant, Guy de	EL0520
Hormone	Pratt, Fletcher	PO0372
Horn of plenty	Grigoriev, Vladimir	GI0130
Horn of time [anthology]	Anderson, Poul	AN0260
Horn of time the hunter	Anderson, Poul	AN0260
Horn of time the hunter	Anderson, Poul	HO0120
Horn of time the hunter	Anderson, Poul	WH0175
Horrer Howce	Saint Clair, Margaret	GA0143
Horror from the hills	Long, Frank Belknap	LO0080
Horror from the middle span	Lovecraft, Howard F.	DE0560
Horrow from the mound	Howard, Robert E.	HO0280
Horse from a different sea	McCaffrey, Anne	MC0165
Horse of a different technicolor	Strete, Craig	GA0100
Horse of air	Dozois, Gardner R.	DO0230
Horse of air	Dozois, Gardner R.	KN0100
Horse of air	Dozois, Gardner R.	KN0308
Horse of air	Dozois, Gardner R.	NE0157
Horse with one leg	Effinger, George Alec	CA0420
Horses	Muir, Edwin	AL0650
Hospital of transplanted hearts	Thomas, D.M.	HA0162
Hostess	Asimov, Isaac	AS0500

How I lost the Second World War and helped turn back the German invasion	Wolfe, Gene	AN0140
How it all went	Benford, Gregory	AS0555
How it felt	Effinger, George Alec	CA0372
How it felt	Effinger, George Alec	EF0210
How like a god	Bloch, Robert	BL0240
How like a god	Bloch, Robert	BL0250
How many miles to Babylon?	Wilhelm, Kate	WI0150
How microx and gigant made the universe expand	Lem, Stanislaw	LE0200
How near is the moon?	Merril, Judith	ME0358
How now purple cow	Pronzini, Bill	AS0555
How shall we conquer?	MacFarlane, Wallace	NE0203
How the heroes die	Niven, Larry	NI0150
How the old world died	Harrison, Harry	GA0148
How the whip came back	Wolfe, Gene	KN0306
How the world was saved	Lem, Stanislaw	ST0220
How to be a soldier	Aldiss, Brian W.	AL0300
How to count on your fingers	Pohl, Frederik	GR0130
How to count on your fingers	Pohl, Frederik	PO0180
How to count on your fingers	Pohl, Frederik	PO0210
How to kill Aunty	Sturgeon, Theodore	ST0320
How to learn Martian	Hockett, Charles F.	GR0130
How xmas ghosts are made	Bunch, David R.	GE0150
How-2	Simak, Clifford D.	AS0585
How-2	Simak, Clifford D.	DI0160
How-4	Simak, Clifford D.	BE0205
How-4	Simak, Clifford D.	GA0190
Howling bounders	Vance, Jack	HA0290
Hub	MacDonald, Philip	MA0191
Huddling place	Simak, Clifford D.	AL0400
Huddling place	Simak, Clifford D.	MO0350
Huddling place	Simak, Clifford D.	SC0210
Huddling place	Simak, Clifford D.	SI1100
Huddling place	Simak, Clifford D.	SI1120
Huge beast	Cartmill, Cleve	MA0191
Hugo winners V.1 [anthology]	Asimov, Isaac	AS0370
Hugo Winners V.2 [anthology]	Asimov, Isaac	AS0400
Hugo winners V.3 [anthology]	Asimov, Isaac	AS0401
human and other things [anthology]	DeGraeff, Allan	DE0250
Human being is the smallest thing	Busby, F.M.	AL0480
Human equation [anthology]	Nolan, William F.	NO0180
Human frailty	Xlebnikov, A.	MA0420
human is	Dick, Philip K.	DI0075
Human man's burden	Sheckley, Robert	CO0760
Human mutant	Paltock, Robert	EV0100
Human operators	Ellison, Harlan	BE0290
Human operators	Ellison, Harlan	EL0440
Human operators	Ellison, Harlan	SI0127
Human operators	VanVogt, A.E.	BE0290
Human operators	VanVogt, A.E.	EL0440
Human operators	VanVogt, A.E.	SI0127
Human pets of Mars	Stone, L.F.	AS0170

Human race has, maybe, thirty-five years left	Lyle, David	AL0665
Human side of the village monster	Bryant, Edward	CA0368
Human zero	Gardner, Erle Stanley	WA0160
Human? [anthology]	Merril, Judith	ME0310
Humanity on Venus	Stapledon, Olaf	MO0320
Humpty Dumpty had a great fall	Long, Frank Belknap	DE0370
Humpty Dumpty had a great fall	Long, Frank Belknap	LO0080
Humpty Dumpty had a great fall	Long, Frank Belknap	SI0820
Hunch	Anvil, Christopher	AN0101
Hunch	Anvil, Christopher	CA0100
Hung like an elephant	Pumilia, Joe	GE0150
Hung like an elephant	Utley, Steven	GE0150
Hunger over sweet waters	Kapp, Colin	NE0304
Hungry guinea pig	Breuer, Miles J., M.D.	CO0400
Hungry house	Bloch, Robert	BL0240
Hunt	Lem, Stanislaw	LE0200
Hunted	MacDonald, John D.	PO0190
Hunter	Fast, Howard	FA0270
Hunter at his ease	Aldiss, Brian W.	HA0164
Hunter gracchus	Kafka, Franz	WH0150
Hunter, come home	McKenna, Richard	KN0130
Hunter, come home	McKenna, Richard	MA0203
Hunter, come home	McKenna, Richard	MC0300
Hunters	Sheldon, Walt	AS0340
Hunting	Cassutt, M.	CA0375
Hunting lodge	Garrett, Randall	MA0465
Hunting lodge	Garrett, Randall	SI0640
Hunting machine	Emshwiller, Carol	BE0208
Hunting problem	Sheckley, Robert	SH0180
Hunting season	Robinson, Frank M.	YE0403
Hurkle is a happy beast	Sturgeon, Theodore	BE0200
Hurkle is a happy beast	Sturgeon, Theodore	BL0120
Hurkle is a happy beast	Sturgeon, Theodore	CO0460
Hurkle is a happy beast	Sturgeon, Theodore	SC0300
Hurkle is a happy beast	Sturgeon, Theodore	SI0780
Hurkle is a happy beast	Sturgeon, Theodore	ST0360
Hurkle is a happy beast	Sturgeon, Theodore	YO0150
Hurricane trio	Sturgeon, Theodore	ST0360
Husband for many wife	Stuart, William W.	HE0100
Hush!	Henderson, Zenna	HE0460
Hussy	Zhuraveleva, Valentina	SH0150
Hyborian age	Howard, Robert E.	HO0160
Hybrid	Laumer, Keith	AL0402
Hybrid	Laumer, Keith	LA0130
Hybrid hyperborean ant	McCardell, R.L.	MO0365
Hyperpilosity	DeCamp, Lyon Sprague	CO0280
Hyperpilosity	DeCamp, Lyon Sprague	DE0070
Hyperspace	Allen, Dick	DA0140
Hyperspherical basketball	Nearing, H., Jr.	MA0192
Hypnoglyph	Anthony, John	DE0500
Hypnoglyph	Anthony, John	MA0330
I always do what Teddy says	Harrison, Harry	DI0240
I always do what Teddy says	Harrison, Harry	HA0270

Immortality .... for scme	McIntosh, J.T.	CO0760
Immortality Inc.	Sheckley, Robert	SH0180
Immortals	Gunn, James E.	PO0374
Immortals of Mercury	Smith, Clark Ashtcn	SM0150
Immunity syndrome	Blish, James	ST0162
Impact	Barnes, Steve	LA0160
Imperscnators	MacApp, C.C.	WI02C6
Implode and peddle	Fyfe, H.B.	NO0330
Impossibility, a study of reason and science	Sullivan, J.F.	ME0150
Impossible highway	Friend, Oscar J.	AS0451
Impossible highway	Frienc, Oscar J.	LE0130
Impossible planet	Dick, Philip K.	AL0480
Impossible puppet show	Aldiss, Brian W.	AL0440
Impossible star	Aldiss, Brian W.	AL0365
Impcssible star	Aldiss, Brian W.	AL0540
Impossible voyage home	Wallace, F.L.	CO0400
Imposter	Dick, Philip K.	AS0070
Imposter	Dick, Philip K.	AS0651
Imposter	Dick, Philip K.	CO0520
Imposter	Dick, Philip K.	CR0101
Imposter	Dick, Philip K.	DI0075
Imposter	Dick, Philip K.	SI0380
Imposter	Dick, Philip K.	WO0210
Impractical joke	DeCamp, Lyon Sprague	DE0130
Impulse	Russell, Eric Frank	CO0250
IMT	Sargent, Pamela	SC0460
In a crooked year	Dozois, Gardner R.	EL1160
In a good cause	Asimov, Isaac	AS0500
In a gcod cause	Asimov, Isaac	HE0130
In a land of clear colors	Sheckley, Robert	DI0230
In a petri dish upstairs	Turner, Gecrge	HA0159
In a quart of water	Telfair, David	MC0150
In a season of calm weather	Bradbury, Ray	BR0100
In alien flesh	Benford, Gregory	WO0419
In Chinistrex Fortronza the people are machines	Bishop, Michael	DI0230
In dark places	Hensley, Jce L.	CL0590
In dark places	Hensley, Jce L.	EL0720
In darkness waiting	Leigh, Stephen	AS0172
In Donovan's time	Grant, Charles L.	KN0316
In entropy's jaws	Silverberg, Robert	CA0231
In entropy's jaws	Silverberg, Robert	CA0234
In hiding	Shiras, Wilmar H.	BL0120
In hiding	Shiras, Wilmar H.	CA0340
In hiding	Shiras, Wilmar H.	KN0480
In hiding	Shiras, Wilmar H.	KNC580
In hiding	Shiras, Wilmar H.	LE0130
In hiding	Shiras, Wilmar H.	SC0212
In hiding	Shiras, Wilmar H.	SL0210
In hiding	Shiras, Wilmar H.	TE0150
In his image	Carr, Terry	SI0123
In his image	Chilson, Robert	AN0108
In his own image	Biggle, Llcyd	BI015C

Infinity box [anthology]	Wilhelm, Kate	WI0165
Infinity of loving	Gerrold, David	EL1160
Infinity zero	Wandrei, Donald	DE0400
Inflexible logic	Maloney, Russell	BR0380
Informal biography of Conan the Cimmerian	Howard, Robert E.	HO0160
Infra Draconis	Gurevich, G.	DU0100
Infra Draconis	Gurevich, G.	WI0280
Infra-medians	Wright, Sewell Peaslee	WO0240
Ingenious patriot	Bierce, Ambrose	AS0555
Ingenious patriot	Bierce, Ambrose	KN0280
Inheritance	Clarke, Arthur C.	CL0130
Inheritance	Clarke, Arthur C.	CL0160
Inheritance	Clarke, Arthur C.	CL0220
Inheritance	Clarke, Arthur C.	CL0250
Initiation	Malzberg, Barry N.	MA0460
Inner landscape [anthology]	anonymous	IN0100
Inner wheel	Roberts, Keith	NE0306
Inner worlds	Morrison, William	BE0205
Innocence	Russ, Joanna	AS0555
Innocence of Father Bangs	Goulart, Ron	GO0100
Innocent arrival	Anderson, Poul	DE0220
Inquiry concerning the curvature of the earth's surface and divers investigations of a metaphysical nature	Price, Roger	ME0360
Ins and outs of the Hadhya city-state	Maddern, Pip	HA0158
Insane ones	Ballard, J.G.	ME0363
Insects	Fast, Howard	FA0270
Insert knob A in hole B	Asimov, Isaac	AS0500
Inside	Carr, Carol	CA0280
Inside	Carr, Carol	KN0308
Inside	Carr, Carol	SI0740
Inside earth	Anderson, Poul	GA0140
Inside John Barth	Stuart, William W.	GA0144
Inside of the earth	Mitchell, Edward Page	MI0250
Inside straight	Anderson, Poul	AN0315
Inside the earth	Clarke, Arthur C.	WI0204
Insidekick	Bone, J.F.	CO0100
Insidekick	Bone, J.F.	GA0145
Inspector	McKimmey, James	EL0200
Inspector's teeth	DeCamp, Lyon Sprague	DE0070
Inspector's teeth	DeCamp, Lyon Sprague	DE0100
Installment plan	Simak, Clifford D.	SI1060
Instead of the cross, the lollipop	Skinner, B.F.	DI0240
Instinct	DelRey, Lester	CO0280
Instinct	DelRey, Lester	KA0070
Instinct	DelRey, Lester	SI0640
Institute	Emshwiller, Carol	MC0150
Institutions	Malzberg, Barry N.	EL1140
Intangibles Inc.	Aldiss, Brian W.	AL0360
Intangibles Inc.	Aldiss, Brian W.	AL0418
Intangibles Inc.	Aldiss, Brian W.	AL0437
Intangibles Inc. [anthology]	Aldiss, Brian W.	AL0418

Invariant	Pierce, John R.	ASO700
Invasion	Ley, Willy	POO240
Invasion	Long, Frank Belknap	DEO40C
Invasion	Long, Frank Belknap	LOOO80
Invasion	Podolny, Roman	GIO130
Invasion from inner space	Koch, Howard	POO376
Invasion from Mars	Koch, Howard	CHO100
Invasion from Mars	Koch, Howard	COO250
Invasion from Mars	Koch, Howard	SAO150
Invasion from Mars [abridged]	Wells, H.G.	KUO100
Invasion of privacy	Shaw, Bob	WOO411
Invasion of the planet of love	Elliot, George P.	MAO199
Investigating the Bidwell endeavors	Bunch, David R.	MEO366
Investigating the curiosity drive	Herzog, Tom	OLO165
Invisible boy	Bradbury, Ray	BRO415
Invisible boy	Bradbury, Ray	DAO230
Invisible dove dancer of Strathpheen Island	Collier, John	DAO230
Invisible girl	Sargent, Pamela	ELO820
Invisible light	Belayev, Alexander	MAO360
Invisible man	Wells, H.G.	KNO130
Invisible man	Wells, H.G.	WEO200
Invisible man	Wells, H.G.	WEO220
Invisible man murder case	Slesar, Henry	DAO230
Invisible men [anthology]	Davenport, Basil	DAO230
Invisible prisoner	LeBlanc, Maurice	DAO230
Ionian cycle	Tenn, William	GRO310
IOU	Wellen, Edward	GAO280
Ipswitch phial	Garrett, Randall	ASO585
Iron chancellor	Silverberg, Robert	SIO300
Iron chancellor	Silverberg, Robert	SIO360
Iron jackass	Brunner, John	BRO550
Iron moon	Elam, Richard M.	ELO120
Iron moon	Elam, Richard M.	ELO140
Iron one	Hamilton, Edmond	ELO180
Iron standard	Padgett, Lewis	GRO220
Irrational numbers [anthology]	Effinger, George Alec	EFO210
Is it the end of the world?	Shore, Wilma	MAO210
Is physics finished?	Rothman, Milton A.	ASO172
Is that what people do?	Sheckley, Robert	PRO160
Is there in truth no beauty?	Blish, James	STO164
Isaac Asimov presents the great science fiction stories. v. 1, 1939 [anthology]	Asimov, Isaac	ASO450
Isaac Asimov presents the great science fiction stories. v. 2, 1940 [anthology]	Asimov, Isaac	ASO451
Isaac Asimov presents the great science fiction stories. v.3, 1941 [anthology]	Asimov, Isaac	ASO452
Isaac Asimov presents the great science fiction stories. v. 1, 1939 [anthology]	Greenberg, Martin Harry	ASO450

Isaac Asimov presents the great science fiction stories. v.3, 1941 [anthology]	Greenberg, Martin Harry	AS0452
Isaac Asimov's masters of science fiction [anthology]	Asimov, Isaac	AS0440
Isaiah	Malzberg, Barry N.	MA0455
Ishmael in love	Silverberg, Robert	SI0760
Ishmael in love	Silverberg, Robert	W00411
Ishmael into the barrens	Lafferty, R.A.	F00130
Island	Jones, Roger	ME0290
Island in the sky	Wellman, Manly Wade	MA0480
Island of Doctor Death	Wolfe, Gene	KN0307
Island of Doctor Death and other stories	Wolfe, Gene	KN0100
Island of Doctor Death and other stories	Wolfe, Gene	NE0156
Island of Dr. Moreau	Wells, H.G.	WE0220
Island of fear	Sambrot, William	SA0270
Island of five colors	Gardner, Martin	CR0230
Island of the crabs	Dneprov, Anatoly	SU0180
Island of the endangered	Ferguson, Dale	Y00150
Island of unreason	Hamilton, Edmond	HA0155
Islands	Grigg, David	HA0158
Islands of space	Campbell, John W.	CA0140
Isolationist	Reynolds, Mack	C00130
Isolationsts	Silverberg, Robert	SI0800
It	Sturgeon, Theodore	AS0451
It	Sturgeon, Theodore	CA0260
It	Sturgeon, Theodore	KN0220
It beccmes necessary	Moore, Ward	ME0362
It could be you	Roberts, Frank	BA0235
It could be you	Roberts, Frank	ME0365
It didn't happen	Brown, Frederic	BR0435
It doesn't really matter	Malzberg, Barry N.	EL0780
It opens the sky	Sturgeon, Theodore	ST0330
It was nothing - really	Sturgeon, Theodore	ST0220
It wasn't my fault	O'Donnell, K.M.	EL0900
It wasn't syzygy	Sturgeon, Theodore	ST0270
"It's a bird! It's a plane!"	Spinrad, Norman	HA0130
It's a good life	Bixby, Jerome	AL0425
It's a good life	Bixby, Jerome	AS0590
It's a good life	Bixby, Jerome	CR0103
It's a good life	Bixby, Jerome	JA0130
It's a good life	Bixby, Jerome	P00300
It's a good life	Bixby, Jerome	P00330
It's a good life	Bixby, Jerome	P00372
It's a good life	Bixby, Jerome	SA0150
It's a good life	Bixby, Jerome	SC0210
It's a good life	Bixby, Jerome	SI0700
It's a great big wonder universe	Aandahl, Vance	MA0200
It's a tough life	Long, Frank Belknap	L00080
It's great to be back	Heinlein, Robert A.	C00730
It's great to be back	Heinlein, Robert A.	HE0250
It's great to be back	Heinlein, Robert A.	HE0340

It's great to be back	Heinlein, Robert A.	KN0190
It's great to be back	Heinlein, Robert A.	PO0293
It's not too late	Clark, John Edward	HA0158
It's such a beautiful day	Asimov, Isaac	AS0500
It's such a beautiful day	Asimov, Isaac	DA0272
It's such a beautiful day	Asimov, Isaac	EN0100
It's such a beautiful day	Asimov, Isaac	PO0373
It's such a beautiful day	Asimov, Isaac	RO0180
Itself	Bacon, E.M.	MO0365
Izzard and the membrane	Miller, Walter M., Jr.	YE0403
J is for Jeanne	Tubb, E.C.	ME0366
J.G.	Price, Roger	ME0361
Jachid and Jachidah	Singer, Isaac Bashevis	AL0665
Jachid and Jachidah	Singer, Isaac Bashevis	DA0200
Jack and Betty	Thurston, Robert	KN0316
Jack fell down	Brunner, John	SA0180
Jack-in-the-box	Bradbury, Ray	BR0280
Jack-in-the-box	Bradbury, Ray	BR0360
Jackal's meal	Dickson, Gordon R.	DI0125
Jackpot	Simak, Clifford D.	SI1180
Jackson Wong's story	Bolsover, John	OB0140
Jacob's bug	Posner, Richard	EL1200
Jade blue	Bryant, Edward	CA0368
Jameson satellite	Jones, N.R.	AS0170
Jamey's visitor	Lytle, B.J.	EL0730
Jamie's smile	Brennert, Alan	CA0275
Jane Saint's travails	Saxton, Josephine	SA0120
January 1975	Malzberg, Barry N.	AS0555
January 1975	Malzberg, Barry N.	MA0455
Jar	Bradbury, Ray	BR0280
Jay score	Russell, Eric Frank	AS0452
Jay score	Russell, Eric Frank	HE0400
Jay score	Russell, Eric Frank	RU0070
Jaycee	Brown, Frederic	BR0435
Jaywalker	Rocklynne, Ross	GA0140
Jazz machine	Matheson, Richard	ME0364
Jean Dupres	Dickson, Gordon R.	NO0401
Jenny among the zeebs	Anmar, Frank	NO0150
Jeremy in the wind	Kneale, Nigel	BR0330
Jerry was a man	Heinlein, Robert A.	HE0190
Jester	Tenn, William	CO0550
Jester	Tenn, William	CO0560
Jesting pilot	Kuttner, Henry	CL0590
Jesting pilot	Kuttner, Henry	KN0190
Jesting pilot	Padgett, Lewis	PA0150
Jet-propelled couch	Lindner, Robert	AL0360
Jetsam	Chandler, A. Bertram	ST0230
Jewbird	Malamud, Bernard	DA0200
Jewbird	Malamud, Bernard	ME0364
Jewel of Bas	Brackett, Leigh	BR0070
Jewels of Gwahlur	DeCamp, Lyon Sprague	HO0220
Jewels of Gwahlur	Howard, Robert E.	HO0220
Jezebel	Leinster, Murray	DE0500
Jigsaw man	Niven, Larry	EL0300

Jigsaw man	Niven, Larry	NI0150
Jilting of Jane	Wells, H.G.	WE0210
Jim and Mary G.	Sallis, James	KN0100
Jim and Mary G.	Sallis, James	KN0307
Jimmy goggles the god	Wells, H.G.	WE0210
Jirel meets magic	Moore, C.L.	SA0220
Jizzle	Wyndham, John	MA0192
Job is ended	Tucker, Wilson	TU0150
Jody after the war	Bryant, Edward	KN0310
Joelle	Anderson, Poul	AS0172
John Grant's little angel	Grove, Walt	PL0150
John of the apocalypse	Benford, Gregory	ZE0150
John of the apocalypse	Benford, James	ZE0150
John Sze's future	Pierce, John R.	C00430
John the revelator	LaFarge, Oliver	MA0191
John Thomas's cube	Leimert, John	C00280
John W. Campbell anthology	Campbell, John W.	CA0140
John Wyndham Omnibus [anthology]	Harris, John Benyon	WY0180
John's other life	Haldeman, Joe W.	EL1060
John's other practice	Marks, Winston K.	BE0205
Johnny on the spot	Long, Frank Belknap	L00080
Join our gang?	Lanier, Sterling E.	AN0101
Join our gang?	Lanier, Sterling E.	CA0100
Joker for hire	Goulart, Ron	G00070
Jokester	Asimov, Isaac	AL0450
Jokester	Asimov, Isaac	AS0310
Jon's world	Dick, Philip K.	DE0530
Jordan	Henderson, Zenna	MA0330
Journal of Ellipsia [excerpt]	Calisher, Hortense	ME0367
Journey	Leinster, Murray	P00371
Journey of ten thousand miles	Mohler, Wil	FE0200
Journey of the soul	Shapiro, N.	EL1130
Journey to another star	Zebrowski, George	EL0800
Journey to another star [anthology]	Elwood, Roger	EL0800
Journey to Babel	Blish, James	ST0162
Journey to Babel	Fontana, D.C.	ST0164
Journey to infinity [anthology]	Greenberg, Martin Harry	GR0190
Journey to the center of the earth	Verne, Jules	BRC520
Journey to the center of the earth	Verne, Jules	L00100
Journey to the heartland	Aldiss, Brian W.	AL0435
Journey to the heartland	Aldiss, Brian W.	CA0373
Journey to the moon [abridged]	DeBergerac, Cyrano	DE0190
Journey to the world underground [excerpt]	Holberg, Ludvig	GU0130
Journey's end	Anderson, Poul	AN0180
Journey's end	Anderson, Poul	AN0280
Journey's end	Anderson, Poul	KN0480
Journey's end	Anderson, Poul	MA0197
Journey's end	Anderson, Poul	MC0180
Journey's end	Anderson, Poul	SI0380
Journey's end	Anderson, Poul	SI0660
Journeys in science fiction [anthology]	Loughlin, Richard L.	L00100

Journeys in science fiction [anthology]	Popp, Lilian M.	L00100
Joy in Mudville	Anderson, Poul	CA0277
Joy in Mudville	Dickson, Gordon R.	CA0277
Joy of living	Nolan, William F.	N00210
Joycelin Shrager story	Disch, Thomas M.	DI0215
Jubilee's story	Lynn, Elizabeth A.	KI0070
Judas	Brunner, John	EL0300
Judas	Brunner, John	M00100
Judas danced	Aldiss, Brian W.	AL0365
Judas canced	Aldiss, Brian W.	SI0123
Judas fish	Scortia, Thomas N.	HA0300
Judas Ram	Merwin, Sam, Jr.	GA0140
Judgement day	Biggle, Lloyd	BI0200
Judgement day	DeCamp, Lyon Sprague	BE0206
Judgement day	DeCamp, Lyon Sprague	DE0070
Judgement day	DeCamp, Lyon Sprague	DE0130
Judgement day	DeCamp, Lyon Sprague	KN0480
Judgement night	Serling, Rod	SE0180
Judgment of Aphrodite	Hoyle, Fred	H00310
Juggernaut	VanVogt, A.E.	C00730
Juke doll	Young, Robert F.	N00210
Jump	Earls, William	AN0108
June 6, 2016	England, G.A.	M00410
Jungle doctor	Young, Robert F.	BE0206
Jungle journey	Wyndham, John	M00320
Jungle substitute	Aldiss, Brian W.	GA0148
Junior	Abernathy, Robert	MA0465
Junior	Abernathy, Robert	ME0356
Junior achievement	Lee, William	AN0102
Junior achievement	Lee, William	AS0590
Junior achievement	Lee, William	CA0100
Junior partner	Goulart, Ron	G00150
Junkmakers	Teichner, Albert	GA0280
Junkyard	Simak, Clifford D.	GA0141
Jupiter five	Clarke, Arthur C.	CL0130
Jupiter five	Clarke, Arthur C.	CL0220
Jupiter five	Clarke, Arthur C.	CL0400
Jupiter five	Clarke, Arthur C.	SI0520
Jury of five	Hoyle, Fred	H00310
Juryrigged	Haldeman, Joe W.	HA0137
Just curious	Schmitz, James H.	HA0232
Kalcar, World of Antares	Hamilton, Edmond	W00360
Kaleidoscope	Bradbury, Ray	BR0415
Kaleidoscope	Bradbury, Ray	C00280
Kangaroo court	Kidd, Virginia	KN0301
Kappa nu nexus	Davidson, Avram	C00720
Kappa nu nexus	Klass, Morton	C00720
Katy dialogues	Goulart, Ron	G00070
Kazam collects	Kornbluth, Cyril M.	CA0420
Kazam collects	Kornbluth, Cyril M.	K00130
Kazam collects	Kornbluth, Cyril M.	P00293
Kazoo	Sallis, James	M00163
Keep out	Brown, Frederic	C00400

Love story in three acts	Gerrold, David	N00401
Love that universe	Clarke, Arthur C.	CL0530
Love they Vimp	Nourse, Alan E., M.D.	N00390
Love, incorporated	Sheckley, Robert	KA0070
Love, incorporated	Sheckley, Robert	PL0150
Love, incorporated	Sheckley, Robert	PL0155
Lovemaker	Eklund, Gordon	EL0180
Lovemaking	Pohl, Frederik	PL0155
Lover when you're near me	Matheson, Richard	BF0203
Lover when you're near me	Matheson, Richard	GA0141
Low grade ore	O'Donnell, Kevin, Jr.	AS0173
Low grade ore	O'Donnell, Kevin, Jr.	AS0440
Low-flying aircraft	Ballard, J.G.	BA0205
Low-flying aircraft [anthology]	Ballard, J.G.	BA0205
Lower than angels	Budrys, Algis	EN0100
Lower than angels	Budrys, Algis	SI0440
Luana	Thomas, Gilbert	MA0206
Luana	Thomas, Gilbert	ME0367
Lucifer	Zelazny, Roger	ZE0180
Luck of Ignatz	DelRey, Lester	DE0310
Luck of Ignatz	DelRey, Lester	W00300
Luckiest man in Denv	Kornbluth, Cyril M.	KN0190
Luckiest man in Denv	Kornbluth, Cyril M.	K00C70
Luckiest man in Denv	Kornbluth, Cyril M.	MC0280
Luckiest man in Denv	Kornbluth, Cyril M.	SI0126
Luckiest man in Denv	Kornbluth, Cyril M.	WA0130
Luger is a 9mm automatic handgun with a parabellum action	Mundis, Jerrold J.	M00166
Luggage store	Bradbury, Ray	BR0230
Lukundoo	White, Edward Lucas	KN0490
Lulu	Simak, Clifford D.	SI1080
Lulu	Simak, Clifford D.	SI1180
Lulungomeena	Dickson, Gordon R.	LE0220
Lulungomeena	Dickson, Gordon R.	SI0400
Lunar trap	Elam, Richard M.	EL0120
Lunar trap	Elam, Richard M.	EL0140
Lunatic assignment	Dorman, Sonya	MA0208
Luncheon in the sepulcher	Disch, Thomas M.	DI0260
Lunians	Boulle, Pierre	B00200
Lydectes: on the nature of sport	Effinger, George Alec	EF0210
Lysenko maze	Grinnell, David	C00400
Lysenko maze	Grinnell, David	CU0070
Lysenko maze	Wollheim, Donald A.	KA0070
M and M, seen as a low-yield thermonuclear device	Varley, John	KN0318
M is for many	Russ, Joanna	CA0372
M-1	Wilson, Gahan	FE0230
Mab Gallen recalled	Wilder, Cherry	KI0070
Macauley circuit	Silverberg, Robert	SI0640
Macauley circuit	Silverberg, Robert	SI0860
MacDonough's Song	Kipling, Rudyard	C00640
Machine	Campbell, John W.	CA0130
Machine	Campbell, John W.	EL0520
Machine	Jakes, John	BE0203

Machine	Jakes, John	JA0070
Machine and men [anthology]	Roberts, Keith	RO0150
Machine made	McIntosh, J.T.	CA0230
Machine made	McIntosh, J.T.	CO0160
Machine made	McIntosh, J.T.	WI0202
Machine stops	Forster, E.M.	AL0665
Machine stops	Forster, E.M.	CO0460
Machine stops	Forster, E.M.	CO0640
Machine stops	Forster, E.M.	HA0210
Machine stops	Forster, E.M.	HO0119
Machine stops	Forster, E.M.	KN0190
Machine stops	Forster, E.M.	KU0100
Machine stops	Forster, E.M.	SC0212
Machine stops	Forster, E.M.	WH0150
Machine stops	Forster, E.M.	WI0250
Machine that was lovely	Wells, Robert	OB0140
Machine that won the war	Asimov, Isaac	AS0500
Machine that won the war	Asimov, Isaac	MA0201
Machineries of joy	Bradbury, Ray	BR0200
Machineries of joy [anthology]	Bradbury, Ray	BR0200
Machines of loving grace	Dozois, Gardner R.	DO0230
Machines of loving grace	Dozois, Gardner R.	KN0311
Machismo on Byronia	Gardner, Martin	AS0173
Machmen	Schmitz, James H.	SC0180
Mad moon	Weinbaum, Stanley G.	MO0290
Mad moon	Weinbaum, Stanley G.	WE0150
Mad moon	Weinbaum, Stanley G.	WE0158
Mad planet	Leinster, Murray	MO0400
Made in U.S.A.	McIntosh, J.T.	BO0100
Made in U.S.A.	McIntosh, J.T.	DE0250
Made in U.S.A.	McIntosh, J.T.	GA0220
Made to measure	Gault, William Campbell	GA0140
Maelstrom II	Clarke, Arthur C.	CL0530
Maelstrom II	Clarke, Arthur C.	KE0100
Maelstrom II	Clarke, Arthur C.	ME0366
Magic child	Grant, Charles L.	EL0940
Magic city	Bond, Nelson S.	PO0293
Magic passes	Herbst, Steve	CL0110
Magic shoes	Saparin, Victor	MA0360
Magic shop	Wells, H.G.	WE0210
Magic shop	Wells, H.G.	WE0250
Magic, Inc.	Heinlein, Robert A.	HE0370
Magic, Inc.	Heinlein, Robert A.	HE0430
Magician's song	McAlister, Patricia	EL0900
Magnetosphere	Hoyle, Fred	HO0310
Magnificent possession	Asimov, Isaac	AS0280
Magus	Ciardi, John	ME0366
Maid to measure	Knight, Damon	AS0555
Maid to measure	Knight, Damon	KN0600
Maiden voyage	Rankine, John	NE0302
Mail supremacy	Peirce, Hayford	AS0555
Mail supremacy	Peirce, Hayford	BE0301
Mainchance	Tate, Peter	MC0150

Make a prison	Block, Lawrence	ME0360
Make mine Mars	Kornbluth, Cyril M.	K00130
Make mine Mars	Kornbluth, Cyril M.	K00160
Make room for me	Sturgeon, Theodore	ST0325
Make room! make room!	Harrison, Harry	SC0250
Maker of gargoyles	Smith, Clark Ashton	SMC150
Making it all the way into the future on Gaxton Falls of the red planet	Malzberg, Barry N.	N00404
Making it through	Malzberg, Barry N.	EL0500
Making it to Gaxton Falls on the Red Planet in the year of our lord	Malzberg, Barry N.	MA0455
Making the connections	Malzberg, Barry N.	MA0455
Maladjusted classroom	Nearing, H., Jr.	MA0193
Malatesta collection	Zelazny, Roger	WH0180
Male response	Aldiss, Brian W.	AL0390
Malf	Ing, D.	B00240
Malice afore thought	Grinnell, David	ME0260
Malignant marauder	Leinster, Murray	W00390
Malley system	DeFord, Miriam Allen	EL0300
Man	Bradbury, Ray	BL0120
Man	Bradbury, Ray	B00300
Man against tomorrow [anthology]	Nolan, William F.	N00200
Man for the moon	Webb, Leland	PL0150
Man from nowhere	Long, Frank Belknap	L00080
Man from outside	Williamson, Jack	LE0220
Man from the South	Dahl, Roald	KN0490
Man from when	Plachta, Danny	AS0555
Man from within	Pilachta, Dannie	W00407
Man in a quandary	Stecher, L.J., Jr.	GA0143
Man in asbestos: an allegory of the future	Leacock, Stephen	D00100
Man in his time	Aldiss, Brian W.	AL0365
Man in his time	Aldiss, Brian W.	AL0540
Man in his time	Aldiss, Brian W.	KN0480
Man in his time	Aldiss, Brian W.	NE0152
Man in space	Lang, Daniel	ME0359
Man in the jar	Knight, Damon	D00165
Man in the jar	Knight, Damon	GA0142
Man in the jar	Knight, Damon	KN0070
Man in the jar	Knight, Damon	KN0600
Man in the moon	Norton, Henry	C00250
Man in the moon	Reynolds, Mack	LE0220
Man in the moone	Godwin, Francis	DE0370
Man in the Rorschach shirt	Bradbury, Ray	KA0070
Man in the sky	Budrys, Algis	DI0130
Man inside	McAllister, Bruce	AS0555
Man inside	McAllister, Bruce	HA0162
Man manifold	Young, Peter	OB0140
Man must die	Clute, John	M00166
Man must die	Clute, John	SI0124
Man of destiny	Christopher, John	GA0140
Man of destiny	Christopher, John	LE0220
Man of distinction	Shaara, Michael	GA0143
Man of parts	Gold, H.L.	HE0160

Man of parts	Gold, H.L.	SI0125
Man of slow feeling	Wilding, M.	BA0240
Man of talent	Silverberg, Robert	BL0210
Man of the Renaissance	Guin, Wyman	SI0121
Man of the stars	Moskowitz, Samuel	MO0290
Man of the year million	Wells, H.G.	ST0210
Man on bridge	Aldiss, Brian W.	AL0365
Man on bridge	Aldiss, Brian W.	AL0540
Man on bridge	Aldiss, Brian W.	NE0301
Man on the 99th floor	Ballard, J.G.	BA0210
Man on top	Bretnor, Reginald	AS0555
Man on top	Bretnor, Reginald	ME0361
Man on top	Bretnor, Reginald	RO0130
Man overboard	Collier, John	MA0200
Man said to the universe [poem]	Crane, Stephen	SA0150
Man spekith	Wilson, Richard	WO0410
Man to my wounding	Anderson, Poul	AN0260
Man to my wounding	Anderson, Poul	HA0145
Man underneath	Lafferty, R.A.	BE0290
Man unwept [anthology]	Cook, Stanley J.	WH0150
Man unwept [anthology]	Whaley, Stephen V.	WH0150
Man upstairs	Bradbury, Ray	BR0230
Man upstairs	Bradbury, Ray	BR0360
Man who	Garnett, David S.	NE0326
Man who always knew	Budrys, Algis	BE0206
Man who always knew	Budrys, Algis	KN0540
Man who ate the world	Pohl, Frederik	KO0160
Man who ate the world	Pohl, Frederik	PO0260
Man who awoke	Manning, Lawrence	AS0170
Man who came back	Silverberg, Robert	BE0300
Man who came early	Anderson, Poul	AN0260
Man who came early	Anderson, Poul	DI0110
Man who came early	Anderson, Poul	KE0100
Man who came early	Anderson, Poul	KN0280
Man who came early	Anderson, Poul	MA0196
Man who came early	Anderson, Poul	SI0120
Man who collected "The Shadow"	Pronzini, Bill	WA0160
Man who collected Poe	Bloch, Robert	BL0240
Man who collected the first of September 1973	Bringsvaerd, Tor Age	HA0166
Man who could not see devils	Russ, Joanna	MC0150
Man who could turn back the clock	Farley, Ralph Milner	AS0555
Man who could work miracles	Wells, H.G.	KN0280
Man who could work miracles	Wells, H.G.	WE0200
Man who could work miracles	Wells, H.G.	WE0210
Man who could work miracles	Wells, H.G.	WE0250
Man who devoured books	Sladek, John T.	KA0070
Man who evolved	Hamilton, Edmond	AS0170
Man who evolved	Hamilton, Edmond	HA0155
Man who found Proteus	Roher, Robert	ME0365
Man who had no idea	Disch, Thomas M.	CA0238
Man who hated machines	Boulle, Pierre	BO0200
Man who learned loving	Sturgeon, Theodore	NE0155
Man who learned loving	Sturgeon, Theodore	WA0100

Manipulation	Kingston, John	NE0303
Manipulation	Roberts, Keith	RO0150
Manna	Phillips, Peter	CO0130
Manna	Phillips, Peter	KN0430
Manna	Phillips, Peter	SI0960
Manners of the age	Fyfe, H.B.	CO0280
Manor of roses	Swann, Thomas Burnett	FE0200
Manscarer	Roberts, Keith	AL0402
Manscarer	Roberts, Keith	ME0290
Manscarer	Roberts, Keith	RO0150
Mansion of forgetfulness	Lemon, M.D.	MO0365
Mantage	Matheson, Richard	KO0160
Manuscript found in a vacuum	Hubbard, P.M.	MA0193
Many mansions	Kimberly, Gail	EL0700
Many mansions	Silverberg, Robert	CA0370
Many mansions	Silverberg, Robert	SI0980
Many mansions	Wolfe, Gene	KN0319
Many splendored thing	Isaacs, Linda	AS0172
Many worlds of Andre Norton [anthology]	Elwood, Roger	NO0250
Many worlds of Andre Norton [anthology]	Norton, Andre	NO0250
Many worlds of Barry Malzberg [anthology]	Malzberg, Barry N.	MA0460
Many worlds of Poul Anderson [anthology]	Anderson, Poul	AN0280
Many worlds of Poul Anderson [anthology]	Elwood, Roger	AN0280
Many worlds of science fiction [anthology]	Bova, Ben	BO0260
Maracot deep	Doyle, Arthur Conan	KU0100
Marathon photograph	Simak, Clifford D.	SI0830
March hare mission	McCormack, F.	KN0580
Marching in	Asimov, Isaac	AS0230
Marching morons	Kornbluth, Cyril M.	AL0650
Marching morons	Kornbluth, Cyril M.	AM0513
Marching morons	Kornbluth, Cyril M.	BE0202
Marching morons	Kornbluth, Cyril M.	KO0070
Marching morons	Kornbluth, Cyril M.	SC0211
Margenes	DeFord, Miriam Allen	DE0210
Margin for error	Padgett, Lewis	CO0130
Mariana	Leiber, Fritz, Jr.	LE0100
Mariana	Leiber, Fritz, Jr.	ME0201
Mariana	Leiber, Fritz, Jr.	ME0360
Marionettes, Inc.	Bradbury, Ray	BR0170
Mark Gable foundation	Szilard, Leo	HA0210
Mark Gable foundation	Szilard, Leo	PO0240
Mark Gable foundation	Szilard, Leo	SZ0150
Mark of Gideon	Blish, James	ST0163
Mark of the beast	Kipling, Rudyard	PR0150
Mark VII	Derleth, August W.	DE0430
Marooned	Campbell, John W.	CA0150
Marooned off Vesta	Asimov, Isaac	AS0200
Marooned off Vesta	Asimov, Isaac	RO0240
Marriage-mender	Bradbury, Ray	BR0400
Mars by moonlight	Pohl, Frederik	PO0260

Maturity	Sturgeon, Theodore	C00670
Maugham obsession	Derleth, August W.	DE0430
Maverick	Dickson, Gordon R.	FI0100
Maxwell equations	Dneprov, Anatoly	DI0280
Maxwell equations	Dneprov, Anatoly	MA0360
May I please speak to Nina?	Bulychev, Kirill	BU0070
May the best man win	Schmidt, Stanley	OL0150
Maybe Jean-Baptiste Pierre Antoine de Monet, Chevalier de Lemarck, was a little bit right	Scott, Robin	KN0306
Maybe just a little one	Bretnor, Reginald	MA0193
Maze	Dybek, Stuart	KN0317
Mazel Tov revolution	Haldeman, Joe W.	HA0137
Mazes	LeGuin, Ursula K.	SI0480
McGillahee's brat	Bradbury, Ray	CA0280
McIlvaine's star	Derleth, August W.	DE0430
McIlvaine's star	Derleth, August W.	DE0590
MCMLV	Tucker, Wilson	TU0150
McNamara's fish	Goulart, Ron	MA0203
Me	Schenck, Hilbert, Jr.	ME0360
Me, myself and I	Tenn, William	TE0180
Meadow	Bradbury, Ray	BR0400
Mealtime	Ellison, Harlan	EL0340
Meaning of the word	Yarbro, Chelsea Quinn	YA0100
Meaning of the word "impossible"	Ley, Willy	SC0300
Meanwhile, we eliminate	Offutt, Andrew J.	EL0720
Meathouse man	Martin, George R.R.	CA0236
Meathouse man	Martin, George R.R.	KN0318
Mechanical answer	MacDonald, John D.	GR0280
Mechanical bride	Leiber, Fritz, Jr.	C00550
Mechanical bride	Leiber, Fritz, Jr.	EL1100
Mechanical house	Derleth, August W.	DE0430
Mechanical mice	Hugi, Maurice A.	AS0452
Mechanical mice	Hugi, Maurice A.	HE0100
Mechanical mice	Hugi, Maurice A.	HE0170
Mechanical mice	Russell, Eric Frank	CA0255
Mechanical sweetheart	Alper, Gerald Arthur	SC0450
Med service	Leinster, Murray	K00160
Medal for Horatius	Hall, William C.	ST0210
Meddler	Niven, Larry	NI0120
Meddlers	Kornbluth, Cyril M.	K00130
Meddlers	Kornbluth, Cyril M.	K00130
Media man	Vinge, Joan D.	VI0070
Medic	Gunn, James E.	GU0160
Medicine dancer	Brown, Bill	ME0260
Medicine for melancholy	Bradbury, Ray	BR0270
Medicine for melancholy	Bradbury, Ray	BR0400
Medicine for melancholy	Bradbury, Ray	BR0415
Medicine for melancholy [anthology]	Bradbury, Ray	BR0280
Meeting	Kornbluth, Cyril M.	AS0401
Meeting	Kornbluth, Cyril M.	BE0291
Meeting	Pohl, Frederik	AS0401
Meeting	Pohl, Frederik	BE0291
Meeting my brother	Krapivin, Vladislav	PA0210

Meeting my brother [I'm going to meet my brother]	Krapivin, Vladislav	MO0150
Meeting of minds	McCaffrey, Anne	MC0165
Meeting of relations	Collier, John	MA0330
Meeting of the board	Nourse, Alan E., M.D.	NO0360
Meeting of the minds	Sheckley, Robert	WI0206
Meeting the aliens on Algol VI	Schaeffer, Robin	EL1140
Meeting with Medusa	Clarke, Arthur C.	BO0210
Meeting with Medusa	Clarke, Arthur C.	CA0231
Meeting with Medusa	Clarke, Arthur C.	CA0234
Meeting with Medusa	Clarke, Arthur C.	CL0200
Meeting with Medusa	Clarke, Arthur C.	CL0530
Meeting with Medusa	Clarke, Arthur C.	HA0164
Meeting with Medusa	Clarke, Arthur C.	NE0158
Megan's world	Randall, Marta	CR0250
Meihem in Ce Klasrum [sic]	Edwards, Dolton	AS0700
Mellonta tauta	Poe, Edgar Allan	FR0070
Mellonta tauta	Poe, Edgar Allan	GU0130
Mellonta tauta	Poe, Edgar Allan	MO0380
Mellonta tauta	Poe, Edgar Allan	PO0100
Mellonta tauta	Poe, Edgar Allan	SA0150
Melting	Wolfe, Gene	KN0315
Memo to secretary	DeGraw, Pat	MA0206
Memorial	Sturgeon, Theodore	CO0520
Memorial	Sturgeon, Theodore	PO0293
Memorial	Sturgeon, Theodore	WA0130
Memory	Anderson, Poul	AN0165
Memory	Sturgeon, Theodore	CR0200
Memory of golden sunshine	Bulmer, Kenneth	NE0319
Men against the stars	Wellman, Manly Wace	DI0130
Men against the stars	Wellman, Manly Wade	GR0220
Men against the stars [anthology]	Greenberg, Martin Harry	GR0220
Men and machines [anthology]	Silverberg, Robert	SI0640
Men and the mirror	Rocklynne, Ross	AS0170
Men are different	Bloch, Alan	AS0340
Men are different	Bloch, Alan	CO0550
Men are different	Bloch, Alan	CO0560
Men in space	Lasswell, Horace D.	ST0210
Men inside	Malzberg, Barry N.	NE0202
Men like gods	Wells, H.G.	WE0250
Men of good value	Priest, Christopher	NE0326
Men of good will	Bova, Ben	BO0250
Men of good will	Bova, Ben	DI0110
Men of good will	Lewis, M.R.	DI0110
Men of Greywater Station	Martin, George R.R.	MA0540
Men of Greywater Station	Martin, George R.R.	MA0540
Men of iron	Endore, Guy	MA0330
Men of space and time	Bleiler, Everett F.	BL0100
Men of the moon	Irving, Washington	FR0070
Men of the ten books	Vance, Jack	BE0202
Men of the ten books	Vance, Jack	WI0201
Men return	Vance, Jack	AL0405
Men return	Vance, Jack	SI0121

Men return	Vance, Jack	VA0250
Men who murdered Mohammed	Bester, Alfred	BE0400
Men who murdered Mohammed	Bester, Alfred	CE0100
Men who murdered Mohammed	Bester, Alfred	HA0130
Men who murdered Mohammed	Bester, Alfred	MA0193
Men who murdered Mohammed	Bester, Alfred	SI1000
Men who murdered Mohammed	Bester, Alfred	SU0150
Menace from earth	Heinlein, Robert A.	AS0590
Menace from earth	Heinlein, Robert A.	HE0310
Menace from earth	Heinlein, Robert A.	HE0340
Menace from earth	Heinlein, Robert A.	MC0280
Menace from earth [anthology]	Heinlein, Robert A.	HE0310
Menace of the machine	Butler, Samuel	EV0100
Menagerie	Blish, James	ST0162
Menagerie	Roddenberry, Gene	ST0164
Mercenary	Reynolds, Mack	HA0145
Merchant	Slesar, Henry	AS0555
Merchants of Venus	Pohl, Frederik	AC0200
Merchants of Venus	Pohl, Frederik	HO0110
Mercurian	Long, Frank Belknap	WO0270
Mercy flight to Luna	Elam, Richard M.	EL0160
Mercyship	Page, Gerald W.	DA0270
Merman	DeCamp, Lyon Sprague	DE0070
Mesmeric revelation	Poe, Edgar Allan	PO0100
Mess of porridge	Dorman, Sonya	MC0150
Message	Anthony, Piers	AN0106
Message	Asimov, Isaac	AS0310
Message	Hall, Frances	AN0106
Message from charity	Lee, William M.	KE0100
Message from the stars	Copper, B.	DA0271
Message in secret	Anderson, Poul	AN0230
Message of joy	Cover, Arthur Byron	GE0150
Metafusion	Runyon, Charles W.	DE0267
Metal	Olsen, Robert R.	NE0208
Metal man	Williamson, Jack	CL0100
Metal man	Williamson, Jack	EL0520
Metal man	Williamson, Jack	RO0240
Metal man	Williamson, Jack	WI0310
Metallic muse [anthology]	Biggle, Lloyd	BI0150
Metamorphosis	Blish, James	ST0163
Metamorphosis	Kafka, Franz	PR0150
Metamorphosis of earth	Smith, Clark Ashton	DE0340
Metamorphosite	Russell, Eric Frank	DE0340
Metamorphosite	Russell, Eric Frank	GR0190
Metamorphosite	Russell, Eric Frank	RU0070
Meteor	Powers, William T.	AS0700
Meteor	Wyndham, John	WY0210
Meteor girl	Williamson, Jack	WI0310
Method bit in "b"	Wolfe, Gene	KN0308
Methuselah's children	Heinlein, Robert A.	HE0340
Metropolitan nightmare	Benet, Stephen Vincent	HO0119
Metropolitan nightmare	Benet, Stephen Vincent	MC0280
Mewhu's jet	Sturgeon, Theodore	CO0130
Mewhu's jet	Sturgeon, Theodore	PO0295

Moon-voyage   Kepler, Johannes   EV0100
Mooncup   Murphy, S.R.   EN0070
Moonduel   Leiber, Fritz, Jr.   ME0366
Moondust, the smell of hay, and   Disch, Thomas M.   ST0230
    dialectical materialism

Moongate   Wilhelm, Kate   KN0320
Moonrakers   Anderson, Poul   AN0165
Moonwalk   Fyfe, H.B.   KN0630
Moonwalk   Fyfe, H.B.   NO0270
Morality   Sturgeon, Theodore   ST0300
More light   Blish, James   MC0150
More science fiction tales [anthology]   Elwood, Roger   EL0920
More soviet science fiction   Prokofieva, R.   PR0150
    [anthology]
More than human   Sturgeon, Theodore   KN0480
More than human [anthology]   Sturgeon, Theodore   ST0300
More women of wonder [anthology]   Sargent, Pamela   SA0220
Morning glory   Wolfe, Gene   MC0150
Morning of the day they did it   White, E.B.   B00151
Morning rush or Happy Birthday, dear   Saye, Lee   EL1200
    Leah
Morphology of the Kirkham wreck   Schenck, Hilbert, Jr.   CA0238
Morrier's bitch   Fox, J.   SA0120
Mortal and the monster   Dickson, Gordon R.   DE0280
Mortal engines [anthology]   Lem, Stanislaw   LE0200
Mortal immortal   Shelley, Mary   M00320
Morthylla   Smith, Clark Ashton   SM0150
Mory   Bishop, Michael   GR0040
Most beautiful music   Mackenroth, Nancy   EL0840
Most beautiful woman in the world   Wilhelm, Kate   WI0150
Most forgettable story in the world   Lafferty, R.A.   EL0360
Most primitive   Russell, Ray   EL0720
Moth   Wells, H.G.   WE0210
Moth race   Hill, Richard   EL0220
Mothballed spaceship   Harrison, Harry   AS0750
Mother   Farmer, Philip Jose   CH0100
Mother   Farmer, Philip Jose   KA0070
Mother   Farmer, Philip Jose   M00350
Mother   Farmer, Philip Jose   P00150
Mother   Farmer, Philip Jose   SC0450
Mother   Farmer, Philip Jose   SI0123
Mother and child   Vinge, Joan D.   KN0316
Mother earth   Asimov, Isaac   AS0280
Mother earth   Asimov, Isaac   GR0190
Mother earth wants you   Farmer, Philip Jose   EL0500
Mother Hilton's littul kittons   Smith, Cordwainer   SM0180
Mother of invention   Godwin, Tom   AM0514
Mother of necessity   Oliver, Chad   C00430
Mother of necessity   Oliver, Chad   MC0400
Mother of toads   Smith, Clark Ashton   SM0150
Mother to the world   Wilson, Richard   KN0100
Mother to the world   Wilson, Richard   KN0303
Mother to the world   Wilson, Richard   NE0154
Motherbeast   Sky, Kathleen   LA0160

Muted horn	Davis, Dorothy Salisbury	FA0215
Muten	Russell, Eric Frank	BR0460
Mutiny	Bakhnov, Vladlen	MA0390
My boat	Russ, Joanna	WO0417
My boy friend's name is Jello	Davidson, Avram	MA0194
My brother Leopold	Pangborn, Edgar	SI0500
My brother Paulie	Ellison, Harlan	EL0360
My brother's wife	Tucker, Wilson	TU0150
My colleague	Grigoriev, Vladimir	GI0100
My darling Hecate	Guin, Wyman	MA0465
My dear Emily	Russ, Joanna	MA0202
My dream of flying to Wake Island	Ballard, J.G.	BA0205
My eyes, they burn!	Bertin, Eddy C.	WO0150
My father, the cat	Slesar, Henry	FA0215
My fear is great	Sturgeon, Theodore	ST0360
My first aeroplane	Wells, H.G.	WE0210
My friend Bobby	Nourse, Alan E., M.D.	NO0360
My friend, Klatu	Yep, Laurence	EL1080
My friend, Klatu	Yep, Laurence	EL1240
My friend Zarathustra	Sallis, James	KN0313
My lady green sleeves	Pohl, Frederik	DE0250
My lady of the psychiatric sorrows	Aldiss, Brian W.	CA0374
My name is Legion	DelRey, Lester	PO0293
My object all sublime	Anderson, Poul	AN0160
My object all sublime	Anderson, Poul	CO0760
My own, my native land	Anderson, Poul	EL0530
My sister's brother	Farmer, Philip Jose	FA0240
My son, the physicist	Asimov, Isaac	AS0500
My sweet lady Jo	Waldrop, Howard	CA0371
My trial as a war criminal	Szilard, Leo	ME0362
My trial as a war criminal	Szilard, Leo	SZ0150
Mysogynist	Gunn, James E.	HA0234
Mysterious doings in the Metropolitan museum	Leiber, Fritz, Jr.	CA0372
Mysterious gem	Street, Claire Edwin	EL1040
Mysterious message	Anderson, Poul	AN0200
Mysterious message	Dickson, Gordon R.	AN0200
Mysterious visions [anthology]	Greenberg, Martin Harry	WA0160
Mysterious visions [anthology]	Olander, Joseph D.	WA0160
Mysterious visions [anthology]	Waugh, Charles G.	WA0160
Mystery diet of the gods: a revelation	Disch, Thomas M.	DI0230
Mystery diet of the gods: a revelation	Sladek, John T.	DI0230
Mystery eyes over earth	Elam, Richard M.	EL0160
Mystery of green crossing	Parnov, Jeremy	MA0390
Mystery of green crossing	Yemtsev, Mikhail	MA0390
Nada	Disch, Thomas M.	MA0204
Nada	Disch, Thomas M.	OL0165
Nail and the oracle	Sturgeon, Theodore	PL0150
Naked sun	Asimov, Isaac	AS0560
Naked time	Black, John D.F.	ST0161
Naked time	Blish, James	ST0162
Naked to the invisible eye	Effinger, George Alec	EF0240

Neighbor	Simak, Clifford D.	SI1130
Nellthu	Boucher, Anthony	KN0220
Nellthu	Boucher, Arthony	MA0195
Nemesis	Clarke, Arthur C.	CL0160
Neon	Ellison, Harlan	EL0320
Nerves	DelRey, Lester	FI0095
Nerves	DelRey, Lester	HE0100
Nerves	DelRey, Lester	SC0211
Neutral planet	Silverberg, Robert	SI0340
Neutrino bomb	Cooper, Ralph S.	C00430
Neutron star	Niven, Larry	AS0400
Neutron star	Niven, Larry	AS0645
Neutron star	Niven, Larry	SA0150
Neutron stars [anthology]	Fitzgerald, Gregory	FI0095
Neutron tide	Clarke, Arthur C.	CL0530
Never ending penny	Wolfe, Bernard	ME0361
Never ending penny	Wolfe, Bernard	PL0150
Never on Mars	Harris, John Benyon	CA0170
Never underestimate	Sturgeon, Theodore	C00280
Never underestimate	Sturgeon, Theodore	C00640
Never-ending western movie	Sheckley, Robert	P00290
New accelerator	Wells, H.G.	DA0230
New accelerator	Wells, H.G.	DE0190
New accelerator	Wells, H.G.	DE0370
New accelerator	Wells, H.G.	JA0130
New accelerator	Wells, H.G.	WE0200
New accelerator	Wells, H.G.	WE0210
New accelerator	Wells, H.G.	WE0250
New age	Allen, Dick	AL0650
New apples in the garden	Neville, Kris	KN0280
New Arcadia	DeCamp, Lyon Sprague	DE0130
New arrivals, old encounters	Aldiss, Brian W.	AL0440
New arrivals, old encounters [anthology]	Aldiss, Brian W.	AL0440
New Atlantis	Bacon, Francis	DE0370
New Atlantis	LeGuin, Ursula K.	CA0235
New Atlantis	LeGuin, Ursula K.	SI0720
New Atlantis	LeGuin, Ursula K.	W00120
New Atlantis [anthology]	Silverberg, Robert	SI0720
New Atlantis [anthology]	Wolfe, Gene	W00120
New Atlantis [excerpt]	Bacon, Francis	GU0130
New awareness [anthology]	Warrick, Patricia	WA0100
New blood	Gunn, James E.	GU0160
New constellations [anthology]	Disch, Thomas M.	DI0230
New constellations [anthology]	Naylor, Charles	DI0230
New dimensions 1 [anthology]	Silverberg, Robert	NE0201
New dimensions 2 [anthology]	Silverberg, Robert	NE0202
New dimensions 3 [anthology]	Silverberg, Robert	NE0203
New dimensions 4 [anthology]	Silverberg, Robert	NE0204
New dimensions 5 [anthology]	Silverberg, Robert	NE0205
New dimensions 7 [anthology]	Silverberg, Robert	NE0207
New dimensions 8 [anthology]	Silverberg, Robert	NE0208
New dimensions 9 [anthology]	Silverberg, Robert	NE0209
New dreams this morning [anthology]	Blish, James	BL0210

New encyclopaedist   Becker, Stephen   ME0365
New father Christmas   Aldiss, Brian W.   AL0540
New father Christmas   Aldiss, Brian W.   WA0130
New folks' home   Simak, Clifford D.   AN0103
New folks' home   Simak, Clifford D.   SI1080
New game   Lightner, A.M.   B00300
New game   Lightner, A.M.   FU0100
New game   Lightner, A.M.   FU0100
New improved sun [anthology]   Disch, Thomas M.   DI0240
New lo!   Goulart, Ron   MA0193
New men for mars   Silverberg, Robert   SI0920
New mind [anthology]   Elwood, Roger   EL0940
New murders for old   Carr, John Dickson   WA0160
New New York New Orleans   Effinger, George Alec   EL0940
New New York New Orleans   Effinger, George Alec   EF0180
New prime   Vance, Jack   SI0560
New prime   Vance, Jack   VA0250
New reality   Harness, Charles L.   BE0201
New reality   Harness, Charles L.   SI0127
New reality   Harness, Charles L.   SU0150
New ritual   Seabright, Idris   MA0193
New s.f. [anthology]   Jones, Langdon   J00150
New signal station   Gansovsky, Sever   GI0100
New sound   Beaumont, Charles   MC0400
New Soviet science fiction [anthology]   anonymous   NE0280
New stories from the twilight zone   Serling, Rod   SE0150
    [anthology]
New tales of space and time   Healy, Raymond J.   HE0130
    [anthology]
New voices in science fiction   Martin, George R.R.   MA0520
    [anthology]
New voices 2 [anthology]   Martin, George R.R.   MA0521
New wine   Christopher, John   CR0100
New women of wonder [anthology]   Sargent, Pamela   SA0230
New writings in SF 1 [anthology]   Carnell, John   NE0301
New writings in SF 19   Carnell, John   NE0319
New writings in sf 2 [anthology]   Carnell, John   NE0302
New writings in SF 26 [anthology]   Bulmer, Kenneth   NE0326
New writings in SF 3 [anthology]   Carnell, John   NE0303
New writings in SF 4 [anthology]   Carnell, John   NE0304
New writings in SF 5 [anthology]   Carnell, John   NE0305
New writings in SF 6 [anthology]   Carnell, John   NE0306
New writings in sf 7 [anthology]   Carnell, John   NE0307
New writings in SF 8 [anthology]   Carnell, John   NE0308
New writings in SF 9 [anthology]   Carnell, John   NE0309
New year's fairy tale   Dudintsev, Vladimir   MA0360
New York A.D. 2660   Gernsback, Hugo   CL0590
New York A.D. 2660   Gernsback, Hugo   CU0070
New York A.D. 2660   Gernsback, Hugo   WA0130
New York Times   Platt, Charles   KN0311
Newsocrats: confessions of a eunuch   Wyal, Pg   ED0150
    dreamer
Next in line   Bradbury, Ray   BR0280
Next in line   Bradbury, Ray   BR0360

Nine hundred grandmothers	Lafferty, R.A.	WO0407
Nine lives	LeGuin, Ursula K.	HA0162
Nine lives	LeGuin, Ursula K.	KA0070
Nine lives	LeGuin, Ursula K.	NE0155
Nine lives	LeGuin, Ursula K.	SU0150
Nine lives	LeGuin, Ursula K.	WA0130
Nine lives	LeGuin, Ursula K.	WH0150
Nine lives	LeGuin, Ursula K.	WO0410
Nine tales of space and time [anthology]	Healy, Raymond J.	HE0160
Nine tomorrows [anthology]	Asimov, Isaac	AS0530
Nine-finger Jack	Boucher, Anthony	BE0202
Nine-finger Jack	Boucher, Anthony	WA0160
Ninth galaxy reader [anthology]	Galaxy Science Fiction Magazine	GA0148
Ninth galaxy reader [anthology]	Pohl, Frederik	GA0148
Ninth symphony of Ludwig Van Beethoven and other lost songs	Scholz, Carter	CA0374
Nither your Jenny nor mine	Ellison, Harlan	EL0400
Nize kitty	Nourse, Alan E., M.D.	EL1130
No biz like show biz	Biggle, Lloyd	BI0100
No charge for alterations	Gold, H.L.	WH0175
No connection	Asimov, Isaac	AS0280
No connection	Asimov, Isaac	BL0120
No different flesh	Henderson, Zenna	HE0490
No different flesh	Henderson, Zenna	MA0205
No direction home	Spinrad, Norman	CA0231
No direction home	Spinrad, Norman	CA0234
No direction home	Spinrad, Norman	HA0164
No fire burns	Davidson, Avram	ME0360
No future in it [anthology]	Brunner, John	BR0550
No hiding place	Chalker, Jack L.	DE0267
No home-like place	Girard, Dean	PO0430
No jokes on Mars	Blish, James	BL0125
No jokes on Mars	Blish, James	DA0270
No land of Nod	Springer, Sherwood	ST0180
No life of their own	Simak, Clifford D.	AS0590
No life of their own	Simak, Clifford D.	SI1060
No limits [anthology]	Ferman, Joseph	FE0260
No man pursueth	Moore, Ward	MA0196
No matter where you go	Rogers, Joel Townsley	MA0199
No mind of man [anthology]	Carr, Terry	CA0310
No moon for me	Miller, Walter M., Jr.	SL0130
No morning after	Clarke, Arthur C.	CL0280
No morning after	Clarke, Arthur C.	CL0310
No morning after	Clarke, Arthur C.	CL0340
No morning after	Clarke, Arthur C.	DE0530
No one believed	Thompson, Will	ME0260
No one said forever	Felice, C.	KI0070
No particular night or morning	Bradbury, Ray	BR0170
No place for magic	Proctor, Maurice	WA0160
No place like earth	Beynon, John	CA0230
No place like earth	Wyndham, John	WI0201
No place like earth [anthology]	Carnell, John	CA0230

Noonday devil	O'Neil, Dennis	EL1020
Nor dust corrupt	McConnell, James	BE0208
Nor iron bars	Blish, James	BL0200
Nor iron bars a cage	Goldin, Stephen	GO0030
Nor iron bars a cage	Hensel, C.T.	GO0030
Nor limestone islands	Lafferty, R.A.	CA0368
Nor the many-colored fires of a star ring.	Martin, George R.R.	DA0140
North wind	Oliver, Chad	NO0230
Northern chess	Lee, Tanith	SA0120
Not a petal falls	Bireley, Richard	NO0404
Not a prison make	Martino, Joseph P.	AN0106
Not a prison make	Martino, Joseph P.	GR0250
Not counting bridges	Fish, Robert L.	AS0555
Not final	Asimov, Isaac	AS0280
Not final	Asimov, Isaac	CL0500
Not final	Asimov, Isaac	CO0340
Not final	Asimov, Isaac	KN0480
Not final!	Asimov, Isaac	KN0580
Not fit for children	Smith, Evelyn E.	GA0141
Not for an age	Aldiss, Brian W.	AL0365
Not for an age	Aldiss, Brian W.	AL0540
Not for an age	Aldiss, Brian W.	OBC140
Not in the literature	Anvil, Christopher	AN0103
Not long before the end	Niven, Larry	NE0155
Not only dead men	VanVogt, A.E.	CH0100
Not only dead men	VanVogt, A.E.	CO0250
Not snow nor rain	DeFord, Miriam Allen	DE0210
Not there	Metcalfe, John	DE0560
Not to be opened	Young, Robert F.	BE0201
Not with a bang	Fast, Howard	FA0270
Not with a bang	Fast, Howard	FA0300
Not with a bang	Knight, Damon	AS0340
Not with a bang	Knight, Damon	CA0340
Not with a bang	Knight, Damon	CO0130
Not with a bang	Knight, Damon	KN0070
Not with a bang	Knight, Damon	KN0250
Not yet the end	Brown, Frederic	AL0411
Not yet the end	Brown, Frederic	BR0435
Note for the milkman	Carroll, Sidney	BR0380
Note on "Hans Phaall"	Poe, Edgar Allan	MO0320
Notes for a novel about the first ship ever to Venus	Malzberg, Barry N.	CA0368
Notes leading down to the conquest	Malzberg, Barry N.	NE0203
Notes leading down to the events at Bedlam	Malzberg, Barry N.	MA0455
Notes on a restless urge	Wissner, Robert	CL0110
Nothing	Herbert, Frank	HE0520
Nothing for my noon meal	Ellison, Harlan	EL0240
Nothing for my noon meal	Ellison, Harlan	EL0340
"Nothing happens on the moon"	Ernst, Paul	CO0280
Nothing in the rules	DeCamp, Lyon Sprague	DE0070
Nothing sirius	Brown, Frederic	BR0435
Nothing sirius	Brown, Frederic	BR0490

Omnilingual	Piper, H. Beam	HA0250
Omnilingual	Piper, H. Beam	SA0210
Omnilingual	Piper, H. Beam	ST0210
On binary digits and human habits	Pohl, Frederik	PO0210
On camera	Novotny, John	CO0490
On handling the data	Hirshfield, Henry I.	CR0104
On handling the data	Mateyko, G. M.	CR0104
On lethal space clouds	Shapley, Harlow	DO0160
On Messenger Mountain	Dickson, Gordon R.	DI0125
On shooting particles beyond the world	Eberhart, Richard	AL0650
On the air	Malzberg, Barry N.	NE0200
On the campaign trail	Malzberg, Barry N.	MA0455
On the dotted line	Biggle, Lloyd	BI0200
On the downhill side	Ellison, Harlan	EL0320
On the downhill side	Ellison, Harlan	NE0158
On the feasibility of coal-driven power stations	Frisch, O.R.	PO0240
On the fourth planet	Bone, J.F.	CO0760
On the fourth planet	Bone, J.F.	ME0364
On the Gem Planet	Smith, Cordwainer	DO0165
On the Gem Planet	Smith, Cordwainer	GA0146
On the Martian problem	Garrett, Randall	AS0173
On the Martian problem	Garrett, Randall	AS0440
On the moon	Tsiolkovsky, Konstantin	MA0330
On the road	Hartmann, Gregor	RY0100
On the road to Honeyville	Wilhelm, Kate	KN0311
On the storm planet	Smith, Cordwainer	DO0170
On the street of serpents	Bishop, Michael	GE0180
On the wall of the lodge	Blish, James	SI0380
On the wall of the lodge	Kidd, Virginia	SI0380
On the wheel	Knight, Damon	NO0402
On Venus, have we got a Rabbi	Tenn, William	DA0200
On wheels	Jakes, John	JA0070
On writing fantasy	Norton, Andre	NO0250
Once a Greech	Smith, Evelyn E.	GA0340
Once and future tales [anthology]	Ferman, Edward L.	FE0200
Once around the moon	Phillips, Y.	ST0230
Once was	Malec, Alexander	MA0450
One afternoon at Utah Beach	Ballard, J.G.	PR0160
One afternoon in Busterville	Grasty, William K.	EL1120
One at a time	Lafferty, R.A.	CA0420
One at a time	Lafferty, R.A.	KN0304
One blink of the moon	Aldiss, Brian W.	AL0440
One face	Niven, Larry	NI0120
One face	Niven, Larry	SI0127
One hundred years of science fiction [anthology]	Knight, Damon	KN0280
100 Great Science Fiction short short stories [anthology]	Asimov, Isaac	AS0555
100 Great Science Fiction short short stories [anthology]	Greenberg, Martin Harry	AS0555
100 Great Science Fiction short short stories [anthology]	Olander, Joseph D.	AS0555

```
102 H-bombs                                  Disch, Thomas M.        DI0210
One leg too many                             Alexander, W.           C00130
One less                                     Rosckhvatsky, Igor      GI0130
One life, furnished in early poverty         Ellison, Harlan         EL0260
One life, furnished in early poverty         Ellison, Harlan         KN0100
One life, furnished in early poverty         Ellison, Harlan         KN0308
One life, furnished in early poverty         Ellison, Harlan         W00412
One love have I                              Young, Robert F.        KE0100
One million A.D. [poem]                       anonymous              ST0210
One ninety-eight ($1.98)                     Porges, Arthur          MA0194
One of the books                             Matheson, Richard       GA0340
One of those days                            Nolan, William F.       ME0363
One ordinary day, with peanuts               Jackson, Shirley        KN0480
One ordinary day, with peanuts               Jackson, Shirley        MA0195
One ordinary day, with peanuts               Jackson, Shirley        ME0201
One ordinary day, with peanuts               Jackson, Shirley        ME0356
One race show                                Jakes, John             JA0070
One reason why we lost                       Stine, G. Harry         ME0358
One station of the way                       Leiber, Fritz, Jr.      HA0161
One step from earth                          Harrison, Harry         HA0220
One step from earth [anthology]              Harrison, Harry         HA0220
One Sunday in Neptune                        Panshin, Alexei         SI0940
One Sunday in Neptune                        Panshin, Alexei         W00410
One thousand dollars a plate                 McKenty, Jack           GA0144
One thousand miles up                        Robinson, Frank M.      BE0205
1937 A.D.!                                   Sladek, John T.         HA0160
1972 annual world's best SF                  Saha, Arthur W.         W00412
   [anthology]
1972 annual world's best SF                  Wollheim, Donald A.     W00412
   [anthology]
1973 annual world's best SF                  Wollheim, Donald A.     W00413
   [anthology]
1974 annual world's best SF                  Saha, Arthur W.         W00414
   [anthology]
1974 annual world's best SF                  Wollheim, Donald A.     W00414
   [anthology]
1975 annual world's best SF                  Wollheim, Donald A.     W00415
   [anthology]
1976 annual world's best sf [anthology]      Wollheim, Donald A.     W00416
1977 annual world's best sf [anthology]      Wollheim, Donald A.     W00417
1979 annual world's best sf [anthology]      Saha, Arthur W.         W00419
1979 annual world's best sf [anthology]      Wollheim, Donald A.     W00419
1980 president                               DeFord, Miriam Allen    DE0210
1980 president                               DeFord, Miriam Allen    OL0150
One way journey                              Silverberg, Robert      SI0760
One way street                               Bixby, Jerome           BE0205
One way to Mars                              Bloch, Robert           MO0380
One who returns                              Berry, John             MA0201
One who waits                                Bradbury, Ray           DE0400
One-A [1-A]                                  Disch, Thomas M.        SA0100
One-to-ten affair                            Gilbert, Michael        WA0160
Oneiromachia                                 Aiken, Conrad           ME0362
Ones who walk away from Omelas               LeGuin, Ursula K.       AS0401
Ones who walk away from Omelas               LeGuin, Ursula K.       NE0200
```

Other worlds, other gods [anthology]	Mohs, Mayo	MO0100
Other worlds, others seas [anthology]	Suvin, Darko	SU0180
Others	Holly, J.H.	EL1000
Ottmar balleau X 2	Bamber, George	ME0362
Ouch!	Anthony, Piers	WI0250
Ounce of cure	Nourse, Alan E., M.D.	NO0360
Ounce of dissension	Loran, Martin	BA0235
Ounce of dissension	Loran, Martin	WI0206
Ounce of prevention	Carter, Paul A.	DE0400
Our fair city	Heinlein, Robert A.	HE0420
Our fair city	Heinlein, Robert A.	ME0230
Our first death	Dickson, Gordon R.	DI0100
Our lady of the endless sky	Duntemann, Jeff	NO0404
Our neighbor by David Copperfield	Wolfe, Gene	HA0159
Our times	Pronzini, Bill	HO0110
Our war with Monaco	Mitchell, Edward Page	MI0250
Out from the Ganymede	Malzberg, Barry N.	NE0202
Out in space	Varshavsky, Ilya	GI0100
Out of night	Campbell, John W.	CA0110
Out of night	Campbell, John W.	CA0130
Out of order	Brunner, John	BR0550
Out of the cradle, endlessly orbiting	Clarke, Arthur C.	CL0470
Out of the cradle, endlessly orbiting	Clarke, Arthur C.	CO0190
Out of the sun	Clarke, Arthur C.	CL0280
Out of the sun	Clarke, Arthur C.	CL0310
Out of the sun	Clarke, Arthur C.	CL0340
Out of the sun	Clarke, Arthur C.	SI0440
Out of this world 1 [anthology]	Owen, Mably	WI0201
Out of this world 1 [anthology]	Williams-Ellis, Amabel	WI0201
Out of this world 10 [anthology]	Pearson, Michael	WI0210
Out of this world 10 [anthology]	Williams-Ellis, Amabel	WI0210
Out of this world 2 [anthology]	Owen, Mably	WI0202
Out of this world 2 [anthology]	Williams-Ellis, Amabel	WI0202
Out of this world 3 [anthology]	Owen, Mably	WI0203
Out of this world 3 [anthology]	Williams-Ellis, Amabel	WI0203
Out of this world 4 [anthology]	Owen, Mably	WI0204
Out of this world 4 [anthology]	Williams-Ellis, Amabel	WI0204
Out of this world 5 [anthology]	Owen, Mably	WI0205
Out of this world 5 [anthology]	Williams-Ellis, Amabel	WI0205
Out of this world 6 [anthology]	Owen, Mably	WI0206
Out of this world 6 [anthology]	Williams-Ellis, Amabel	WI0206
Out of this world 7 [anthology]	Owen, Mably	WI0206
Out of this world 7 [anthology]	Williams-Ellis, Amabel	WI0206
Out, wit!	Myers, Howard L.	AN0109
Out, wit!	Myers, Howard L.	HA0165
Outbreeders	Silverberg, Robert	SI0760
Outbreeders	Silverberg, Robert	SI0840
Outer becoming inner [poem]	Bronk, William	SA0150
Outer concentriac	Gotschalk, Felix C.	NE0204
Outer limit	Doar, Graham	CO0130
Outer limits of space	Edelson, Edward	AL0650
Outer reaches [anthology]	Derleth, August W.	DE0470
Outside	Aldiss, Brian W.	AL0365
Outside	Aldiss, Brian W.	AL0540

Place of pain	Shiel, M.P.	MO0320
Place of the gods	Benet, Stephen Vincent	AS0590
Place of the gods	Benet, Stephen Vincent	SA0270
Place of the tigress	Mayne, Isobel	OB0140
Place where Chicago was	Harmon, Jim	GA0149
Place where Chicago was	Harmon, Jim	MC0280
Place with no name	Ellison, Harlan	EL0280
Place with no name	Ellison, Harlan	EL0320
Placement test	Laumer, Keith	LA0130
Placement test	Laumer, Keith	WH0175
Placet is a crazy place	Brown, Frederic	AS0650
Placet is a crazy place	Brown, Frederic	PO0120
Placet is a crazy place	Brown, Frederic	WI0201
Plagiarist	Phillips, Peter	CR0230
Plague	Keller, Teddy	AN0101
Plague	Keller, Teddy	CA0100
Plague	Laumer, Keith	AN0109
Plague	Laumer, Keith	NO0240
Plague	Leinster, Murray	CO0280
Plague of cars	Tushnet, Leonard	NE0201
Plague of masters	Anderson, Poul	AN0230
Plan for the assassination of Jacqueline Kennedy	Ballard, J.G.	BA0120
Plan for the assassination of Jacqueline Kennedy	Ballard, J.G.	ME0290
Planet Arcadia	Disch, Thomas M.	DI0215
Planet called Cervantes	Keith, John	NE0326
Planet for sale	Nielson, Niels E.	WO0150
Planet named Shayol	Smith, Cordwainer	AM0513
Planet named Shayol	Smith, Cordwainer	SM0180
Planet of doubt	Weinbaum, Stanley G.	SI0940
Planet of doubt	Weinbaum, Stanley G.	WE0158
Planet of forgetting	Schmitz, James H.	WO0406
Planet of no return	Anderson, Poul	AN0400
Planet passage	Wollheim, Donald A.	GA0370
Planet passage	Wollheim, Donald A.	WO0270
Planet story	Wilhelm, Kate	SI0480
Planet story	Wilhelm, Kate	WI0180
Planetary effulgence	Russell, Bertrand	ME0363
Planetary exchange [poem]	Jones, LeRoi	SA0150
Planetoid idiot	Gotlieb, P.	SI0900
Planetoid of dooms	Colladay, Morrison	CO0130
Planets of wonder [anthology]	Carr, Terry	CA0320
Planners	Wilhelm, Kate	KN0100
Planners	Wilhelm, Kate	KN0303
Planners	Wilhelm, Kate	NE0154
Planners	Wilhelm, Kate	WI0150
Planting time	Adams, P.	AL0410
Planting time	Adams, P.	ST0220
Planting time	Nightingale, Charles	AL0410
Planting time	Nightingale, Charles	ST0220
Plants	Leinster, Murray	GR0220
Plastic abyss	Wilhelm, Kate	WI0135
Plastic age	Goldsmith, Howard	EL0460

Plato's stepchildren	Blish, James	STO164
Plattner story	Wells, H.G.	WEO200
Plattner story	Wells, H.G.	WEO210
Plattner story	Wells, H.G.	WEO250
Plausible improbable	Wilhelm, Kate	WIO150
Play's the thing	Bloch, Robert	BLO250
Play's the thing	Hoyle, Fred	HOO310
Playback	Clarke, Arthur C.	CLO530
Playboy book of science fiction and fantasy [anthology]	Playboy Magazine	PLO150
Playground	Bradbury, Ray	DEO500
Playground	Bradbury, Ray	KAO070
Playmate	Croutch, Leslie A.	DEO160
Plaything	Niven, Larry	ASO555
Plaything	Niven, Larry	NIO120
Pleasant dreams	Robin, Ralph	COO280
Please stand by	Goulart, Ron	MAO202
Pleasure garden of Felipe Sagittarius	Colvin, James	MOO162
Plenitude	Worthington, Will	MCO280
Plenitude	Worthington, Will	MEO201
Plenitude	Worthington, Will	MEO360
Plenitude	Worthington, Will	SUO150
Pliable animal	Harrison, Harry	HAO270
Plot	Herzog, Tom	KAO070
Plot	Herzog, Tom	MEO366
Plot for a novel	Varshavsky, Ilya	NEO280
Plot is the thing	Bloch, Robert	BLO240
Plot to save the world	Brownstein, Michael	DIO250
Plum duff	VanDresser, Peter	DEO310
Plumrose	Goulart, Ron	GOO130
Plutonian drug	Smith, Clark Ashton	DEO470
Plutonian terror	Williamson, Jack	WIO310
Pocketful of stars [anthology]	Knight, Damon	KNO460
Pod and the barrier	Sturgeon, Theodore	STO320
Pod in the barrier	Sturgeon, Theodore	STO330
Poem rocket	Ginsberg, Allen	ALO665
Poem rocket [poem]	Ginsberg, Allen	SAO150
Poet in the hologram in the middle of prime time	Bryant, Edward	EDO150
Poet in the hologram in the middle of prime time	Bryant, Edward	NOO402
Poets of Millgrove, Iowa	Sladek, John T.	MOO162
Point of focus	Silverberg, Robert	SIO340
Point of focus	Silverberg, Robert	WIO206
Point of view	Weinbaum, Stanley G.	WEO158
Poison belt [anthology]	Doyle, Arthur Conan	DOO160
Polaris of the snows	Stilson, C.B.	MOO400
Police operation	Piper, H. Beam	NOO300
Politeness	Brown, Frederic	BRO430
Political machine	Jakes, John	JAO070
Political science fiction [anthology]	Greenberg, Martin Harry	GRO250
Political science fiction [anthology]	Warrick, Patricia	GRO250
Politics	Leinster, Murray	CUO070

Politics	Leinster, Murray	JA0130
Polity and custom of the Camiroi	Lafferty, R.A.	OL0150
Polity and custom of the Camiroi	Lafferty, R.A.	SI0380
Pollock and the Porroh man	Wells, H.G.	WE0210
Polly Plus	Garrett, Randall	AS0180
Polly Plus	Garrett, Randall	AS0440
Polyfilla [poem]	Morgan, Edwin	BE0500
Pond water	Brunner, John	EL0200
Pool of the black one	DeCamp, Lyon Sprague	HO0190
Pool of the black one	Howard, Robert E.	HO0190
Poor little warrior!	Aldiss, Brian W.	AL0365
Poor little warrior!	Aldiss, Brian W.	AL0450
Poor little warrior!	Aldiss, Brian W.	AL0540
Poor little warrior!	Aldiss, Brian W.	KN0490
Poor little warrior!	Aldiss, Brian W.	MA0198
Poor little warrior!	Aldiss, Brian W.	SI0120
Poor man, beggar man	Russ, Joanna	CA0368
Poor man, beggar man	Russ, Joanna	NE0157
Poor planet	McIntosh, J.T.	CO0610
Poor superman	Leiber, Fritz, Jr.	HE0400
Poor superman	Leiber, Fritz, Jr.	LE0100
Pop goes the weasel	Hoskins, Robert	BE0301
Poppa needs shorts	Richmond, Walt	MC0400
Poppa needs shorts	Richmond, Walt	ME0364
Population control, 1986	Paredes, Horacio V.	SA0300
Population implosion	Cogswell, Theodore R.	BE0299
Population implosion	Offutt, Andrew J.	SU0150
Pork chop tree	Schmitz, James H.	SC0190
Portable novels of science [anthology]	Wollheim, Donald A.	W00330
Portable phonograph	Clark, Walter Van Tilburg	BR0380
Portable phonograph	Clark, Walter Van Tilburg	CR0200
Portable phonograph	Clark, Walter Van Tilburg	HO0100
Portable phonograph	Clark, Walter Van Tilburg	KN0540
Portable phonograph	Clark, Walter Van Tilburg	R00210
Portable phonograph	Clark, Walter Van Tilburg	SA0150
Portals of tomorrow [anthology]	Derleth, August W.	DE0500
Portobello Road	Spark, Muriel	ME0362
Portrait of the artist	Harrison, Harry	BL0210
Portrait of the artist	Harrison, Harry	HA0270
Poseidon project	Rackham, John	NE0309
Positive feedback	Anvil, Christopher	MC0400
Positive feedback	Anvil, Christopher	MI0180
Possessed	Clarke, Arthur C.	AL0410
Possessed	Clarke, Arthur C.	CL0310
Possessed	Clarke, Arthur C.	CL0370
Possessed	Clarke, Arthur C.	CL0400
Possible world of science fiction [anthology]	Conklin, Groff	C00340

Prometheus	Farmer, Philip Jose	M00100
Prometheus rebound	Galouye, Daniel F.	HA0300
Promised planet	Young, Robert F.	YO0180
Prone	Reynolds, Mack	C00720
Prone	Reynolds, Mack	HA0260
Prone	Reynolds, Mack	HA0290
Proof	Cleeve, Brian	C00340
Proof	Clement, Hal	AS0645
Proof	Clement, Hal	HA0232
Proof positive	Greene, Graham	MA0330
Proof positive	Malec, Alexander	MA0450
Propagandist	Leinster, Murray	C00220
Propagandist	Leinster, Murray	C00340
Propagandist	Leinster, Murray	GA0370
Proper santa claus	McCaffrey, Anne	MC0165
Proper study	Asimov, Isaac	AS0250
Proper study	Holly, Joan C.	EL0860
Prophet of Zorayne	Dixon, Terry	EL1120
Prophets of doom	Gernsback, Hugo	SC0300
Prose bowl	Malzberg, Barry N.	PR0210
Prose bowl	Pronzini, Bill	PR0210
Prospector's special	Sheckley, Robert	AS0575
Protect me from my friends	Brunner, John	BR0550
Protected species	Fyfe, H.B.	AL0410
Protected species	Fyfe, H.B.	AL0450
Protected species	Fyfe, H.B.	AS0700
Protected species	Fyfe, H.B.	CA0105
Protective temporal strike	Giannattasio, Gerard E.	N00404
Protest	Bulychev, Kirill	BU0070
Protest note	Laumer, Keith	LA0100
Proteus island	Weinbaum, Stanley G.	WE0158
Proteus islands	Weinbaum, Stanley G.	WE0150
Protocols of the elders of Britain	Brunner, John	W00416
Protoplasma	Derleth, August W.	DE0430
Prototaph	Laumer, Keith	AN0106
Prototaph	Laumer, Keith	AS0555
Prott	Saint Clair, Margaret	C00520
Prott	Saint Clair, Margaret	CR0100
Proud robot	Padgett, Lewis	HE0100
Proud robot	Padgett, Lewis	PA0180
Proust syndrome	Goldsmith, Howard	EL0640
Provincial's wings	Shefner, Vadim	NE0280
Proving ground	Gansovsky, Sever	R00270
Prowler in the city at the edge of the world	Bloch, Robert	EL0440
Prowler in the city at the edge of the world	Ellison, Harlan	EL0300
Prowler in the city at the edge of the world	Ellison, Harlan	EL0440
Prowler of the wastelands	Vincent, Harl	M00380
Proxima Centauri	Leinster, Murray	AS0170
Proxima Centauri	Leinster, Murray	LE0160
Proxy intelligence	VanVogt, A.E.	VA0140

Quiet revolution for death	Dann, Jack	NE0208
Quietus	Rocklynne, Ross	AS0451
Quietus	Rocklynne, Ross	HE0100
Quietus	Rocklynne, Ross	HE0170
Quincurx	Disch, Thomas M.	DI0215
Quincunx	Disch, Thomas M.	J00150
Quis custodiet...?	Saint Clair, Margaret	C00460
Quit zoomin' those hands through the air	Finney, Jack	B00100
Quit zoomin' those hands through the air	Finney, Jack	C00310
Quit zoomin' those hands through the air	Finney, Jack	FI0070
Quit zoomin' those hands through the air	Finney, Jack	L00100
Quite late one spring night	Curlovich, John M.	KN0317
Quixote and the windmill	Anderson, Poul	AN0325
R is for rocket	Bradbury, Ray	BR0300
R is for rocket [anthology]	Bradbury, Ray	BR0300
R.U.R.	Capek, Karel	C0C550
R.U.R.	Capek, Karel	KU0100
Rabbits to the moon	Banks, Raymond E.	MA0330
Rabble-dowser	McCaffrey, Anne	EL0980
Race around the sun	Elam, Richard M.	EL0160
Radiant enemies	Starzl, R.F.	M00290
Radiation blues	Cogswell, Theodore R.	ME0361
Radical center	Reynolds, Mack	OL0150
Rag thing	Grinnell, David	AS0340
Rag thing	Grinnell, David	C00280
Raid takes place at midnight	Varshavsky, Ilya	MA0420
Railways up on Cannis	Kapp, Colin	WI0202
Rain check	Merril, Judith	SA0180
Rain check	Padgett, Lewis	PA0150
Rain magic	Gardner, Erle Stanley	EL0480
Rain, rain go away	Ellison, Harlan	EL0340
Rain, rain, go away	Asimov, Isaac	AS0250
Rainbird	Lafferty, R.A.	GA0146
Rainbow gold	Rice, Jane	MA0200
Rainmaker	Reese, John	HE0400
Rainy day revolution no. 39	Cozzi, Luigi	W00150
Rake	Goulart, Ron	MA0205
Rammer	Niven, Larry	BE0290
Ramparts	Bailey, Hilary	CA0372
Random guest	Wyndham, John	CE0100
Random guest	Wyndham, John	SU0150
Random guest	Wyndham, John	WY0150
Random sample	Caravan, T.P.	AS0340
Randy's syndrome	Aldiss, Brian W.	AL0418
Randy-Tandy man	Rocklynne, Ross	CA0370
Ranging	Jakes, John	EL0200
Ranging	Jakes, John	EN0100
Ransom	Fyfe, H.B.	MA0192
Ransom	Fyfe, H.B.	MC0180
Rape of the solar system	Stone, L.F.	W00270

Report on the nature of the lunar surface	Brunner, John	ST0230
Report to headquarters	Malzberg, Barry N.	MA0455
Report to headquarters	Malzberg, Barry N.	NE0205
Request for proposal	Lewis, Anthony R.	OL0150
Requiem	Hamilton, Edmond	EL0340
Requiem	Hamilton, Edmond	HA0155
Requiem	Heinlein, Robert A.	HE0100
Requiem	Heinlein, Robert A.	HE0170
Requiem	Heinlein, Robert A.	HE0280
Requiem	Heinlein, Robert A.	HE0340
Requiem	Heinlein, Robert A.	JA0130
Requiem for Methusaleh	Blish, James	ST0163
Rescue	Edmondson, G.C.	MA0197
Rescue operation	Harrison, Harry	AS0651
Rescue operation	Harrison, Harry	HA0270
Rescue operation	Harrison, Harry	MC0400
Rescue party	Clarke, Arthur C.	CL0130
Rescue party	Clarke, Arthur C.	CL0220
Rescue party	Clarke, Arthur C.	CL0310
Rescue party	Clarke, Arthur C.	CL0400
Rescue party	Clarke, Arthur C.	C00730
Rescue party	Clarke, Arthur C.	P00190
Rescue party	Clarke, Arthur C.	W00210
Rescued girls of refugee	McCaffrey, Anne	EL1160
Rescued girls of refugee	McCaffrey, Anne	EL1240
Rescuer	Porges, Arthur	AL0450
Rescuer	Porges, Arthur	AS0651
Resident physician	White, James	AL0410
Resident witch	Schmitz, James H.	CA0360
Rest is silence	Grant, Charles L.	NE0160
Rest of the robots [anthology]	Asimov, Isaac	AS0560
Restricted clientele	Crossen, Kendall F.	CR0200
Restricted clientele	Crossen, Kendall F.	OL0150
Resurgence of Miss Ankle-strap wedgie	Ellison, Harlan	EL0400
Resurrection	VanVogt, A.E.	AM0515
Resurrection	VanVogt, A.E.	KN0480
Resurrection	VanVogt, A.E.	KN0580
Resurrection	VanVogt, A.E.	SI0600
Resurrection of Jimber-Jaw	Burroughs, Edgar Rice	BU0180
Resurrection of Jimber-Jaw	Burroughs, Edgar Rice	M00320
Retreat from earth	Clarke, Arthur C.	CL0200
Retreat syndrome	Dick, Philip K.	DI0083
Retreat to the stars	Brackett, Leigh	CR0200
Retro man	Eklund, Gordon	NE0207
Retrograde evolution	Simak, Clifford D.	SI1160
Retrograde summer	Varley, John	CA0235
Retrograde summer	Varley, John	VA0280
Return	Henderson, Zenna	HE0490
Return	McGuire, John J.	SC0400
Return	Piper, H. Beam	SC0400
Return engagement	DelRey, Lester	GA0146
Return from oblivion	Serling, Rod	SE0180
Return of a legend	Gallun, Raymond Z.	BR0080

Roaches	Disch, Thomas M.	DI0260
Roaches	Disch, Thomas M.	ME0366
Road of the eagles	Howard, Robert E.	HO0250
Road to nightfall	Silverberg, Robert	FA0215
Road to nightfall	Silverberg, Robert	SI0280
Road to nightfall	Silverberg, Robert	SI0330
Road to nightfall	Silverberg, Robert	SI0760
Road to science fiction v.1 [anthology]	Gunn, James E.	GU0130
Road to the sea	Clarke, Arthur C.	CL0470
Roads must roll	Heinlein, Robert A.	FI0095
Roads must roll	Heinlein, Robert A.	HE0100
Roads must roll	Heinlein, Robert A.	HE0220
Roads must roll	Heinlein, Robert A.	HE0280
Roads must roll	Heinlein, Robert A.	HE0340
Roads must roll	Heinlein, Robert A.	KN0570
Roads must roll	Heinlein, Robert A.	LO0100
Roads must roll	Heinlein, Robert A.	SC0210
Roads of destiny	Henry, O.	PR0150
Roads, the roads, the beautiful roads	Davidson, Avram	KN0305
Robbie	Asimov, Isaac	AS0430
Robbie	Asimov, Isaac	CO0550
Robbie	Asimov, Isaac	CO0560
Robbie	Asimov, Isaac	DE0160
Robert Heinlein omnibus [anthology]	Heinlein, Robert A.	HE0350
Robert Sheckley omnibus [anthology]	Sheckley, Robert	SH0130
Robin Hood, F.R.S.	Clarke, Arthur C.	CL0280
Robin Hood, F.R.S.	Clarke, Arthur C.	CL0340
Robing	Holmes, H. H.	GR0280
Robinson	Rome, David	BA0240
Robley	Varshavsky, Ilya	PA0210
Robnic	Boucher, Anthony	BO0120
Roborocts	Parry, Jay A.	AS0175
Robot and the man [anthology]	Greenberg, Martin Harry	GR0280
Robot A1-76 goes astray	Asimov, Isaac	AS0560
Robot humor	Zubkov, E.	MA0420
Robot who wanted to know	Boyd, Felix	FA0215
Robot's return	Williams, Robert Moore	GR0280
Robot's return	Williams, Robert Moore	HE0100
Robot's return	Williams, Robert Moore	HE0170
Robot's return	Williams, Robert Moore	MA0550
Robot's story	Wolfe, Gene	EL0220
Robotniks	Bakhnov, Vladlen	MA0390
Robots are here	Carr, Terry	HA0130
Robots don't bleed	Groves, J.W.	CA0230
Robots have no tails [anthology]	Padgett, Lewis	PA0180
Rock diver	Harrison, Harry	PO0190
Rock diver	Harrison, Harry	SI0420
Rock god	Ellison, Harlan	EL0320
Rocket	Bradbury, Ray	BR0300
Rocket man	Bradbury, Ray	BR0300
Rocket man	Ludwig, Edward W.	DE0160
Rocket of 1955	Kornbluth, Cyril M.	AS0452
Rocket of 1955	Kornbluth, Cyril M.	AS0555

Rocket of 1955	Kornbluth, Cyril M.	CE0100
Rocket of 1955	Kornbluth, Cyril M.	K00070
Rocket of 1955	Kornbluth, Cyril M.	K00100
Rocket rider	Coombs, Charles	FU0100
Rocket summer	Bradbury, Ray	BR0230
Rocket to the sun	VanDresser, Peter	DE0310
Rocketeers have shaggy ears	Bennett, Keith	BR0080
Rocketeers have shaggy ears	Bennett, Keith	GR0310
Rockets to where?	Merril, Judith	ME0359
Rocking-horse winner	Lawrence, D.H.	WH0150
Rod Serling's the twilight zone [anthology]	Gibson, Walter B.	SE0180
Rod Serling's the twilight zone [anthology]	Serling, Rod	SE0180
Rodent laboratory	Platt, Charles	M00165
Rodney Parish for hire	Ellison, Harlan	EL0440
Rodney Parish for hire	Hensley, Joe L.	EL0440
Roger Bacon formula	Pratt, Fletcher	C00130
Rogue Leonardo	Lack, G.L.	NE0302
Rogue moon	Budrys, Algis	SC0212
Rogue psi	Schmitz, James H.	WH0175
Rogue ship	VanVogt, A.E.	KN0540
Rogue ship	VanVogt, A.E.	MA0480
Rogue tomato	Bishop, Michael	NE0205
Rogues in the house	Howard, Robert E.	H00160
Roller ball murder	Harrison, William	HA0166
Roller coaster	Bester, Alfred	WH0180
Romance in a twenty-first century used car lot	Young, Robert F.	WI0245
Romance in a twenty-first century used car lot	Young, Robert F.	Y00180
Romance of Dr. Tanner	Goulart, Ron	CA0368
Romance of the first radical	Lang, Allan Kim	ME0150
Roog	Dick, Philip K.	DI0075
Roog	Dick, Philip K.	DI0083
Roog	Dick, Philip K.	SI0600
Room	Russell, Eric Frank	PL0150
Room	Russell, Ray	AS0555
Room	Russell, Ray	N00200
Roommates	Harrison, Harry	DI0250
Roommates	Harrison, Harry	MC0400
Rooms of paradise	Watson, Ian	HA0159
Rooms of paradise [anthology]	Harding, Lee	HA0159
Root of ampoi	Smith, Clark Ashton	SM0150
Rope enough	Collier, John	ME0310
Rope of glass	Zebrowski, George	SC0460
Rope's end	DeFord, Miriam Allen	DE0220
Rorqual Maru	Bass, T.J.	W00413
Rose Bowl-Pluto hypothesis	Latham, Philip	KN0305
Rose by any other name	Anvil, Christopher	ME0361
Rose for Ecclesiastes	Zelazny, Roger	AL0665
Rose for Ecclesiastes	Zelazny, Roger	MA0204
Rose for Ecclesiastes	Zelazny, Roger	MA0360
Rose for Ecclesiastes	Zelazny, Roger	SC0210

Russian science fiction 1968 [anthology]	Magidoff, Robert	MA0390
Russian science fiction 1969 [anthology]	Magidoff, Robert	MA0420
Rust	Kelleam, Joseph E.	AS0450
Rust	Kelleam, Joseph E.	GR0280
Rust	Kelleam, Joseph E.	NO0240
Rustle of wings	Brown, Frederic	DE0500
Rutherford [excerpt]	Stewart, D.	BA0240
Ruum	Porges, Arthur	BR0520
Ruum	Porges, Arthur	CR0100
Ruum	Porges, Arthur	CR0170
Ruum	Porges, Arthur	WI0201
S is for space [anthology]	Bradbury, Ray	BR0330
S-F: the year's greatest science fiction and fantasy, 1956 [anthology]	Merril, Judith	ME0356
S-F: the year's greatest science fiction and fantasy, 1957 [anthology]	Merril, Judith	ME0357
S-F: the year's greatest science fiction and fantasy, 1958 [anthology]	Merril, Judith	ME0358
S-F: the year's greatest science fiction and fantasy, 1959 [anthology]	Merril, Judith	ME0359
S.R.O.	Ellison, Harlan	EL0280
Sacheverell	Davidson, Avram	DA0233
Sacheverell	Davidson, Avram	DA0240
Sacheverell	Davidson, Avram	MA0204
Sack	Morrison, William	HE0400
Sack	Morrison, William	PO0295
Sacred city of cats (from Time cat)	Alexander, Lloyd	DE0160
Sad story of dramatic critic	Wells, H.G.	WE0210
Safe at any speed	Niven, Larry	AS0555
Safe at any speed	Niven, Larry	NI0150
Safety engineer	Boult, S. Kye	G00030
Sail on! Sail on!	Farmer, Philip Jose	AL0401
Sail on! Sail on!	Farmer, Philip Jose	KN0160
Sail on! Sail on!	Farmer, Philip Jose	SI1040
Sail the tide of mourning	Lupoff, Richard A.	NE0205
Sail the tide of mourning	Lupoff, Richard A.	CA0235
Sail 25	Vance, Jack	VA0220
Saint 505	Clark, John	ME0290
Saint Katy the virgin	Steinbeck, John	BR0380
Saline solution	Laumer, Keith	LA0100
Saliva tree	Aldiss, Brian W.	NE0151
Sally	Asimov, Isaac	AS0500
Sally	Asimov, Isaac	WH0180
Salty's sweep	Darnay, A.	DE0267
Salvage in space	Williamson, Jack	WI0310
Sam Hall	Anderson, Poul	AN0160
Sam Hall	Anderson, Poul	C00550
Sam Hall	Anderson, Poul	C00560

Scarab in the city of time	Randall, Marta	NE0200
Scarab in the city of time	Rancall, Marta	NE0205
Scarfie's world	Aldiss, Brian W.	ME0366
Scarlet dream	Moore, C.L.	CR0230
Scarlet lunes	Coblentz, Stanton A.	F00100
Scarlet plague	London, Jack	C00280
Scaro	Sturgeon, Theodore	ST0270
Scattershot	Bear, Greg	CA0375
Scattershot	Bear, Greg	W00419
Scent of sarsaparilla	Bradbury, Ray	BR0100
Scent of sarsaparilla	Bradbury, Ray	R00210
Schedule	Walton, Harry	GR0220
Schematic man	Pohl, Frederik	HA0162
Schizoid creator	Smith, Clark Ashton	SM0150
Schlossie	Laurance, Alice	LA0160
School and society through science fiction [anthology]	Greenberg, Martin Harry	OL0165
School and society through science fiction [anthology]	Olander, Joseph D.	OL0165
School and society through science fiction [anthology]	Warrick, Patricia	OL0165
Schrodinger's cat	LeGuin, Ursula K.	CA0372
Schumann computer	Niven, Larry	NI0120
Schwartz between the galaxies	Silverberg, Robert	DE0265
Schwartz between the galaxies	Silverberg, Robert	SI0540
Science [poem]	Jeffers, Robinson	SA0150
Science and sorcery [anthology]	Ford, Garret	F00100
Science fair	Vinge, Verror	KN0309
Science fiction [poem]	Amis, Kingsley	SA0150
Science fiction adventures in dimension [anthology]	Conklin, Groff	C00370
Science fiction adventures in mutation [anthology]	Conklin, Groff	C00400
Science fiction argosy [anthology]	Knight, Damon	KN0480
Science fiction bestiary [anthology]	Silverberg, Robert	SI0780
Science fiction by gaslight [anthology]	Moskowitz, Samuel	M00365
Science fiction by scientists [anthology]	Conklin, Groff	C00430
Science fiction carnival [anthology]	Brown, Frederic	BR0460
Science fiction carnival [anthology]	Reynolds, Mack	BR0460
Science fiction discoveries [anthology]	Pohl, Carol	P00290
Science fiction discoveries [anthology]	Pohl, Frederik	P00290
Science fiction emphasis 1 [anthology]	Gerrold, David	GE0180
Science fiction emphasis 1 [anthology]	Goldin, Stephen	GE0180
Science fiction for people who hate science fiction [anthology]	Carr, Terry	CA0340
Science fiction for telepaths	Blake, E. Michael	AS0555
Science fiction galaxy [anthology]	Conklin, Groff	C00460
Science fiction hall of fame. v.1 [anthology]	Silverberg, Robert	SC0210
Science fiction hall of fame. v.2A [anthology]	Bova, Ben	SC0211

Science fiction hall of fame. v.2B [anthology]	Bova, Ben	SC0212
Science fiction horror movie pocket computer	Wilson, Gahan	HA0164
Science fiction novellas [anthology]	Harrison, Harry	HA0250
Science fiction novellas [anthology]	McNelly, Willis	HA0250
Science fiction oddities	Conklin, Groff	CO0490
Science fiction of Edgar Allan Poe [anthology]	Beaver, Harold	PO0100
Science fiction of Edgar Allan Poe [anthology]	Poe, Edgar Allan	PO0100
Science fiction of the forties [anthology]	Pohl, Frederik	PO0293
Science fiction of the forties [anthology]	Greenberg, Martin Harry	PO0293
Science fiction of the forties [anthology]	Olander, Joseph D.	PO0293
Science fiction omnibus on pollution	anonymous	SC0250
Science fiction omnibus. The best science fiction stories: 1949,1950 [anthology]	Bleiler, Everett F.	BL0120
Science fiction omnibus. The best science fiction stories: 1949,1950 [anthology]	Dikty, T.E.	BL0120
Science fiction reader [anthology]	Harrison, Harry	HA0260
Science fiction reader [anthology]	Pugner, Carol	HA0260
Science fiction roll of honor [anthology]	Pohl, Frederik	SC0300
Science fiction showcase [anthology]	Kornbluth, Mary	KO0160
Science fiction stories	Elam, Richard M.	EL0120
Science fiction story [poem]	Ackerson, Duane	HA0167
Science fiction story for Joni Mitchell	Jakubowski, Maxim	JO0150
Science fiction subtreasury [anthology]	Tucker, Wilson	TU0150
Science fiction tales [anthology]	Elwood, Roger	EL1040
Science fiction terrors tales [anthology]	Conklin, Groff	CO0520
Science fiction thinking machines [anthology]	Conklin, Groff	CO0550
Science fiction through the ages 1 [anthology]	Evans, I.O.	EV0100
Science fiction: contemporary mythology [anthology]	Greenberg, Martin Harry	WA0130
Science fiction: contemporary mythology [anthology]	Olander, Joseph D.	WA0130
Science fiction: contemporary mythology [anthology]	Warrick, Patricia	WA0130
Science fiction: the future [anthology]	Allen, Dick	AL0665
Science fiction: the great years [anthology]	Pohl, Carol	PO0120
Science fiction: the great years [anthology]	Pohl, Frederik	PO0120

Science fiction: the great years v.2 [anthology]	Pohl, Carol	PO0295
Science fiction: the great years v.2 [anthology]	Pohl, Frederik	PO0295
Science fictional Sherlock Holmes	anonymous	SC0300
Science fictional solar system [anthology]	Asimov, Isaac	AS0575
Science fictional solar system [anthology]	Greenberg, Martin Harry	AS0575
Science fictional solar system [anthology]	Waugh, Charles G.	AS0575
Scientist divides	Wandrei, Donald	WA0130
"Scientists are stupid"	Campbell, John W.	AN0105
Scoop	Cave, P.L.	DA0272
Scorner's seat	Lafferty, R.A.	EL1020
Scrabo	Timperley, R.	DA0272
Scraping at the bones	Budrys, Algis	HA0168
Scrawny one	Boucher, Anthony	MA0490
Scream	Gordon, Giles	MO0165
Scream	Wilhelm, Kate	HA0167
Scream	Wilhelm, Kate	KN0313
Screaming woman	Bradbury, Ray	BR0330
Screwfly solution	Sheldon, Raccoona	BE0303
Screwfly solution	Sheldon, Raccoona	CA0237
Screwtop	McIntyre, Vonda N.	CR0250
Screwtcp	McIntyre, Vonda N.	MC0285
Screwtop	McIntyre, Vonda N.	SA0230
Sculptors of life	West, Wallace	CO0550
Scythe	Bradbury, Ray	BR0280
Scythe	Sandrelli, Sandro	WO0150
Sea bright	Moore, Hal R.	MA0205
Sea change	Chandler, A. Bertram	HA0300
Sea change	Scortia, Thomas N.	AL0510
Sea change	Scortia, Thomas N.	WA0130
Sea home	Lee, William M.	MA0208
Sea of faces	Silverberg, Robert	CA0371
Sea raiders	Wells, H.G.	CL0100
Sea raiders	Wells, H.G.	DO0100
Sea raiders	Wells, H.G.	WE0200
Sea raiders	Wells, H.G.	WE0210
Sea raiders	Wells, H.G.	WE0250
Sea thing	VanVogt, A.E.	VA0205
Sea thing [anthology]	VanVogt, A.E.	VA0205
Sea wreck	Jesby, Edward	KN0480
Sea's furthest end	Broderick, Damien	NE0301
Seafarer	Penman, Thomas	NE0326
Seafarer	Smith, Ritchie	NE0326
Sealman	Masefield, John	MA0330
Search	Brown, Frederic	BR0430
Search	Simonds, Bruce	ME0365
Search	VanVogt, A.E.	VA0180
Search for illusion	Asimov, Isaac	AL0480
Searcher	Schmitz, James H.	SC0190
Searchlight	Heinlein, Robert A.	HE0340

Seven science fiction novels of H.G. Wells [anthology]	Wells, H.G.	WE0220
Seven trips through time and space [anthology]	Conklin, Groff	CO0610
Seven wonders of the universe	Mallette, Mose	MA0206
Seven-day terror	Lafferty, R.A.	JA0130
Seven-day terror	Lafferty, R.A.	ME0363
Seventeen x infinity [anthology]	Conklin, Groff	CO0640
Seventh Galaxy Reader [anthology]	Galaxy Science Fiction Magazine	GA0146
Seventh Galaxy Reader [anthology]	Pohl, Frederik	GA0146
Seventh victim	Sheckley, Robert	KA0070
Seventh victim	Sheckley, Robert	MC0400
Seventh victim	Sheckley, Robert	NOC200
Seventh victim	Sheckley, Robert	SH0210
Seventy years of decpop	Farmer, Philip Jose	AC0200
Several murders of Roger Ackroyd	Malzberg, Barry N.	AS0440
Several ways and the sun	Planchat, Henry-Luc	NE0207
Sex and/or Mr. Morrison	Emshwiller, Carol	EL0300
Sex and/or Mr. Morrison	Emshwiller, Carol	SA0240
Sex opposite	Sturgeon, Theodore	ST0270
Sexual implications of the charge of the light brigade	Farmer, Philip Jose	FA0240
SF 12 [anthology]	Merril, Judith	ME0367
SF the best of the best part 2 [anthology]	Merril, Judith	ME0201
SF, The spirit of youth	Paul, Frank R.	SCC300
SF: authors' choice 2 [anthology]	Harrison, Harry	HA0232
SF: authors' choice 3 [anthology]	Harrison, Harry	HA0233
SF: authors' choice 4 [anthology]	Harrison, Harry	HA0234
Shab Guido G.	Asimov, Isaac	AS0250
Shadow and the flash	London, Jack	DA0230
Shadow kingdom	Howard, Robert E.	HO0160
Shadow lay	Fitzgerald, E.D.	OB0140
Shadow of space	Farmer, Philip Jose	FA0245
Shadow of space	Farmer, Philip Jose	WA0130
Shadow of wings	Silverberg, Robert	SI0360
Shadow on the Fancher twins	Mitchell, Edward Page	MI0250
Shadow on the moon	Henderson, Zenna	HE0490
Shadow out of time	Lovecraft, Howard P.	WO0330
Shadow show	Simak, Clifford D.	SI1160
Shadow world	Simak, Clifford D.	CO0150
Shadows	Brackett, Leigh	BRO095
Shadows	Sargent, Pamela	CA0265
Shadows [anthology]	Grant, Charles L.	GR0040
Shadows of the past	Yefremov, Ivan	MA0360
Shaffery among the immortals	Pohl, Frederik	MA0210
Shaffery among the immortals	Pohl, Frederik	NE0158
Shaka!	Oliver, Chad	EL0580
Shake hands with the man on the moon	Leyson, Burr	FUC100
Shaker revival	Jonas, Gerald	DI0250
Shaker revival	Jonas, Gerald	MI0180
Shaker revival	Jonas, Gerald	SI0121
Shaker revival	Jonas, Gerald	WO0411

Sheriff of Canyon Gulch	Dickson, Gordon R.	AN0280
Sheriff of Canyon Gulch	Dickson, Gordon R.	NO0240
Sheriff of Canyon Gulch	Dickson, Gordon R.	SI0780
Shifting parameters in disappearance and memory	Haas, C.	CA0373
Shifting seas	Weinbaum, Stanley G.	WE0150
Shifting seas	Weinbaum, Stanley G.	WE0158
Shining one	Schachner, Nat	EL1240
Shining ones	Clarke, Arthur C.	CL0530
Shining ones	Clarke, Arthur C.	ME0365
Ship of disaster	Bayley, Barrington J.	MO0164
Ship of shadows	Leiber, Fritz, Jr.	AS0401
Ship of shadows	Leiber, Fritz, Jr.	FE0110
Ship of shadows	Leiber, Fritz, Jr.	WO0410
Ship sails at midnight	Leiber, Fritz, Jr.	DE0470
Ship sails at midnight	Leiber, Fritz, Jr.	LE0100
Ship that turned aside	Peyton, Green	CO0130
Ship who sang	McCaffrey, Anne	AL0650
Ship who sang	McCaffrey, Anne	SA0240
Ship-sister, star-sister	Silverberg, Robert	EL1200
Shipshape home	Matheson, Richard	CO0280
Shipwright	Kingsbury, Donald	CA0241
Shock	Kuttner, Henry	DE0470
Shock	Kuttner, Henry	KU0130
Shock treatment	McComas, J. Francis	HE0160
Shock treatment	McComas, J. Francis	MA0330
Shocking thing [anthology]	Knight, Damon	KN0490
Shoddy lands	Lewis, C.S.	FI0090
Shoddy lands	Lewis, C.S.	HA0210
Shoddy lands	Lewis, C.S.	MA0196
Shopdropper	Nelson, Alan	CO0190
Shoppe keeper	Ellison, Harlan	MO0155
Shore	Bradbury, Ray	BR0230
Shoreline at sunset	Bradbury, Ray	ME0360
Shores beneath [anthology]	Sallis, James	SA0080
Shores of night	Scortia, Thomas N.	BE0206
Shores of tomorrow [anthology]	Silverberg, Robert	SI0800
Short happy lives of Eustace Weaver	Brown, Frederic	BR0435
Short history of the bolo fighting machines	Laumer, Keith	LA0070
Short in the chest	Seabright, Idris	CO0310
Short in the chest	Seabright, Idris	CO0640
Short in the chest	Seabright, Idris	SI0125
Short life	Donovan, Francis	CR0103
Short ones	Banks, Raymond E.	GR0250
Short ones	Banks, Raymond E.	MA0195
Short ones	Banks, Raymond E.	SI0127
Short-short story of mankind	Steinbeck, John	AL0450
Short-short story of mankind	Steinbeck, John	ME0359
Shortsighted	Hoyle, Fred	HO0310
Shortstack	Richmond, L.	CO0140
Shortstack	Richmond, Walt	CO0140
Shortstack	Richmond, Walt	KE0100
Shortstack	Richmond, Walt	KE0100

Six cubed plus one	Rankine, John	NE0307
Six fingers of time	Lafferty, R.A.	GA0280
Six fingers of time [anthology]	Galaxy Science Fiction Magazine	GA0280
Six great short novels of science fiction	Conklin, Groff	C00670
Six great short science fiction novels [anthology]	Conklin, Groff	C00700
Six haiku [poems]	Anderson, Karen	SA0150
Six haiku [poems]	Anderson, Karen	AS0340
Six matches	Strugatsky, Arkady	PR0180
Six science fiction plays [anthology]	Elwood, Roger	EL1100
Six-fingered jacks	James, E.R.	WI0204
Sixth Galaxy Reader [anthology]	Galaxy Science Fiction Magazine	GA0145
Sixth Galaxy Reader [anthology]	Gold, H.L.	GA0145
Sixth palace	Silverberg, Robert	SI0280
Sixth palace	Silverberg, Robert	SI0360
Sixth palace	Silverberg, Robert	SIC400
Sixth sense	Coney, Michael G.	W00410
Sixty-four square madhouse	Leiber, Fritz, Jr.	IF0100
Sixty-third street station	Davidson, Avram	DA0240
Skag with the queer head	Leinster, Murray	C00400
Skeleton	Bradbury, Ray	BR0280
Skeleton	Bradbury, Ray	BR0415
Skeleton men of Jupiter	Burroughs, Edgar Rice	M00380
Sketches among the ruins of my mind	Farmer, Philip Jose	DI0260
Sketches among the ruins of my mind	Farmer, Philip Jose	N00403
Skills of Xanadu	Sturgeon, Theodore	SI0124
Skinburn	Farmer, Philip Jose	FA0240
Skinny people of Leptophlebo Street	Lafferty, R.A.	KN0316
Skirmish	Simak, Clifford D.	AL0450
Skirmish	Simak, Clifford D.	C00550
Skirmish	Simak, Clifford D.	C00560
Skirmish	Simak, Clifford D.	SI1120
Skirmish	Simak, Clifford D.	SI1160
Skirmish [anthology]	Simak, Clifford D.	SI1120
Skirmish on a summer morning	Shaw, Bob	SH0160
Skulking permit	Sheckley, Robert	SH0210
Sky	Lafferty, R.A.	NE0157
Sky	Lafferty, R.A.	NE0201
Sky	Lafferty, R.A.	SI0560
Sky is burning	Ellison, Harlan	EL0340
Sky is burning	Ellison, Harlan	EL0360
Sky lift	Heinlein, Robert A.	HE0310
Sky lift	Heinlein, Robert A.	KN0160
Sky people	Anderson, Poul	AN0160
Sky people	Anderson, Poul	MA0330
Sky's an Oyster; the stars are pearls	Bischoff, Dave	AS0555
Skyghosts and dusk-devils	Brennert, Alan	ED0150
Skyhook	Gloeckner, Carolyn	EL0960
Skylark of space [excerpt]	Smith, Evelyn E.	SC0300
Skysign	Blish, James	HAC2C0
Slan	VanVogt, A.E.	VA0210

Spock must die!	Blish, James	ST0164
Spock's brain	Blish, James	ST0161
Spontaneous reflex	Strugatsky, Arkady	DU0100
Spooky	Reynolds, Mack	EL0820
Sport [poem]	Utley, Steven	HA0166
Spot of konfrontation	Aldiss, Brian W.	AL0440
[spot]	Wilson, Gahan	EL0220
Spring came to Blue Ridge early this year	Arnold, Charles	KN0313
Spud and Cochise	LaFarge, Oliver	MA0330
Spud failure definite	Peart, Noel	OB0140
Spy story	Sheckley, Robert	PL0150
SQ	LeGuin, Ursula K.	LA0160
SQ	LeGuin, Ursula K.	WO0419
Square pony express	Gotschalk, Felix C.	NE0209
Square root of brain	Leiber, Fritz, Jr.	MO0164
Square root of brain	Leiber, Fritz, Jr.	WO0409
Squire of Gothos	Blish, James	ST0164
Squirrel cage	Disch, Thomas M.	ME0290
Sredni Vashtar	Saki	SA0150
SRL AD	Matheson, Richard	BR0460
Stabbed alive	Flynn, Rancal	HA0158
Stair trick	Clingerman, Mildred	AS0340
Stair trick	Clingerman, Mildrec	MA0192
Stalin in the soul	LeGuin, Ursula K.	HO0110
Stampec caution	Gallun, Raymond Z.	CO0150
Stanley toothbrush	Carr, Terry	SI0740
STAPLE farm	Dneprov, Aratoly	SU0180
Star	Clarke, Arthur C.	AL0401
Star	Clarke, Arthur C.	AS0370
Star	Clarke, Arthur C.	CA0340
Star	Clarke, Arthur C.	CL0200
Star	Clarke, Arthur C.	CL0280
Star	Clarke, Arthur C.	CL0310
Star	Clarke, Arthur C.	CL0340
Star	Clarke, Arthur C.	CR0104
Star	Clarke, Arthur C.	DO0130
Star	Clarke, Arthur C.	KN0160
Star	Clarke, Arthur C.	SA0150
Star	Wells, H.G.	BR0520
Star	Wells, H.G.	DO0130
Star	Wells, H.G.	GU0130
Star	Wells, H.G.	KU0100
Star	Wells, H.G.	SI0680
Star	Wells, H.G.	WE0200
Star	Wells, H.G.	WE0210
Star	Wells, H.G.	WE0250
Star beast	Anderson, Poul	AN0325
Star begotten	Wells, H.G.	WE0250
Star bride	Boucher, Anthony	AS0555
Star bright	Clifton, Mark	AS0590
Star bright	Clifton, Mark	GA0141
Star bright	Clifton, Mark	SA0150
Star bright	Williamson, Jack	AS0450

Star ducks	Brown, Bill	BE0201
Star ducks	Brown, Bill	CR0170
Star dummy	Boucher, Anthony	CO0280
Star fourteen [anthology]	Pohl, Frederik	PO0330
Star gypsies	Gresham, W. L.	MA0193
Star light	Asimov, Isaac	NE0304
Star maker	Stapledon, Olaf	ST0150
Star of life	Hamilton, Edmond	AL0510
Star of stars [anthology]	Pohl, Frederik	PO0300
Star of wonder	May, Julian	DI0130
Star party	Lory, Robert	WO0405
Star pit	Delany, Samuel R.	DE0255
Star pit	Delany, Samuel R.	SI0124
Star plunderer	Anderson, Poul	AL0410
Star road [anthology]	Dickson, Gordon R.	DI0125
Star science fiction stories 1 [anthology]	Pohl, Frederik	PO0371
Star science fiction stories 2 [anthology]	Pohl, Frederik	PO0372
Star science fiction stories 3 [anthology]	Pohl, Frederik	PO0373
Star science fiction stories no. 4 [anthology]	Pohl, Frederik	PO0374
Star science fiction stories no. 6	Pohl, Frederik	PO0376
Star ship	Anderson, Poul	AL0480
Star short novels [anthology]	Pohl, Frederik	PO0400
Star train	Mendelson, Drew	AS0180
Star Trek reader [anthology]	Blish, James	ST0161
Star Trek reader II [anthology]	Blish, James	ST0162
Star Trek reader III [anthology]	Blish, James	ST0163
Star Trek reader IV [anthology]	Blish, James	ST0164
Star-crossed lover	Stuart, William W.	CO0760
Star-linked	Fyfe, H.B.	NO0330
Star-mouse	Brown, Frederic	BR0080
Star-mouse	Brown, Frederic	BR0435
Star-mouse	Brown, Frederic	HE0100
Star-splitter	Frost, Robert	AL0650
Staras flonderans	Wilhelm, Kate	KN0301
Starbirth	Goldbarth, Albert	DI0230
Starbride	Boucher, Anthony	SL0210
Starcrossed	Zebrowski, George	EL0180
Stardance	Robinson, Jeanne	BE0303
Stardance	Robinson, Jeanne	CA0237
Stardance	Robinson, Spider	BE0303
Stardance	Robinson, Spider	CA0237
Starfog	Anderson, Poul	AN0165
Starfog	Anderson, Poul	AN0295
Starlacy	Martin, George R.R.	PO0290
Starlight, star bright	Bester, Alfred	MA0193
Starlit corridor [anthology]	Mansfield, Roger	MA0470
Starpit	Delany, Samuel R.	ME0367
Starry messenger [anthology]	Ryan, Charles C.	RY0100
Stars and darkness	Chang, G.	CA0373
Stars and under [anthology]	Crispin, Edmund	CR0170

Stars are calling, Mr. Keats	Young, Robert F.	YO0180
Stars are the styx	Sturgeon, Theodore	GA0140
Stars below	LeGuin, Ursula K.	DO0165
Stars below	LeGuin, Ursula K.	KN0314
Stars, like dust	Asimov, Isaac	AS0558
Stars, like dust	Asimov, Isaac	AS0620
Stars, won't you hide me?	Bova, Ben	BO0250
Stars, my destination	Bester, Alfred	BO0151
Starscape with frieze of dreams	Young, Robert F.	KN0308
Starshine [anthology]	Sturgeon, Theodore	ST0320
Starsong	Saberhagen, Fred	WO0409
Start in life	Sellings, Arthur	AL0425
Starthinker 9	Coney, Michael G.	WE0290
Starting from scratch	Sheckley, Robert	AS0555
Starting line	Clarke, Arthur C.	CL0280
Starting line	Clarke, Arthur C.	CL0340
State of grace	Wilhelm, Kate	KN0319
State of grace	Wilhelm, Kate	WI0180
State of the art	Malzberg, Barry N.	MA0455
State of the art	Malzberg, Barry N.	NE0204
State of the art on alyssum	Randall, Marta	NE0207
State of ultimate peace	Nabors, William	HA0145
Stations of the nightmare: Part 1	Farmer, Philip Jose	EL0580
Stations of the nightmare: Part 2: the Startouched	Farmer, Philip Jose	EL0581
Stations of the nightmare: Part 3: The Evolution of Paul Eyre	Farmer, Philip Jose	EL0582
Statistician's day	Blish, James	HA0164
Statue for father	Asimov, Isaac	AS0250
Status quondam	Miller, P. Schuyler	HE0130
Steam-driver boy	Sladek, John T.	NO0402
Steel	Matheson, Richard	NO0210
Steel brother	Dickson, Gordon R.	NO0330
Steel sonnets	Duntemann, Jeff	KN0317
Stella	White, Ted	EL0300
Stella	White, Ted	EL0500
Stella	White, Ted	EL0760
Stella blue	Carrington, Grant	MO0155
Stellar 1 [anthology]	DelRey, Judy-Lynn	DE0265
Stellar 3 [anthology]	DelRey, Judy-Lynn	DE0267
Stellar 4 [anthology]	DelRey, Judy-Lynn	DE0268
Stellar science fiction stories [anthology]	DelRey, Judy-Lynn	DE0275
Stellar short novels [anthology]	DelRey, Judy-Lynn	DE0280
Stentorii luggage	Barrett, Neal, Jr.	GA0250
Stepson of space	Gallun, Raymond Z.	PO0190
Stepson of space	Gallun, Raymond Z.	PO0293
Steve Weinraub and the secret empire	Effinger, George Alec	EF0240
Stevie and the dark	Henderson, Zenna	HE0460
Stick for Harry Eddington	Oliver, Chad	HA0232
Stickeney and the critic	Clingerman, Mildred	DE0500
Still life	Russell, Eric Frank	CO0100
Still trajectories	Aldiss, Brian W.	AL0365
Still trajectories	Aldiss, Brian W.	CL0100

Sunken land	Leiber, Fritz, Jr.	SI0620
Sunken universe	Blish, James	KN0630
Sunout	Williams, Eric	NE0305
Sunrise on Mercury	Silverberg, Robert	SI0760
Sunrise on Mercury	Silverberg, Robert	SI0940
Sunrise on Mercury [anthology]	Silverberg, Robert	SI0860
Sunset harp	Bradbury, Ray	BR0100
Sunward	Coblentz, Stanton A.	WO0270
Super-neutron	Asimov, Isaac	AS0280
Superiority	Clarke, Arthur C.	CL0130
Superiority	Clarke, Arthur C.	CL0160
Superiority	Clarke, Arthur C.	CL0220
Superiority	Clarke, Arthur C.	CL0250
Superiority	Clarke, Arthur C.	CL0310
Superiority	Clarke, Arthur C.	DE0590
Superiority	Clarke, Arthur C.	GR0250
Suppliant in space	Sheckley, Robert	WO0414
Supply point	Mooney, B.	DA0272
Supremacy of Uruguay	White, E.B.	BR0330
Sure thing	Asimov, Isaac	AS0440
Surface tension	Blish, James	AS0645
Surface tension	Blish, James	BL0180
Surface tension	Blish, James	CH0100
Surface tension	Blish, James	CO0670
Surface tension	Blish, James	GA0141
Surface tension	Blish, James	HA0260
Surface tension	Blish, James	HO0119
Surface tension	Blish, James	SC0210
Surface tension	Blish, James	YE0404
Survival	Beynon, John	CA0230
Survival	Wyndham, John	BE0203
Survival	Wyndham, John	WY0210
Survival from infinity [anthology]	Elwood, Roger	EL1140
Survival kit	Pohl, Frederik	PO0260
Survival on a primitive planet	Tofte, Arthur	EL1140
Survival problems	Neville, Kris	CA0372
Survival ship	Merril, Judith	HE0400
Survival ship	Merril, Judith	MA0550
Survival ship	Merril, Judith	RO0180
Survival U	Fischer, John	AL0650
Survival, A.D. 2000	Reynolds, Mack	EL1140
Survivor	Moudy, Walter F.	GR0250
Survivor	Moudy, Walter F.	KE0100
Survivor	Moudy, Walter F.	ME0366
Survivor I	Ellison, Harlan	EL0440
Survivor I	Slesar, Henry	EL0440
Susan	Bevan, Alistair	ME0366
Susceptibility	MacDonald, John D.	GA0140
Susie's reality	Stickgold, Bob	IF0170
Susie's reality	Stickgold, Bob	KA0070
Swan song	Yarbro, Chelsea Quinn	YA0100
Swap	Goulart, Ron	GO0100
Swastika!	Aldiss, Brian W.	AL0365
Swastika!	Aldiss, Brian W.	NO0401

Tale of the ragged mountains	Poe, Edgar Allan	FR0070
Tale of the ragged mountains	Poe, Edgar Allan	PO0100
Tale of the ragged mountains	Poe, Edgar Allan	SI0620
Tale of the thirteenth floor	Nash, Ogden	MA0330
Talent	Sturgeon, Theodore	AS0340
Talent of Harvey	Fast, Howard	FA0270
Talent of Harvey	Fast, Howard	FA0300
Tales beyond time [anthology]	DeCamp, Catherine Crook	DE0160
Tales beyond time [anthology]	DeCamp, Lyon Sprague	DE0160
Tales from the White Hart [anthology]	Clarke, Arthur C.	CL0430
Tales of Conan [anthology]	DeCamp, Lyon Sprague	HO0250
Tales of Conan [anthology]	Howard, Robert E.	HO0250
Tales of known space [anthology]	Niven, Larry	NI0150
Tales of science and sorcery [anthology]	Smith, Clark Ashton	SM0150
Tales of ten worlds [anthology]	Clarke, Arthur C.	CL0470
Tales of the distant past	Podolny, Roman	MA0390
Tales of three planets [anthology]	Burroughs, Edgar Rice	BU0130
Tales of time and space [anthology]	Olney, Ross R.	OL0180
Talking stone	Asimov, Isaac	DE0220
Tanar of Pellucidar	Burroughs, Edgar Rice	BU0100
Tangle hold	Wallace, F.L.	GA0220
Tangled web	Schmitz, James H.	SC0180
Tank trapeze	Moorcock, Michael	HA0233
Tarfu's last show	Boston, Bruce	ED0150
Target generation	Simak, Clifford D.	SI1160
Tarrying	Scortia, Thomas N.	EL0700
Tartarus of Maids	Melville, Herman	SA0150
Taste of Armageddon	Blish, James	ST0161
Taxpayer	Bradbury, Ray	BR0230
Tea in a space-ship	Kirkup, James	MA0470
Tea tray in the sky	Smith, Evelyn E.	GA0141
Teacher	Sidney, Kathleen M.	KN0318
Teaching prime	Kelley, Leo P.	OL0165
Teamwork	Yore, Mary Jane	EL0460
Technical error	Clarke, Arthur C.	CL0130
Technical error	Clarke, Arthur C.	CL0220
Technical error	Clarke, Arthur C.	CL0400
Technical error	Clarke, Arthur C.	PO0293
Technical slip	Beynon, John	CO0310
Technical slip	Wyndham, John	CA0280
Teddy bear	Gunn, James E.	GU0100
Teddysaurs	Hamilton-Peterson, J.	DA0270
Tee Vee Man	Hargreaves, H.A.	CA0210
Teen-age outer space stories [anthology]	Furman, A.L.	FU0100
Teen-age science-fiction stories [anthology]	Elam, Richard M.	EL0140
Teen-age space adventures	Furman, A.L.	FU0130
Teen-age super science stories [anthology]	Elam, Richard M.	EL0160
Teeth of despair	Davidson, Avram	CO0490
Teeth of despair	Klein, Sidrey	CO0490

Three poems	Dillingham, Peter	NE0209
Three portraits and a prayer	Pohl, Frederik	FI0090
Three portraits and a prayer	Pohl, Frederik	GA0146
Three portraits and a prayer	Pohl, Frederik	PO0180
Three prophetic novels [anthology]	Wells, H.G.	WE0230
Three soldiers	Poyer, D.C.	RY0100
Three times infinity [anthology]	Margulies, Leo	MA0485
Three trips in time and space [anthology]	anonymous	TH0210
Three ways	Aldiss, Brian W.	AL0440
3-part puzzle	Dickson, Gordon R.	DI0125
3000 years of fantasy and science fiction [anthology]	DeCamp, Lyon Sprague	DE0190
Threepenny-piece	Stevens, James	MA0191
Through a window	Wells, H.G.	WE0210
Through channels	Matheson, Richard	CO0520
Through other eyes	Lafferty, R.A.	SI0660
Through time and space with Ferdinand Feghoot--twice!	Briarton, Grendel	AS0172
Through time and space with Ferdinand Feghoot--twice!	Briarton, Grendel	AS0440
Through time and space with Ferdinand Feghoot	Briarton, Grendel	MA0198
Through time and space with Ferdinand Feghoot	Briarton, Grendel	MC0180
Through the purple cloud	Williamson, Jack	WI0310
Throwback	DeCamp, Lyon Sprague	DE0130
Throwback	DeCamp, Lyon Sprague	ST0210
Throwback	DeFord, Miriam Allen	CR0230
Throwback	Elwood, Roger	EL1120
Thunder and roses	Sturgeon, Theodore	AS0651
Thunder and roses	Sturgeon, Theodore	AS0700
Thunder and roses	Sturgeon, Theodore	CA0105
Thunder and roses	Sturgeon, Theodore	ST0360
Thunder-thieves	Asimov, Isaac	ME0359
Thundering worlds	Hamilton, Edmond	HA0155
Thus I refute Beelzy	Collier, John	WH0150
Thus love betrays us	MacLennan, Phyllis	BE0291
Thus love betrays us	MacLennan, Phyllis	MA0210
Thus love betrays us	MacLennan, Phyllis	WO0413
Thus we frustrate Charlemagne	Lafferty, R.A.	RO0180
Thus we frustrate Charlemagne	Lafferty, R.A.	SI0120
Thus we frustrate Charlemagne	Lafferty, R.A.	SU0150
Thuvia,maid of Mars	Burroughs, Edgar Rice	BU0200
Ticket to anywhere	Knight, Damon	K00160
Ticket to anywhere	Knight, Damon	SI0400
Ticket to Tranal	Sheckley, Robert	SH0130
Tiddlywink warriors	Anderson, Poul	AN0200
Tide of death	Doyle, Arthur Conan	DO0160
Tie that binds	Whitley, George	EA0100
Tiger by the tail	Henderson, Gene L.	B00300
Tiger by the tail	Nourse, Alan E., M.D.	AS0340
Tiger by the tail	Nourse, Alan E., M.D.	CO0370
Tiger by the tail	Nourse, Alan E., M.D.	GA0141

Tiger by the tail [anthology]	Nourse, Alan E., M.D.	N00390
Tiger god	Serling, Rod	SE0180
Tiger green	Dickson, Gordon R.	DI0100
Tiger green	Dickson, Gordon R.	DI0115
Tiger ride	Blish, James	P00293
Tiger ride	Blish, James	PR0210
Tiger ride	Knight, Damon	P00293
Tiger ride	Knight, Damon	PR0210
Tilting island	Bennett, G.J.	M00365
Tilting island	Vivian, T.J.	M00365
Timaios (excerpt)	Plato	DE0190
Time and Hagakure	Utley, Steven	AS0173
Time and stars [anthology]	Anderson, Poul	AN0335
Time and the riddle [anthology]	Fast, Howard	FA0270
Time bind	Dorman, Sonya	KN0313
Time brother	Jones, Raymond F.	EL0540
Time bum	Kornbluth, Cyril M.	K00130
Time bum	Kornbluth, Cyril M.	K00160
Time considered as a helix of semi-precious stones	Delany, Samuel R.	AS0400
Time considered as a helix of semi-precious stones	Delany, Samuel R.	DE0255
Time considered as a helix of semi-precious stones	Delany, Samuel R.	NE0155
Time considered as a helix of semi-precious stones	Delany, Samuel R.	SA0080
Time considered as a helix of semi-precious stones	Delany, Samuel R.	W00409
Time deer	Strete, Craig	HA0167
Time deer	Strete, Craig	NE0161
Time enough	Knight, Damon	KN0070
Time enough	Knight, Damon	KN0250
Time exposures	Tucker, Wilson	AS0585
Time exposures	Tucker, Wilson	CA0368
Time for sale	Farley, Ralph Milmer	EL0520
Time fuze	Garrett, Randall	AL0510
Time heals	Anderson, Poul	SI1000
Time in advance	Tenn, William	AL0425
Time in advance	Tenn, William	AS0585
Time in the round	Leiber, Fritz, Jr.	GA0142
Time in thy flight	Bradbury, Ray	BR0330
Time is the traitor	Bester, Alfred	AL0430
Time is the traitor	Bester, Alfred	P00295
Time lag	Anderson, Poul	AN0305
Time lag	Anderson, Poul	MA0201
Time locker	Padgett, Lewis	HE0100
Time locker	Padgett, Lewis	HE0170
Time locker	Padgett, Lewis	PA0180
Time machine	Bradbury, Ray	BR0300
Time machine	Jones, Langdon	KN0100
Time machine	Jones, Langdon	KN0305
Time machine	Wells, H.G.	KU0100
Time machine	Wells, H.G.	SC0211
Time machine	Wells, H.G.	WE0210

Time machine	Wells, H.G.	WE0220
Time machine	Wells, H.G.	WE0230
Time machine	Wells, H.G.	WE0240
Time machine	Wells, H.G.	WE0270
Time machine [excerpt]	Wells, H.G.	AL0665
Time machine [selection]	Wells, H.G.	SI1000
Time machine [selections]	Wells, H.G.	KN0160
Time of going away	Bradbury, Ray	BR0400
Time of his life	Eisenberg, Larry	SI0120
Time of passage	Ballard, J.G.	OL0170
Time of passage [anthology]	Greenberg, Martin Harry	OL0170
Time of passage [anthology]	Olander, Joseph D.	OL0170
Time of the big sleep	Andrevon, Jean Pierre	KN0490
Time of the eye	Ellison, Harlan	EL0240
Time of the eye	Ellison, Harlan	EL0360
Time out of mind	Boulle, Pierre	BO0200
Time out of mind and other stories [anthology]	Boulle, Pierre	BO0200
Time piece	Haldeman, Joe W.	DI0110
Time probe	Clarke, Arthur C.	CL0500
Time probe [anthology]	Clarke, Arthur C.	CL0500
Time pussy	Asimov, Isaac	AS0280
Time scale	Abramov, Aleksandr	BE0020
Time scale	Abramov, Sergei	BE0020
Time shards	Benford, Gregory	CA0376
Time to come [anthology]	Derleth, August W.	DE0530
Time to keep	Wilhelm, Kate	WI0150
Time to live	Haldeman, Joe W.	HA0137
Time to live	Haldeman, Joe W.	OL0170
Time to rest	Harris, John Benyon	DE0400
Time to rest	Wyndham, John	WY0210
Time tombs	Ballard, J.G.	BA0215
Time tombs	Ballard, J.G.	IF0102
Time trap	Harness, Charles L.	SI0120
Time trap	Kuttner, Henry	AL0405
Time travel	Niven, Larry	AL0650
Time travel and the law	Kornbluth, Cyril M.	GR0130
Time travel for pedestrians	Nelson, Ray	EL0220
Time waits for Winthrop	Tenn, William	GA0310
Time waits for Winthrop [anthology]	Galaxy Science Fiction Magazine	GA0310
Time waits for Winthrop [anthology]	Pohl, Frederik	GA0310
Time wants a skeleton	Rocklynne, Ross	AS0452
Time wants a skeleton	Rocklynne, Ross	AS0650
Time's arrow	Clarke, Arthur C.	CL0130
Time's arrow	Clarke, Arthur C.	CL0220
Time's arrow	Clarke, Arthur C.	CL0400
Time-travel happens	Phillips, A.M.	HE0100
Timed clock	VanVogt, A.E.	VA0150
Timeless stories for today and tomorrow [anthology]	Bradbury, Ray	BR0380
Timescape	Butler, M.	EN0070
Timescape	Engdahl, Sylvia	EN0070

To sleep, perchance to dream	Mackenroth, Nancy	EL0680
To sleep, perchance to dream	Mackenroth, Nancy	EL0760
To sport with Amaryllis	Hill, Richard	KN0305
To the Chicago abyss	Bradbury, Ray	AL0665
To the Chicago abyss	Bradbury, Ray	BR0200
To the Chicago abyss	Bradbury, Ray	FE0110
To the dark star	Silverberg, Robert	EL0200
To the dark star	Silverberg, Robert	HA0161
To the dark star	Silverberg, Robert	SI0360
To the dark tower came	Wolfe, Gene	KN0319
To the end of time [anthology]	Davenport, Basil	ST0150
To the end of time [anthology]	Stapledon, Olaf	ST0150
To the moon, 1969 [poem]	Deutsch, Babette	SA0150
To the mountains	Haney, Laura	CL0110
To the pump room with Jane	Watson, Ian	NE0326
To the pure	Knight, Damon	KN0600
To the rescue	Goulart, Ron	G00070
To the stars [anthology]	Silverberg, Robert	SI0900
To the world of Zzzd	Street, Claire Edwin	EL1220
To walk a city's street	Simak, Clifford D.	W00413
To walk the night	Sloane, William Milligan	SL0150
To whom this may come	Bellamy, Edward	FR0070
To worlds beyond [anthology]	Silverberg, Robert	SI0920
Toads of Grimmerdale	Norton, Andre	N00250
Tobermory	Saki	L00100
Toe to tip, tip to toe, pip-pop as you go	Nolan, William F.	N00150
Tolliver's travels	Fenton, Frank	HE0130
Tolliver's travels	Petracca, Joseph	HE0130
Tomb tapper	Blish, James	BL0180
Tomb tapper	Blish, James	BL0200
Tomb-spawn	Smith, Clark Ashton	SM0150
Tomorrow [anthology]	Elwood, Roger	EL1100
Tomorrow and tomorrow [anthology]	Knight, Damon	KN0540
Tomorrow and tomorrow and tomorrow	Vonnegut, Kurt, Jr.	AL0650
Tomorrow and tomorrow and tomorrow	Vonnegut, Kurt, Jr.	B00100
Tomorrow is a million years	Ballard, J.G.	EL0200
Tomorrow is here to stay	Crossen, Kendall F.	CR0230
Tomorrow is yesterday	Blish, James	ST0161
Tomorrow the stars [anthology]	Heinlein, Robert A.	HE0400
Tomorrow today [anthology]	Zebrowski, George	ZE0150
Tomorrow x 4 [anthology]	Knight, Damon	KN0570
Tomorrow's alternatives [anthology]	Elwood, Roger	EL1200
Tomorrow's child	Bradbury, Ray	DA0271
Tomorrow's children	Anderson, Poul	AN0180
Tomorrow's children	Anderson, Poul	AN0280
Tomorrow's children	Anderson, Poul	SI0700
Tomorrow's children	Schongut, Emanuel	AS0590
Tomorrow's children	Waldrop, F.N.	SI0700
Tomorrow's children [anthology]	Asimov, Isaac	AS0590
Tomorrow's gift	Cooper, Edmund	P00374
Tomorrow's Wall Street Journal	Fast, Howard	FA0270
Tomorrow's worlds [anthology]	Silverberg, Robert	SI0940

Tomorrow, inc. [anthology]	Greenberg, Martin Harry	GRO300
Tomorrow, inc. [anthology]	Olander, Joseph D.	GRO300
Tomus	Robinett, Stephen	KNO319
Tongue of beast	Claudy, Carl H.	DE0310
Tonight the sky will fall	Galouye, Daniel F.	AL0510
Tonight the stars revolt!	Fox, Gardner F.	AL0411
Too far	Brown, Frederic	MA0195
Too long at the fair	Wellen, Edward	NOC404
Tools of the trade	Jones, Raymond F.	SL0180
Tooth	Dewey, G. Gordon	MA0192
Top	Albee, George Summer	COC760
Top secret	Grinnell, David	CO0250
Top stand-by job	Dick, Philip K.	DIO083
Total environment	Aldiss, Brian W.	CL0590
Total environment	Aldiss, Brian W.	MI0180
Total environment	Aldiss, Brian W.	WO0409
Total experience kick	Platt, Charles	KE0100
Total experience kick	Platt, Charles	ME0290
Total experience kick	Platt, Charles	MO0162
Total recall	Sternig, Larry	FU0130
Totally rich	Brunner, John	FI0090
Totally rich	Brunner, John	SIO330
Totem and taboo	Farmer, Philip Jose	FAC240
Totenbuch	Figueredo, A. Parra y	EL0220
Toto, I have a feeling we're not in Kansas anymore	Millar, Jeff	KNO317
Touch of infinity [anthology]	Fast, Howard	FA0300
Touch of nutmeg makes it	Collier, John	KNO490
Touch of peace	Vickory, S.	WH0150
Touch of strange	Sturgeon, Theodore	FE0230
Touch of strange [anthology]	Sturgeon, Theodore	STO330
Touch of your hand	Sturgeon, Theodore	STO330
Touched with fire	Bradbury, Ray	BRO280
Touchstone	Carr, Terry	MA0204
Tough old man	Hubbard, L. Ron	NOC300
Tourist trade	Tucker, Wilson	BE0202
Tourist trade	Tucker, Wilson	HE0400
Toward infinity [anthology]	Knight, Damon	KNO580
Toward the beloved city	Farmer, Philip Jose	EL0560
Toward the beloved city	Farmer, Philip Jose	EL1240
Toward the beloved city	Farmer, Philip Jose	FA0240
Tower	Scortia, Thomas N.	EL0540
Tower of the elephant	Howard, Robert E.	HO0160
Town where no one got off	Bradbury, Ray	BRO400
Toy for Juliette	Bloch, Robert	EL0300
Toy for Juliette	Bloch, Robert	EL0440
Toy for Juliette	Ellison, Harlan	EL0440
Toy shop	Harrison, Harry	ME0363
Toy theater	Wolfe, Gene	KNO309
Toys	Purdom, Tom	CA0360
Toys	Purdom, Tom	SA0180
Toys for Debbie	Kyle, David A.	IF0102
Trace	Bixby, Jerome	AS0555

Treasury of great science fiction v.2 [anthology]	Boucher, Anthony	B00151
Treasury of science fiction [anthology]	Conklin, Groff	C00730
Treasury of science fiction classics	Kuebler, Harold W.	KU0100
Treat [poem]	Kerr, Walter H.	MA0205
Treaty in Tartessos	Anderson, Karen	MA0203
Tree men of Potee	Holberg, Lewis	DE0370
Tree of life	Eisenstein, Phyllis	BE0301
Tree trunks	Gallagher, John	ME0364
Trefoil company	Davidson, Avram	DA0235
Trematode a critique of modern S-F	Bester, Alfred	BE0203
Trends	Asimov, Isaac	AS0230
Trends	Asimov, Isaac	AS0450
Trends	Asimov, Isaac	CL0100
Trends	Asimov, Isaac	DI0220
Trends	Asimov, Isaac	GR0220
Trends	Asimov, Isaac	ST0230
Trespass	Anderson, Poul	BE0201
Trespass	Dickson, Gordon R.	BE0201
Triad [anthology]	VanVogt, A.E.	VA0210
Triangle [anthology]	Asimov, Isaac	AS0620
Tricentennial	Haldeman, Joe W.	AN0140
Tricentennial	Haldeman, Joe W.	HA0137
Tricentennial	Haldeman, Joe W.	NE0162
Tricentennial	Haldeman, Joe W.	P00430
Trick or treaty	Laumer, Keith	IF0100
Trick or two	Novotny, John	MA0330
Tricky tonnage	Jameson, Malcolm	HA0290
Trigger tide	Guin, Wyman	C00280
Triggerman	Bone, J.F.	AN0150
Triggerman	Bone, J.F.	CA0100
Triggerman	Bone, J.F.	GR0250
Triggerman	Bone, J.F.	L00100
Triggerman	Bone, J.F.	ME0359
Trigononomy	Moore, Raylyn	EL1060
Trip one	Grendon, Edward	C00160
Trip one	Grendon, Edward	SL0180
Trip to the city	Laumer, Keith	LA0130
Trip to the city	Laumer, Keith	WH0180
Trip, trap	Wolfe, Gene	KN0302
Triple moons of Deneb II	Charney, David H.	EL1040
Trippers	Shaeffer, R.	EL0860
Trips	Silverberg, Robert	FE0170
Trips	Silverberg, Robert	SI0540
Trips	Silverberg, Robert	SI0620
Trips in time [anthology]	Silverberg, Robert	SI0960
Triptych	Malzberg, Barry N.	SI0120
Triumph of time	Blish, James	BL0190
Triumphant head	Saxton, Josephine	MC0150
Triumphant head	Saxton, Josephine	SA0230
Triumphs of a taxidermist	Wells, H.G.	WE0210
Troll road	Bernott, Jean	LA0160
Trolley	Bradbury, Ray	BR0330

Visitor	Bradbury, Ray	BR0170
Visitor	Reynolds, Mack	ZE0150
Visitor from outer space	Kayantsev, A.	DU0100
Visitors from outer space	Voltaire	EV0100
Vitanuls	Brunner, John	MO0100
Vitanuls	Brunner, John	OL0170
Voice from the curious cube	Bond, Nelson S.	AS0555
Voice from the gallery	Brownlow, Catherine	OB0140
Voice in the earphones	Schramm, Wilbur	SA0270
Voice in the garden	Ellison, Harlan	EL0360
Voice in the night	Hodgson, William Hope	MO0365
Voice of the dolphins [anthology]	Szilard, Leo	SZ0150
Voice of the lobster	Kuttner, Henry	CR0200
Voice of the sonar in my vermiform appendix	Farmer, Philip Jose	FA0240
Voices from the cliff	Leahy, John Martin	FO0100
Voices of time	Ballard, J.G.	AM0512
Voices of time	Ballard, J.G.	BA0120
Voices of time	Ballard, J.G.	BA0150
Voices of time	Ballard, J.G.	IN0100
Voices of time	Ballard, J.G.	KN0280
Voices of time	Ballard, J.G.	SI0121
Volcano dances	Ballard, J.G.	ME0366
Volpla	Guin, Wymar	GA0142
Von Kempelen and his discovery	Poe, Edgar Allan	PO0100
Voortrekkers	Anderson, Poul	FE0170
Vortex blasters	Smith, Edward E.	MO0350
Vortex new stories science fiction [anthology]	Bearne, C.G.	BE0020
Vox populi	Malzberg, Barry N.	MA0455
Voyage of the "Deborah Pratt"	DeFord, Miriam Allen	DE0210
Voyage of the Bagel	Gardner, Martin	AS0180
Voyage of the space beagle	VanVogt, A.E.	VA0210
Voyage that lasted six hundred years	Wilcox, Don	LE0220
Voyage to Laputa [excerpt]	Swift, Jonathan	GU0130
Voyage to Sfanomoe	Smith, Clark Ashton	DE0370
Voyage to the moon	DeBergerac, Cyrano	MO0320
Voyage to the moon	Rostand, Edmund	MO0320
Voyage to the moon [excerpt]	DeBergerac, Cyrano	GU0130
Voyagers in time [anthology]	Silverberg, Robert	SI1000
Voyages	Sauer, Rob	SA0300
Voyages and travels of Sir John Manceville [excerpt]	anonymous	GU0130
W-A-V-E-R	Kupferberg, Tuli	ME0367
Wabbler	Leinster, Murray	CL0500
Wabbler	Leinster, Murray	CR0102
Wabbler	Leinster, Murray	ME0230
Wabbler	Leinster, Murray	PO0293
Wages of synergy	Sturgeon, Theodore	ST0180
Wages of synergy	Sturgeon, Theodore	ST0325
Waging of the peace	Pohl, Frederik	PO0260
Waif	Leiber, Fritz, Jr.	EL0680
Wait	Reed, Kit	MA0198
Wait	Reed, Kit	ST0210

With the night mail	Kipling, Rudyard	GU0130
With the night mail	Kipling, Rudyard	HO0119
With the night mail	Kipling, Rudyard	KN0280
With these hands	Kornbluth, Cyril M.	BL0210
With these hands	Kornbluth, Cyril M.	CU0070
With these hands	Kornbluth, Cyril M.	DO0130
With these hands	Kornbluth, Cyril M.	KO0070
With these hands	Kornbluth, Cyril M.	KO0100
With these hands	Kornbluth, Cyril M.	MO0155
With these hands	Kornbluth, Cyril M.	SI0125
Within the pyramid	Miller, R. Dewitt	HE0100
Without a thought	Saberhagen, Fred	SI0640
Witness	Russell, Eric Frank	MO0350
Witnesses	Sansom, William	BR0380
Wizard of scorpio	Akers, Alan Burt	WO0180
Wizard of Venus	Burroughs, Edgar Rice	BU0130
Wizards of Pung's Corners	Pohl, Frederik	BO0100
Wizards of Pung's Corners	Pohl, Frederik	PO0260
Wizards of Pung's Corners	Pohl, Frederik	SU0150
Wolf in the fold	Blish, James	ST0161
Wolf pack	Miller, Walter M., Jr.	ME0260
Wolf tracks	Gaither, Donald	AS0180
Wolf tracks	Gaither, Donald	AS0440
Wolfram	Anderson, Poul	AN0250
Wolfram hunters	Hoch, Edward D.	EL0560
Wolfshead [anthology]	Howard, Robert E.	HO0280
Wolfshead [anthology]	Lord, Glenn	HO0280
Wolves of Nakesht	Frank, J.	SA0120
Woman from Altair	Brackett, Leigh	BR0070
Woman in sunlight with mandoline	Aldiss, Brian W.	KN0312
Woman of the white waste	Morgan, T.J.	SA0120
Woman waiting	Emshwiller, Carol	KN0307
Woman who loved the moon	Lynn, Elizabeth A.	SA0120
Woman's place	Clifton, Mark	GA0340
Woman's rib	Scortia, Thomas N.	BE0291
Womb to tomb	Wesley, Joseph	AN0108
Womb to tomb	Wesley, Joseph	HA0162
Womb, with a view	Utley, Steven	GE0150
Women men don't see	Tiptree, James, Jr.	HA0167
Women men don't see	Tiptree, James, Jr.	SA0230
Women of wonder [anthology]	Sargent, Pamela	SA0240
Wonder horse	Byram, George	ME0201
Wonder horse	Byram, George	ME0358
Wonderbird	Budrys, Algis	EL0440
Wonderbird	Ellison, Harlan	EL0440
Wonderful corot	Mitchell, Edward Page	MIC250
Wonderful death of Dudley Stone	Bradbury, Ray	BR0280
Wonderful dog suit	Hall, Donald	ME0365
Wonderful ice cream suit	Bradbury, Ray	BR0415
Wonderful ice-cream suit	Bradbury, Ray	BR0400
Wonderful world of Robert Sheckley [anthology]	Sheckley, Robert	SH0210
Wonderful, all-purpose transmogrifer	Malzberg, Barry N.	FE0170
Wondermakers [anthology]	Hoskins, Robert	HO0119

World's best science fiction: 1966 [anthology]	Carr, Terry	W00406
World's best science fiction: 1966 [anthology]	Wollheim, Donald A.	W00406
World's best science fiction: 1967 [anthology]	Carr, Terry	W00407
World's best science fiction: 1967 [anthology]	Wollheim, Donald A.	W00407
World's best science fiction: 1969 [anthology]	Carr, Terry	W00409
World's best science fiction: 1969 [anthology]	Wollheim, Donald A.	W00409
World's best science fiction: 1970 [anthology]	Carr, Terry	W00410
World's best science fiction: 1970 [anthology]	Wollheim, Donald A.	W00410
World's best science fiction: 1971 [anthology]	Carr, Terry	W00411
World's best science fiction: 1971 [anthology]	Wollheim, Donald A.	W00411
Worlds apart [anthology]	Owen, Mably	WI0280
Worlds apart [anthology]	Williams-Ellis, Amabel	WI0280
Worlds near and far [anthology]	Carr, Terry	CA0420
Worlds of Clifford D. Simak [anthology]	Simak, Clifford D.	SI1180
Worlds of If	Weinbaum, Stanley G.	SI0740
Worlds of If	Weinbaum, Stanley G.	WE0150
Worlds of If	weinbaum, Stanley G.	WE0158
Worlds of maybe [anthology]	Silverberg, Robert	SI1040
Worlds of Monty Wilson	Nolan, William F.	AS0555
Worlds of Robert A. Heinlein [anthology]	Heinlein, Robert A.	HE0440
Worlds of Robert F. Young [anthology]	Young, Robert F.	YO0180
Worlds of science fiction [anthology]	Mills, Robert P.	MI0150
Worlds of the imperium	Laumer, Keith	KN0160
Worlds of tomorrow [anthology]	Derleth, August W.	DE0590
Worlds of wonder [anthology]	Harrison, Harry	HA0290
Worlds to come [anthology]	Knight, Damon	KN0630
Worlds to kill	Ellison, Harlan	EL0280
Worm	Keller, David H., M.D.	CA0260
Worm	Keller, David H., M.D.	R00240
Worm that flies	Aldiss, Brian W.	EL0200
Worm that flies	Aldiss, Brian W.	W00409
Worrywart	Simak, Clifford D.	C00310
Worrywart	Simak, Clifford D.	CR0101
Wound	Fast, Howard	AL0405
Wound	Fast, Howard	FA0270
Wreck of the Ship John B.	Robinson, Frank M.	HA0160
Writer as teacher	Sallis, James	CL0110
Writing of the rat	Blish, James	BL0125
Written in the stars	Young, Robert F.	YO0180
Wrong way street	Niven, Larry	NI0120
Wrong world	McIntosh, J.T.	C00140
Wrong-way street	Niven, Larry	GA0148

Wrong-way street	Niven, Larry	SI1000
Wrong-way street	Niven, Larry	ST0230
X marks the pedwalk	Leiber, Fritz, Jr.	KE0100
X yes	Disch, Thomas M.	DI0215
Xenofreak / Xenophobe	Bryant, Edward	EL0660
Xi effect	Latham, Philip	ALC400
Xi effect	Latham, Philip	BL0100
Xi effect	Latham, Philip	CR0100
Xong of Xugan	Russell, Ray	EL0640
Xong of Xuxan	Russell, Ray	H00120
Yachid and Yechida	Singer, Isaac Bashevis	ME0365
Yahrzeit	Malzberg, Barry N.	EL1160
Ye phantasie writer and his catte	McClintic, Winona	MA0198
Ye who would sing	Foster, Alan Dean	RYC100
Year 2000 [anthology]	Harrison, Harry	HA0300
Year after tomorrow	Carmel, Carl	DE0310
Year after tomorrow [anthology]	DelRey, Lester	DE0310
Year after tomorrow [anthology]	Matschat, Cecile	DE0310
Year day	Kuttner, Henry	KU0130
Year of the jackpot	Heinlein, Robert A.	AL0650
Year of the jackpot	Heinlein, Robert A.	CA0340
Year of the jackpot	Heinlein, Robert A.	GA0141
Year of the jackpot	Heinlein, Robert A.	HE0310
Year of the jackpot	Heinlein, Robert A.	KN0490
Year of the jackpot	Heinlein, Robert A.	SI1020
Year of the jackpot	Heinlein, Robert A.	W00210
Year's best S-F; the 6th annual [anthology]	Merril, Judith	ME0361
Year's best S-F; the 7th annual [anthology]	Merril, Judith	ME0362
Year's best S-F; the 8th annual [anthology]	Merril, Judith	ME0363
Year's best S-F; the 8th annual [anthology]	Merril, Judith	ME0363
Year's best S-F; the 9th annual [anthology]	Merril, Judith	ME0364
Year's best S-F; the 10th annual [anthology]	Merril, Judith	ME0365
Year's best S-F; the 11th annual [anthology]	Merril, Judith	ME0366
Year's best science fiction novels 1952 [anthology]	Bleiler, Everett F.	YE0403
Year's best science fiction novels 1953 [anthology]	Bleiler, Everett F.	YE0404
Year's best science fiction novels 1954 [anthology]	Bleiler, Everett F.	YE0405
Year's best science fiction novels 1952 [anthology]	Dikty, T.E.	YE0403
Year's best science fiction novels 1953 [anthology]	Dikty, T.E.	YE0404
Year's best science fiction novels 1954 [anthology]	Dikty, T.E.	YE0405
Years	Young, Robert F.	HA0165
"Years draw nigh"	DelRey, Lester	DE0340

Abernathy, Robert
    Rotifers   SIO420
    Single combat   KNO19C
    Single combat   MIO18C
    Strange exodus   ALO480

Abramov, Aleksandr
    Time scale   BEO02C

Abramov, Sergei
    Time scale   BEO020

Ackerman, Forrest J.
    Best science fiction of 1973   ACO20C
        [anthology]
    Mute question   CRO20C
    Mute question   SIO70C

Ackerson, Duane
    DNA [poem]   HAO167
    Future sportsman's manual   EDO15C
    Science fiction story [poem]   HAO167
    Sign at the end of the universe   ASO555
    Sign at the end of the universe   GEO15C

Adams, Louis J.A.
    Dark conception   MAO204

Adams, P.
    Planting time   ALO410
    Planting time   STO22C

Addobati, Michael
    Side view of a circle   NCO4C4

Adlard, Mark
    Theophilus   BEO50C

Aickman, Robert
    Cicerones   DEO56C

Aiken, Conrad
    Mr. Arcularis   KNO450
    Oneiromachia   MEO362

Aiken, J.
    Elephant's ear   DIO260

Akers, Alan Burt
    Wizard of scorpio   WOO180

Albee, George Summer
    Top   COO76C

Aldani, Lino
    Good night Sophie   R00270

Aldiss, Brian W.
    Ahead   AL0540
    Aimez-vous Holman Hunt   SI0480
    Airs of earth [anthology]   AL03CC
    All about Venus [anthology]   AL0310
    All the world's tears   AL0375
    Always somebody there   EL1180
    Amen and out   AL0375
    Amen and out   ALU44C
    Amen and out   W00407
    And the stagnation of the heart   CA0360
    And the stagnation of the heart   HA020C
    Another little boy   AL0365
    Another little boy   M00162
    Aperture moment   SI0480
    Appearance of life   AL0435
    Appearance of life   WE0290
    Appearance of life   wC0417
    As for our fatal continuity   AL0375
    As for our fatal continuity   HA0165
    Astounding analog reader. V.1   AS0650
       [anthology]
    Astounding analog reader. V.2   AS0651
       [anthoogy]
    Auto-Ancestral fracture   HA0232
    Backwater   AL0435
    Basis for negotiation   AL030C
    Basis for negotiation   AL0540
    Best fantasy stories [anthology]   AL0360
    Best science fiction stories of Brian   AL0365
       W. Aldiss [anthology]
    Best SF: 1967 [anthology]   HA0160
    Best SF: 1968 [anthology]   HA0161
    Best SF: 1969 [anthology]   HA0162
    Best SF: 1970 [anthology]   HA0163
    Best SF: 1971 [anthology]   HA0164
    Best SF: 1972 [anthology]   HA0165
    Best SF: 1973 [anthology]   HA0166
    Best SF: 1974 [anthology]   HA0167
    Best SF: 1975 the ninth annual   HA0168
       [anthology]
    Book of Brian Aldiss [anthology]   AL0375
    Brian Aldiss omnibus (2) [anthology] AL039C
    Burning question   GR0250
    But who can replace a man?   KN0160
    But who can replace a man?   WI0202
    But without orifices   SI0480
    Cardiac arrest   AL0375
    Castle scene with penitents   KN0312
    Chinese perspective   PR0160
    Circulation of the blood   HA02CC
    Comic inferno   AL0375

Aldiss, Brian W.

Confluence	ME0367
Cosmic inferno	GA0147
Creatures of apogee	AL0435
Danger: religion!	AL0437
Danger: religion!	IN0100
Dark soul of the night	CA0275
Decade, the 1940's [anthology]	AL0400
Decade, the 1950's [anthology]	AL0401
Decade, the 1960's [anthology]	AL0402
Diagrams for three enigmatic stories	FE0170
Dumb show	AL0540
Dumb show	DO0100
Enigma 1	AL0435
Enigma 2	AL0435
Enigma 3	AL0435
Enigma 4	AL0435
Enigma 5	AL0435
Equator	HA0100
Ergot show	NO0402
Ergot show	ST0220
Evil earths [anthology]	AL0405
Expensive delicate ship	AL0435
Expensive delicate ship	NO0403
Full sun	CA0260
Full sun	KN0302
Galactic empires, v.1 [anthology]	AL0410
Galactic empires, v.2 [anthology]	AL0411
Game of God	AL0300
Gesture of farewell	AL0425
Girl and robot with flowers	AL0365
Heresies of the huge God	AL0405
Heresies of the huge God	GA0149
Heresies of the huge God	SI0380
Heresies of the huge God	SI0580
Heresies of the huge God	SI0600
Hothouse	SI0700
Hothouse	WI0204
House that Jules built	HA0161
How to be a soldier	AL0300
Hunter at his ease	HA0164
Impossible puppet show	AL0440
Impossible star	AL0365
Impossible star	AL0540
In the arena	AL0375
In the arena	IF0102
Incentive	SI0560
Indifference	AL0440
Indifference	HA0159
Intangibles Inc.	AL0360
Intangibles Inc.	AL0418
Intangibles Inc.	AL0437
Intangibles Inc. [anthology]	AL0418
International smile	AL0300
International smile	WI0245

Aldiss, Brian W.
        Introducing SF [anthology]   AL0425
        Journey to the heartland   AL0435
        Journey to the heartland   CA0373
        Judas danced   AL0365
        Judas danced   SI0123
        Jungle substitute   GA0148
        Kind of artistry   AL0300
        Kind of artistry   AL0540
        Kind of artistry   MA0202
        Lambeth blossom   SC0450
        Last orders   AL0435
        Last orders [anthology]   AL0435
        Let's be frank   NE0201
        Let's be frank   NE0358
        Listen with big brother   HA0167
        Live? Our computers will do that for us   AL0435
        Live? Our computers will do that for us   KN0315
        Male response   AL0390
        Man in his time   AL0365
        Man in his time   AL0540
        Man in his time   KN0480
        Man in his time   NE0152
        Man on bridge   AL0365
        Man on bridge   AL0540
        Man on bridge   NE0301
        Moment of eclipse   AL0365
        Monsters of Ingratitude IV   NC0404
        Monsters of Ingratitude IV   AL0435
        Multi-value motorway   MO0163
        My lady of the psychiatric sorrows   CA0374
        Neanderthal planet   AL0418
        Neanderthal planet   AL0437
        Neanderthal planet [anthology]   AL0437
        Nebula award stories two [anthology]   NE0152
        New arrivals, old encounters   AL0440
        New arrivals, old encounters   AL0440
            [anthology]
        New father Christmas   AL0540
        New father Christmas   WA0130
        Night that all time broke out   EL0300
        Night that all time broke out   SI0420
        Non-isotropic   AL0440
        Non-stop   AL0390
        Not for an age   AL0365
        Not for an age   AL0540
        Not for an age   CB0140
        O moon of my delight   AL0300
        Old hundredth   AL0300
        Old hundredth   AL0365
        Old hundredth   AL0540
        Old hundredth   DO0165
        Old hundredth   HA0234
        Old hundredth   NE0361
        One blink of the moon   AL0440

Aldiss, Brian W.

Aldiss, Brian W.
        Ten-story jigsaw   ME0359
        There is a tide   AM0515
        Thing under the glacier   DA0271
        Three coins in enigmatic fountains   NE0326
        Three ways   AL0440
        Total environment   CL0590
        Total environment   MI0180
        Total environment   WO0409
        Underprivileged   AL0375
        Underprivileged   KN0190
        Unreal estates   AM0513
        Village swindler   AL0402
        Waiting for the universe to begin   SI0480
        What you get for your dollar   DI0240
        Where the lines converge   DI0260
        Where the lines converge   RY0100
        Who can replace a man?   AL0365
        Who can replace a man?   AL0540
        Who can replace a man?   AS0070
        Who can replace a man?   HA0260
        Who can replace a man?   HA0290
        Who can replace a man?   MC0400
        Who can replace a man?   SI0640
        Who can replace a man? [anthology]   AL0540
        Wired for sound   AL0435
        Woman in sunlight with mandoline   KN0312
        Working in the spaceship yards   HA0162
        Worm that flies   EL0200
        Worm that flies   WO0409
        Young soldier's horoscope   KN0312

Alexander, Lloyd
        Sacred city of cats (from Time cat)   DE0160

Alexander, W.
        One leg too many   CO0130

Allan, Grant
        Pausodyne   DE0370

Allen, Dick
        Backward, into beasts evolving [poem]   HA0167
        Hyperspace   DA0140
        Looking ahead [anthology]   AL0650
        New age   AL0650
        Science fiction: the future [anthology]   AL0665
        When I first read   ME0367

Allen, Grant
        Thames valley catastrophe   MO0365

Allen, Lori
        Looking ahead [anthology]   AL0650

Allen, Marijane
    Neanderthal   ST021C

Allen, Steve
    Public hating   ME02C1
    Public hating   ME0356

Allison, Ruth
    Loolies are here   KN010C
    Loolies are here   KN0301
    Loolies are here   PR0210

Allred, J.
    When I was in your mind   AN014C

Alper, Gerald Arthur
    Mechanical sweetheart   SC0450

Alpert, Hollis
    Simian problem   COC64C

Alterman, Peter S.
    Binding energy   NE02C9

Altov, Henrik
    Icarus and Daedalus   GI013C
    Master builder   SU018C

Amis, Kingsley
    Hemingway in space   AL0402
    Hemingway in space   ME0361
    Mason's life   HA0166
    Report [poem]   HA0164
    Science fiction [poem]   SA015C
    Somthin strange   HA021C
    Spectrum 1 [anthology]   AMC51C
    Spectrum 2 [anthology]   AMU511
    Spectrum 3 [anthology]   AM0512
    Spectrum 4 [anthology]   AM0513
    Spectrum 5 [anthology]   AM0514
    Unreal estates   AM0513

Ammons, A.R.
    Misfit [poem]   SA015C

Anderson, Karen
    Landscape with sphinxes   AS0555
    Landscape with sphinxes   MA0202
    Murphy's hall   PR021C
    Origin of the species   MA0193
    Piebald hippogriff   NE0363
    Six haiku [poems]   SAC15C
    Six haiku [poems]   AS0340
    Treaty in Tartessos   MA0203

Anderscn, Poul

Escape from orbit	AN0335
Escape the morning	HA0260
Escape the morning	HA0290
Eutopia	EL0300
Eve times four	AN0335
Eve times four	WH0180
Fair exchange	EL0582
Fatal fulfillment	AN0160
Fatal fulfillment	FI010C
Faun	AN0305
Flandry of Terra [anthology]	AN0230
Flight to forever	YE0403
Fcr the duration	AN0325
Game of glory	AN0230
Garden in the void	MO0290
Genius	EL0120
Genius	CO016C
Ghetto	NO0230
Goat song	AN025C
Goat song	AS0401
Goat song	NE0158
Goat song	WA0130
Goat song	WO0413
Gypsy	AN0325
Gypsy	BO0245
Gypsy	DI0130
Gypsy	SI0900
Helping hand	CO0220
Helping hand	CO0340
Helping hand	GR0250
Her strong enchantments failing	AN0280
Hiding place	AN0160
Hiding place	AN0340
High ones	AN0260
High treason	HA0200
Hcme	AN0305
Hcme	HO0110
Homeward and beyond [anthology]	AN0250
Hcrn of time [anthology]	AN0260
Hcrn of time the hunter	AN0260
Hcrn of time the hunter	HC0120
Horn of time the hunter	WH0175
I tell you, it's true	NO0402
Immortal game	MA0194
In hoka signo vinces	AN020C
In the shadow	AN0305
Innocent arrival	DE022C
Inside earth	GA0140
Inside straight	AN0315
Interloper	DE047C
Joelle	AS0172
Jcurney's end	AN0180
Jcurney's end	AN0280
Jcurney's end	KN0480

Anderson, Poul

Journey's end	MA0197
Journey's end	MC0180
Journey's end	SI0380
Journey's end	SI0660
Joy in Mudville	CA0277
Kings who die	AN0315
Kings who die	ME0363
Kings who die	SC0300
Kyrie	AN0160
Kyrie	EL0200
Kyrie	EN0100
Kyrie	SI0520
Kyrie	W00409
Last monster	LE0220
Last of the deliverers	AN0160
Last of the deliverers	GR0250
License	AN0315
Life cycle	SI0440
Little knowledge	BE0290
Little knowledge	W00412
Live coward	CO0100
Lodestar	AS0750
Long remembering	AN0250
Long remembering	K00160
Long remembering	SI0960
Longest voyage	AN0160
Longest voyage	AN0180
Longest voyage	AN0280
Longest voyage	AS0370
Lord of a thousand sons	AL0411
Man to my wounding	AN0260
Man to my wounding	HA0145
Man who came early	AN0260
Man who came early	DI0110
Man who came early	KE0100
Man who came early	KN0280
Man who came early	MA0196
Man who came early	SI0120
Many worlds of Poul Anderson [anthology]	AN0280
Martian crown jewels	B00150
Martian crown jewels	CL0180
Martian crown jewels	SC0400
Martyr	CR0104
Martyr	MA0200
Master key	AN0340
Matius	AN0260
Memory	AN0165
Message in secret	AN0230
Moonrakers	AN0165
Murphy's hall	AN0250
Murphy's hall	PR0210
My object all sublime	AN0160
My object all sublime	C00760

Anderson, Poul

My own, my native land	EL0580
Mysterious message	AN0200
Nebula award stories four [anthology]	NE0154
Night face	AN0295
Night face [anthology]	AN0295
Night piece	MI015C
No truce with kings	AN0335
No truce with kings	AS0400
Passing the love of women	EL0581
Peat bog	AN0250
Peat bog	GR014C
Peek! I see you!	AN0250
Pirate	AN0250
Plague of masters	AN0230
Planet of no return	AN04CC
Problem of pain	BE0299
Problem of pain	EL056C
Problem of pain	MA0210
Problem of pain	CL017C
Progress	AN0260
Pugilist	FC045C
Queen of air and darkness	AN0180
Queen of air and darkness	AN0280
Queen of air and darkness	AN0305
Queen of air and darkness	AS04C1
Queen of air and darkness	CA0231
Queen of air and darkness	CA0234
Queen of air and darkness	FE0110
Queen of air and darkness	NE0157
Queen of air and darkness [anthology]	AN0305
Quixote and the windmill	AN0325
Sam Hall	AN0160
Sam Hall	C0055C
Sam Hall	C0056C
Sensitive man	AN0165
Sensitive man	FI0095
Serpent in Eden	EL098C
Serpent in Eden	EL1240
Seven conquests [anthology]	AN0315
An adventure in science fiction	
Sharing of flesh	AN0295
Sharing of flesh	AS040C
Sharing of flesh	MA055C
Sheriff of Canyon Gulch	AN0200
Sheriff of Canyon Gulch	AN0280
Sheriff of Canyon Gulch	N00240
Sheriff of Canyon Gulch	SI078C
Sister planet	AL031C
Sister planet	MA0475
Sky people	AN0160
Sky people	MA033C
Star beast	AN0325
Star plunderer	AL041C
Star ship	AL0480

Anderson, Poul
    Starfog   AN0165
    Starfog   AN0295
    Strange bedfellows   AN0315
    Strangers from earth [anthology]   AN0325
    Sun invisible   AN037C
    Sunjammer   AN0104
    Swordsman of lost terra   WO0360
    Terminal guest   TE015C
    Territory   AN0340
    Three cornered wheel   AN037C
    Tiddlywink warriors   AN0200
    Time and stars [anthology]   ANC335
    Time heals   SI100C
    Time lag   AN0305
    Time lag   MA0201
    Tinkler   DE059C
    Tomorrow's children   AN0180
    Tomorrow's children   ANC28C
    Tomorrow's children   SI07CC
    Trader to the stars   AN0340
    Trader to the stars [anthology]   AN034C
    Tragedy of errors   AN0295
    Trespass   EE0201
    Trouble twisters   AN0370
    Trouble twisters [anthology]   AN0370
    Turning point   AN0335
    Turning point   CO014C
    Un-man   GR010C
    Visitor   AN025C
    Voortrekkers   FE017C
    War of two worlds   AN04CC
    War of two worlds [anthology]   AN0400
    Wildcat   AN0315
    Windmill   EL1020
    Wingless on Avalon   EL054C
    Wings of victory   AN025C
    Wolfram   AN025C
    World named Cleopatra   AN0130
    World named Cleopatra   AN028C
    World without stars   AN0400
    Yo ho hoka!   ANC20C

Andrevon Jean Pierre
    Observation of Quadragnes   RC027C

Andrevon, Jean Pierre
    Time of the big sleep   KN049C

Andrew, William
    Right thing   OB014C

Andreyev, Leonid
    Abyss   KN049C

Arnason, Eleanor
    Ace 167   KN0315
    Clear day in the motor city   DI0240
    Going down   KN0319
    House by the sea   KN0316
    Warlord of Saturn's moons   SA0230

Arnold, Charles
    Spring came to Blue Ridge early this   KN0313
        year

Aroeste, Jean L.
    All our yesterdays   ST0164

Arrhenius, Svante
    Destinies of the stars   AL0310

Arthur, Robert [pseud. of Ray Bradbury]
    Evolution's end   AS0452
    Evolution's end   CR0200
    Evolution's end   WA0100
    Fire balloons   WA0100
    Postpaid to paradise   AS0451
    Postpaid to paradise   MA0191
    Wheel of time   BR0460

Ash, Paul
    Big sword   AN0514
    Big sword   CO0100
    Wings of a bat   W00407

Ashby, Richard
    Commencement night   AN0514
    Commencement night   CO0160
    Master race   SL0180

Ashe, Tamsin
    Quality of mercy   SC0460

Ashley, Mike
    Souls in metal [anthology]   AS0070

Ashley, Richard
    Master race   FU0130

Asimov, Isaac
    All the troubles of the world   AS0530
    All the troubles of the world   H00110
    All the troubles of the world   WI0206
    Anniversary   AS0200
    Anniversary   R00240
    Asimov's choice: astronauts & androids AS0172
        [anthology]
    Asimov's choice: black holes &   AS0173
        bug-eyed monsters [anthology]

Asimov, Isaac

Asimov, Isaac

Dces a bee care?	AS025C
Dreaming is a private thing	AS0310
Dreaming is a private thing	BL0210
Dreaming is a private thing	GR0300
Dreaming is a private thing	ME0201
Dreaming is a private thing	ME0356
Dreamworld	MA0195
Dying night	AS0200
Each an explorer	AS025C
Each an explorer	ME0357
Each an explorer	SI052C
Early Asimov [anthology]	AS0280
Earth is room enough	AS0335
Earth is room enough [anthology]	AS0310
End of eternity	AS0335
Endochronic properties of resublimated thiotimoline	AS0280
Escape	AS0430
Everest	AS0250
Evidence	AS0430
Evidence	GR0250
Evidence	N00210
Evidence	WI025C
Evitable conflict	AS0430
Exile to hell	AS025C
Exile to hell	AS0555
Eyes do more than see	AS05CC
Eyes do more than see	AS0555
Eyes do more than see	MA0205
Eyes do more than see	ME0366
Far ends of time and earth [anthology]	ASC335
Feeling of power	AM0511
Feeling of power	AS053C
Feeling of power	WI021C
Feminine intuition	AS0230
Feminine intuition	FE0230
Fifty short science fiction tales [anthology]	AS0340
First law	AS0560
First law	FA0215
Flies	AS0500
Flies	C0052C
Fcundation	AL0410
Founding father	AS025C
Fcunding father	KE0100
Franchise	AS0310
Franchise	EL0480
Franchise	GR0250
Fun they had	AS02CC
Fun they had	AS031C
Fun they had	AS0340
Fun they had	E00100
Fun they had	C0031C
Fun they had	L0010C

Asimov, Isaac

Fun they had	SU0150
Galley slave	AS0560
Galley slave	C00550
Galley slave	C00700
Galley slave	GA0310
Gentle vultures	AS0530
Gentle vultures	SI0440
Gimmicks three	AS0310
Good taste	AS0172
Graduated robot [anthology]	EL0780
Greatest asset	AS0250
Greatest asset	BE0291
Green patches	AS0500
Half-baked publisher's delight	AS0555
Half-breed	AS0280
Half-breed on Venus	AS0280
Hazing	AS0280
Hell-fire	AS0310
"Nobody here but...."	AS0500
"Nobody here but...."	PO0371
Heredity	AS0280
Heredity	PO0190
History	AS0280
Homo sol	AS0280
Homo sol	C00280
Hostess	AS0500
Hostess	GA0140
Hugo winners V.1 [anthology]	AS0370
Hugo Winners V.2 [anthology]	AS0400
Hugo winners V.3 [anthology]	AS0401
I'm in Marsport without Hilda	AS0530
I, robot [anthology]	AS0430
Ideas die hard	GA0142
Ideas die hard	ST0230
Imaginary	AS0280
Immortal bard	AL0425
Immortal bard	AS0310
In a good cause	AS0500
In a good cause	HE0130
Insert knob A in hole B	AS0500
Isaac Asimov presents the great science fiction stories. v. 1, 1939 [anthology]	AS0450
Isaac Asimov presents the great science fiction stories. v. 2, 1940 [anthology]	AS0451
Isaac Asimov presents the great science fiction stories. v.3, 1941 [anthology]	AS0452
Isaac Asimov's masters of science fiction [anthology]	AS0440
It's such a beautiful day	AS0500
It's such a beautiful day	DA0272
It's such a beautiful day	EN0100

Asimov, Isaac

It's such a beautiful day	P00373
It's such a beautiful day	R00180
Jokester	AL0450
Jokester	AS0310
Key	FE0110
Key	MA0206
Key item	AS0250
Kid stuff	AS0310
Last question	AL0510
Last question	AS0200
Last question	AS0310
Last question	AS0530
Last question	DE0190
Last question	SC0300
Last trump	AS0310
Legal rites	AS0280
Legal rites	MA0490
Lenny	AS0560
Lenny	EL0520
Lenny	EL1240
Lenny	FO0240
Let's get together	AS0560
Let's get together	ME0358
Let's not	AS0250
Liar	AS0430
Liar	AS0452
Liar	JA0130
Liar	ME0310
Liar	MC0230
Liar	MO0350
Liar	SI0660
Life and times of Multivac	AS0230
Light verse	AS0250
Little lost robot	AS0430
Little lost robot	CR0101
Little lost robot	CR0170
Little man on the subway	AS0280
Little man on the subway	FO0100
Living space	AS0310
Living space	H00120
Living space	SI1040
Living space	WI0203
Loint of paw	AS0555
Loint of paw	MA0197
Machine that won the war	AS0500
Machine that won the war	MA0201
Magnificent possession	AS0280
Marching in	AS0230
Marooned off Vesta	AS0200
Marooned off Vesta	R00240
Martian way	AS0200
Martian way	AS0430
Martian way	AS0470
Martian way	AS0558

Asimov, Isaac

Martian way	KN063C
Martian way	SC0212
Martian way [anthology]	AS0470
Message	AS031C
Mirror-image	AS020C
Misbeggotten missionary	C0016C
Misbeggotten missionary	HE0400
Misbeggotten missionary	SA015C
Missing item	AS0173
Missing item	AS044C
Monkey's finger	AS0250
Mother earth	AS028C
Mother earth	GR0190
My son, the physicist	AS05CC
Naked sun	AS0560
Nebula award stories eight [anthology]	NE0158
Nightfall	AL0450
Nightfall	AS020C
Nightfall	AS0452
Nightfall	AS05C0
Nightfall	AS0650
Nightfall	AS070C
Nightfall	CA0255
Nightfall	HA026C
Nightfall	HE010C
Nightfall	KN012C
Nightfall	MA055C
Nightfall	SC021C
Nightfall	SI068C
Nightfall, and other stories [anthology]	AS0500
Nine tomorrows [anthology]	ASC530
No connection	AS0280
No connection	BL012C
Not final	AS0280
Not final	CL050C
Not final	C0034C
Not final	KN048C
Not final!	KN0580
Old-fashioned	AS0230
1C0 Great Science Fiction short short stories [anthology]	AS0555
Pate de fois gras	AS0645
Pause	AS025C
Pause	DE0530
Pebble in the sky	AS0335
Pebble in the sky	AS0620
Prime of life	AS023C
Prisoners of the stars v.2 [anthology]	AS0558
Profession	AS053C
Profession	BC0245
Profession	OL0165
Proper study	AS0250
Rain, rain, go away	AS025C

Asimov, Isaac

Reason	AL0400
Reason	AL048C
Reason	AS0430
Reason	KN0160
Reason	P00293
Red queen's race	AS028C
Red queen's race	KN048C
Red queen's race	FR0150
Rejection slips	AS0530
Rest of the robots [anthology]	AS0560
Ring around the sun	ASC28C
Risk	AS0560
Robbie	AS0430
Robbie	C00550
Robbie	C00560
Robbie	DE0160
Runaround	AS0430
Runaround	M00200
Runaround	SU015C
Sally	AS050C
Sally	WH018C
Satisfaction guaranteed	AS031C
Search for illusion	AL048C
Secret sense	AS028C
Segregationist	AS05CC
Segregationist	HA0161
Shah Guido G.	AS025C
Silly asses	AS025C
Singing bell	AS0585
Singing bell	MA0195
Someday	AS031C
Someday	HAC29C
Spell my name with an S	AS0530
Star light	NEC3C4
Stars, like dust	AS0558
Stars, like dust	AS062C
Statue for father	AS0250
Strange playfellow	AS0451
Stranger in paradise	AS023C
Stranger in paradise	IF017C
Stranger in paradise	W00415
Strikebreaker	AS050C
Strikebreaker	C00640
Strikebreaker	MA055C
Suckerbait	AS047C
Super-neutron	AS028C
Sure thing	AS044C
Take a match	AS025C
Take a match	NE0202
Talking stone	DE022C
Tercentenary incident	AS023C
That thou art mindful of him	AS0070
That thou art mindful of him	AS0230
That thou art mindful of him	FE017C

Asimov, Isaac

Thiotimoline and the space age	ME0361
Thiotimoline to the stars	AS0250
Thiotimoline to the stars	AS0750
13 crimes of science fiction [anthology]	AS0585
Robot A1-76 goes astray	AS0560
Satisfaction guaranteed	AS0560
Science fictional solar system [anthology]	AS0575
Suckerbait	AS0558
Thunder-thieves	ME0359
Time pussy	AS0280
Tomorrow's children [anthology]	AS0590
Trends	AS0280
Trends	AS0450
Trends	CL0100
Trends	DI0220
Trends	GR0220
Trends	ST0230
Triangle [anthology]	AS0620
Tunnel [anthology]	EL122C
2430 A.D	AS0250
Ugly little boy	AS0530
Ugly little boy	AS0590
Ugly little boy	MI0150
Ultimate speed limit	DA014C
Unto the fourth generation	AS0500
Unto the fourth generation	CA02CC
Unto the fourth generation	MA0330
Up-to-date sorcerer	AS0500
Up-to-date sorcerer	MA0198
Victory unintentional	AS0560
Victory unintentional	CA0255
Victory unintentional	LE0220
Victory unintentional	SA0210
Waterclap	AS0230
Waterclap	AS0575
Waterclap	WO0411
Watery place	AS0310
Weapon too dreadful to use	AS0280
Weapon too dreadful to use	HA010C
What if	AS0500
What if	CO0370
What if	CO0043
What is this thing called love?	AS0500
What is this thing called love?	CO0049
Where do we go from here? [anthology]	AS0645
Winnowing	AS0230
Youth	AS0470
Youth	AS0558

Atherton, John

Waste not, want not	FL0150

Attanasio, A.A.
    Blood's horizon   NE0207
    Interface   SI048C

Auden, W.H.
    Curse [poem]   HA0166
    Moon landing [poem]   SA015C
    Unknown citizen [poem]   SA015C

Auerbach, Arnold M.
    Day Rembrandt went public   CU007C
    Day Rembrandt went public   ME0363
    If "Hair" were revived in 2016   HA0164

Bacon, E.M.
    Itself   MO0365

Bacon, Francis
    New Atlantis   DE0370
    New Atlantis [excerpt]   GU013C
    Utopian science fiction   EV010C

Bacon, Gertrude
    Gorgon's head   RO0180

Bade, William L.
    Ambition   CC0370

Baen, James
    Best from Galaxy volume 4 [anthology]   GA010C

Bagley, Simon
    Welcome, Conrad   OL0150

Bailey, Hilary
    Doctor Gelabius   ME0290
    Dogman of Islington   CA028C
    Dr. Gelabius   MO0164
    Fall of Frenchy Steiner   ME0367
    In reason's ear   MO0166
    Ramparts   CA0372

Baker, Russell
    Ms found in a bus   ME0363
    Sinister metamorphosis   ME0365

Bakhnov, Vladlen
    Beware of the ahs!   NE028C
    Cheap sale   NE028C
    Mutiny   MA039C
    Robotniks   MA039C
    Speaking of demonology   MA042C
    Unique   MA042C

Ballard, J.G.

Assassination of John Fitzgerald Kennedy considered as a downhill motor race	AL0402
Assassination of John Fitzgerald Kennedy considered as a downhill motor race	BA0120
Assassination of John Fitzgerald Kennedy considered as a downhill motor race	HA0160
Assassination of John Fitzgerald Kennedy considered as a downhill motor race	ME0290
Assassination of John Fitzgerald Kennedy considered as a downhill motor race	OL0150
Atrocity exhibition	BA0120
Beach murders	BA0205
Best short stories of J.G. Ballard [anthology]	BA0120
Billenium	BA0120
Billenium	BA0150
Billenium	CL0590
Billenium	CR0170
Billenium	CU0070
Billenium	KN0190
Billenium	SA0300
Billenium	SI1020
Billenium	WA0130
Billenium	WI0204
Build-up	BA0150
Build-up	BO0100
Build-up	SU0150
Cage of sand	BA0120
Cage of sand	BA0150
Cage of sand	EA0210
Cage of sand	DI0250
Cage of sand	SI0380
Chronopolis	BA0120
Chronopolis	BA0150
Chronopolis	CE0100
Chronopolis [anthology]	BA0150
Cloud-sculptors of Coral D	BA0120
Cloud-sculptors of Coral D	MA0208
Cloud-sculptors of Coral D	ME0367
Cloud-sculptors of Coral D	NE0153
Comsat angels	BA0205
Concentration City	BA0120
Dead astronaut	BA0205
Death module	MO0165
Deep end	BA0120
Deep end	BA0150
Drowned giant	BA0120
Drowned giant	BA0150
Drowned giant	CA0280

Ballard, J.G.

Drowned giant	ME0366
Drowned giant	NE0151
Drowned world	BA0185
End game	BA0120
End game	BA0150
End game	BA0215
Escapment	BA0210
Garden of time	AL0425
Garden of time	BA0120
Garden of time	BA0150
Garden of time	MA0202
Garden of time	SA0150
Greatest television show on earth	BA0205
Illuminated man	MA0204
Insane ones	NE0363
Killing ground	HA0162
Killing ground	MO0166
Last world of Mr. Goddard	BA0215
Life and death of God	BA0205
Low-flying aircraft	BA0205
Low-flying aircraft [anthology]	BA0205
Man on the 99th floor	BA0210
Manhole	BA0120
Manhole 69	BA0150
Minus one	BA0215
My dream of flying to Wake Island	BA0205
Now wakes the sea	BA0150
Now wakes the sea	BA0215
Now wakes the sea	MA0203
One afternoon at Utah Beach	PR0160
Overloaded Man	BA0120
Passport to eternity [anthology]	BA0210
Place and a time to die	BA0205
Plan for the assassination of Jacqueline Kennedy	BA0120
Plan for the assassination of Jacqueline Kennedy	ME0290
Prima belladonna	ME0357
Question of re-entry	BA0210
Recognition	EL0300
Sound sweep	BA0150
Sound sweep	KN0540
Sound sweep	ME0201
Sound sweep	ME0360
Souvenir	PL0150
Storm-bird, storm-dreamer	BA0150
Subliminal man	BA0120
Subliminal man	BA0215
Subliminal man	GR0300
Subliminal man	KA0070
Subliminal man	SI0680
Sudden afternoon	BA0215
Terminal beach	BA0120
Terminal beach	BA0150

Ballard, J.G.
    Terminal beach   BA0215
    Terminal beach   ME0365
    Terminal beach   SI012C
    Terminal beach [anthology]   BA0215
    Thirteen for Centaurus   BA0120
    Thirteen for Centaurus   CL0100
    Thirteen to Centaurus   BA0210
    Thirteen to Centaurus   EL0840
    Thousand dreams of Stellavista   BA0210
    Time of passage   CL017C
    Time tombs   BA0215
    Time tombs   IF0102
    Tomorrow is a million years   EL0200
    Track 12   AL0450
    Track 12   BA0210
    Ultimate city   BA0205
    Venus hunters   BA0215
    Voices of time   AM0512
    Voices of time   BA0120
    Voices of time   BA0150
    Voices of time   IN010C
    Voices of time   KN0280
    Voices of time   SI0121
    Volcano dances   ME0366
    Waiting grounds   SI056C
    Watch towers   BA0210
    Watchtowers   BA015C
    Why I want to fuck Ronald Reagan   BA0120
    Wind from nowhere   BA0185
    You and me and the continuum   ME0290
    You: Coma: Marilyn Monroe   ME0367
    You: Coma: Marilyn Monroe   MO0162
    Zone of terror   BA015C

Balmer, Edwin
    When worlds collide   KU0100

Bamber, George
    Ottmar balleau X 2   ME0362

Bangs, J.K.
    Glance ahead; being a christmas tale   ME0150
        of A.D. 3568

Banister, Manly
    Escape to earth   H0013C

Banks, Michael A.
    Lost and found   AS0175

Banks, Raymond E.
    Christmas trombone   BE0205
    Double dome   DE025C
    Littlest people   BE020C5

Banks, Raymond E.
    Rabbits to the moon   MA0330
    Short ones   GR0250
    Short ones   MA0195
    Short ones   SI0127
    This side up   GA0144
    Walter Perkins is here!   NO0150

Bar-David, S.
    Dagger of the mind   ST0161

Barbet, Pierre
    Problem in bionics   WC0150

Barclay, Alan
    Only an echo   CA0170

Barfoot, John
    Coils   KN0313
    Crystallization of the myth   KN0311
    House   KN0317

Barnes, Bruce
    After the wreck of the stellar queen   HA0158

Barnes, Steve
    Impact   LA0160

Barr, R.
    Doom of London   MC0365
    Revolt of the...   MC0410

Barr, Stephen
    Back of our heads   CO0720
    Callahan and the wheelies   CO0490
    Homing instinct of Joe Vargo   AM0510
    I am a nucleus   GA0143

Barrett, Neal, Jr.
    Greyspun's gift   WC0411
    Nightbeat   SI0480
    Stentorii luggage   GA0250

Barthelme, Donald
    Balloon   AL0665
    Balloon   ME0367
    Game   ME0366
    Game   SA0100
    Genius   HA0164

Basch, Joan Patricia
    Matog   MA0206

Bass, T.J.
    Rorqual Maru   WO0413

Bearne, C.G.
        Vortex new stories science fiction   BE0020
        [anthology]

Beaumont, Charles [pseud. of C. Nutt]
        Blood brother   PL0150
        Crooked man   PL0150
        Free dirt   FE0230
        Keeper of the dream   DE0530
        Last word   AL0405
        Last word   MA0195
        Mass for mixed voices   NO0200
        Mourning song   ME0364
        New sound   MC0400
        Vanishing American   CL0590
        Vanishing American   DA0230
        Vanishing American   MA0195
        You can't have them all   AL0360
        You can't have them all   PL0155

Beaver, Harold
        Science fiction of Edgar Allan Poe   PO0100
        [anthology]

Beaves, J.M.
        Passion play   CA0372

Becker, Stephen
        New encyclopaedist   ME0365

Beer, Patricia
        After death [poem]   HA0165

Beerbohm, Max
        Ten years ago   HA0166

Behrens, William W., III
        Limits to growth [excerpt]   AL0650

Belaval, Emilio S.
        Purple child   SA0300

Belayev, Alexander
        Hoity-toity   DU0100
        Invisible light   MA0360
        Over the abyss   DI0280

Belcher, C. Davis
        Price   KN0305

Bell, Eric Temple
        Ultimate catalyst   CO0430

Bellamy, Edward
        Blindman's world   DE0370

Bellamy, Edward
    Looking backward [excerpt]   GU0130
    To whom this may come   FR007C

Belling, M.
    Rape patrol   SA0120

Bemelmans, Ludwig
    Putzi   ER0380

Benedict, Myrle
    Sit by the fire   FA0215

Benet, Stephen Vincent
    Angel was a yankee   ME0230
    By the waters of Babylon   CL010C
    By the waters of Babylon   KN019C
    By the waters of Babylon   SA015C
    Metropolitan nightmare   H00119
    Metropolitan nightmare   MC028C
    Nightmare for future reference: TE015C
        A....poem
    Nightmare number three   H00119
    Nightmare number three [poem]   SA015C
    Place of the gods   ASC59C
    Place of the gods   SA0270

Benford, Gregory
    And the sea like mirrors   EL0220
    Calibrations and exercises   NE020C
    Calibrations and exercises   NE0209
    Cambridge, 1:58 a.m.   SI048C
    Dark sanctuary   P0043C
    Deeper than the darkness   MI0180
    Doing Lennon   CA0235
    Hiss of dragon   CA0238
    How it all went   AS0555
    If the stars are gods   CA0371
    If the stars are gods   NE016C
    In alien flesh   W00419
    John of the apocalypse   ZE015C
    Knowing her   NE0207
    Knowing her   CL017C
    Nobody lives on Burton street   MI018C
    Nobody lives on Burton street   W00411
    Noon-coming   CA0375
    Seascape   DA014C
    Threads of time   SI083C
    Time shards   CA0376
    West wind, falling   CA0368
    What did you do last year?   CA0373
    White creatures   NE0205

Benford, James
    John of the apocalypse   ZE0150

Bester, Alfred
    Five million, two hundred seventy-one   BE0400
      thousand and nine [5,271,009]
    Five million, two hundred seventy-one   FE0230
      thousand and nine [5,271,009]
    Five million, two hundred seventy-one   P00150
      thousand and nine [5,271,009]
    Five million, two hundred seventy-one   SI0123
      thousand and nine [5,271,009]
    Flowered thundermug   N0018C
    Fondly fahrenheit   AM0512
    Fondly fahrenheit   BE0400
    Fondly fahrenheit   HA0232
    Fondly fahrenheit   KN0490
    Fondly fahrenheit   MA0194
    Fondly fahrenheit   SC0210
    Four-hour fugue   AN0140
    Four-hour fugue   BE0400
    Four-hour fugue   HA0167
    Four-hour fugue   W00415
    Hell is forever   BE0400
    Hobson's choice   CR0101
    Hobson's choice   KN0540
    Hobson's choice   MA0192
    Hobson's choice   SI0580
    Light fantastic v.1 [anthology]   BE0400
    Men who murdered Mohammed   BE0400
    Men who murdered Mohammed   CE01CC
    Men who murdered Mohammed   HA0130
    Men who murdered Mohammed   MA0198
    Men who murdered Mohammed   SI1000
    Men who murdered Mohammed   SU015C
    Ms. fond in a champagne bottle   BE0400
    Oddy and Id   BE0201
    Oddy and Id   SI0820
    Of time and Third Avenue   BE02C2
    Of time and Third Avenue   KN0160
    Pi man   MA0199
    Pi man   SI012C
    Push of a finger   AS0650
    Roller coaster   WH018C
    Something up there likes me   AS0750
    Something up there likes me   BE0299
    Starlight, star bright   MA0193
    Stars,my destination   B00151
    They don't make life like they used to   MA0203
    They don't make life like they used to   ME0364
    Time is the traitor   AL0480
    Time is the traitor   F00295
    Trematode a critique of modern S-F   BE0203
    Will you wait?   MA033C

Bevan, Alistair
    Susan   ME0366

Beynon, John [pseud. of John Beynon Harris]
    No place like earth   CA0230
    Survival   CA0230
    Technical slip   C00310

Bierce, Ambrose
    Damned thing   CL0100
    Damned thing   GU0130
    Damned thing   KU0100
    Irgenious patriot   AS0555
    Ingenious patriot   KN0280
    Mcxon's master   BR0520
    Mcxon's master   C00550
    Mcxon's master   EL0520
    Mcxon's master   H00119
    Mcxon's master   KN0160
    Mcxon's master   LC0100
    Occurrence at Owl Creek Bridge   KN0450
    Oil of dog   KN0490
    Psychological shipwreck   FR0070

Biggle, Lloyd
    And madly teach   BI0100
    And madly teach   MA0206
    Beachhead in Utopia   EL0980
    Botticelli horror   BI0150
    D.F.C.   BI0200
    Double edged rope   BI0100
    Eye for an eye   BI0100
    Eye for an eye   EL0680
    First love   BI0100
    Frayed string on the stretched   CA0231
       forefinger of time
    Frayed string on the stretched   CA0234
       forefinger of time
    Galaxy of strangers [anthology] BI0100
    In his own image   BI0150
    In his own image   MA0208
    Judgement day   BI0200
    Leading man   BI0150
    Metallic muse [anthology]   BI0150
    Monument   AN0101
    Monument   CA0100
    Nebula award stories seven [anthology] NE0157
    No biz like show biz   BI0100
    On the dotted line   BI0200
    Orphan of the void   BI0150
    Perfect punishment   BI0200
    Petty larceny   BI0200
    Round trip to Esidarap   BI0100
    Round trip to Esidarap   WI0203
    Rule of the door   BI0200
    Rule of the door [anthology]   BI0200
    Secret weapon   BI0200
    Slight case of limbo   BI0200

Bishop, Michael
        Blooded on Arachne   SI0480
        Cathadonian odyssey   WO0415
        Collaborating   HA0159
        Contributors to Plenum four   NE0205
        Death and designation among the Asadi   IF017C
        Death and designation among the Asadi   WO0414
        E = MC (squared) [poem]   SA0150
        House of compassionate sharers   BE0303
        House of compassionate sharers   CA0237
        In Chinistrex Fortronza the people are   DI023C
            machines
        In the Lilliputian asylum   KN0315
        Mory   GR0C40
        Old folks at home   CA0241
        Old folks at home   CA0375
        On the street of serpents   GE018C
        Rogue tomato   NE02C5
        Samurai and the willows   BE0302
        Three dream woman   NE0203
        Window in Dante's hell   HA0166
        Window in Dante's hell   KN0312
        Window in Dante's hell   OL0170

Bixby, Jerome
        Angels in the jets   F0015C
        Angels in the jets   WH018C
        Holes around Mars   AL0401
        Holes around Mars   AS0645
        Holes around Mars   CO022C
        Holes around Mars   CO0310
        It's a good life   AL0425
        It's a good life   AS059C
        It's a good life   CR0103
        It's a good life   JA013C
        It's a good life   FC03CC
        It's a good life   P00330
        It's a good life   F00372
        It's a good life   SA015C
        It's a good life   SC0210
        It's a good life   SI0700
        Old testament   IF010C
        One way street   BE0205
        Page and player   N00270
        Trace   AS0555

Black, John D.F.
        Naked time   ST0161

Blackie, J.
        Space pilot   MA047C

Blake, E. Michael
        Legend of Lonnie and the seven-ten   GE015C
            split

329

Blake, E. Michael
    Science fiction for telepaths   AS0555
    Translator   EL0880

Blake, William
    Infant sorrow   WH0150

Bland, Frederic
    Fifteenth wind of March   FE0200

Bleiler, Everett F.
    Best science fiction stories: 1950   BE0200
    Best science fiction stories: 1951   BE0201
    Best science fiction stories: 1952   BE0202
    Best science fiction stories: 1953   BE0203
    Imagination unlimited [anthology]   BL0100
    Men of space and time   BL0100
    Science fiction omnibus. The best   BL0120
        science fiction stories: 1949,1950
        [anthology]
    Year's best science fiction novels   YE0403
        1952 [anthology]
    Year's best science fiction novels   YE0404
        1953 [anthology]
    Year's best science fiction novels   YE0405
        1954 [anthology]

Blish, James
    All our yesterdays   ST0162
    Alternative factor   ST0164
    Amok time   ST0161
    And some were savages   BL0125
    Anywhen [anthology]   BL0125
    Apple   ST0163
    Arena   ST0161
    Assignment: earth   ST0161
    Balance of terror   ST0162
    Battle of the unborn   C00400
    Beanstalk   CR0230
    Beep   AL0411
    Beep   BL0200
    Beep   N00300
    Beep   SL0210
    Best science fiction stories   BL0180
        [anthology]
    Box   C00280
    Box   SI0300
    Bread and circuses   ST0164
    Bridge   AM0515
    Bridge   AS0575
    Bridge   AS0651
    By any other name   ST0163
    Case of conscience   CR0100
    Catspaw   ST0161
    Changeling   ST0163

Elish, James

Charlie's law	ST0162
Cities in flight [anthology]	BL019C
City on the edge of forever	ST0161
Cloud minders	ST0163
Common time	AL0450
Common time	BL0180
Common time	EL0200
Common time	DC013C
Common time	SI0560
Common time	SI0680
Common time	SI0900
Common time	WA013C
Conscience of the king	ST0162
Court martial	ST0161
Dagger of the mind	ST0162
Dark night of the soul	BL0210
Day of the dove	ST0164
Deadly years	ST0163
Devil in the dark	ST0162
Doomsday machine	ST0161
Dusk of idols	EL0125
Dusk of idols	SI0127
Earthman, come home	BL019C
Earthman, come home	SC0212
Elaan of Troyius	ST0163
Empath	ST0164
Enemy within	ST0161
Enterprise incident	ST0162
Errand of mercy	ST0161
For the world is hollow and I have touched the sky	ST0161
Friday's child	ST0161
FYI	EE05CC
FYI	P00372
Galactic cluster [anthology]	EL02CC
Galileo seven	ST0164
Genius heap	GA0145
Get out of my sky	MA0475
Getting along	EL022C
Glitch	ST022C
Hero's life	HA020C
How beautiful with banners	BL0125
How beautiful with banners	EL018C
How beautiful with banners	FI009C
How beautiful with banners	KN0301
How beautiful with banners	SC0300
Immunity syndrome	ST0162
Is there in truth no beauty?	ST0164
Journey to Babel	ST0162
King of the hill	BL0200
Last gunfight	ST0161
Let that be your last battlefield	ST0163
Life for the stars	EL019C
Lights of Zetar	ST0163

Bloch, Robert

Broomstick ride	BLO24C
Catnip	ELO24C
Cold chills [anthology]	BLO25C
Crime machine	GA0146
Daybroke	BLO24C
Daybroke	FO0300
Daybroke	FO033C
Daybroke	SCO3CC
Double whammy	BLO250
Edifice complex	ELO24C
Ego trip	BLO25C
Enoch	BLO24C
Fear planet	DEO40C
Forever and amen	ACO2CC
Forever and amen	ELO25C
Forever and amen	ELO3CC
Forever and amen	ELO5OC
Forever and amen	ELO760
Funnel of God	BLO24C
Goddess of wisdom	BLO24C
Gods are not mocked	BLO25C
Head	CAO275
Hell-bound train	ELO24C
Hell-bound train	ASO37C
How like a god	BLO24C
How like a god	BLO25C
Hungry house	ELO240
I do not love thee, Doctor Fell	BEO206
I like blondes	PLO155
In the cards	BLO250
Learning maze	ELO250
Learning maze	ELO84C
Man who collected Poe	BLO24C
Model	BLO250
Movie people	ELO25C
Mr. Steinway	BLO24C
Nightmare number four	KO016C
One way to Mars	MO038C
Oracle	ELO250
Past master	BLO24C
Past master	ELO48C
Picture	GRO040
Play's the thing	BLO25C
Plot is the thing	BLO24C
Prowler in the city at the edge of the world	ELO440
See how they run	BLO250
Sorceror's apprentice	ELC24C
Space-born	BLO250
Space-born	ELO54C
Strange flight of Richard Clayton	ASO45C
Strange flight of Richard Clayton	MO035C
Strange island of Dr. Nork	MAO490
That hell-bound train	FEO230

Bloch, Robert
    Toy for Juliette   BL0300
    Toy for Juliette   BL0440
    Way of life   FA0215
    Word of honor   BL0240
    Word of honor   FL015C
    You got to have brains   BL0240
    Yours truly, Jack the Ripper   BL0240

Block, Lawrence
    Make a prison   ME0360

Boardman, Tom V.
    Connoisseur's science fiction   B00100
      [anthology]

Boehm, Herb
    Air raid   AS0173
    Air raid   AS0440

Boles, N.
    Two years to Gala   EL1040

Bolsover, John
    Jackson Wong's story   OB0140

Bond, Nelson S.
    Abduction of Abner Green   BR0460
    And lo! The bird   DE040C
    And lo! the bird   SI042C
    Conqueror's isle   GA037C
    Conqueror's isle   PR015C
    Cunning of the beast   M00100
    Day we celebrate   C0034C
    Magic city   PC0293
    Monster from nowhere   SU015C
    Pilgrimage   AS0450
    Pilgrimage   RO024C
    Priestess who rebelled   M00410
    This is the land   DE047C
    This is the land   DE0500
    Voice from the curious cube   AS0555

Bono, Paul
    Mars stone   AS0555

Bone, J.F.
    Founding father   C00720
    Gamesman   EL064C
    High priest   EL1120
    High priest   EL1240
    Insidekick   C00100
    Insidekick   GA0145
    On the fourth planet   C00760
    On the fourth planet   ME0364

Bone, J.F.
    Prize for Edie   ME0362
    Triggerman   AN0150
    Triggerman   CA0100
    Triggerman   GR025C
    Triggerman   L001C0
    Triggerman   ME0359

Bone, Jesse
    Piece de resistance   AS0180

Booth, Philip
    Let the trees   [poem]   SA015C

Borges, Jorge Luis
    Circular ruins   HA0210
    Circular ruins   KN045C
    Circular ruins   ME0366
    Library of Babel   SI0680
    Lottery in Babylon   CA0280

Borgese, Elisabeth Mann
    True self   GA0145
    Twin's wail   P00300
    Twin's wail   P00330
    Twin's wail   P00376

Borski, Robert
    In the crowded part of heaven GE018C
    Trolls   ST0220

Boston, Bruce
    Tarfu's last show   ED015C

Boucher, Anthony [pseud. of W.A.P. White]
    Ambassadors   AS0340
    Ambassadors   CR0230
    Anomaly of the empty man   SC0400
    Balaam   CR0103
    Balaam   HE0160
    Balaam   M00100
    Barrier   AM0513
    Barrier   C00670
    Best from fantasy and science fiction MA0191
       1st series [anthology]
    Best from fantasy and science fiction MA0192
       2nd series [anthology]
    Best from fantasy and science fiction MA0193
       3rd series [anthology]
    Best from fantasy and science fiction MA0194
       4th series [anthology]
    Best from fantasy and science fiction MA0195
       5th series [anthology]
    Best from fantasy and science fiction MA0196
       6th series [anthology]

Boucher, Anthony [pseud. of W.A.P. White]
    Best from fantasy and science fiction   MA0197
      7th series [anthology]
    Best from fantasy and science fiction   MA0198
      8th series [anthology]
    Bite   B00120
    Books   ME0364
    Compleat werewolf   B00120
    Compleat werewolf   ME0230
    Compleat werewolf [anthology]   B00120
    Conquest   P00372
    Expedition   B00120
    First   AS0555
    Gandolphus   MA0330
    Ghost of me   B00120
    Ghost of me   ME0260
    Greatest tertian   C00250
    Khartoum: a prose limerick   SC0450
    Mary Celestial   PR0210
    Mr. Lupescu   B00120
    Nellthu   KN0220
    Nellthu   MA0195
    Nine-finger Jack   BE0202
    Nine-finger Jack   WA0160
    Other inauguration   C00520
    Pink caterpillar   B00120
    Public eye   DE0220
    Q.U.R.   B00120
    Q.U.R.   HE0100
    Quest for Saint Aquin   CR0104
    Quest for Saint Aquin   HE0130
    Quest for Saint Aquin   KN0280
    Quest for Saint Aquin   MI0150
    Quest for Saint Aquin   MC0100
    Quest for Saint Aquin   SC0210
    Robnic   B00120
    Scrawny one   MA0490
    Shape in time   NO0150
    Snulbug   AS0452
    Snulbug   B00120
    Snulbug   MA0193
    Star bride   AS0555
    Star dummy   C00280
    Starbride   SL0210
    Transfer point   CR0200
    Transfer point   SI0126
    Treasury of great science fiction   B00150
      V. 1. [anthology]
    Treasury of great science fiction v.2   B00151
      [anthology]
    We print the truth   B00120

Boufigliolli, Kyril
    Blastoff   ME0290

Boulle, Pierre
    Age of wisdom   BO0200
    Diabolical weapon   BO0200
    E = MC (squared)   BO0200
    Enigmatic saint   EO0200
    Hallucination   BO0200
    Love and gravity   BO0200
    Lunians   BO0200
    Man who hated machines   EO0200
    Man who picked up pins   EO0200
    Miracle   EO0200
    Perfect robot   BO0200
    Time out of mind   BO0200
    Time out of mind and other stories   BO0200
        [anthology]

Boult, S. Kye
    Safety engineer   GO0030

Bova, Ben
    Aliens [anthology]   BO0210
    Analog Annual [anthology]   BO0240
    Analog 9 [anthology]   AN0109
    Best of Analog [anthology]   AN014C
    Blood of tyrants   BO0250
    Brillo   EL044C
    Build me a mountain   PO0450
    But what if we tried it?   DA014C
    Dueling machine   HA0145
    Exiles   BO0245
    Fifteen miles   BO025C
    Fifteen miles   HA016C
    Fifteen miles   KN046C
    Forward in time [anthology]   BO025C
    Great supersonic zeppelin race   EL068C
    Last decision   DE0268
    Last decision   DE0275
    Man who saw Gunga Din thirty times   EL1060
    Many worlds of science fiction   BO026C
        [anthology]
    Men of good will   BO025C
    Men of good will   DI0110
    Next logical step   BO025C
    Perfect warrior   BO0250
    Science fiction hall of fame. v.2A   SC0211
        [anthology]
    Science fiction hall of fame. v.2B   SC0212
        [anthology]
    Sightseers   EL072C
    Slight miscalculation   EO025C
    Slight miscalculation   HA0130
    Stars, won't you hide me?   BO0250
    System   AS0555
    Test in orbit   BO025C
    Weathermakers   BO025C

Eova, Een
    Where is everybody?   ME0364
    Zero gee   BO0250
    Zero gee   EL0220

Bowen, Elizabeth
    Cherry soul   MA0192

Boy's Life
    Boy's life book of outer space stories   BO0300

Eoyd, Felix
    Rcbot who wanted to know   FA0215

Boyd, John [pseud. of Boyd Bradfield Upchurch]

Boyd, Lyle
    Chain reaction   PO0240

Boyd, William C.
    Chain reaction   PO0240

Brackett, Leigh
    All the colors of the rainbow   BR0095
    All the colors of the rainbow   DE0250
    All the colors of the rainbow   FE0260
    Best of Leigh Brackett [anthology]   BR0070
    Best of planet stories no. 1   BR0080
        [anthology]
    Book of Skaith   ER0090
    Child of the green light   CA0255
    Citadel of lost ages   BR0095
    Come sing the moons of Moravenn   EL1000
    Dancing girl of Ganymede   BR0095
    Enchantress of Venus   BR0070
    Enchantress of Venus   BR0095
    Enchantress of Venus   MA0480
    Ginger star   ER0090
    Halfling   BR0095
    Halfling   PO0293
    Halfling [anthology]   BR0095
    Hounds of Skaith   ER0090
    How bright the stars   EL0700
    Jewel of Bas   BR0070
    Lake of the gone forever   AL0480
    Lake of the gone forever   BR0095
    Lake of the gone forever   SA0220
    Last days of Shandakor   BR0070
    Lorelei of the red mist   BR0080
    Lorelei of the red mist   MA0485
    Lorelei of the red mist   NC0180
    "Mommies and daddie"   EL0640
    Mcon that vanished   ER0070
    Moon that vanished   WC0360
    Other people   BE0208

339

Brackett, Leigh

Queer ones	BR007C
Reavers of Skaith	BR009C
Retreat to the stars	CR020C
Shadows	ER0095
Shannach, the last	BR007C
Sword of Rhiannon	AL051C
Terror out of space	WO0300
Tweener	BR007C
Vanishing Venusians	BR007C
Veil of Astellar	BR007C
Veil of Astellar	CA0320
Woman from Altair	BR007C

Bradbury, Ray

All summer in a day	AL051C
All summer in a day	AS059C
All summer in a day	BR0270
All summer in a day	ER04CC
All summer in a day	MA0194
All summer in a day	SA03CC
Almost the end of the world	BR0100
Almost the end of the world	ER0200
And so died Riabouchinska	ER020C
And the moon be still as bright	EL0120
And the moon be still as bright	BR0230
And the rock cried out	ER010C
And the rock cried out	ER0415
And the sailor, home from the sea	BR020C
And this did Dante do	NO0401
Anthem sprinters	BR020C
Anthem sprinters	ER0415
April witch	BR013C
April witch	BR040C
Asleep in Armageddon	CO0340
Bad day for sales	BR017C
Beggar on the O.Connell Bridge	ER020C
Best of all possible worlds	ER020C
Big black and white game	BR013C
Big black and white game	BR04CC
Black ferris	KN0220
Boys, raise giant mushrooms in your cellar!	BR020C
Changeling	NO0210
Christ, old student in a new school	EL0220
Christus Apollo	MO010C
Chrysalis	ER0330
Cistern	BR0280
Cistern	BR0360
City	BR0170
Come into my cellar	BR0330
Come into my cellar	CO0640
Come into my cellar	GA0146
Concrete mixer	BR0170
Crowd	ER028C

Bradbury, Ray

Crowd	BR036C
Dandelion wine	BR0415
Dark they were and golden-eyed	BR010C
Dark they were and golden-eyed	BR0270
Dark they were and golden-eyed	BR0330
Dark they were and golden-eyed	BR04CC
Day it rained forever	BR010C
Day it rained forever	BR027C
Day it rained forever	BR04CC
Day it rained forever [anthology]	BR010C
Dead man	BR036C
Death and the maiden	BR020C
Dia de muerte	BR020C
Doodad	ELC48C
Doodad	M0038C
Dragon	BR040C
Drummer boy of Shiloh	BR020C
Drummer boy of Shiloh	R0021C
Dwarf	BR028C
Dwarf	BR0415
Dwellers in silence	EE020C
Dwellers in silence	BL012C
Earth men	BR023C
Earth men	KN058C
Embroidery	BR04CC
Emissary	BR028C
En la noche	BR040C
End of the beginning	BR030C
Exiles	DE037C
Fever dream	BR040C
Fever dream	BR0415
Final sceptre, a lasting crown	FE023C
Fire balloons	CR010C
Fire balloons	MC0180
Fire balloons	WA01CC
First night of lent	BR040C
Flight of ravens	BR020C
Flying machine	BR040C
Fog horn	BR040C
Fog horn	BR0415
Fog horn	SA015C
Forever and the earth	C00130
Fox and the forest	BR017C
Fox and the forest	BR0415
Frost and fire	BR030C
Fruit at the bottom of the bowl	BR040C
Fruit at the bottom of the bowl	BR0415
Garbage collector	BR04CC
Gift	BR040C
Golden apples of the sun	BR013C
Golden apples of the sun	BR040C
Golden apples of the sun [anthology]	BR013C
Golden kite, the silver wind	BR040C
Great collision of Monday last	BR040C

Bradbury, Ray

Great fire	BR040C
Great wide world over there	BR040C
Green morning	BR0230
Hail and farewell	BR0400
Hail and farewell	BR0415
Handler	BR0360
Handler	MA0490
Headpiece	BR040C
Here there be tygers	HE0130
Highway	BR0170
Highway	MC040C
Holiday	DE040C
Homecoming	BR028C
I see you never	BR04CC
I sing the body electric	FI0095
I, Mars	NO023C
Icarus Montgolfier Wright	BR0330
Illustrated man	BRC17C
Illustrated man	BR0415
Illustrated man [anthology]	BRC17C
Illustrated man [excerpt]	WH015C
Illustrated woman	BR0200
In a season of calm weather	BR010C
In this sign	EL056C
In this sign	LE022C
Interim	BR023C
Invisible boy	BR0415
Invisible boy	DA023C
Jack-in-the-box	BR028C
Jack-in-the-box	BR0360
Jar	BR028C
Kaleidoscope	BR0415
Kaleidoscope	CO028C
Lake	BRC28C
Lake	BR0360
Last night of the world	BRC17C
Let's play "poison"	BR0360
Lifework of Juan Diaz	BR02CC
Little journey	GA0140
Little mice	BR04CC
Little mice	BR0415
Locusts	BR023C
Lombstone	BR0360
Long rain	BR03CC
Long years	BR023C
Lorelei of the red mist	BR008C
Lorelei of the red mist	MA0485
Lorelei of the red mist	NO018C
Luggage store	BR023C
Machineries of joy	BR02CC
Machineries of joy [anthology]	BR0200
Man	BL012C
Man	BO0300
Man in the Rorschach shirt	KAC07C

Bradbury, Ray
Man upstairs	BRO28C
Man upstairs	BRO36C
Marionettes, Inc.	BRO17C
Marriage-mender	BRO40C
Mars is heaven!	BLO12C
Mars is heaven!	KNO63C
Mars is heaven!	SCO21C
Martian chronicles [anthology]	BRO23C
McGillahee's brat	CAO28C
Meadow	BRO40C
Medicine for melancholy	BRC27C
Medicine for melancholy	BRO40C
Medicine for melancholy	BRO415
Medicine for melancholy [anthology]	BRO28C
Million-year picnic	POO293
Million-year picnic	PRO150
Miracle of rare device	MIO15C
Murderer	BRO40C
Musicians	BRO23C
Naming of names	ACO24C
Naming of names	STO180
Next in line	BRO28C
Next in line	BRO36C
Night	BRO36C
Night meeting	BRO415
Night meeting	COO37C
No particular night or morning	BRO170
October country [anthology]	BRC28C
Off season	BRO23C
Old ones	BRO23C
One who waits	DEO40C
Other foot	BEO2C2
Other foot	BRC13C
Other foot	BRO17C
Other foot	BRO33C
Other foot	BRO40C
Other foot	DEO25C
Other foot	DEO25C
Payment in full	AOO20C
Pedestrian	ALO401
Pedestrian	BRO38C
Pedestrian	BRO4CC
Pedestrian	FIOO9C
Pedestrian	MIO18C
Perchance to dream	BRC1CC
Perhaps we are going away	BRO20C
Pillar of fire	BRO33C
Piper	HAO1CC
Playground	DEO5CC
Playground	KAOO7C
Powerhouse	BRO40C
Punishment without crime	COO52O
R is for rocket	BRO3CC
R is for rocket [anthology]	BRO3CC

Bradbury, Ray

Referent	BR0100
Rocket	BR0300
Rocket man	BR030C
Rocket summer	BR0230
S is for space [anthology]	BR0330
Scent of sarsaparilla	BR0100
Scent of sarsaparilla	RO0210
Screaming woman	BR0330
Scythe	BR0280
Serious search for weird worlds	ME0361
Settlers	BR0230
Shape of things	GR0310
Shore	BR0230
Shoreline at sunset	ME0360
Silent town	BR0230
Skeleton	BR0280
Skeleton	BR0415
Small assassin	BR0280
Small assassin	BR0360
Small assassin	BR0415
Small assassin	TE0150
Small assassin [anthology]	BR0360
Smile	DE059C
Smile	RO0180
Smiling people	BR0360
Some live like Lazarus	BP0200
Sound of summer running	BR030C
Sound of thunder	CA034C
Sound of thunder	CR0170
Sound of thunder	DO01C0
Sound of thunder	RO0180
Strawberry window	BR01CC
Subterfuge	FO015C
Summer night	BR0230
Sun and shadow	BR040C
Sun and shadow	BR0415
Sunset harp	BR01CC
Taxpayer	BR0230
There was an old woman	BR0280
There will come soft rains	BR0415
There will come soft rains	CR02CC
There will come soft rains	PO0190
Third expedition	BR0230
Time in thy flight	BR0330
Time machine	BR030C
Time of going away	BR04CC
Timeless stories for today and tomorrow [anthology]	BR0380
To the Chicago abyss	AL0665
To the Chicago abyss	BR02CC
To the Chicago abyss	FE0110
Tomorrow's child	DA0271
Touched with fire	BR0280
Town where no one got off	BR0400

Bradbury, Ray
        Trolley   BR033C
        Twice twenty-two [anthology]   ERC4CC
        Tyrannosaurus Rex   BRC200
        Uncle Einar   BRO28C
        Uncle Einar   BRO30C
        Usher II   ERO23C
        Vacation   PLO15C
        Veldt   ERO415
        Veldt   DAO272
        Veldt   MEC26C
        Vignettes of tomorrow   DEO4CC
        Vintage Bradbury [anthology]   BRO415
        Visitor   ERO17C
        Wake for the living   MCO35C
        Watchers   BRO23O
        Watchful poker chip of H. Matisse   BRO28C
        Watchful poker chip of H. Matisse   BRO415
        Way in the middle of the air   DEO25C
        Wilderness   ENO1CC
        Wilderness   SLO21C
        Wind   BRO28O
        Wonderful death of Dudley Stone   BRO28C
        Wonderful ice cream suit   BRO415
        Wonderful ice-cream suit   BRO4CC
        Yela   DEO47C
        Ylla   ERO415
        Zero hour   CRO101
        Zero hour   DOO1CC

Bradfield, Scott
        Halcyon in a mirror at midnight   EDO15C

Bradley, Marion Zimmer
        Day of the butterflies   WOO18C
        Phoenix   WHO175
        Wind people   KNO16C
        Wind people   SAO240

Brand, Jonathan
        Encounter with a hick   ELO3CC
        Long day in court   IFO10C

Erand, Thomas
        Don Slow and his electric girl getter   ELO18O

Brantingham, J.
        Chicken of the tree   CAO376

Brennert, Alan
        In this image   CAO265
        Jamie's smile   CAO275
        Skyghosts and dusk-devils   EDO15C

Bronk, William
    Outer becoming inner [pcem]   SA0150

Bronson, Donna
    Canis familiaris   ED0150

Bronte, Emily
    Death of Augusta   SA0120

Brosnar, J.
    Conversation on a starship in Warpdrive ST0220

Broughton, Rhoda
    Behold it was a dream   ME0260

Brown, Bill
    Medicine dancer   ME0260
    Star ducks   EE0201
    Star ducks   CR0170

Brown, Fredric
    Abominable   BR0435
    Abominable   ME0361
    All good BEMS   BR0490
    Angelic angleworm   BR0430
    Angels and spaceships [anthology]   BR0430
    Answer   BR0435
    Answer   CR0102
    Answer   CR0170
    Arena   AL0400
    Arena   AL0425
    Arena   BR0435
    Arena   CH0100
    Arena   CO0520
    Arena   MA0550
    Arena   SC0210
    Arena   SI0100
    Arena   WH0150
    Armageddon   AS0452
    Armageddon   BR0430
    Armageddon   BR0435
    Best of Frederic Brown [anthology]   BR0435
    Come and go mad   BR0435
    Come and go mad   BR0490
    Come and go mad   MA0490
    Crisis, 1999   DE0220
    Daisies   BR0430
    Dark interlude   GA0140
    Dark interlude   PR0210
    Daymare   BR0490
    Double standard   ME0364
    Double standard   FL0155
    Earthmen bearing gifts   BR0435
    Earthmen bearing gifts   CO0760
    Earthmen bearing gifts   GA0146

Brown, Fredric

End	BRO435
Etaoin Shrdlu	BRO435
Etaoin Shrdlu	PRO150
Expedition	MA0197
Experiment	BRO435
Gateway to darkness	MA0480
Geezenstacks	BRO435
Hall of mirrors	BRO435
Hall of mirrors	POO150
Hat trick	BRO430
Honeymoon in the hell	GA0140
Imagine	BRO435
Imagine: a poem	MA0195
Immortality	CE0100
It didn't happen	BRO435
Jaycee	BRO435
Keep out	COO400
Kleine Nachtmusik	BRO435
Knock	BL0120
Knock	BRO435
Knock	BRO490
Last Martian	GA0140
Letter to a phoenix	BRO435
Letter to a Phoenix	GRO190
Mouse	BE0200
Mouse	BL0120
Nightmare in time	ME0362
Nightmare in yellow	BRO435
Not yet the end	AL0411
Not yet the end	BRO435
Nothing sirius	BRO435
Nothing sirius	BRO490
Paradox lost	BRO460
Pattern	BRO430
Pattern	BRO435
Pattern	SA0300
Pi in the sky	BRO435
Pi in the sky	BRO490
Pi in the sky	POO293
Placet is a crazy place	ASO650
Placet is a crazy place	POO120
Placet is a crazy place	WI0201
Politeness	BRO430
Preposterous	BRO430
Puppet show	BRO435
Puppet show	KE0100
Puppet show	MCO180
Puppet show	OL0180
Puppet show	PL0150
Puppet show	WI0250
Rebound	BRO435
Recessional	BRO435
Reconciliation	BRO430
Reconciliation	BRO435

Brown, Fredric
    Rustle of wings   DE050C
    Science fiction carnival [anthology]   BRO460
    Search   BRO430
    Sentence   BRO430
    Short happy lives of Eustace Weaver   BRO435
    Solipsist   BRO43C
    Something green   MO0290
    Space on my hands [anthology]   BRO490
    Star-mouse   BRO080
    Star-mouse   BRO435
    Star-mouse   HE010C
    Too far   MA0195
    Waveries   CO0250
    Waveries   MC040C
    Waveries   SA0150
    Weapon   AS0340
    Weapon   CO0280
    Weapon   SA01C0
    Yehudi principle   BRO43C
    Yehudi principle   BRO435

Brown, J.G.
    From Frankenstein to Andromeda   BRO52C
    [anthology]

Brown, Rosel George
    David's daddy   ME0361
    Flower arrangement   GA0145
    Fruiting body   FE020C

Brown, Terrence L.
    Synergy sculture   KN032C

Browning, John S.
    Burning bright   GR0280

Brownjohn, Alan
    To see the rabbit   MA0470

Brownlow, Catherine
    Voice from the gallery   CB014C

Brownstein, Michael
    Plot to save the world   DI0250

Broxon, M.D.
    Book of Padriaq   DE0267
    Night is cold, the stars are far away   BE0300
    Night is cold, the stars are far away   CA0372
    Singularity   AS0180
    Source material   AS0555
    Stones have names   CA0265

Brunner, John

Badman	BRO550
Badman	WIO205
Better mousetrap	IFO100
Coincidence day	ANO105
Elected silence	BRO55C
Fair	BRO550
Fair	HAO234
Inception of the epoch of Mrs. Bedonebyasyoudid	BEO500
Iron jackass	BRO550
Jack fell down	SAO180
Judas	ELO300
Judas	MOO1CO
Last lonely man	MEO365
Last lonely man	CLO170
Last lonely man	WOO405
Lostling	ELO68C
No future in it [anthology]	BRO55C
Out of order	BRO55C
Pond water	ELO200
Protect me from my friends	BRO55C
Protocols of the elders of Britain	WOO416
Puzzle for spacemen	BRO550
Puzzle for spacemen	MCO180
Report on the nature of the lunar surface	BRO520
Report on the nature of the lunar surface	BRO55C
Report on the nature of the lunar surface	HOO120
Report on the nature of the lunar surface	MEO361
Report on the nature of the lunar surface	STO230
Stimulus	BRO550
Stimulus	WIO206
Such stuff	AMO513
Such stuff	KAO07C
Such stuff	MEO363
Totally rich	FIOO9C
Totally rich	SIO380
Vitanuls	MOO100
Vitanuls	CLO170
Wasted on the young	GAO148
What are friends for?	CAO265
What friends are for?	BEO300
Windows of heaven	ALO45C
Windows of heaven	BRO550
You'll take the high road	THO21C

Brunner, K.Houston

Thou good and faithful	NOO27C

Campbell, John W.
    Night   AL0405
    Night   CA016C
    Night   M00350
    Night   SI0560
    Other eyes watching   AS0170
    Out of night   CA0110
    Out of night   CA0130
    Piracy preferred   CA0115
    Prologue to Analog [anthology] AN0150
    Rebellion   CA0130
    Solarite   CA0115
    Space beyond   CA0150
    Space beyond [anthology]   CA0150
    "Scientists are stupid"   AN0105
    Twilight   CA016C
    Twilight   SC0210
    Twilight   SI0460
    Twilight   SI0680
    Twilight   WA0130
    Twilight   WH0150
    Who goes there?   CA0110
    Who goes there?   CA0160
    Who goes there?   SC0211
    Who goes there?   SC0300
    Who goes there? [anthology]   CAC16C

Campbell, Ramsey
    Dead letters   GRCC4C
    Little voice   GR004C
    Murders   NE0326

Campton, D.
    Cradle ship   DA0272
    Walk in the woods   DA0272

Cantine, Holley
    Double, double, toil and trouble MA0200
    Double, double, toil and trouble ME0361

Capek, Karel
    Absolute at large   KN012C
    R.U.R.   CO0550
    R.U.R.   KU010C
    System   MC0320

Capote, Truman
    Miriam   TE0150

Caravan, T.P.
    Court of Tartary   MA0204
    Random sample   AS034C

Carlson, Esther
    Museum piece   PR0150

Carlson, William
    Call from Kerlyana   GO0030
    Dinner at Helen's   SC0450
    First mission   EL086C

Carmel, Carl
    Year after tomorrow   DE031C

Carneiro, Andre
    Darkness   HA0165
    Darkness   NO0402

Carnell, John
    Gateway to the stars [anthology]   CA017C
    Gateway to tomorrow [anthology]   CA02C0
    Lambda I [anthology]   CA021C
    New writings in SF 1 [anthology]   NE0301
    New writings in SF 19   NE0319
    New writings in sf 2 [anthology]   NE03C2
    New writings in SF 3 [anthology]   NE0303
    New writings in SF 4 [anthology]   NE0304
    New writings in SF 5 [anthology]   NE0305
    New writings in SF 6 [anthology]   NE0306
    New writings in sf 7 [anthology]   NE0307
    New writings in SF 8 [anthology]   NE0308
    New writings in SF 9 [anthology]   NE0309
    No place like earth [anthology]   CA0230

Carr, Carol
    Inside   CA028C
    Inside   KN0308
    Inside   SI074C
    Look, you think you've got troubles DA02CC
    Look, you think you've got troubles KE010C
    Look, you think you've got troubles KN010C
    Look, you think you've got troubles KN0305
    Look, you think you've got troubles KN046C
    Look, you think you've got troubles SI010C
    Look, you think you've got troubles ST022C
    Some are born cats   CA026C
    Some are born cats   EL104C

Carr, John Dickson
    New murders for old   WA016C

Carr, Robert Spencer
    Easter eggs   BL012C

Carr, Terry
    Answer   EL120C
    Best science fiction novellas of the   CA0241
       year no. 1 [anthology]
    Best science fiction of the year no.1 CA0231
       [anthology]

Carr, Terry

Best science fiction of the year no.4 [anthology]	CA0234
Best science fiction of the year no.5 [anthology]	CA0235
Best science fiction of the year no.6 [anthology]	CA0236
Best science fiction of the year no.7 [anthology]	CA0237
Best science fiction of the year no.8 [anthology]	CA0238
Brown Robert	SI0125
Castle in the stars	EL118C
City of yesterday	SI030C
Classic science fiction [anthology]	CA0255
Colors of fear	NE02C4
Creatures from beyond [anthology]	CA026C
Dance of the changer and the three	CH01CC
Dance of the changer and the three	EL02CC
Dance of the changer and the three	NE0154
Dance of the changer and the three	SI0400
Dance of the changer and the three	WA013C
Dance of the changer and the three	WC04C9
Fellowship of the stars [anthology]	CA0265
Hop-friend	AS0575
Hop-friend	KN046C
Hop-friend	MA0202
Hop-friend	SI0100
Ides of tomorrow [anthology]	CA0275
In his image	SI0123
Infinite arena [anthology]	CA0277
Into the unknown [anthology]	CA0280
No mind of man [anthology]	CA031C
Ozymandias	EL0220
Ozymandias	SIC7CC
Planets of wonder [anthology]	CA0320
Rejoice, rejoice, we have no choice	EL074C
Rejoice, rejoice, we have no choice	SI0126
Robots are here	HA013C
Saving worlds	EL102C
Science fiction for people who hate science fiction [anthology]	CA034C
Some are born cats	CA026C
Some are born cats	EL1040
Stanley toothbrush	SI074C
They live on levels	CA0420
They live on levels	NE0200
They live on levels	NE0203
This side of infinity [anthology]	CA036C
Touchstone	MA0204
Universe 1 [anthology]	CA0368
Universe 3 [anthology]	CA037C
Universe 4 [anthology]	CA0371
Universe 5 [anthology]	CA0372
Universe 6 [anthology]	CA0373

Carr, Terry
    Universe 7 [anthology]   CA0374
    Universe 8 [anthology]   CA0375
    Universe 9 [anthology]   CA0376
    Winds at starmont   CA031C
    World's best science fiction: 1965   W00405
        [anthology]
    World's best science fiction: 1966   W00406
        [anthology]
    World's best science fiction: 1967   W004C7
        [anthology]
    World's best science fiction: 1969   W004C9
        [anthology]
    World's best science fiction: 1970   W0041C
        [anthology]
    World's best science fiction: 1971   WC0411
        [anthology]
    Worlds near and far [anthology]   CA042C

Carrington, Grant
    After you've stood on the log at the   AS0555
        Center of the Universe, what is
        there left to do ?
    Stella blue   M00155

Carroll, Sidney
    None before me   BR038C
    Note for the milkman   BR038C

Carter, Angela
    Executioner's beautiful daughter   HA0167

Carter, Lin
    Martian El Dorado of Parker Wintley   W0018C

Carter, Paul A.
    Last objective   AL04CC
    Man who rode the trains   DE0560
    Ounce of prevention   CEC4CC

Cartmill, Cleve
    Deadline   P00293
    Green cat   DE047C
    Huge beast   MA0191
    Link   GR014C
    Link   GR0250
    Link   HE010C
    Number nine   LE013C
    Oscar   AS034C
    Overthrow   GR0190
    You can't say that   HE013C

Cartur, Peter
    Mist   AS034C
    Mist   C0037C

Carver, J. A.
    Love Rogo   FU016C

Cassell, R.V.
    War in the air   MI015C

Cassutt, M.
    Hunting   CA0375

Castell, Daphne
    Come up and see me   MC015C
    Who's in there with me?   ME0290

Causey, James
    Felony   BE0205
    Show must go on   NC0210
    Teething ring   AS034C
    Teething ring   GA0141

Cave, P.L.
    Scoop   DA0272

Cawood, Hap
    Synchromocracy   ME0365

Cerf, Christopher
    Vintage anthology of science fantasy   CE010C

Chain, Julian
    Captives   ST0210

Chalker, Jack L.
    Dance band on the Titanic   AS044C
    Dance band on the Titanic   W00419
    No hiding place   DE0267

Chambers, Robert W.
    Demoiselle D'ys   MO026C
    Third eye   ME015C

Chandler, A. Bertram
    All laced up   BA0235
    Cage   AL045C
    Cage   CO076C
    Cage   MA0197
    Cage   MA055C
    Castaway   C0037C
    Critical angle   ST0230
    Fall of knight   FA0215
    False dawn   GR0190
    Finishing touch   CA020C
    Giant killer   AS065C
    Giant killer   PR015C
    Grimes at Glenrowan   AS0175
    Half pair   AL045C

Chandler, A. Bertram
    Jetsam   ST0230
    Late   HA0232
    Left-hand way   HA016C
    No room in the stable   AS0172
    Sea change   HA030C

Chang, G.
    Stars and darkness   CA0373

Chapman, Steve
    Autopsy in transit   KN0317
    Burger creature   KN0312
    Right-handed wrist   KN032C
    Testing.....one,two,three,four   AN0108

Charney, David H.
    Mommy loves ya   EL120C
    Triple moons of Deneb II   EL1040

Charnock, Graham
    Chinese boxes   KN0308

Charteris, Leslie
    Convenient monster   WA016C

Chatrian, Alexander
    Han Schnap's spy glass   M0038C

Cheetham, Anthony
    Bug-eyed monsters [anthology]   CH010C

Cheever, John
    Enormous radio   BR0380
    Enormous radio   HA021C

Cherryh, C.J.
    Cassandra   W00419
    Dreamstone   SA0120

Chesterton, G.K.
    Finger of stone   WA0160

Chilson, Robert
    In his image   AN01C8
    People reviews   CA0374

Chin, M.L.
    Best is yet to be   RY01C0

Christie, Agatha
    Last seance   ME026C
    Red signal   WA0160

Clarke, Arthur C.

Deep range	P00300
Deep range	P00330
Deep range	PC0373
Deep range	YC0150
Defenestration of Ermintrude Inch	CL0430
Dial "F" for Frankenstein	CL0530
Dial "F" for Frankenstein	FL0150
Dog star	CL0310
Dog star	CL0470
Dog star	SC0300
Earth and the overlords	CL0160
Earthlight	CL0130
Earthlight	CL0190
Encounter at dawn	CL0130
Encounter at dawn	CL0160
Encounter at dawn	CL0310
Encounter at dawn	CL0220
Exile of the eons	CL0250
Exile of the eons	CL0370
Expedition to earth	CL0160
Expedition to earth [anthology]	CL0250
Fall of moondust	CL0190
Feathered friend	CL0280
Feathered friend	CL0340
Fires within	CL0130
Fires within	CL0220
Fires within	CL0400
Fires within	C00460
Fires within	DE0590
Food of the gods	CL0530
Forgotten enemy	AL0450
Forgotten enemy	CL0370
Forgotten enemy	CL0400
Forgotten enemy	CR0170
Forgotten enemy	HA0234
Forgotten enemy	SL0210
Freedom of space	CL0280
Freedom of space	CL0340
From the ocean, from the stars [anthology]	CL0280
Golden age	CL0160
Green fingers	CL0280
Green fingers	CL0340
Green fingers	SA0210
Hate	CL0200
Hate	CL0470
Haunted space suit	AS0340
Herbert George Morley Robert Wells, Esq.	CL0530
Hide and seek	AS0651
Hide and seek	CA0200
Hide and seek	CL0130
Hide and seek	CL0160
Hide and seek	CL0200

Clarke, Arthur C.
    Hide and seek   CL0220
    Hide and seek   CL0250
    Hide and seek   CL0310
    Hide and seek   SL0180
    History lesson   AL0665
    History lesson   CL0130
    History lesson   CL0200
    History lesson   CL0220
    History lesson   CL0250
    History lesson   CO0280
    History lesson   HO0100
    History lesson   RO0210
    I remember Babylon   CL0310
    I remember Babylon   CL0470
    I remember Babylon   ME0361
    I remember Babylon   PL0150
    I remember Babylon   PL0155
    Inheritance   CL0130
    Inheritance   CL0160
    Inheritance   CL0220
    Inheritance   CL0250
    Inside the earth   WI0204
    Into the comet   CL0200
    Into the comet   CL0470
    Jupiter five   CL0130
    Jupiter five   CL0220
    Jupiter five   CL0400
    Jupiter five   SI0520
    Last command   CL0530
    Last generation   CL0160
    Let there be light   CL0470
    Light of darkness   CL0530
    Longest science-fiction story ever   CL0530
        told
    Loophole   CL0160
    Loophole   CL0250
    Loophole   CO0730
    Love that universe   CL0530
    Maelstrom II   CL0530
    Maelstrom II   KE0100
    Maelstrom II   ME0366
    Man who ploughed the sea   CL0370
    Man who ploughed the sea   CL0430
    Meeting with Medusa   BO0210
    Meeting with Medusa   CA0231
    Meeting with Medusa   CA0234
    Meeting with Medusa   CL0200
    Meeting with Medusa   CL0530
    Meeting with Medusa   HA0164
    Meeting with Medusa   NE0158
    Moving spirit   CL0370
    Moving spirit   CL0430
    Nemesis   CL0160
    Neutron tide   CL0530

Clarke, Arthur C.

Next tenants	CL013C
Next tenants	CL022C
Next tenants	CL043C
Nine billion names of god	CL028C
Nine billion names of god	CL031C
Nine billion names of god	CL034C
Nine billion names of god	CR0101
Nine billion names of god	D0010C
Nine billion names of god	KN028C
Nine billion names of god	MC010C
Nine billion names of god	P00371
Nine billion names of god	SC0210
Nine billion names of god	SL021C
Nine billion names of god	ST021C
Nine billion names of god	WA01CC
Nine billion names of god	WI02C6
Nine billion names of god [anthology]	CL031C
No morning after	CL028C
No morning after	CL031C
No morning after	CL034C
No morning after	DE053C
Obsolescence of man	AL065C
Other side of the sky	B00151
Other side of the sky	CL028C
Other side of the sky [anthology]	CL034C
Other tiger	DE050C
Out of the cradle, endlessly orbiting	CL047C
Out of the cradle, endlessly orbiting	C0019C
Out of the sun	CL028C
Out of the sun	CL031C
Out of the sun	CL034C
Out of the sun	SI0440
Pacifist	CL013C
Pacifist	CL022C
Pacifist	CLC43C
Pacifist	FA0215
Parasite	CL037C
Parasite	CL040C
Passer-by	CL028C
Passer-by	CL034C
Patent pending	CE010C
Patent pending	CL031C
Patent pending	CL043C
Patent pending	GR0300
Playback	CL053C
Possessed	AL0410
Possessed	CL031C
Possessed	CL037C
Possessed	CLC4CC
Possible, that's all!	DA0140
Prelude to Mars	CL037C
Prelude to Mars [anthology]	CL037C
Prelude to space	CL016C
Prelude to space	CL037C

Clarke, Arthur C.

Publicity campaign	CL028O
Publicity campaign	CL034C
Quarantine	AS0172
Quarantine	AS044C
Question of residence	CL028O
Question of residence	CL034C
Reach for tomorrow [anthology]	CL040C
Refugee	CL020C
Refugee	CL028O
Refugee	CL034C
Reluctant orchid	CL013O
Reluctant orchid	CL022C
Reluctant orchid	CL031O
Reluctant orchid	CL043C
Report on planet three	WI0245
Rescue party	CL013O
Rescue party	CL022O
Rescue party	CL031C
Rescue party	CL040C
Rescue party	C00730
Rescue party	F00190
Rescue party	W00210
Retreat from earth	CL020O
Reunion	CL053O
"If I forget thee, oh earth"	AL0405
"If I forget thee, oh earth"	CL010C
"If I forget thee, oh earth"	CL022C
"If I forget thee, oh earth"	CL025O
"If I forget thee, oh earth"	CL031O
"If I forgot thee, oh earth"	CL016C
Road to the sea	CL047C
Robin Hood, F.R.S.	CL028C
Robin Hood, F.R.S.	CL034C
Sands of Mars	CL019O
Sands of Mars	CL037C
Saturn rising	AS0575
Saturn rising	CL047C
Second dawn	CL016C
Second dawn	CL020C
Second dawn	CL025C
Second dawn	CL037O
Secret	CL053C
Security check	CL028C
Security check	CL034O
Security check	CU0070
Seeker of the sphinx	YE0403
Sentinel	AL0480
Sentinel	AM0512
Sentinel	CL013O
Sentinel	CL016C
Sentinel	CLC2CC
Sentinel	CL022C
Sentinel	CL025O
Sentinel	CL031C

Clarke, Arthur C.

Sentinel	KN0630
Sentinel	SI068C
Sentinel	SU0150
Shining ones	CL0530
Shining ones	ME0365
Silence, please	CL0130
Silence, please	CL022C
Silence, please	CL0430
Sleeping beauty	CL0430
Slight case of sunstroke	CL0470
Songs of distant earth	CL028C
Songs of distant earth	CL0340
Special delivery	CL0280
Special delivery	CL034C
Star	AL0401
Star	AS037C
Star	CA0340
Star	CL02CC
Star	CL028C
Star	CL031C
Star	CL0340
Star	CR0104
Star	D0013C
Star	KN0160
Star	SA015C
Starting line	CL028C
Starting line	CL034C
Summertime on Icarus	CL020C
Summertime on Icarus	CL031C
Summertime on Icarus	CL047C
Summertime on Icarus	C00430
Sunjammer	CA0277
Sunjammer	CL02CC
Sunjammer	EL052C
Sunjammer	EL124C
Sunjammer	HA026C
Sunjammer	HA029C
Sunjammer	N0023C
Sunjammer	W00406
Superiority	CL0130
Superiority	CL016C
Superiority	CL022C
Superiority	CL0250
Superiority	CL0310
Superiority	DE059C
Superiority	GR0250
Take a deep breath	CL028C
Take a deep breath	CL034C
Take a deep breath	CL050C
Tales from the White Hart [anthology]	CL043C
Tales of ten worlds [anthology]	CL047C
Technical error	CL0130
Technical error	CL022C
Technical error	CL040C

Clarke, Arthur C.
    Technical error   P00293
    Thirty seconds-thirty days   ST018C
    This earth of majesty   MA0195
    Time probe   CL05CC
    Time probe [anthology]   CL05OC
    Time's arrow   CL0130
    Time's arrow   CL022C
    Time's arrow   CL04CC
    Transcience   CL028C
    Transcience   CL0310
    Transcience   CL034C
    Transcience   LE022C
    Transit of earth   CL053C
    Transit of earth   CL0170
    Transit of earth   W00412
    Travel by wire   CL02CC
    Trouble with the natives   CL0370
    Trouble with the natives   CL0400
    Trouble with time   AL0425
    Trouble with time   CL031C
    Trouble with time   CL047C
    Ultimate melody   CL0370
    Ultimate melody   CL0430
    Ultimate melody   EL048C
    Ultimate melody   M00155
    Venture to the moon   CL020C
    Venture to the moon   CL028C
    Venture to the moon   CL0340
    Venture to the moon   MA0197
    Venture to the moon   ST023C
    Walk in the dark   CL031C
    Walk in the dark   CL037C
    Walk in the dark   CLC4CC
    Walk in the dark   C0022C
    Walk in the dark   C0034C
    Walk in the dark   SI0900
    Wall of darkness   CL028C
    Wall of darkness   CL031C
    Wall of darkness   CL034C
    Wall of darkness   M00260
    Wall of darkness   SI074C
    Watch this space   CL0280
    Watch this space   CL034C
    Whacky   CL020C
    What goes up?   CL037C
    What goes up?   CL043C
    Who can replace a man?   CL013C
    Who's there?   CL031C
    Who's there?   CL047C
    Who's there?   WI0203
    Wind from the sun   CL053C
    Wind from the sun [anthology]   CL053C

Claudy, Carl H.
    Land of no shadow   DE031C
    Master minds of Mars   DE031C
    Tongue of beast   DE031C

Cleaver, P.
    Clone of espers   DA0273
    Harmony aggro   DA0271

Cleeve, Brian
    Angela's satyr   ME0363
    Cold front   GR022C
    Critical factor   PC0372
    Hot planet   AM0513
    Hot planet   GA0147
    Hot planet   ME0364
    Proof   CO034C

Clem, Ralph
    City 2000 A.D. [anthology]   CL059C

Clement, Hal [pseud. of Harry Clement Stubbs]
    Answer   CC055C
    Attitude   GR031C
    Dust rag   AS0645
    Fireproof   AL040C
    Foundling stars   IF0102
    Lecture demonstration   AS075C
    Logical life   DE0265
    Longline   CA014C
    Proof   AS0645
    Proof   HA0232

Clifton, Mark
    Civilized   DE05CC
    Clerical error   BE020C
    Clerical error   MA0465
    Conquerer   EE02C3
    Conquerer   CO028C
    Conqueror   SI07CC
    Crazy Joey   ME0260
    Hang head, vandal!   ME0363
    How allied   CO014C
    Sense from thought divine   AM0511
    Sense from thought divine   ME0201
    Sense from thought divine   ME0356
    Star bright   AS059C
    Star bright   GA0141
    Star bright   SA015C
    We're civilized!   AL0410
    What have I done?   AS0651
    What have I done?   ME0230
    What now, little man   ME036C
    What thin partitions   MC0260
    Woman's place   GA034C

Clingan, C.C.
        High bank   EL0180

Clingerman, Mildred
        Birds can't count   MA0195
        Birds can't count   ME0356
        First lesson   MA0330
        Last prophet   MA0195
        Letters from Laura   BO1051
        Minister without portfolio   CO0250
        Minister without portfolio   EA01CC
        Minister without portfolio   SL0210
        Mr. Sakrison's halt   MAC196
        Stair trick   AS0340
        Stair trick   MA0192
        Stickeney and the critic   DE05CC
        Wild wood   MA0197
        Wild wood   MC0180
        Word   DE0500

Clinton, Ed M.,Jr.
        Small world of M-75   CC0400

Cloete, Stuart
        Blast   CO0670

Clough, Roy L., Jr.
        Bait   NCO3CC

Clute, John
        Man must die   MO0166
        Man must die   SI0124

Coates, Robert M.
        Hour after Westrly   BRO38C

Coblentz, Stanton A.
        Scarlet lunes   FO010C
        Sunward   WC0270

Cochrane, William E.
        Minister west   AS0172

Cogswell, G.R.
        Contact point   EL11CC

Cogswell, Theodore R.
        Big stink   DE0250
        Blowup blues   ME0361
        Burning   KN046C
        Cabbage patch   KN0490
        Consumer's report   SA03CC
        Contact point   EL1100
        Early bird   AS0750
        Early bird   HA0166

Cogswell, Theodore R.
        Faex Delenda est [poem]   HA0165
        Limiting factor   CC0400
        Limiting factor   GA0142
        Minimum sentence   GA0141
        Population implosion   BE0299
        Probability zero! The population   AS075C
            implosion
        Radiation blues   ME0361
        Spectre general   N00330
        Spectre general   SC0212
        Wall around the world   AL045C
        Wall around the world   HA029C
        Wall around the world   ME026C
        You know Willie   ME0201
        You know Willie   ME0358

Cohn, Gary
        Rules of Moopsball   KN0318

Cole, Everett B.
        Exile   EE0205
        Exile   DI016C

Coleman, Barbara J.
        Single changes   HA0158

Coles, David
        Critical path   NE0319

Colin, Vladimir
        Contact   SU0180

Collacay, Morrison
        Planetoid of dooms   C00130

Collier, John
        Evening primrose   MI015C
        Green thoughts   KN0480
        Incident on a lake   AL0360
        Interpretation of a dream   KN0450
        Interpretation of a dream   ME026C
        Invisible dove dancer of Strathpheen   DA023C
            Island
        Man overboard   MA02CC
        Meeting of relations   MA033C
        Rope enough   ME0310
        Thus I refute Beelzy   WH015C
        Touch of nutmeg makes it   KN0490

Collyn, George
        In passage of the sun   M00163
        In the passage of the sun   SA010C
        Singular quest of Martin Borg   ME0290
        Singular quest of Martin Borg   M00162

Colvin, James
    Mountain   M00163
    Pleasure garden of Felipe Sagittarius   M00162

Conesa, Lisa
    Eyes of a woman-from a portrait by   HA0167
        Picasso [poem]

Coney, Michael G.
    Mind prison   NE0319
    Oh, Valinda!   W00413
    Sharks of Pentreath   W00412
    Sixth sense   W00410
    Starthinker 9   WE0290
    Those good old days of liquid fuel   W00417
    Whatever became of the McGowans?   W00411

Conklin, Groff
    Another part of the galaxy [anthology] C00100
    Big book of science fiction [anthology] C00130
    Elsewhere and elsewhen [anthology]   C00140
    Fifty short science fiction tales   AS0340
        [anthology]
    5 unearthly visions [anthology]   C00150
    Giants unleashed [anthology]   C00160
    Great science fiction about doctors   C00190
        [anthology]
    Great stories of space travel   C00220
        [anthology]
    Invaders of earth [anthology]   C00250
    Omnibus of science fiction [anthology] C00280
    Operation future [anthology]   C00310
    Possible world of science fiction   C00340
        [anthology]
    Science fiction adventures in   C00370
        dimension [anthology]
    Science fiction adventures in mutation C00400
        [anthology]
    Science fiction by scientists   C00430
        [anthology]
    Science fiction galaxy [anthology]   C00460
    Science fiction oddities   C00490
    Science fiction terrors tales   C00520
        [anthology]
    Science fiction thinking machines   C00550
        [anthology]
    Selection from Science fiction   C00560
        thinking machines [anthology]
    Seven come infinity [anthology]   C00580
    Seven trips through time and space   C00610
        [anthology]
    Seventeen x infinity [anthology]   C00640
    Six great short novels of science   C00670
        fiction

Conklin, Groff
    Six great short science fiction novels   CO0700
      [anthology]
    13 above the night [anthology]   CO0720
    Treasury of science fiction   CO0730
      [anthology]
    12 great classic of science fiction   CO0760
    Way home [anthology]   ST0360

Conner, Michael
    Extinction of confidence, the exercise   DI0230
      of honesty
    Last   NE0209
    Vamp   KN0319

Conquest, Robert
    Spectrum 1 [anthology]   AM0510
    Spectrum 2 [anthology]   AM0511
    Spectrum 3 [anthology]   AM0512
    Spectrum 4 [anthology]   AM0513
    Spectrum 5 [anthology]   AM0514

Conway, Gerard F.
    Mindship   CA0368

Cook, Glen
    And dragons in the sky   CL0110
    In the wind   ZE0150

Cook, Stanley J.
    Man unwept [anthology]   WH0150

Cook, Stephen
    Final flower   BA0235

Coombs, Charles
    Rocket rider   FU0100

Coon, Carleton S.
    Future of the races of man   ST0210

Coon, Gene L.
    Devil in the dark   ST0164
    Piece of the action   ST0164

Cooper, B.L.
    Error in punctuation   DE0267

Cooper, Edmund
    Intruders   ST0230
    Tomorrow's gift   PO0374

Cooper, Ralph S.
    Neutrino bomb   CO0430

Coover, Robert
    Pedestrian accident   HA0163

Copparc, A.E.
    Adam and Eve and pitch me   TE0150

Coppel, Alfred
    Dreamer   BE0203
    Exile   SL0210
    Last night of summer   W00210
    Rebel of Valkyr   AL0410
    What goes up?   F00100

Copper, B.
    Message from the stars   DA0271

Coren, Alan
    Owing to circumstances beyond our   HA0167
       control, 1948 has been unavoidably
       detained

Corman, Cid
    Compass [poem]   SA0150

Correa, Hugo
    Alter ego   KA0070

Correy, Lee [pseud. of G. Harry Stine]
    Easy way out   AN0106
    Something in the sky   EA0100
    "And a star to steer by"   DI0130

Corwin, Norman
    Belles letters, 2272   N00150

Cotton, John
    Columbus on St. Domenica [poem] HA0165
    Report back   HA0162

Cottrell, C.L.
    Danger! Child at large   F00376

Coulson, Juanita
    Uraguyen and I   LA0160

Counselman, Mary Elizabeth
    Handful of silver   DE0560
    Unwanted   MA0490

Coupling, J.J.
    Mr. Kincaid's past   ME0260
    Period piece   BL0120
    To be a man   HA0300

Courtney, Robert
    Rover I will be   DI0130

Couzyn, Jeni
    Day we embarked for Cythera [poem]   BE0500
    Heresies of the huge God [poem]   BE0500

Cover, Arthur Byron
    Gee, isn't he the cutest little thing? G0003C
    Gross love story   GE015C
    Message of joy   GE015C

Cowie, George R.
    Demobilization   F001CC

Cowper, Richard
    Custodians   HA0168
    Custodians   W00416
    Hertford manuscript   W00417

Cox, Arthur Jean
    Blight   DE053C
    Occurrence at the Owl Creek rest home P00290

Cox, Irving, Jr.
    Hole in the sky   DE053C
    Like gods they came   SL018C

Cox, Jean
    Fame   KN0306

Cozzi, Luigi
    Rainy day revolution no. 39   W00150

Craig, William
    Fall of Japan   AL065C

Crane, Robert
    Purple fields   P00372

Crane, Stephen
    Man said to the universe [poem]   SA015C

Crispin, Edmund [pseud. of R.B. Montgomery]
    Best SF Five science fiction stories   CR0104
      [anthology]
    Best SF Four science fiction stories   CR0103
      [anthology]
    Best SF science fiction stories   CR0100
      [anthology]
    Best SF Three science fiction stories CR0102
      [anthology]
    Best SF Two science fiction stories   CR0101
      [anthology]
    Stars and under [anthology]   CR017C

```
Dahl, Roald
     Great automatic grammatisator          CE0100
     Great automatic grammatisator          WI0245
     In the ruins                           ME0366
     Man from the South                     KN0490
     Sound machine                          BR0380
     William and Mary                       FI0090

Daley, John Bernard
     Man who liked lions                    ME0357

Dance, Clifton, Jr. M.D.
     Brothers                               C00190

Daniel, Molly
     Winter housecleaning                   CL0110

Dann, Jack
     Drum lollipop                          KN0311
     Dybbuk dolls                           NE0205
     Faces forward                          EL0660
     Faces forward                          PR0210
     Faster than light [anthology]          DA0140
     Flower that missed the morning         EL0820
     Fragmentary blue                       ED0150
     Future power [anthology]               DA0170
     Good old days                          EL0800
     I'm with you in Rockland               SC0450
     Immortal [anthology]                   DA0180
     Od                                     EL0980
     Quiet revolution for death             NE0200
     Quiet revolution for death             NE0208
     Thirty-three and one-third             EL0860
     Timetipping                            SI0480
     Wandering stars [anthology]            DA0200
     Whirl cage                             KN0310
     Yellowhead                             DI0230

Danton, W.
     Bend of time                           EL0920

Danzig, Allan
     Great Nebraska sea                     AM0513
     Great Nebraska sea                     ME0364

Darlington, Daniel A.
     Patent rights                          AS0555

Darnay, A.
     Salty's sweep                          DE0267

Daulton, G.
     Death-trap                             M00365
```

Davenport, Basil
    Invisible men [anthology]   DA0230
    To the end of time [anthology]   ST0150

Davidson, Avram
    Apres nous   DA0240
    Apres nous   MA020C
    Best from fantasy and science fiction MA0202
        12th series [annthology]
    Best from fantasy and science fiction MA0203
        13th series [anthology]
    Best from fantasy and science fiction MA0204
        14th series [anthology]
    Best of Avram Davidson [anthology]   DA0235
    Big Sam   MC0150
    Bottle full of kismet   DA0240
    Bounty hunter   AL0411
    Bounty hunter   FA0215
    Bumberboom   WO0407
    Ceaseless stone   AS0585
    Certificate   DA0240
    Certificate   MA0330
    Climacteric   DA024C
    Dagon   DA0238
    Dagon   MA0199
    Dr. Morris Goldpepper returns   DA0240
    Gaslin day   KN0306
    Golem   DA0200
    Golem   DA0235
    Golem   JA0130
    Golem   KN0220
    Golem   MA0195
    Golem   ME0201
    Golem   ME0356
    Goobers   DA0240
    Goslin day   DA020C
    Grantha sighting   DA0238
    Grantha sighting   EA010C
    Grantha sighting   MA0198
    Help! I am Dr. Morris Goldpepper   DA0235
    Help! I am Dr. Morris Goldpepper   GA0142
    Help! I a'm Dr. Morris Goldpepper   SI0580
    House the Blakeneys built   DA0240
    House the Blakeneys built   MA0205
    House the Blakeneys built   MA055C
    I do not hear you, sir   RO0210
    I weep, I cry, I glorify   DA0238
    In which the lodge is tiled   DA0238
    Kappa nu nexus   CO0720
    King's evil   DA0235
    King's evil   MA0196
    King's evil   MC0180
    Lemuria revisited   DA0238
    Lord of Central Park   DA0238
    Love called this thing   CA0340

Davidson, Avram

Love called this thing	GA0145
Mr. Stillwell's stage	MA0197
My boy friend's name is Jello	MA0194
Naples	GR0040
Necessity of his condition	DA0235
No fire burns	ME0360
Now let us sleep	DA0235
Now let us sleep	FE0260
Now let us sleep	ME0358
Now let us sleep	MI015C
Now let us sleep	OL0170
Ogre	DA0235
Ogre and the vly	DA0240
Or all the seas with oysters	AS0370
Or all the seas with oysters	CE0100
Or all the seas with oysters	GA0143
Or all the seas with oysters	ME0359
Or all the seas with oysters	SI0420
Or the grasses grow	DA0235
Or the grasses grow	DE0220
Or the grasses grow	KO0160
Paramount Ulj	DA0240
Partial comfort	DA0238
Phoenix and the mirror	DA0235
Power of every root	DA0240
Power of every root	HA0233
Redward Edward papers [anthology]	DA0238
Rite of spring	KN0100
Rite of spring	KN0308
Roads, the roads, the beautiful roads	KN0305
Sacheverell	CA0238
Sacheverell	DA0240
Sacheverell	MA0204
Sensible man	FL0150
Singular events	DA0238
Singular events which occurred in the hovel on the alley off of Eye Street	MA0202
Sixty-third street station	DA0240
Sources of the Nile	DA0235
Sources of the Nile	DA0240
Sources of the Nile	KN0460
Sources of the Nile	KN0570
Sources of the Nile	MA0201
Strange seas and shores [anthology]	DA0240
Tail-tied kings	DA0240
Tail-tied kings	GA0146
Take wooden indians	DA0240
Take wooden indians	GA0144
Teeth of despair	CO0490
13th brumaire	DA0238
Trefoil company	DA0235
Unknown law	DA0235
Up Christopher to madness	EL0440

Davidscn, Avram
    Vat   DA0240
    What strange stars and skies   DA0235
    What strange stars and skies   MA0203
    Yc-ho and up   DA024C

Davis, Chandler
    Adrift on the policy level   GR025C
    Adrift on the policy level   MC0400
    Adrift on the policy level   PO0240
    Hexamnion   NO04C1
    Last year's grave undug   CO0043C
    Letter to Ellen   CO0550
    Letter to Ellen   CO056C
    Letter to Ellen   PC0293

Davis, Dorothy Salisbury
    Muted horn   FA0215

Davis, Grania
    Last one in is a rotten egg   LA0160
    Young love   KN0313

Davis, Hank
    Tc plant a seed   KN0311

Davis, Richard
    Space 1 [anthology]   DA027C
    Space 2 [anthology]   DA0271
    Space 3 [anthology]   CA0272
    Space 4 [anthology]   DA0273

Davis, Robert L.
    Teratohippus   BE0291

Davis, W.F.
    Ask and it may be given   WA01CC

Davy, John
    Venus mystery for scientists   AL031C

DeBergerac, Cyrano
    Journey to the moon [abridged]   CE019C
    Voyage to the moon   MO0320
    Voyage to the moon [excerpt]   GU013C

DeCamp, Catherine Crook
    Icarus [a Greek myth retold by   CE016C
        Catherine Crook DeCamp]
    Tales beyond time [anthclogy]   CE016C

DeCamp, Lyon Sprague
    Ameba   DE0C7C
    Animal-cracker plot   DE0100
    Aristotle and the gun   DE0130

DeCamp, Lyon Sprague

DeCamp, Lyon Sprague
    Lament by a maker   MA0195
    Language for time travelers   DE0070
    Language for time travelers   GR0130
    Let's have fun   DE0130
    Little green men   DE0070
    Living fossil   NC0240
    Merman   DE0070
    New Arcadia   DE0130
    Nothing in the rules   DE0070
    People of the black circle   HC0190
    Perpetual motion   DE0100
    Pool of the black one   HC0190
    Red nails   HC0220
    Reluctant shaman   DE0070
    Reward of virtue   DE0070
    Slithering shadow   HC0190
    Sorcerers [poem]   MC0150
    Summer wear   BE0201
    Summer wear   CE0100
    Tales beyond time [anthology]   DE0160
    Tales of Conan [anthology]   HC0250
    Thing of custom   DE0130
    Thing of custom   FA0215
    Thing of custom   FI0090
    3000 years of fantasy and science CE0190
       fiction [anthology]
    Throwback   DE0130
    Throwback   ST0210
    Two yards of dragon   DE0070
    Warrior race   AS0451
    Weissonbroch spectacles   DA0230

DeCles, Jon
    Cruelty   MC0180

DeCourcy, Dorothy
    Rat race   CO0130

DeCourcy, John
    Rat race   CO0130

Dee, Roger
    Interlopers   AL0411
    Problem on Balak   GA0141
    Unwelcome tenant   AS0340
    Unwelcome tenant   ME0230

Defoe, Daniel
    Friendly demon   MA0191

DeFord, Miriam Allen
    Apotheosis of Ki   DE0210
    Apotheosis of Ki   MC0180
    Beast in view   EL0980

Delany, Samuel R.
    Corona   AL0650
    Corona   DE0255
    Dog in a fisherman's net   DE0255
    Driftglass   CL0100
    Driftglass   DE0255
    Driftglass   DO0170
    Driftglass [anthology]   DE0255
    High weir   DE0255
    High weir   HO0120
    Night and the loves of Joe Dicostanzo MC0150
    Night and the loves of Joe Dicostanzo DE0255
    Power of the nail   EL0440
    Star pit   DE0255
    Star pit   SI0124
    Starpit   ME0367
    Time considered as a helix of   AS0400
        semi-precious stones
    Time considered as a helix of   DE0255
        semi-precious stones
    Time considered as a helix of   NE0155
        semi-precious stones
    Time considered as a helix of   SA0080
        semi-precious stones
    Time considered as a helix of   WO0409
        semi-precious stones
    We, in some strange power's employ,   DE0255
        move on a rigorous line

Dell, Dudley [pseud. of H.L. Gold]
    Biography project   GA0140

Dellinger, Paul
    little knowledge   AS0555

DelRey, Judy-Lynn
    Stellar 1 [anthology]   DE0265
    Stellar 3 [anthology]   DE0267
    Stellar 4 [anthology]   DE0268
    Stellar science fiction stories   DE0275
        [anthology]
    Stellar short novels [anthology]   DE0280

DelRey, Lester
    Alien   FO0372
    And it come out here   CO0370
    And it come out here   SI1000
    Best of C.L. Moore [anthology]   MO0170
    Best science fiction stories of the EE0290
        year, 1972 [anthology]
    Best science fiction stories of the BE0291
        year, 2d annual collection
        [anthology]

DelRey, Lester

Best science fiction stories of the year, 3rd annual collection [anthology]	BE0299
Best science fiction stories of the year, fourth annual collection [anthology]	EE0300
Best science fiction stories of the year, fifth annual collection [anthology]	BE0301
Dark mission	AS0451
Day is done	AS0645
Day is done	CO0310
Day is done	GR0140
Dead ringer	GA0142
Evensong	EL0300
Evensong	MC0100
Fcr I am a jealous people	PO0400
Helen O'Loy	AS0070
Helen O'Loy	DE0190
Helen O'Loy	JA0130
Helen O'Loy	ME0230
Helen O'Loy	FO0150
Helen O'Loy	FR0150
Helen O'Loy	SC0210
Helping hand	PO0374
Hereafter, inc.	AS0452
Icealist	PO0371
Instinct	CO0280
Instinct	KA0070
Instinct	SI0640
Into thy hands	GR0280
Into thy hands	LE0220
Keepers of the house	SI0380
Kindness	DE0310
Kindness	MC0350
Last true god	AL0650
Luck of Ignatz	DE0310
Luck of Ignatz	WO0300
Mcnster	HE0400
Monster	SC0300
My name is Legion	PO0293
Natural advantage	WO0417
Nerves	FI0095
Nerves	HE0100
Nerves	SC0211
Over the top	AS0700
Pcund of cure	PO0372
Psalm	ME0361
"Years draw nigh"	DE0340
Renegade	ST0210
Return engagement	GA0146
Seat of judgement	FE0260
Smallest god	CA0255

DelRey, Lester
    Still waters   WI0202
    Though dreamers die   GR0280
    Tc avenge man   GA0148
    Wings of night   C00130
    Wings of night   C0022C
    Year after tomorrow [anthology]   DE031C

Ceming, Richard
    Shape of things that came   B0015C
    Shape of things that came   MC018C

Demmon, Calvin
    Servo   EC015C

Dempsey, Hank
    CWACC strikes again   AN01C6
    Defensive bomber   NC0403

Dentinger, Stephen
    Future is ours   SA018C

Denton, Kit
    Burning spear   BA0235

Derleth, August W.
    Adventure of the ball of Nostradamus   SC040C
    Acventure of the snitch in time   DE022C
    Adventure of the snitch in time   SC040C
    Beachheads in space [anthology]   CE034C
    Beyond time and space [anthology]   DEC37C
    By rocket to the moon   DE043C
    Corner for Lucia   DE0430
    Detective and the senator   DE0430
    Eye for history   DE043C
    Far boundaries [anthology]   DE040C
    Ferguson's capsules   DE0430
    Harrigan's file [anthology]   CE043C
    Hcuse in the valley   EL052C
    Invaders from the microcosm   DE0430
    "Who shall I say is calling?"   ME031C
    Man who rode the saucer   CE043C
    Mark VII   DE043C
    Martian artifact   DE043C
    Maugham obsession   DE043C
    McIlvaine's star   DE043C
    McIlvaine's star   DEC59C
    Mechanical house   DE043C
    Other side of the wall   DE0430
    Outer reaches [anthology]   CE0470
    Fenfield misadventure   CE043C
    Portals of tomorrow [anthology]   DE050C
    Protoplasma   DE043C
    Remarkable dingdong   CEC43C
    Time to come [anthology]   DEC53C

Derleth, August W.
 Travelers by night [anthology]   DE0560
 Traveller in time   DE0430
 Worlds of tomorrow [anthology] DE0590

Dern, Daniel P.
 Yes sir that's my   NE0208
 Yes sir that's my   NE020C

Deutsch, A.J.
 Subway named Mobius   AS0645
 Subway named Mobius   CO028C
 Subway named Mobius   CR0103
 Subway named Mobius   KN028C

Deutsch, Babette
 To the moon, 1969 [poem]   SA015C

Deutsch, R. H.
 Watches   F00100

DeVet, Charles V.
 Second game   AS0585
 Special feature   CO058C

DeWeese, G.
 Midnight bicyclist   RY010C
 When you wish upon a star   DE0267

Dewey, G. Gordon
 Tooth   MA0192

Dexter, Ralph W.
 Eltonian pyramid   ST021C

Dick, Philip K.
 Adjustment team   DI0075
 Autofac   DI0075
 Autofac   DI0085
 Autofac   DI0250
 Autofac   SI03CC
 Best of Philip K. Dick [anthology] DI0075
 Beyond lies the wub   DI0075
 Beyond lies the wub   DI0083
 Book of Philip K. Dick [anthology] DI0075
 Breakfast at twilight   DI0075
 Breakfast at twilight   DI0075
 Captive market   DI0083
 Captive market   GR03CC
 Colony   AL051C
 Colony   DI0075
 Commuter   DI0075
 Crack in space   DI0078
 Crawlers   DI0083
 Days of Perky Pat   DI0075

Dick, Philip K.

Dick, Philip K.
    Roog   SI060C
    Second variety   AM0511
    Second variety   DI0075
    Second variety   DI0085
    Second variety   YE0405
    Service call   DI0075
    Shell game   DI0075
    Top stand-by job   DI0083
    Turning wheel   DI0075
    Unteleported man   DI0078
    Upon the dull earth   DI0083
    Variable man   DI0085
    Variable man [anthology]   DI0085
    War game   AS0585
    War game   DI0083
    War veteran   DI0083
    We can remember it for you wholesale   DI0083
    We can remember it for you wholesale   FE023C
    We can remember it for you wholesale   MA0206
    We can remember it for you wholesale   NE0152
    We can remember it for you wholesale   SI0124
    We can remember it for you wholesale   WO040C
    World of talent   DI0085

Dickens, Charles
    Rat that could speak   MA0191

Dickey, James
    Apollo [poem]   SA015C

Dickinson, Joseph
    Three for the stars   MA0202

Dickson, Gordon R.
    Act of creation   DI0115
    Adventure of the misplaced hound   AN020C
    Adventure of the misplaced hound   SC040C
    Ancient, my enemy   DI0100
    Ancient, my enemy [anthology]   DI01CC
    Ballad of the Shoshonee   ME0361
    Black Charlie   GA0144
    Black Charlie   KN0280
    Black Charlie   MC0155
    Bleak and barren land   DI01CC
    Brother Charlie   DI0115
    Brothers   AS075C
    Building on the line   DI0125
    Call him lord   AN0106
    Call him lord   DI0115
    Call him lord   GR0250
    Call him lord   NE0152
    Catch   DI0125
    Christmas present   DI0125
    Christmas present   EN010C

Dickson, Gordon R.

Combat SF [anthology]	DI0110
Computers don't argue	AL0402
Computers don't argue	AN0105
Computers don't argue	AS0651
Computers don't argue	HO0120
Computers don't argue	NE0151
Computers don't argue	RO0210
Computers don't argue	WA0130
Danger! human!	SI0320
Dolphin's way	DI0115
Don Jones	AN0200
Dreamsman	ME0360
Dreamsman	PO0376
Earthman's burden [anthology]	AN0200
Enter a pilgrim	BE0300
Friendly man	DI0100
Gordon R. Dickson's SF best [anthology]	DI0115
Half a hoka	SC0400
Haunted village	MA0201
Hilifter	AN0103
Hilifter	DI0115
Hilifter	DI0125
Hilifter	SA0150
Home from the shore	ME0363
Honorable death	KN0460
Honorable death	SI0125
Idiot solvent	CO0720
Idiot solvent	DI0115
In hoka signo vinces	AN0200
In the bone	DI0100
In the bone	DI0115
Jackal's meal	DI0125
Jean Dupres	NO0401
Joy in Mudville	CA0277
Law-twister shorty	BO0260
Love me true	DI0100
Lulungomeena	LE0220
Lulungomeena	SI0400
Maverick	FI0100
Monkey wrench	AL0450
Monkey wrench	DI0100
Mortal and the monster	DE0280
Mousetrap	DI0125
Mysterious message	AN0200
Nebula winners twelve [anthology]	NE0162
Odd ones	DI0100
Of the people	DI0115
On Messenger Mountain	DI0125
Our first death	DI0100
Present state of igneous research	AN0140
Ricochet on Miza	DI0110
Sheriff of Canyon Gulch	AN0180
Sheriff of Canyon Gulch	AN0280
Sheriff of Canyon Gulch	NO0240

Dickson, Gordon R.
    Sheriff of Canyon Gulch   SI0780
    Sleight of wit   AN0101
    Sleight of wit   CA0100
    Soldier, ask not   AS0400
    Star road [anthology]   DI0125
    Steel brother   AO0330
    Things which are Caesar's   AN0190
    Three   MC0180
    3-part puzzle   DI0125
    Tiger green   CI0100
    Tiger green   DI0115
    Trespass   BE0201
    Twig   DE0265
    Twig   WO0415
    Warrior   HA0234
    Warrior   ME0366
    Warrior   WO0180
    Whatever gods there be   DI0125
    Yo ho hoka!   AN0200

Diefendorf, David
    Fables   DI0230

Dighton, Ralph
    Sierra Sam   ME0360

Dikty, T.E.
    Best science fiction stories and   BE0205
        novels: 1955
    Best science fiction stories and   BE0206
        novels: 1956
    Best science fiction stories: 1950 BE0200
    Best science fiction stories: 1951 BE0201
    Best science fiction stories: 1952 BE0202
    Best science fiction stories: 1953 BE0203
    Best science-fiction stories and   BE0208
        novels, ninth series
    Earth's natural satellite   DI0220
    Every boy's book of outer space   DI0130
        stories [anthology]
    Five tales from tomorrow [anthology] DI0160
    Great science fiction stories about DI0190
        Mars [anthology]
    Great science fiction stories about DI0220
        the moon [anthology]
    Imagination unlimited [anthology]   BL0100
    Red planet   DI0190
    Science fiction omnibus. The best   BL0120
        science fiction stories: 1949,1950
        [anthology]
    Year's best science fiction novels   YE0403
        1952 [anthology]
    Year's best science fiction novels   YE0404
        1953 [anthology]

Dikty, T.E.
    Year's best science fiction novels   YE0405
        1954 [anthology]

Dillingham, Peter
    House   P00430
    I graver   NE0208
    Three poems   NE0209

Dillon, John
    Late great future [anthology]   FI0090

Disch, Thomas M.
    Angouleme   HA0164
    Apollo   DI0215
    Asian shore   DI0215
    Asian shore   HA0163
    Asian shore   HA0250
    Asian shore   KN0306
    Asian shore   SA0080
    Birds   DI0215
    Birds   HA0166
    Bone of contention   DI0210
    Casablanca   SI0123
    Chanson perpetuelle   DA0180
    Colors   DI0215
    Come to Venus melancholy   FI0090
    Contest   M00162
    Dangerous flags   DI0210
    Death and the single girl   DI0215
    Demi-urge   DI0210
    Descending   AL0402
    Descending   NE0365
    Descent of the West End   M00162
    Displaying the flag   DI0215
    Early science fiction stories of   DI0210
        Thomas M. Disch [anthology]
    Emancipation: a romance of the times   NE0201
        to come
    Empty room   M00162
    Et in Arcadia ego   HA0234
    Feathers from the wings of an angel   DI0215
    Final audit   DI0210
    Five eggs   KN0301
    5 eggs   DI0210
    Genetic code   DI0210
    Getting into death   DI0215
    Getting into death [anthology]   DI0215
    In praise of New York   EL0720
    Invaded by love   DI0210
    Joycelin Shrager story   DI0215
    Leader of the revolution   DI0210
    Let us quickly hasten to the gate of   DI0215
        ivory
    Linda and Daniel and Spike   M00164

Disch, Thomas M.

Luncheon in the sepulcher	DI0260
Man who had no idea	CA0238
Master of the Milford altarpiece	DI0215
Moondust, the smell of hay, and dialectical materialism	ST0230
Mutability	PR0160
Mystery diet of the gods: a revelation	DI0230
Nada	MA0204
Nada	CL0165
New constellations [anthology]	DI0230
New improved sun [anthology]	DI0240
Now is forever	WO0405
102 H-bombs	DI0210
One-A [1-A]	SA0100
Persistence of desire	DI0215
Planet Arcadia	DI0215
Pressure of time	KN0307
Princess' carillon	DI0210
Puppies of Terra	DI0210
Pyramids for Minnesota: a serious proposal	DI0240
Quincunx	DI0215
Quincunx	JO0150
Return of the Medusae	DI0210
Roaches	DI0260
Roaches	ME0366
Ruins of earth [anthology]	DI0250
Santa Claus compromise	HA0168
Sightseers	DI0210
Slaves	DI0215
Squirrel cage	ME0290
Strangeness [anthology]	DI0260
Things lost	EL0220
Two poems	EL1020
Utopia: Never!	DI0210
Vacation on earth	ME0367
Vamp	DI0210
White Fang goes dingo	DI0210
X yes	DI0215

Dixon, Richard

Destination: Amaltheia [anthology]	DI0280

Dixon, Terry

Hate is a sandpaper ice cube with polkadots of love on it	NO0150
Prophet of Zorayne	EL1120

Dneprov, Anatoly

Crabs on the island	MO0150
Crabs take over the island	MA0420
Formula for immortality	NE0280
Formula of immortality	GI0130
Heroic feat	MA0390

Dostoevsky, Fyodor
    Dream of a ridiculous man   KN0450

Doyle, Arthur Conan
    American's tale   WA016C
    Blurring of the lines   DC016C
    Dead world   DC0160
    Diary of the dying   D00160
    Disintegration machine   H00119
    Disintegration machine   L0010C
    Great awakening   D0016C
    Great Keinplatz experiment   C00190
    Los amigos fiasco   M00320
    Lost world   BR052C
    Maracot deep   KU010C
    Poison belt [anthology]   D0016C
    Professor Challenger stories   DC0160
    Submerged   CC016C
    Tide of death   D0016C

Dozois, Gardner R.
    Another world [anthology]   DC0165
    Best science fiction stories of the   EE0302
        year, 6th annual collection
        [anthology]
    Best science fiction stories of the   EE0303
        year, 7th annual collection
        [anthology]
    Chains of the sea   D0023C
    Chains of the sea   EF015C
    Day in the life [anthology]   D00170
    Dream at noonday   D0023C
    Dream at noonday   KN0307
    Flash point   D0023C
    Future power [anthology]   DA017C
    Horse of air   DC023C
    Horse of air   KN010C
    Horse of air   KN0308
    Horse of air   NE0157
    In a crooked year   EL1160
    King Harvest   NE0202
    Kingdom by the sea   DC023C
    Kingdom by the sea   KN031C
    Last day of July   D00230
    Last day of July   NE0203
    Machines of loving grace   D0C23C
    Machines of loving grace   KN0311
    Man who waved hello   D0023C
    Special kind of morning   D00230
    Special kind of morning   NE02CC
    Special kind of morning   NE0201
    Special kind of morning   SI0124
    Storm   D00230
    Storm   EL1240
    Strangers   NE02C4

Dozois, Gardner R.
        Visible man   DO0230
        Visible man [anthology]   DO0230
        Where no sun shines   DO0230
        Where no sun shines   KN0306

Drake, David
        Butcher's bill   DI0110
        Denkirch   DE0560

Draper, Hal
        Ms Fnd in a lbry   CO0640

Dressler, Daniel
        White army   GA0370
        White army   WO0240

Driscoll, Dennis
        Going up   ME0358

Drury, Allan
        Something   MA0200

Dryfoos, Dave
        Bridge crossing   FO0190

Dudintsev, Vladimir
        New year's fairy tale   MA0360

duMaurier, Daphne
        Birds   DI0250

Dunsany, Edward J., Lord
        Misadventure   MA0194

Duntemann, Jeff
        Our lady of the endless sky   NO0404
        Steel sonnets   KN0317

Durrell, Lawrence
        High Barbary   ME0362

Dutt, Violent L.
        Soviet science fiction [anthology]   DU0100

Dyalhis, Neitzin
        When the green star waned   DE0370

Dybek, Stuart
        Maze   KN0317

Dye, Charles
        Syndrome Johnny   GA0140

Earl, Stephen
    Walkabout   OB0140

Earle, W.
    In re state vs. Forbes   M00365

Earley, George W.
    Encounters with aliens [anthology]   EA0100

Earls, William
    Jump   AN0108
    Traffic problem   CL059C
    Traffic problem   HA0163
    Traffic problem   HA026C

Eberhart, Richard
    On shooting particles beyond the world AL0650

Edelson, Edward
    Outer limits of space   AL0650

Edelstein, Scott
    Age of Libra   PO029C
    Exhibition   N00403
    Future pastimes [anthology]   ED015C
    Slime dwellers   CL059C

Edmondson, G.C.
    Galactic Calabash   CO049C
    Rescue   MA0197
    Ringer   EA010C

Edwards, Dolton
    Meihem in Ce Klasrum [sic]   AS0700

Edwards, Kelley
    Counterspy   CR0102

Effinger, George Alec
    All the last wars at once   CA0231
    All the last wars at once   CA0234
    All the last wars at once   CA0368
    All the last wars at once   EF024C
    All the last wars at once   KA007C
    All the last wars at once   SI1020
    All the last wars at once   WA013C
    And us, too, I guess   EF015C
    And us, too, I guess   EF021C
    Ashes all my lust   CA0265
    At the bran foundry   EF021C
    At the bran foundry   NE0203
    Awesome menace of the polarizer   EF018C
    B.K.A. the master   EF018C
    Biting down hard on truth   EF021C
    Biting down hard on truth   KN0315

Effinger, George Alec
    Chains of the sea [anthology]   EF015C
    Chase our blues away   EF018C
    Contentment, satisfaction, cheer,   EF018C
        well-being, gladness, joy, comfort,
        and not having to get up early any
        more
    Contentment, satisfaction, cheer,   DA0170
        well-being, gladness, joy, comfort,
        and not having to get up early any
        more
    Contest results   EF018C
    Curtains   EF021C
    Curtains   HA0145
    Dirty tricks [anthology]   EF018C
    Early to bed   CL0110
    F(x) = (11/15/67)   NE0202
    f(x)=(11/15/67) x=her, f(x)=0   NE0200
    f(x)=(11/15/67): x=her, f(x)=0   EF024C
    Ghost writer   CA037C
    Ghost writer   EF0240
    Ghost writer   MO0155
    Hard times   EF021C
    Heartstop   EF018C
    Horse with one leg   CA0420
    How it felt   CA0372
    Hcw it felt   EF021C
    Ibid   CA0374
    Irrational numbers [anthology]   EF021C
    Last full measure   AS0180
    Lights out   EF024C
    Live, from Berchtesgaden   EF018C
    Live, from Berchtesgaden   KN0100
    Live, from Berchtesgaden   KN031C
    Live, from Berchtesgaden   SI0124
    Lydectes: on the nature of sport EF021C
    Mixed feelings [anthology]   EF0240
    Mom's differentials   MA052C
    Mothers' march on ecstasy   EF0180
    Mothers' march on ecstasy   NE02C5
    Naked to the invisible eye   EF024C
    New New York New Orleans   ELC94C
    New New York New Orleans   EF018C
    Paradise last   DA020C
    Sand and stones   CL0110
    Sand and stones   EF0180
    Steve Weinraub and the secret empire EF0240
    Strange ragged saintliness   EF018C
    Things go better   EF024C
    Things go better   KN0311
    Timmy was eight   EF018C
    25 crunch split right on two   EF021C
    Two sadnesses   EF0240
    Wednesday, November 15, 1967   DI025C
    Wednesday, November 15, 1967   EF0240

Elam, Richard M.
    Day the flag fell   EL0140
    Expedition Pluto   EL0160
    First men into space   EL0160
    Flight of the Centaurus   EL0160
    Ghost ship of space   EL0160
    Hands across the deep   EL0120
    Hands across the deep   EL0140
    Iron moon   EL0120
    Iron moon   EL0140
    Lunar trap   EL0120
    Lunar trap   ELC140
    Mercy flight to Luna   EL0160
    Mystery eyes over earth   EL0160
    Peril from outer space   EL0160
    Project ocean floor   ELC120
    Project ocean floor   EL0140
    Race around the sun   EL0160
    Red sands   EL0120
    Red sands   ELC140
    Science fiction stories   EL0120
    Sol's little brother   EL0120
    Sol's little brother   EL0140
    Space steward   EL0160
    Strange men   EL0120
    Strange men   EL0140
    Teen-age science-fiction stories   EL0140
        [anthology]
    Teen-age super science stories   EL0160
        [anthology]
    Venusway   EL0120
    Venusway   ELC140
    What time is it?   EL0120
    What time is it?   ELC140

Elder, Joseph
    Eros in orbit [anthology]   EL018C
    Farthest reaches [anthology]   ELC20C

Elgin, Suzette Haden
    For the sake of grace   W0041C

Ellanby, Boyd [pseud. of Lyle & William Boyd]
    Category Phoenix   YE04C4
    Chain reaction   P0024C

Ellern, W.B.
    Moon prospector   CI022C

Ellin, Stanley
    Blessington method   WA016C

Elliot, George P.
    Fag   MI0150
    Invasion of the planet of love   MA0199

Elliot, John
    A for Andromeda [selections]   ER0520

Elliott, Bruce
    Battle of the S....S   CR0230
    Devil was sick   CR0200
    Fearsome fable   MA0191

Elliott, Chandler
    Day on death highway   GA0147
    Inanimate objection   AM0510

Elliott, George P.
    Among the dangs   ME0362
    NRACP   DE0250
    Sandra   B00150

Elliott, Rose Bedrick
    Baby killers   CR0230

Ellis, H.F.
    Space-crime continuum   C00490

Ellison, Harlan
    "Repent, Harlequin!" said the   AL0665
        ticktockman
    "Repent, Harlequin!" said the   AS0400
        ticktockman
    "Repent, Harlequin!" said the   EL0240
        ticktockman
    "Repent, Harlequin!" said the   EL0420
        ticktockman
    "Repent, Harlequin!" said the   GA0149
        ticktockman
    "Repent, Harlequin!" said the   GR0250
        ticktockman
    "Repent, Harlequin!" said the   H00100
        ticktockman
    "Repent, Harlequin!" said the   MC0400
        ticktockman
    "Repent, Harlequin!" said the   NE0151
        ticktockmen
    "Repent, Harlequin!" said the   R00180
        ticktockman
    "Repent, Harlequin!" said the   SA0150
        ticktockman
    "Repent, Harlequin!" said the   SU0150
        ticktockman
    "Repent, Harlequin!" said the   W00406
        ticktockman
    Adrift just off the islets of   AS0401
        Langerhans: Latitude 38 54' N,
        Longitude 77 00' 13" W

Ellison, Harlan

Acrift just off the islets of Langerhans: latitude 38 54' N, longitude 77 at 00' 13" W	EL032C
Again, dangerous visions [anthology]	EL0220
All the sounds of fear	EL0340
All the sounds of fear	EL0400
All the sounds of fear	ME0363
Alone against tomorrow [anthology]	EL024C
Along the scenic route	EL028C
Along the scenic route	EL0320
Approaching oblivion [anthology]	EL0260
Are you listening?	CA028C
Are you listening?	EL024C
Are you listening?	EL028C
Asleep: with still hands	EL028C
At the mouse circus	EL0320
At the mouse circus	NE02CC
At the mouse circus	NE0201
Back to the drawing boards	EL0340
Back to the drawing boards	EL036C
Basilisk	EL032C
Basilisk	HA0145
Battle without banners	EL036C
Battle without banners	EL0400
Battlefield	EL0340
Battlefield	SI102C
Beast that shouted love at the heart of the world	AS040C
Beast that shouted love at the heart of the world [anthology]	EL028C
Beast that shouted love at the heart of the world	EL0280
Beast that shouted love at the heart of the world	SI0380
Big Sam was my friend	EL0380
Big Sam was my friend	EL038C
Bleeding stones	EL032C
Blind bird, blind bird, go away from me!	EL04CC
Blind lightning	EL024C
Blind lightning	SI044C
Boy and his dog	EL028C
Boy and his dog	NE0155
Boy and his dog	SU015C
Boy and his dog	WO0410
Bright eyes	EL024C
Bright eyes	EL0420
Brillo	EL0440
Catman	EL0260
City on the edge of forever	EL110C
Cold friend	EL026C
Come to me not in winter's white	EL044C
Commuter's problem	EL0340
Corpse	EL0320

Ellison, Harlan

Ellison, Harlan

Ellison, Harlan

Pretty Maggie Moneyeyes	EL0320
Pretty Maggie Moneyeyes	EL0380
Pretty Maggie Moneyeyes	ELC380
Pretty Maggie Moneyeyes	EL04CC
Pretty Maggie Moneyeyes	HA0160
Pretty Maggie Moneyeyes	MC018C
Pretty Maggie Moneyeyes	NE0153
Prowler in the city at the edge of the world	EL030C
Prowler in the city at the edge of the world	EL0440
Punky & the Yale men	EL0400
Rain, rain go away	EL034C
Region between	FI010C
Resurgence of Miss Ankle-strap wedgie	EL04CC
Riding the dark train out	EL04CC
Rock god	EL0320
Rodney Parish for hire	EL0440
Run for the stars	EL028C
Runesmith	EL044C
S.R.O.	EL0280
Santa Claus vs. S.P.I.D.E.R	EL0280
Seeing	CA0236
Seeing	CA0275
Seeing	WE0290
Shatterday	NE0161
Shattered like a glass goblin	EL0280
Shattered like a glass goblin	ELC320
Shattered like a glass goblin	KN01CC
Shattered like a glass goblin	KN0304
Shattered like a glass goblin	MC040C
Shoppe keeper	MO0155
Silent in Gehenna	BO026C
Silent in Gehenna	EL026C
Silent in Gehenna	HO0110
Silent in Gehenna	PO0450
Silver corridor	ELC24C
Silver corridor	EL0340
Sky is burning	EL0340
Sky is burning	ELC360
Sleeping dogs	BE030C
Sleeping dogs	EL042C
Soldier	KE0100
Soldier [originally, Soldier from tomorrow]	EL0360
Song the Zombie sang	EL0440
Street scene	EL044C
Survivor I	EL0440
Time of the eye	EL024C
Time of the eye	EL0360
Toy for Juliette	EL0440
Try a dull knife	EL024C
Try a dull knife	EL028C
Universe of Robert Blake	EL04CC

Ellison, Harlan
    Up Christopher to madness   EL0440
    Very last day of a good woman   EL0240
    Very last day of a good woman   EL0340
    Voice in the garden   EL0360
    Wanted in surgery   EL0420
    We mourn for anyone   EL0360
    What I did on my vacation this summer, EL0400
        by Little Bobby Hirschhorn, age 27
    Whimper of whipped dogs   EL0320
    White on white   EL0280
    Wind beyond the mountains   EL0340
    Wine has been left open too long and   CA0373
        the memory has gone flat
    Wonderbird   EL0440
    World of the myth   EL0380
    World of the myth   EL0380
    Worlds to kill   EL0280
    You are what you write   CL0110

Elmslie, Kenward
    Accident vertigo   DI0250

Elwood, Roger
    Adrift in space and other stories   EL0460
        [anthology]
    Alien earth [anthology]   EL0480
    And walk now gently through the fire   EL0500
        [anthology]
    Androids, time machines, and blue   EL0520
        giraffes [anthology]
    Ariel   EL1240
    Ariel   NE0204
    Children of infinity [anthology]   EL0540
    Chronicles of a comer [anthology]   EL0560
    Continuum 1 [anthology]   EL0580
    Continuum 2 [anthology]   EL0581
    Continuum 3 [anthology]   EL0582
    Crisis [anthology]   EL0640
    Dystopian Visions [anthology]   EL0660
    Epoch [anthology]   SI0480
    Far side of time [anthology]   EL0680
    Flame tree planet [anthology]   EL0700
    Future city [anthology]   EL0720
    Future kin [anthology]   EL0740
    Gifts of Asti [anthology]   EL0760
    Journey to another star [anthology]   EL0800
    Killer plants [anthology]   EL0820
    Learning maze [anthology]   EL0840
    Long night of waiting [anthology]   EL0860
    Many worlds of Andre Norton [anthology] N00250
    Many worlds of Poul Anderson   AN0280
        [anthology]
    Mind angel [anthology]   EL0880
    Missing world [anthology]   EL0900

Elwood, Roger
    More science fiction tales [anthology]   EL0920
    New mind [anthology]   EL0940
    Night of the sphinx [anthology]   EL0960
    Omega [anthology]   EL0980
    Other side of tomorrow [anthology]   EL1000
    Saving worlds [anthology]   EL1020
    Science fiction tales [anthology]   EL1040
    Showcase [anthology]   EL1060
    Signs and wonders [anthology]   EL1080
    Six science fiction plays [anthology]   EL1100
    Strange gods [anthology]   EL1120
    Survival from infinity [anthology]   EL1140
    Ten tomorrows [anthology]   EL1160
    Throwback   EL1120
    Tomorrow [anthology]   EL1100
    Tomorrow's alternatives [anthology]   EL1200
    Visions of tomorrow [anthology]   EL1240

Emmett, Elizabeth
    Enchantment   ME0361

Emshwiller, Carol
    Al   KN0100
    Al   KN0310
    Animal   KN0304
    But soft, what light...   HA0234
    Chicken Icarus   ME0367
    Childhood of the human hero   EL1060
    Childhood of the human hero   NE0159
    Day at the beach   ME0201
    Day at the beach   ME0360
    Debut   KN0306
    Debut   SA0230
    Hunting machine   BE0203
    Institute   MC0150
    Lib   MC0166
    Pelt   KN0460
    Pelt   ME0359
    Sex and/or Mr. Morrison   EL0300
    Sex and/or Mr. Morrison   SA0240
    Woman waiting   KN0307

Emtsev, M.
    Pale Neptune equation   NE0280

Endore, Guy
    Day of the dragon   YO0150
    Men of iron   MA0330

Enever, J. E.
    Giant meteor impact   AN0106

Engdahl, Sylvia
    Anywhere, anywhen [anthology]   EN0070

Engcahl, Sylvia
    Beckoning trail   EN010C
    Timescape   EN0070
    Universe ahead [anthology]   EN010C

Englanc, G.A.
    Darkness and dawn   MO04CC
    June 6, 2016   MO041C

Erckmann, Emile
    Hans Schnap's spy glass   MO038C

Ernst, Paul
    "Nothing happens on the moon"   C0028C
    Microscopic giants   C0052C

Eshbach, Lloyd
    Dust   SC03CC

Etchison, Dennis
    Country of the strong   NE0304
    Damechild   N0015C
    Fires of night   C0028C
    Nighthawk   GR0040
    Ocd boy out   NE0302

Eustace, R.
    Where the air quivered   MO0365

Eustis, Helen
    Mr. Death and the redheaded woman BR038C

Evans, E.E.
    Shed   DE016C
    Shed   SL021C

Evans, I.O.
    Science fiction through the ages 1 EV01CC
        [anthology]

Exter, Maureen
    Night of the sphirx   EL096C
    Spacer's dance   EL064C

Fabricant, Noah D.
    Great science fiction about doctors C0019C
        [anthology]

Fairfax, John
    All Adam again [poem]   BE050C
    Twelve stations from gemini [poem] BE050C

Fairman, Paul W.
    Brothers beyond the void   DE059C
    Missing symbol   STC230

Fancett, E.
    Museum piece   DA027C
    Refugees   DA0271

Farber, Jerry
    Gorman   HA0163
    Gorman   OL0165

Farber, Sharon N.
    Born again   AS018C

Farley, C.
    DILOPS are coming   EN0070

Farley, Ralph Milmer
    Liquid fire   LE013C
    Liquid fire   SI070C
    Man who could turn back the clock   AS0555
    Time for sale   EL0520

Farmer, Philip Jose
    After King Kong fell   EL0980
    After King Kong fell   HA0167
    After King Kong fell   NE0160
    Alley man   FA024C
    Attitudes   MA0193
    Blasphemers   FA0245
    Book of Philip Jose Farmer [anthology]   FA0240
    Bowl bigger than earth   FA0245
    Brass and gold   FA024C
    Don't wash the carats   FAC24C
    Don't wash the carats   KN0100
    Don't wash the carats   KN0303
    Down in the black gang   FA0245
    Down in the blank gang [anthology]   FA0245
    Exclusive interview with Lord   FA0240
        Greystoke
    Father's in the basement   FA024C
    Father's in the basement   KN0311
    Few miles   FA0245
    Forward the beloved city   EL1080
    How deep the grooves   FA0245
    King of beasts   Y0015C
    King of the beasts   GA0148
    Mother   CH0100
    Mother   KA0070
    Mother   M0035C
    Mother   PC015C
    Mother   SC045C
    Mother   SI0123
    Mother earth wants you   ELC5CC
    My sister's brother   FA0240
    Obscure life and hard times of Kilgore FA024C
        Front
    Only who can make a tree?   FA0240

Farmer, Philip Jose
 Oogenesis of Bird City OL015C
 Open to me, my sister FE020C
 Opening the door EL054C
 Prometheus FA0245
 Prometheus MC018C
 Prometheus MO01CC
 Riders of the purple wage AS040C
 Riders of the purple wage EL030C
 Riverworld FA0245
 Sail on! Sail on! AL04C1
 Sail on! Sail on! KN0160
 Sail on! Sail on! SI1040
 Seventy years of decpop AC020C
 Sexual implications of the charge FA024C
  of the light brigade
 Shadow of space FA0245
 Shadow of space WA0130
 Sketches among the ruins of my mind DI0260
 Sketches among the ruins of my minc NC0403
 Skinburn FA0240
 Sliced-crosswise only-on-Tuesday world BE029C
 Sliced-crosswise only-on-Tuesday world CA0231
 Sliced-crosswise only-on-Tuesday world CA0234
 Sliced-crosswise only-on-Tuesday world NE02CC
 Sliced-crosswise only-on-Tuesday world NE0201
 Sliced-crosswise only-on-Tuesday world SI0128
 Stations of the nightmare: Part 1 EL058C
 Stations of the nightmare: Part 2: EL0581
  the Startouched
 Stations of the nightmare: Part 3: EL0582
  The Evolution of Paul Eyre
 Sumerian oath FA024C
 Sumerian oath NC0402
 Totem and taboo FA0240
 Toward the beloved city EL056C
 Toward the beloved city EL124C
 Toward the beloved city FA0240
 Voice of the sonar in my vermiform FA0240
  appendix

Farnsworth, Mona
 All roads M0026C

Farrell, James F.
 Benefactor of humanity ME0365

Fast, Howard
 Cato the Martian CO0640
 Cato the Martian FA0270
 Cato the Martian SA015C
 Cephes 5 FA0270
 Cephes 5 FA030C
 Cold, cold box FA0270
 Cold, cold box WI0206

Fast, Howard

Echinomastus contentii	FA0270
Egg	FA027C
Egg	FA0300
First men	AL0450
First men	KAC070
First men	MI0150
First men	OL0165
General Hardy's profession	FA0270
General Hardy's profession	FA030C
General zapped an angel	FA0270
General zapped an angel	GR0250
Hole in the floor	FA0270
Hole in the floor	FA0300
Hoop	FA027C
Hoop	FA0300
Hunter	FA0270
Insects	FA0270
Interval	FA027C
Large ant	AL0401
Large ant	AM0513
Large ant	FA027C
Large ant	ME0361
Martian shop	FA027C
Martian shop	MA033C
Matter of size	FA027C
Matter of size	FA030C
Mind of God	FA027C
Mind of God	FA030C
Mohawk	FA0270
Mouse	FA027C
Mouse	Y0015C
Movie house	FA0270
Not with a bang	FA027C
Not with a bang	FA0300
Of time and cats	FA027C
Pragmatic seed	FA0270
Pragmatic seed	FA0300
Price	FA0270
Price	FA0300
Show cause	FA0270
Show cause	FA030C
Sight of Eden	FA027C
Talent of Harvey	FA0270
Talent of Harvey	FA0300
Time and the riddle [anthology]	FA0270
Tomorrow's Wall Street Journal	FA027C
Touch of infinity [anthology]	FA030C
Trap	FA0270
UFO	FA0270
UFO	FA030C
Vision of Milty Boil	FA0270
Wound	AL0405
Wound	FA027C

Fast, Jon
    Earthblossom   CI0230

Fawcett, Douglas
    Anarchist; or, the doom of the great   WI0280
        city

Feder, Moshe
    Sandial   KN0316

Fehrenbach, T.R.
    Remember the Alamo!   AN0101
    Remember the Alamo!   CA0100
    Remember the Alamo!   GR0250
    Remember the Alamo!   RO0210

Feiffer, Jules
    Dog eat dog   ME0364
    Looking backward   ME0362

Feldman, Arthur
    Mathematicians   AS0340

Felice, C.
    David and Lindy   CA0375
    No one said forever   KI0070

Felsen, Henry Gregor
    Spaceman cometh   CO0640

Fennel, Erik
    Doughnut jockey   BL0120

Fenton, Frank
    Chicken or the egghead   HE0160
    Tolliver's travels   HE0130

Ferguson, Dale
    Island of the endangered   Y00150

Ferman, Edward L.
    Best from fantasy and science fiction MA0210
        20th series [anthology]
    Best from fantasy and science fiction, FE0110
        a special 25th anniversary
        [antholoy]
    Best from fantasy and science fiction, MA0205
        15th series [anthology]
    Best from fantasy and science fiction, MA0208
        18th series [anthology]
    Final stage [anthology]   FE0170
    Graven images [anthology]   GR0070
    Once and future tales [anthology]   FE0200

Ferman, Edward L.
    Twenty years of the magazine of   FE023C
       fantasy and science fiction
       [anthology]

Ferman, Joseph
    No limits [anthology]   FE026C

Fessier, Michael
    Fascinating stranger   LE0130

Fiedler, Leslie
    Cross the border, close the gap   ALU650

Figueredo, A. Parra y
    Totenbuch   EL0220

Filer, Burt K.
    Backtracked   SU015C
    Backtracked   WO0409
    Eye of the beholder   EL0220
    Hot potato   BE0290
    Hot potato   EC0260
    Sun   KN046C

Finch, Christopher
    Landscape of shallows   MO0165

Fink, David Harold, M.D.
    Compound B   CO019C
    Compound B   HE016C

Finney, Charles G.
    Captivity   MA0201

Finney, Jack
    Behind the news   FI007C
    Contents of the dead man's pocket   FI0070
    Cousin Len's wonderful adjective cellar ALC36C
    Cousin Len's wonderful adjective cellar FI007C
    Dash of spring   FI007C
    Double take   PL015C
    Face in the photo   ME0363
    I'm scared   FI007C
    I'm scared   HE04CU
    Of missing persons   FI0070
    Of missing persons   ME0356
    Of missing persons   OL018C
    Other wife   ME036C
    Quit zoomin' those hands through the BO0100
       air
    Quit zoomin' those hands through the CO031C
       air
    Quit zoomin' those hands through the FI0070
       air

Fox, Gardner F.
    Tonight the stars revolt!   AL0411

Fox, J.
    Morrien's bitch   SA012C

Frank, J.
    Wolves of Nakesht   SA012C

Franke, Herbert W.
    Paradise 3000   WO0150
    Slum   R0027C

Franklin, H. Bruce
    Future perfect [anthology]   FR007C

Frede, R.
    Oh, lovelee appearance of the lass   GR007C
       from the north countree

Free, Colin
    Weather in the underworld   BA0235
    Weather in the underworld   WO0405

Friborg, Albert Compton
    Careless love   BE0205
    Careless love   DI0160
    Careless love   MA0194
    Push-button passion   DI016C

Friedberg, Gertrude
    Wayward cravat   AS0590

Friedman, Bruce Jay
    Foot in the door   PL0150
    Killer in the TV set   PL015C
    Yes, we have no Ritchard   FE023C

Friedman, Stuart
    Beautiful, beautiful, beautiful!   AS034C
    Beautiful, beautiful, beautiful!   DE059C

Friend, Oscar J.
    Giant anthology of science fiction MA048C
    Impossible highway   AS0451
    Impossible highway   LE013C

Frisch, O.R.
    On the feasibility of coal-driven   P00240
       power stations

Fritch, Charles E.
    Birthday present   N0020C
    Castaway   N0023C
    Geever's flight   N0021C

Fritch, Charles E.
    If at first you don't succeed,to hell   AS0555
        with it !
    Misfortune cookie   AS0555

Frith, U.
    Emergency society   ST0220

Frost, Robert
    Star-splitter   AL0650

Furman, A.L.
    Teen-age outer space stories   FU0100
        [anthology]
    Teen-age space adventures   FU0130

Furnas, J.C.
    Laocoon complex   BR0380
    Laocoon complex   ME0260

Fyfe, H.B.
    Afterthought   ME0230
    Bureau of slick tricks   GR0310
    Implode and peddle   N00330
    In value deceived   C00340
    In value deceived   GA0370
    In value deceived   SL0210
    Locked out   GR0220
    Manners of the age   C00280
    Mconwalk   KN063C
    Moonwalk   N00270
    Protected species   AL0410
    Protected species   AL0450
    Protected species   AS0700
    Protected species   CA0105
    Ransom   MA0192
    Ransom   MC0180
    Star-linked   N00330
    Well-Oiled machine   BR0460

Gaither, Donald
    Wolf tracks   AS0180
    Wolf tracks   AS0440

Galaxy Science Fiction Magazine
    Bodyguard [anthology]   GA0190
    Fifth Galaxy Reader [anthology]   GA0144
    Five galaxy short novels [anthology]   GA0220
    Fcurth Galaxy Reader [anthology]   GA0143
    Galaxy reader of science fiction   GA0140
        [First] [anthology]
    Mind partner [anthology]   GA0250
    Ninth galaxy reader [anthology]   GA0148
    Second Galaxy Reader of Science   GA0141
        Fiction [anthology]

Galaxy Science Fiction Magazine
    Seventh Galaxy Reader [anthology]   GA0146
    Six fingers of time [anthology]   GA0280
    Sixth Galaxy Reader [anthology]   GA0145
    Tenth galaxy reader [anthology]   GA0149
    Third Galaxy Reader [anthology]   GA0142
    Time waits for Winthrop [anthology]   GA0310
    World couldn't be [anthology]   GA0340

Gallagher, John
    Tree trunks   ME0364

Gallant, Joseph
    Stories of scientific imagination   GA0370
       [anthology]

Gallun, Raymond Z.
    Asteroid of fear   N00270
    Davy Jones' ambassador   SI0420
    Derelict   MO0200
    Old faithful   AS0170
    Old faithful   BL0100
    Old faithful   P00120
    Operation Pumice   C00340
    Return of a legend   ER0080
    Return of a legend   N00330
    Scarab   C00550
    Seeds of the dusk   AS0650
    Seeds of the dusk   HE0100
    Seeds of the dusk   SI0940
    Stamped caution   C00150
    Stepson of space   P00190
    Stepson of space   P00293
    Trail blazer   N00270

Galouye, Daniel F.
    City of force   GA0190
    Diplomatic coop   HA0232
    Prometheus rebound   HA0300
    Sanctuary   MA0194
    Sitting duck   GA0280
    Tonight the sky will fall   AL0510

Gamow, George
    Heart on the other side   P00240

Gansovsky, Sever
    Day of anger   SH0150
    Day of wrath   FA0210
    New signal station   GI0100
    Proving ground   R00270

Gardner, Erle Stanley
    Human zero   WA0160
    Rain magic   EL0480

Gardner, Martin
    Case of the defective Doyles   AS0440
    Devil and the trombone   AS0555
    Island of five colors   CR0230
    Machismo on Byronia   AS0173
    No-sided professor   CE0100
    No-sided professor   MA0191
    Nc-sided professor   SU0150
    Ocm   AS0555
    Thang   AS0555
    Thang   BL012C
    Third Dr. Moreau   AS0175
    Voyage of the Bagel   AS018C

Gardner, T.S.
    Last woman   MO0410

Garis, H.R.
    Professor Jonkin's cannibal plant   MO0365

Garnett, Bill
    Singular   NO0404

Garnett, David S.
    Man who   NE0326

Garrett, Randall
    After a few words   AS0651
    All about "The Thing"   ME0357
    Best policy   SI044C
    Case of identity   AN01C4
    Fighting division   AN01C5
    Great Klandnar race   CA0277
    Hail to the chief   OL0150
    Hot argument   ME0360
    Hunting lodge   MA0465
    Hunting lodge   SI064C
    Ipswitch phial   AS0585
    Muddle of the wood   MC018C
    On the Martian problem   AS0173
    On the Martian problem   AS044C
    Polly Plus   AS018C
    Polly Plus   AS0440
    Sound decision   AN015C
    Sound decision   CA0100
    Sound decision   FR0210
    Sound decision   SA0210
    Time fuze   AL051C
    Tin Lizzie   DI019C

Gary, Romain
    Decadence   ME0365

Gault, William Campbell
    Fog   CL013C
    Made to measure   GA0140
    Title fight   FA0215

Gehm, Barry
    Home on LaGrange   P00430

Gehman, Richard
    HicKory, dicKory, Kerouac   ME02C1
    HicKory, dicKory, Kerouac   ME0359

Geier, Chester S.
    Environment   CO028C

Genberg, Mort
    IBM   ME0364

Gernsback, Hugo
    Extra sensory perfection   MO032C
    New York A.D. 2660   CL0590
    New York A.D. 2660   CU007C
    New York A.D. 2660   WA013C
    Prophets of doom   SC0300

Gerrano, Rob
    Healing orgy   HA0158
    Song and dance   HA0158

Gerrolo, David
    Alternities [anthology]   GE0150
    Infinity of loving   EL116C
    Love story in three acts   NO04C1
    Science fiction emphasis 1 [anthology]   GE018C
    With a finger in my I   EL0220

Ghidalia, Vic
    Ardroids, time machines, and blue   EL0520
        giraffes [anthology]

Giannattasio, Gerard E.
    Protective temporal strike   NO04C4

Gibson, Walter B.
    Rod Serling's the Twilight zone   SE018C
        [anthology]

Giesy, J.U.
    Palos of the dog star pack   MC040C

Gilbert, D.
    Solfy drink, a saffel fragrance   NE0205

Gilbert, Michael
    One-to-ten affair   WA016C

Godwin, Tom
        Cold equations   AS0651
        Cold equations   EE0205
        Cold equations   CR0102
        Cold equations   DE019C
        Cold equations   DI0160
        Cold equations   CO0100
        Cold equations   HA026C
        Cold equations   JA013C
        Cold equations   KE0100
        Cold equations   OL017C
        Cold equations   SC021C
        Cold equations   WA010C
        Gentle captive   EL1080
        Gentle captive   EL124C
        Greater thing   AL0450
        Last victory   BE0208
        Mother of invention   AM0514
        We'll walk again in the moonlight   EL064C
        You created us   BE0206

Goforth, laura
        Love called this thing   CA034C

Goggin, Richard
        Frances Harkins   CO064C
        Frances Harkins   SA015C

Gohman, Fred
        Flying teacup   FU010C

Gold, H.L.
        Day they got Boston   CO064C
        Day they got Boston   GR0250
        Enormous room   WI0280
        Enormous room   YE0405
        Fifth Galaxy Reader [anthology]   GA0144
        Five galaxy short novels [anthology]   GA0220
        Fourth Galaxy Reader [anthology]   GA0143
        Love in the dark   DA023C
        Love in the dark   HA0232
        Love in the dark   FO0190
        Man of parts   HE0160
        Man of parts   SI0125
        Man with English   CA034C
        Man with English   PO0300
        Man with English   FO033C
        Man with English   PO0371
        Man with English   SI082C
        Matter of form   CO0130
        Matter of form   PO012C
        Matter of form   PO0150
        Mind partner [anthology]   GA025C
        No charge for alterations   WH0175
        Perfect murder   CO037C

Goulart, Ron
    Into the shop   GO015C
    Joker for hire   GO0070
    Junior partner   GO0150
    Katy dialogues   GO0070
    Keeping an eye on Janey   GO0150
    Letters to the editor   MA0192
    Lofthouse   GO0070
    McNamara's fish   MA0203
    Monte Cristo complex   GO0150
    Muscadine   GOCC7C
    Muscadine   MA0208
    New lo!   MA0198
    Ncbody starves   GC0070
    Ncbody starves   NOC2CC
    Nutzenbolts [anthology]   GO0100
    Cdd job no.101   GO013C
    Odd job no.101 [anthology]   GO013C
    Passage to Murdstone   GO013C
    Please stand by   MA0202
    Plumrose   GO013C
    Prez   GO0150
    Princess 22   GO0070
    Rake   MAC2C5
    Recurrent suitor   .   DE0220
    Regarding patient 724   GO013C
    Romance of Dr. Tanner   CA0368
    Stockyard blues   GC01CC
    Stungun Slim   CA0371
    Swap   GC010C
    Terminal   GO0070
    Terminal   ME0366
    To the rescue   GC0070
    Trouble with machines   GO0070
    Two days running and then skip a day   GO0100
    Varieties of religious experience   GO013C
    Way things work   GC013C
    What's become of screwloose?   GO0150
        [anthology]
    What's become of screwloose?   GC015C
    Whistler   EL0180
    Whistler   GO0100
    Whole round world   NO0150
    Yes-men of Venus   GO0150

Govan, Christine Noble
    Miss Winters and the wind   BR0380

Grant, Charles L.
    Crowd of shadows   NE0162
    Eldorado   M00155
    Glow of candles, a unicorn's eye   GR007C
    In Donovan's time   KN0316

Grant, Charles l.
    Magic child   EL0940

Grant, Charles L.
    Rest is silence   NE0160
    Shadows [anthology]   GR004C
    Summer of the Irish Sea   ED0150
    Summer of the Irish sea   KN0311

Grass, Gunter
    In the egg   ME0367

Grasty, William K.
    One afternoon in Busterville   EL1120

Graves, Robert
    Shout   HA0210
    Shout   MA0192

Gray, Will H.
    Bees from Borneo   C0028C

Green, Joseph
    Birdlover   EL106C
    Creators   NE0302
    Death in Coventry   EL066C
    Decision makers   SU015C
    Encounter with a carnivore   SI048C
    First light on a darkling plain NE0319
    Haggard honeymoon   NE0301
    Let my people go!   EL100C
    Single combat   DI0110
    Space to move   EL0940
    Treasure hunt   NE0305
    Waiting world   EL074C

Green, Robert M., Jr.
    Apology to Inky   KN0480
    Apology to Inky   MA0206

Greenberg, Martin Harry
    Coming attractions [anthology] GR013C

Greenberg, Alvin
    "Franz Kafka"   HA0163

Greenberg, Martin Harry
    All about the future [anthology] GR010C
    Anthropology through science fiction MA0550
       [anthology]
    Best of John Jakes [anthology]   JA0070
    City 2000 A.D. [anthology]   CL059C
    Coming attractions   GR0100
    Dawn of time [anthology]   GR014C

Greenberg, Martin Harry
        Five science fiction novels [anthology]   GR016C
        Introductory psychology through science   KA0070
            fiction [anthology]
        Isaac Asimov presents the great science   AS0450
            fiction stories. v. 1, 1939
            [anthology]
        Isaac Asimov presents the great science   AS0452
            fiction stories. v.3, 1941
            [anthology]
        Journey to infinity [anthology]   GR019C
        Men against the stars [anthology]   GR0220
        Mysterious visions [anthology]   WA016C
        Neglected visions [anthology]   MA0465
        100 Great Science Fiction short short   AS0555
            stories [anthology]
        Political science fiction [anthology]   GR025C
        Robot and the man [anthology]   GR028C
        School and society through science   CL0165
            fiction [anthology]
        Science fiction of the forties   PO0293
            [anthology]
        Science fiction: contemporary   WA013C
            mythology [anthology]
        Science fictional solar system   AS0575
            [anthology]
        13 crimes of science fiction   AS0535
            [anthology]
        Time of passage [anthology]   CL017C
        Tomorrow, inc. [anthology]   GRC30C
        Travelers of space [anthology]   GR031C

Greenblatt, Jerome
        Zen archer   DI024C

Greene, Graham
        Discovery in the woods   SA0150
        End of the party   HA0210
        End of the party   KN0450
        End of the party   TE0150
        Little place off the Edgeware Road   WA0160
        Proof positive   MA0330
        Under the garden   DI026C

Greenhough, Terry
        Dcll   WE029C

Greer, William W.
        Quads from Vars   BO030C

Gregor, Lee
        Heavy planet   HEC1CO

Grendon, Edward
    Crisis   C00250
    Figure   AS0340
    Open Sesame   DE0400
    Song of the Pewee   DE04CC
    Trip one   C00160
    Trip one   SL0180

Gresham, W. L.
    Star gypsies   MA0193

Greshnov, M.
    Golden lotus, a legend   GI010C

Gribbin, J.
    Climatic threat   E00240

Griffith, A.W.
    Captive audience   GR0300
    Captive audience   MA0193

Griffith, Ann
    Zeritsky's Law   C0028C

Griffith, G.A.
    Corner in lightning   ME015C
    Corner in lightning   MC0365

Griffiths, George
    Honeymoon in space   AL0510

Grigg, David
    Crippled spinner   HA0158
    Islands   HA0158
    Single changes   HA0158

Grigoriev, Vladimir
    Horn of plenty   GI0130
    My colleague   GI010C
    Vanya   GIC10C

Grimm, Christopher
    Bodyguard   GA0190

Grinnell, David
    Extending the holdings   EE02C2
    Lysenko maze   C004CC
    Lysenko maze   CU007C
    Malice afore thought   ME0260
    Rag thing   AS034C
    Rag thing   C00280
    Top secret   C00250

Gross, Marion
    Good provider   AS034C

Gross, Marion
    Good provider   C00370
    Good provider   KE01CC

Grove, Walt
    John Grant's little angel   PL0150

Groves, J.W.
    Robots don't bleed   CA023C

Grow, Julian F.
    Fastest gun dead   ME0362

Grunert, Karl
    Enemies in space   C00250

Guin, Wyman
    Beyond Bedlam   AM0515
    Beyond Bedlam   GA0140
    Delegate from Guapanga   OL0150
    Man of the Renaissance   SI0121
    My darling Hecate   MA0465
    Trigger tide   C00280
    Volpla   GA0142

Gunn, James E.
    Breaking point   GU010C
    Breaking point [anthology]   GU010C
    Cave of night   AS0645
    Cave of night   GU016C
    Cave of night   ME0356
    Cinderella story   GU010C
    Green thumb   GU0100
    Guilt   AS018C
    Hedonist   GU0160
    Immortals   P00374
    Kindergarten   AS0555
    Listeners   GU0100
    Listeners   NE0154
    Man who owed tomorrow   GU0100
    Medic   GU016C
    Misogynist   GA0141
    Monster named Smith   GU010C
    Mysogynist   HA0234
    Nebula award stories ten [anthology] NE016C
    New blood   GU016C
    Old folks   CA028C
    Old folks   HA0165
    Old folks   N00402
    Power and the glory   GU0100
    Road to science fiction v.1 [anthology] GU0130
    Some dreams are nightmares [anthology] GU016C
    Teddy bear   GU010C
    Wherever you may be   GA022C

Haldeman, Joe W.
    Mind of his own   HA0137
    Private war of Private Jacob   HA0137
    Study war no more [anthology]   HA0145
    Summer's lease   HA0137
    Time piece   DI0110
    Time to live   HA0137
    Time to live   OL0170
    To Howard Hughes: a modest proposal HA0137
    To Howard Hughes: a modest proposal HA0145
    Tricentennial   AN0140
    Tricentennial   HA0137
    Tricentennial   NE0162
    Tricentennial   P00430
    26 days, on earth   HA0137
    We are very happy here   HA0166

Hale, Edward Everett
    Brick moon   M00320

Hale, Robert Beverly
    Immediately yours   ME0362

Halkin, J.
    What d'ye think o' Mother Reilly   DA0273

Hall, A.
    Blind spot   M00400

Hall, Donald
    Wonderful dog suit   ME0365

Hall, Frances
    Message   AN0106

Hall, Graham M.
    Sun push   ME0290
    Tennyson effect   M00165

Hall, Steve
    Round billiard table   NE0302

Hall, William C.
    Medal for Horatius   ST0210

Hallstead, William F. III
    Space Lane Cadet   BC0300

Hamburger, Michael
    Report on a supermarket   ME0290

Hamilton, Alex
    Words of warning   HA0165

Hamiltcn, Edmond
    Accursed galaxy   AS0170
    Accursed galaxy   HA0155
    After a judgement day   HA0155
    Alien earth   EL048C
    Alien earth   HA0155
    Best of Edmond Hamilton [anthology] HA0155
    Castaway   HA0155
    Child of the winds   HA0155
    Ccnquest of two worlds   HA0155
    Ccnquest of two worlds   WC0240
    Day of judgement   HA0155
    Dead planet   DE059C
    Dead planet   MC0290
    Devolution   ASC17C
    Easy money   HA0155
    Exile   HA0155
    Exile   LEC220
    Fessenden's worlds   DE037C
    Fessenden's worlds   HA0155
    Forgotten world   MA048C
    He that hath wings   HA0155
    In the world's dusk   HA0155
    In the world's dusk   WC0210
    Iron one   EL108C
    Island of unreason   HA0155
    Kaldar, World of Antares   W00360
    Kingdoms of the stars   CA0320
    Man who evolved   AS0170
    Man who evolved   HA0155
    Man who returned   HA0155
    Man who saw the future   MC038C
    Pro   CI0220
    Pro   HA0155
    Reguiem   MC0350
    Requiem   ELC84C
    Requiem   HA0155
    Seeds from outside   HA0155
    Star of life   AL0510
    Sunfire   R00240
    Thundering worlds   HA0155
    What's is like out there?   HA0155
    What's it like out there?   CA034C
    What's it like out there?   KN016C
    What's it like out there?   SI052C
    What's it like out there?   ST0180

Hamilton-Peterson, J.
    Teddysaurs   CA027C

Hamm, Thelma
    Native son   DE016C

Haney, Laura
    To the mountains   CL0110

Hanks, R.
>   City that loves you   MC0280

Hannigan, D.F.
>   Old Doctor Rutherford   MO0365

Harding, Lee
>   Altered I [anthology]   HA0158
>   Dancing Gerontius   BA0240
>   Evidence   BA0235
>   Liberators   NE0305
>   Night of passage   DA0272
>   Quest   CA0210
>   Rooms of paradise [anthology]   HA0159

Hargreaves, H.A.
>   Dead to the world   WI0210
>   Tee Vee Man   CA0210

Harmon, David P.
>   Piece of the action   ST0164

Harmon, Jim
>   Name your symptom   GA0143
>   Place where Chicago was   GA0149
>   Place where Chicago was   MC0280

Harmon, Seth
>   Moon gold   FU0100

Harned, Theresa
>   Hideous splotch of purple   AS0175

Harness, Charles L.
>   Bookmobile   OL0165
>   Chess-players   WI0210
>   Chessplayers   CO0490
>   Child by chronos   MA0193
>   New reality   BE0201
>   New reality   SI0127
>   New reality   SU0150
>   Ornament to his profession   KN0480
>   Ornament to his profession   ME0367
>   Paradox men   AL0510
>   Probable cause   KN0304
>   Time trap   SI0120

Harper, Richard
>   Samaritan   BO0300

Harper, Ron
>   Samaritan   EN0100

Harris, C.W.
>   Baby on Neptune   WO0270

Harris, John Benyon
    John Wyndham Omnibus [anthology]   WY0180
    Lost machine   RO024C
    Never on Mars   CA017C
    Time to rest   DEC4CC

Harris, Larry M.
    Mex   FA0215

Harris-Burland, J.B.
    Lord Beden's motor   MO0365

Harrison, Harry
    According to his abilities   HA027C
    Ac Astra   BE0300
    Alien agony   AL045C
    All about Venus [anthology]   AL031C
    American dead   HAC3CC
    Apeman, spaceman [anthology]   STU21C
    Astounding [anthology]   AS075C
    Astounding analog reader. V.1   AS065C
        [anthology]
    Astounding analog reader. V.2   AS0651
        [anthology]
    Best SF: 1967 [anthology]   HA016C
    Best SF: 1968 [anthology]   HA0161
    Best SF: 1969 [anthology]   HA0162
    Best SF: 1970 [anthology]   HA0163
    Best SF: 1971 [anthology]   HA0164
    Best SF: 1972 [anthology]   HA0165
    Best SF: 1973 [anthology]   HA0166
    Best SF: 1974 [anthology]   HA0167
    Best SF: 1975 the ninth annual   HA0168
        [anthology]
    Brave newer world   FO013C
    By the falls   HA0233
    By the falls   NE0156
    Captain Bedlam   HA027C
    Captain Honario Harpplayer, R.N.   CL010C
    Captain Honario Harpplayer, R.N.   HA0270
    Captain Honario Harpplayer, R.N.   MA0203
    Commando raid   HA0145
    Decade, the 1940's [anthology]   AL040C
    Decade, the 1950's [anthology]   AL0401
    Decade, the 1960's [anthology]   AL0402
    Ever-branching tree   OL0165
    Final encounter   AL0411
    Final encounter   GA0147
    Final encounter   HA027C
    Four for the future [anthology]   HA0200
    From fanaticism, or for reward   HA022C
    Ghoul squad   HA020C
    Gods themselves throw incense   HA020C
    Greening of the green   PR0160
    Heavy duty   HA022C

Harrison, Harry

How the old world died	GA0148
I always do what Teddy says	DI0240
I always do what Teddy says	HA027C
I always do what Teddy says	SA0210
I have my vigil	HO012C
I have my vigil	MA0208
If	HA026C
If	HA029C
Life preservers	HA022C
Light fantastic [anthology]	HA021C
Make room! make room!	SC0250
Mothballed spaceship	AS0750
Nebula award stories two [anthology]	NE0152
No war, or battle's sound	DI011C
No war, or battle's sound	HA022C
Nova 1 [anthology]	NO0401
Nova 2 [anthology]	NO0402
Nova 3 [anthology]	NO0403
Nova 4 [anthology]	NO0404
One step from earth	HA0220
One step from earth [anthology]	HA022C
Pliable animal	HA027C
Portrait of the artist	EL0210
Portrait of the artist	HA027C
Powers of observation	AN0108
Pressure	HA022C
Pressure	SI0940
Rescue operation	AS0651
Rescue operation	HA027C
Rescue operation	MC0400
Rock diver	FO0190
Rock diver	SI0420
Roommates	DI0250
Roommates	MC0400
Run from the fire	SI0480
Science fiction novellas [anthology]	HA025C
Science fiction reader [anthology]	HA026C
SF: authors' choice 2 [anthology]	HA0232
SF: authors' choice 3 [anthology]	HA0233
SF: authors' choice 4 [anthology]	HA0234
Space rats of the C.C.C.	FE0170
Space rats of the C.C.C.	ST022C
Streets of Ashkelon	HA025C
Streets of Ashkelon	HA027C
Streets of Ashkelon	SI0380
Streets of Ashkelon	WA01C0
Tale of the ending	HA0220
Tale of the ending	HA022C
Toy shop	ME0363
Trainee for Mars	DC013C
Two tales and eight tomorrows [anthology]	HA027C
Unto my manifold dooms	HA027C
Velvet glove	AS007C

Harrison, Harry
    Velvet glove   FA0215
    Velvet glove   SA018C
    Waiting place   HA0220
    Wicked flee   BE029C
    Wicked flee   NE0201
    Wife to the lord   HA0220
    Worlds of wonder [anthology]   HA0290
    Year 2000 [anthology]   HA03CC

harrison, M. John
    Baa baa blocksheep   M00166
    Lamia mutable   EL022C
    Running down   DI0260
    Settling the world   DI024C
    Settling the world   HA0168

Harrison, William
    Roller ball murder   HA0166

Hart, Ellis
    Mourners for hire   EL036C

Hartmann, Gregor
    On the road   RY010C
    Sun-1   NE0203

Hartridge, Jon
    Like father   HA0162

Harvey, Frank
    Death dust   SA027C

Hasford, Gustav
    Heartland   KN0316

Hasse, Henry
    Eyes   FO010C
    He who shrank   AS017C
    He who shrank   HE010C

Hatcher, Jack
    Fuel for the future   GR013C

Haverkos, L.S.
    Error in punctuation   DE0267

Hawkins, Peter
    Circus   CA0170
    Life cycle   CA020C

Hawkins, R.L.
    Simple outside job   AS0173

Heinlein, Robert A.

And he built a crooked house	CA0255
And he built a crooked house	CL0500
And he built a crooked house	HE0220
And he built a crooked house	HE0420
And he built a crooked house	KA0070
And he built a crooked house	SI0740
Ard he built a crooked house	SU0150
Assignment in eternity [anthology]	HE0190
Best of Robert Heinlein [anthology]	HE0220
Beyond doubt	POC190
Black pits of Luna	CO0340
Black pits of Luna	GA0370
Black pits of Luna	HE0250
Black pits of Luna	HE0340
Black pits of Luna	SI0940
Blowups happen	AS0700
Blowups happen	CR0101
Blowups happen	HE0340
Blowups happen	HE0440
By his bootstraps	AM0510
By his bootstraps	CA0255
By his bootstraps	HE0310
By his bootstraps	MA0480
Columbus was a dope	AS0340
Columbus was a dope	HA0100
Columbus was a dope	HE0310
Columbus was a dope	PO0295
Coventry	CO0670
Coventry	HE0340
Coventry	KN0120
Delilah and the space-rigger	HE0250
Delilah and the space-rigger	HE0340
Destination moon	MA0485
Elsewhen	HE0190
Feline	HE0340
Free men	HE0440
Gentlemen, be seated	HE0250
Gentlemen, be seated	HE0340
Goldfish bowl	HE0310
Goldfish bowl	ST0210
Green hills of earth	AL0665
Green hills of earth	HE0220
Green hills of earth	HE0250
Green hills of earth	HE0340
Green hills of earth	HE0350
Green hills of earth	SA0150
Green hills of earth	SA0270
Green hills of earth [anthology]	HE0250
Gulf	HE0190
Gulf	KN0130
It's great to be back	CO0730
It's great to be back	HE0250
It's great to be back	HE0340
It's great to be back	KN0190

Heinlein, Robert A.

It's great to be back	P00293
Jerry was a man	HE0190
L-5 society	P00430
Life-line	AS0450
Lifeline	HE0220
Lifeline	HE0340
Lifeline	HE0440
Logic of empire	HE0250
Logic of empire	HE0340
Long watch	DE0370
Long watch	HE0220
Long watch	HE0250
Long watch	HE0340
Long watch	SC0300
Lost legacy	HE0190
Magic, Inc.	HE0370
Magic, Inc.	HE0430
Man who sold the moon	E00151
Man who sold the moon	HE0220
Man who sold the moon	HE028C
Man who sold the moon	HE0340
Man who sold the moon	HE0350
Man who sold the moon [anthology]	HE0280
Man who traveled in elephants	HE0420
Menace from earth	AS0590
Menace from earth	HE0310
Menace from earth	HE0340
Menace from earth	MC0280
Menace from earth [anthology]	HE0310
Methuselah's children	HE0340
Misfit	AS0450
Misfit	C00160
Misfit	HE0340
Ordeal in space	HE0250
Ordeal in space	HE0340
Ordeal in space	KN0630
Ordeal in space	WI0206
Our fair city	HE0420
Our fair city	ME0230
Past through tomorrow [anthology]	HE0340
Pottage	MA0195
Pottage	ME0356
Project nightmare	HE0310
Puppet masters	HE0370
"Let there be light"	HE0230
Requiem	HE0100
Requiem	HE0170
Requiem	HE0280
Requiem	HE0340
Requiem	JA0130
Roads must roll	FI0095
Roads must roll	HE0100
Roads must roll	HE0220
Roads must roll	HE0280

Henderson, Zenna
    Angels unawares   HE0490
    Anything box [anthology]   HE0460
    Ararat   BE0203
    Ararat   EN0100
    Ararat   WI0203
    Captivity   MA0198
    Captivity   WI0280
    Come on, wagon!   HE0460
    Come on, wagon!   MA0192
    Deluge   HE0490
    Deluge   MA0203
    Food to all flesh   CR0102
    Food to all flesh   CR0170
    Food to all flesh   HE0460
    Gilead   AS0590
    Grunder   HE0460
    Hush!   HE0460
    Jordan   MA0330
    Last step   HE0490
    No different flesh   HE0490
    No different flesh   MA0205
    People: no different flesh [anthology] HE0490
    Pottage   CL0165
    Return   HE0490
    Shadow on the moon   HE0490
    Something bright   DE0160
    Something bright   GA0146
    Something bright   HE0460
    Something bright   ME0361
    Stevie and the dark   HE0460
    Subcommittee   HE0460
    Subcommittee   ME0363
    Substitute   HE0460
    There was a garden   LA0160
    Things   CC0760
    Things   HE0460
    Troubling of the water   HE0490
    Turn the page   HE0460
    Walking Aunt Daid   HE0460
    Wilderness   ME0358

Henneberg, Charles
    Blind pilot   MA0200

Henneberg, Nathalie- Charles
    Ysolde   WO0150

Henri, Adrian.
    Galactic love poem. 2 [poem]   BE0500

Henry, O. [pseud. of William Sidney Porters]
    Roads of destiny   PR0150

Hensel, C.F.
    Harriet   EL1200

Hensel, C.T.
    Nor iron bars a cage   GO0030

Hensley, Joe L.
    Argent blood   AS0555
    In dark places   CL0590
    In dark places   EL0720
    Lord Randy, my son   EL0300
    Midnight bicyclist   RY0100
    Pair   DI0110
    Rodney Parish for hire   EL0440
    Shut the last door   MC0150

Herbert, Frank
    A-W-F unlimited   CO0640
    Book of Frank Herbert [anthology]   HE0520
    Cease fire   KN0160
    Come to the party   WO0419
    Death of a city   EL0720
    Encounter in a lonely place   HE0520
    Featherbedders   AN0107
    Gambling device   HE0520
    Gone dogs   HE0520
    Greenslaves   CH0100
    Looking for something?   HE0520
    Mary Celeste move   AN0104
    Mating call   CO0720
    Murder will in   FI0100
    Nightmare blues   BE0205
    Nothing   HE0520
    Occupation force   HE0520
    Operation syndrome   HE0520
    Passage for piano   HE0520
    Primitives   GA0149
    Rat race   HE0520
    Seed stock   HE0520
    Tactful saboteur   CO0610
    Try to remember   RO0240

Herbst, Steve
    Creation of a future world in The   KN0313
        Tracer
    Magic passes   CL0110
    Old soul   KN0311
    Uneven evening   ED0150
    Uneven evening   HA0164

Hernhuter, Albert
    Texas week   AS0340

Herodotus
    Amazons   MO0410

Hoch, Edward D.
        Bcy who brought love   EL064C
        Computer cops   SA018C
        Forbidden word   WA016C
        Last paradox   AS0555
        Night of the millennium   EL100C
        Wclfram hunters   EL056C
        Zoo   AS0555

Hockett, Charles F.
        Hcw to learn Martian   GR013C

Hodgins, Roderic C.
        History of Doctor Frost   MA02C5

Hodgson, William Hope
        Derelect   CO046C
        Noise in the night   DE037C
        Vcice in the night   MC0365
        Wild man of the sea   DE056C

Hodous, Mike
        Dead end   AN0107

Hoffmar, Lee
        Lost in the marigolds   KN0309
        Soundless evening   EL022C

Hogan, James P.
        Assassin   DE0268
        Assassin   DE0275

Holberg, Lewis
        Tree men of Potee   DE037C

Holberg, Ludvig
        Jcurney to the world uncerground   GU013C
            [excerpt]

Holding, Elisabeth S.
        Strange children   WA016C

Holdstcck, Robert P.
        Travellers   WE029C

Hollancer, John
        Great bear [poem]   SA015C

Hollis, H.H.
        Stoned counsel   EL022C
        Sword game   NE0154
        Sword game   W00409

Hollister, Bernard C.
        Another tomorrow [anthology]   HC010C

Howard, Robert E.
    Black stone   H00280
    Blood-stained God   HC0250
    Cairn on the headland   H00280
    Coming of Conan [anthology]   H0016C
    Conan the adventurer [anthology]   H00190
    Conan the warrior   H00220
    Conan the warrior [anthology]   H00220
    Drums of tombalker   H0019C
    Fire of Asshurbanipal   H00280
    Flame knife   H00250
    Frost-giant's daughter   H00160
    God in the bowl   H00160
    Hawks over Shem   H0025C
    Horror from the mound   H00280
    House of Arabu   H00280
    Hyborian age   HC016C
    Informal biography of Conan the   H00160
        Cimmerian
    Jewels of Gwahlur   H0022C
    King and the oak   HCC16C
    Mirrors of Tuzun   HC016C
    People of the black circle   H00190
    Pool of the black one   H00190
    Queen of the Black Coast   H0016C
    Red Nails   HC022C
    Road of the eagles   H00250
    Rogues in the house   H00160
    Shadow kingdom   H00160
    Slithering Shadow   HC019C
    Tales of Conan [anthology]   HC0250
    Tower of the elephant   H00160
    Valley of the worm   HC028C
    Wolfshead [anthology]   H00280

Howell, Joseph
    Transition trolley   EL106C

Hoyle, Fred
    A for Andromeda [Selections]   BR0520
    Agent 38   HC0310
    Ax   H00310
    Black cloud   BR0520
    Black cloud   F0024C
    Blackmail   HA016C
    Blackmail   H00310
    Cattle trucks   H00310
    Element 79 [anthology]   H00310
    Judgment of Aphrodite   H00310
    Jury of five   H00310
    Magnetosphere   H00310
    Martians   H00310
    Operation   H00310
    Play's the thing   H00310
    Pym makes his point   H00310

Hyde, Gavin
    Sparkie's fall   PO0330

Hyne, C.J.C.
    Lizard   ME0150

Ibraghimbekov, M.
    Santo di Chavez   SH0150

If [magazine]
    If reader of science fiction   IF0100
    [anthology]

Imbert, Enrique Anderson
    Legends from "The Chesire Cat"   DI0230

Ing, D.
    Devil you don't know   CA0238
    Malf   BO0240

Inglis, James
    Night watch   AL0480
    Night watch   NE0303

Ionesco, Eugene
    Flying high   ME0358
    Rhinoceros   WH0150

Irving, Washington
    Conquest by the moon   RO0210
    Men of the moon   FR0070

Irwin, Margaret
    Earlier service   MA0192

Isaacs, Linda
    Many splendored thing   AS0172

Isherwood, Christopher
    I am waiting   BR0380

Ivanov, Vsevolod
    Sisyphus, the son of Aeolus   RO0270

Jackson, A.A
    Sun up   DA0140

Jackson, Clive
    Swordsman of Varnis   BR0460

Jackson, Shirley
    Beautiful stranger   DI0260
    Bulletin   MA0194
    Demon lover   BR0380
    Omen   MA0198

Jackson, Shirley
    One ordinary day, with peanuts   KN0480
    One ordinary day, with peanuts   MA0195
    One ordinary day, with peanuts   ME0201
    One ordinary day, with peanuts   ME0356

Jacobi, Carl
    Gentleman is an EPWA   DE059C
    Street that wasn't there   CA0260
    Tepondicon   DE040C
    Unpleasantness at Carver house   DE056C
    White pinnacle   DE053C

Jacobs, Harvey
    Dress rehearsal   BE03CC
    Egg of the Glak   MA0208
    Girl who drew the gods   ME0366
    Gravity   AL04C2
    Gravity   MO0166
    In seclusion   ME0367
    In seclusion   MO0164

Jacobs, Sylvia
    Pilot and the Bushman   GA014C

Jaffray, Norman R.
    Cowboy Lament   MA0194

Jakes, John
    Best of John Jakes [anthology]   JA007C
    Here is thy sting   JA007C
    Here is thy sting   KN0303
    Highest form of life   JACC7C
    Love is a punch in the nose   JA007C
    Machine   BE0203
    Machine   JA007C
    On wheels   JA007C
    One race show   JAC07C
    Political machine   JA007C
    Ranging   EL02CC
    Ranging   ENC1CC
    Recidivism preferred   JA0C7C
    Sellers of the dream   AM0513
    Sellers of the dream   GR0300
    Sellers of the dream   JA007C
    Stranger with roses   EL1100
    There's no vinism like Chauvinism   JA007C

Jakubowski, Maxim
    Science fiction story for Joni
        Mitchell   J00150

James, Clive
    Rise of airstrip one   HA0167

James, D.L.
    Moon of delirium   CO0340

James, E.R.
    Emergency working   CA0200
    Six-fingered jacks   WI0204

James, Lawrence
    You get lots of yesterdays, lots of   NE0326
       tomorrows, and only one today

James, P.D.
    Murder, 1986   WA0160

Jameson, Malcolm
    Admiral's inspection   JA0100
    Alien envoy   WO0390
    Blind alley   LE0130
    Blind man's buff   EL0100
    Blind man's buff   DI0130
    Blockade runner   JA0100
    Brimstone bill   JA0100
    Bullard of the space patrol [anthology] JA0100
    Bullard reflects   BO0151
    Bullard reflects   CA0277
    Bullard reflects   JA0100
    Bureaucrat   JA0100
    Hobo god   GR0100
    Lillies of life   CO0340
    Orders   JA0100
    Pride   ME0230
    Sorcerer's apprentice   CO0310
    Space war tactics   GR0130
    Tricky tonnage   HA0290
    White mutiny   JA0100

Janifer, Laurence M. [pseud. of Larry Mark Harris]
    Amfortas   EL0980
    Bible after Apocalypse   NE0204
    Civis Obit   EL0660
    Elementary   PR0210
    Few minutes   EL1160
    Fire sale   AS0555
    Gift   EL0660
    Master's choice [anthology]   JA0130
    Question   AS0555
    Story time   EL0800
    Thine alabaster cities gleam   EL0720

Janner, C.R.
    Tumithak in Shawm   AS0170
    Tumithak of the corridors   AS0170

Janvier, Ivan.
    Things   EE0206

Johnson, Robert Barbour
    Far below   MC026C

Johnson, S.S.
    House by the crab apple tree   MA0204
    House by the crab apple tree   SA010C

Johnston, G.
    Vale, Polline!   BA024C

Jonas, Gerald
    Imagination numbers in a real garden   MA0206
       [poem]
    Shaker revival   DI0250
    Shaker revival   MI0180
    Shaker revival   SI0121
    Shaker revival   WC0411

Jones, A.E.
    Created he them   MA0195

Jones, Elis Gwyn
    When the engines had to stop   wI0204

Jones, Langdon
    Biographical note on Ludwig van   MC0165
       Beethoven II
    Coming of the sun   HA0233
    Eye of the lens   MO0166
    Great clock   MO0163
    Hall of machines   ME0290
    New s.f. [anthology]   J0015C
    Time machine   KN010C
    Time machine   KN0305
    Transient   MO0164

Jones, LeRoi
    Planetary exchange [poem]   SA015C

Jones, N.R.
    Hermit of Saturn's ring   WO027C
    Jameson satellite   AS017C

Jones, Raymond F.
    Bowl of Biskies makes a growing boy EL100C
    Correspondence course   HE010C
    Discontinuity   CO058C
    Doomsday's color-press   HO013C
    Farthest horizon   NO027C
    Farthest horizon   SL021C
    Flauna   EL0680
    Gift of the gods   EL0840
    Laughing lion   EL1040
    Lions of Rome   EL070C
    Noise level   AM0514

Keller, David H., M.D.
 Folsom flint [anthology]   KE007C
 Golden key   KE0070
 Landslide   KE007C
 Living machine   W0024C
 Pent house   KE0070
 Piece of linoleum   KE007C
 Psychophonic nurse   C0019C
 Question   KE007C
 Red death   KE007C
 Revolt of the pedestrians   DE0370
 Sarah   KE0070
 Service first   DE047C
 Thing in the cellar   KE007C
 Twins   KE007C
 Unto us a child is born   KE007C
 White city   KE007C
 Worm   CA026C
 Worm   RC0240

Keller, Teddy
 Plague   AN01C1
 Plague   CA0100

Kelley, Leo P.
 Teaching prime   OL0165
 Themes in science fiction [anthology] KE01CC
 Travelin' man   KE0100

Kelly, J.P.
 Death therapy   CA0238

Kennedy, X.J.
 Space: for Martin Green [poem] SA015C

Kent, Morgan
 Family portrait   ME0365

Kepler, Johannes
 Moon-voyage   EV01CC
 Somnium   DE037C
 Somnium, or lunar astronomy [excerpt] GU0130

Kerr, David
 Epiphany for aliens   EL022C

Kerr, Walter H.
 Treat [poem]   MA02C5

Kersh, Gerald
 Bargain with Cashel   ME0364
 Copper Dahlia   CR01C1
 River of riches   ME0359
 Somewhere not far from here ME0366
 Unsafe deposit box   HA021C

Kersh, Gerald
    Unsafe deposit box   ME0363
    Unsafe deposit box   SA027C
    Whatever happened to Corporal Cuckoo?   KN0280
    Whatever happened to Corporal Cuckoo?   PO030C
    Whatever happened to Corporal Cuckoo?   PC0330
    Whatever happened to Corporal Cuckoo?   PO0373

Kessel, J.
    Silver man   RY010C

Kevles, Bettyann
    Mars-station   FU0130

Keyes, Daniel
    Crazy Maro   MA020C
    Flowers for Algernon   AS037C
    Flowers for Algernon   CR0103
    Flowers for Algernon   FI009C
    Flowers for Algernon   KA007C
    Flowers for Algernon   MA0199
    Flowers for Algernon   ME036C
    Flowers for Algernon   SC021C
    Quality of mercy   FR010C

Keyes, Thom
    Period of gestation   MC0164

Kidd, Virginia
    Abendlandes   EL072C
    Ascension: a workday arabesque [poem]   MC0150
    Cholo M   EL112C
    Flowering season   HO0110
    Kangaroo court   KN0301
    Millenial women [anthology]   KI007O
    On the wall of the lodge   SI0380
    Saving worlds [anthology]   EL1020

Killough, Lee
    Cup of hemlock   AS0555
    Tropic of Eden   CA0237

Kimberly, Gail
    Fire fountain   EL0581
    Lady beautiful   EL0840
    Many mansions   EL070C
    Minna in the night sky   EL068O
    Peace, love, and food for the hungry   EL1000
    Where summer song rings hollow   EL066O

King, Marshall
    Beach scene   ME0361

King, S.
    Nona   GR0040

King, Vincent
    Defense mechanism   NE0307
    Defense mechanism   NE0309
    Discontent contingency   NE0319
    Geraniums   EL098C

Kingsbury, D.
    To bring in the steel   CA0238

Kingsbury, Donald
    Shipwright   CA0241
    To bring in the steel   PO043C

Kingston, John
    Manipulation   NE0303

Kinsolving, M.R.
    Walls   EL114C

Kipling, Rudyard
    As easy as A.B.C.   SA015C
    Brushwood boy   KN045C
    Easy as A.B.C.   CO0460
    Easy as A.B.C.   CO064C
    Finest story in the world   HA021C
    Finest story in the world   PR015O
    MacDonough's Song   CO0640
    Mark of the beast   PR015O
    Wireless   LO010C
    With the night mail   EL124C
    With the night mail   GU013C
    With the night mail   HO0119
    With the night mail   KN023C

Kippax, John
    Dusty death   WI0202
    Friday   WI02C1

Kirby, Jack
    Forever people   AL0650

Kirkland, Jack
    Wall of fire   MO026C

Kirkup, James
    Tea in a space-ship   MA0470

Kirs, Alex
    Better than ever   ME0366

Kita, N.
    Empty field   EL0980

Klass, Morton
    In the beginning   ST0210

Klass, Morton
    Kappa nu nexus   CO0720

Klein, Gerard
    Party line   W00150
    Valley of echoes   R00270

Klein, Sidney
    Teeth of despair   CO0490

Klein, T.E.D.
    Renaissance man   DA0271

Kline, Otis Adelbert
    Stolen centuries   M00260
    Vision of Venus   W00330

Kline, T.F.
    Space poem   BA0240

Kneale, Nigel
    Jeremy in the wind   BR0380

Knight, Damon
    Anachron   KN0070
    Anachron   KN0250
    Analogues   CE0100
    Analogues   KN0070
    Ancient madness   GA0148
    Ask me anything   GA0140
    Auto-Da-Fe   GA0149
    Auto-Da-Fe   KN0600
    Babel II   KN0070
    Babel II   KN0250
    Babel II   MI0150
    Babel II   SI0580
    Backward, o time   KN0070
    Backward, o time   KN0600
    Best of Damon Knight [anthology]   KN0070
    Best stories from Orbit, v.1-10   KN0100
        [anthology]
    Beyond tomorrow [anthology]   KN0120
    Big pat boom   GA0146
    Big pat boom   KN0070
    Big pat boom   KN0600
    Cabin boy   AS0590
    Cabin boy   CO0220
    Cabin boy   GA0140
    Cabin boy   KN0070
    Cabin boy   KN0250
    Catch that Martian   CO0280
    Catch that Martian   SI0600
    Century of great short science fiction KN0130
        novels [anthology]
    Century of science fiction [anthology] KN0160

Knight, Damon

Knight, Damon
Man in the jar	KN007C
Man in the jar	KN0600
Mary	DOO17C
Mary	KN007C
Mary	KN0600
Masks	KN007C
Masks	KN046C
Masks	SI0380
Masks	SUC15C
Masks	WA0130
Masks	WC04C9
Natural state	GA031C
Natural state	GRO1CC
Natural state	KN0470
Natural state	KN051U
Natural state	MC028C
Nebula award stories, 1965 [anthology]	NE0151
Night of lies	KN060C
Not with a bang	AS034C
Not with a bang	CA034C
Not with a bang	C00130
Not with a bang	KN007C
Not with a bang	KN025C
On the wheel	NC0402
One hundred years of science fiction [anthology]	KN028C
Orbit 1 [anthology]	KN03C1
Orbit 2 [anthology]	KN0302
Orbit 3 [anthology]	KN0303
Orbit 4 [anthology]	KN0304
Orbit 5 [anthology]	KN0305
Orbit 6 [anthology]	KN0306
Orbit 7 [anthology]	KN0307
Orbit 8 [anthology]	KN0308
Orbit 9 [anthology]	KN0309
Orbit 10 [anthology]	KN031C
Orbit 11 [anthology]	KN0311
Orbit 12 [anthology]	KN0312
Orbit 13 [anthology]	KN0313
Orbit 14 [anthology]	KN0314
Orbit 15 [anthology]	KN0315
Orbit 16 [anthology]	KN0316
Orbit 17 [anthology]	KN0317
Orbit 18 [anthology]	KN0318
Orbit 19 [anthology]	KN0319
Orbit 20 [anthology]	KN0320
Perchance to dream [anthology]	KN0450
Pocketful of stars [anthology]	KN046C
Rule golden	C007CC
Rule golden	HA0145
Rule golden	KN047C
Rule golden	KN051C
Rule golden [anthology]	KNC47C
Science fiction argosy [anthology]	KNC48C

Knight, Damon
       Second-class citizen   STO21C
       Semper Fi   KN0070
       Semper Fi   KN0600
       Shall the dust praise thee?   AS0555
       Shall the dust praise thee?   EL03CC
       Shall the dust praise thee?   MO0100
       Shocking thing [anthology]   KN0490
       Special delivery   CO0310
       Special delivery   KNC07C
       Special delivery   KN0220
       Stranger station   AL065C
       Stranger station   AM0513
       Stranger station   CHC1CC
       Stranger station   ME0357
       Stranger station   SI044C
       They say   KN0319
       Thing of beauty   GA0145
       Thing of beauty   KN0070
       Thing of beauty   KNC25C
       Three novels   KN051C
       Ticket to anywhere   KC016C
       Ticket to anywhere   SIO4CC
       Tiger ride   F00293
       Tiger ride   PR021C
       Time enough   KN007C
       Time enough   KN0250
       To serve man   EE02C1
       To serve man   HA013C
       To serve man   KN007C
       To serve man   KN025C
       To the pure   KNC6CC
       Tomorrow and tomorrow [anthology]   KN0540
       Tomorrow x 4 [anthology]   KN057C
       Toward infinity [antholcgy]   KN0580
       Turning on [anthology]   KNC6CC
       What rough beast?   MA0199
       World without children   GA022C
       Worlds to come [anthology]   KNC630
       You're another   KN025C
       You're another   MA0195
       You're another   MC018C

Knight, David C.
       Amazing Mrs. Mimms   FA0215

Knight, N.L.
       Crisis in Utopia   GR016C

Koch, Howard
       Invasion from inner space   PC0376
       Invasion from Mars   CHO1CC
       Invasion from Mars   CO025C
       Invasion from Mars   SA0150

Kornbluth, Cyril M.

Gomez	KN0540
Gomez	KC0070
Gomez	K00100
Goodly creatures	K00100
I never ast no favors	MA0194
Kazam collects	CA0420
Kazam collects	KC0130
Kazam collects	F00293
Last man left in the bar	K00070
Last man left in the bar	KC0130
Last man left in the bar	SI0120
Little black bag	AS0651
Little black bag	CL0500
Little black bag	C00190
Little black bag	K00070
Little black bag	KC0130
Little black bag	F00120
Little black bag	P00190
Little black bag	SC0210
Luckiest man in Denv	KN0190
Luckiest man in Denv	K00070
Luckiest man in Denv	MC0280
Luckiest man in Denv	SI0126
Luckiest man in Denv	WA0130
Make mine Mars	K00130
Make mine Mars	K00160
Marching morons	AL0650
Marching morons	AM0513
Marching morons	BE0202
Marching morons	K00070
Marching morons	SC0211
Meddlers	K00130
Meddlers	K00130
Meeting	AS0401
Meeting	BE0291
Mile beyond the moon	K00130
Mile beyond the moon [anthology]	K00130
Mindworm	BE0201
Mindworm	KN0280
Mindworm	KC0070
Mindworm	KC0100
Mindworm	SI0660
Ms found in a chinese fortune cookie	AL0450
Ms found in a chinese fortune cookie	MA0197
Mute inglorious Tam	BE0300
Nightmare with Zeppelins	CA0144
Only thing we learn	C00130
Only thing we learn	K00070
Passion pills	KC0130
Passions pills	K00130
Quaker cannon	ME0362
Quaker cannon	PR0210
Remorseful	KC0070
Remorseful	P00372

Kornbluth, Cyril M.
    Rocket of 1955   AS0452
    Rocket of 1955   AS0555
    Rocket of 1955   CE010C
    Rocket of 1955   K00070
    Rocket of 1955   K0010C
    Shark ship   K00070
    Shark ship   K0013C
    Shark ship   KC013C
    Shark ship   SA030C
    Shark ship   SC0250
    Shark ship   SI038C
    Silly season   FE023C
    Silly season   HE04CC
    Silly season   K00070
    Silly season   SI060C
    Slave   KC013C
    Slave   KC013C
    That share of glory   DI013C
    That share of glory   KN063C
    That share of glory   KC01C0
    That share of glory   N0033C
    That share of glory   SI0121
    Theory of rocketry   JA013C
    Theory of rocketry   MA0193
    Thirteen o'clock   K0010C
    Thirteen o'clock   KCC1CC
    Time bum   K0013C
    Time bum   K00160
    Time travel and the law   GR013C
    Two dooms   K0C070
    Two dooms   KCC13C
    Two dooms   K00130
    Virginia   K00130
    Virginia   K00160
    With these hands   BL021C
    With these hands   CU0070
    With these hands   D0013C
    With these hands   K00070
    With these hands   KCC1CC
    With these hands   MC0155
    With these hands   SI0125
    Words of Guru   AS0452
    Words of Guru   K0C07C
    Words of Guru   K0013C
    Words of Guru   TE015C
    World of Myrion Flowers   DE0250
    World of Myrion Flowers   KE01CC
    World of Myrion Flowers   KE010C

Kornbluth, Mary
    Science fiction showcase [anthology]   K00160

Krapivin, Vladislav
    Meeting my brother   PA0210

Krapivin, Vladislav
    Meeting my brother [I'm going to meet   MC0150
       my brother]

Krepps, Robert W.
    Enormous room   WI0280
    Enormous room   YE0405
    Five years in the marmalade   BE0200
    Five years in the marmalade   BL0120

Kress, Nancy
    Delicate shade of Kipney   AS0440

Kruse, Clifton B.
    Dr. Lu-Mie   W0024C

Kubilius, Walter
    Other side   BE0202
    Second chance   SL0180

Kuebler, Harold W.
    Treasury of science fiction classics   KU0100

Kummer, Frederic Arnold Jr.
    Forgiveness of Tenchu Taen   GR0310

Kummer, Frederic Arnold, Jr.
    When time went mad   F00295

Kunitz, Stanley
    Flight of Apollo [poem]   SA0150

Kupferberg, Tuli
    Cinemagicians   ME0367
    Personal   ME0367
    Personal   SU0150
    W-A-V-E-R   ME0367

Kurland, Michael
    Best of Avram Davidson [anthology]   DA0235
    Elementary   PR0210
    Small world   SC0460
    Think only this of me   BE0299
    Think only this of me   SI0127

Kurosaka, Bob
    Those who can, do   ME0366

Kurosaka, Robert T.
    Lot to learn   AS0555

Kuttner, Henry
    Absalom   HE0400
    Absalom   R00180
    Absalom   WH0150

Kuttner, Henry

Ahead of time [anthology]	KU0130
Beauty and the beast	CA0260
By these presents	KU0130
Camouflage	KU0130
Children's hour	B00150
Cold war	C00400
Cross of centuries	MC0100
Cross of centuries	P00300
Cross of centuries	P00330
Cross of centuries	P00374
Cure	KN0480
De profundis	KU0130
Deadlock	KU0130
Don't look now	JA0130
Don't look now	F00293
Dream's end	CR0230
Dream's end	KN0450
Ego machine	BR0460
Gallegher plus	HA0130
Ghost	KU0130
Grome there was	AS0452
Happy ending	BL0120
Happy ending	KN0120
Home is the hunter	KU0130
Home there's no returning	ME0356
Housing problem	BR0380
Jesting pilot	CL0590
Jesting pilot	KN0190
Misguided halo	AS0450
Near miss	ME0358
Or else	CR0100
Or else	KU0130
Or else	SA0100
Piggy bank	B00151
Pile of trouble	KU0130
Private eye	BE0200
Private eye	BL0120
Shock	DE0470
Shock	KU0130
Sword of tomorrow	MA0480
Those among us	NC0210
Time trap	AL0405
Two-handed engine	AL0401
Twonky	AS0070
Twonky	CA0255
Vintage season	AM0515
Vintage season	SC0211
Voice of the lobster	CR0200
We guard the black planet	CA0320
We guard the black planet	M00350
Wild surmise	P00371
Year day	KU0130

Kuykendall, Roger
    We didn't do anything wrong, hardly   AN0150
    We didn't do anything wrong, hardly   CA010C
    We didn't do anything wrong, hardly   HA029C

Kyle, David A.
    Interstellar zoo   GR031C
    Toys for Debbie   IF0102

Lack, G.L.
    Rogue Leonardo   NE0302

LaFarge, Oliver
    John the revelator   MA0191
    Spud and Cochise   MA0330

Lafferty, R.A.
    All pieces of a river shore   KN0308
    All pieces of a river shore   SI0123
    All pieces of a river shore   W00412
    All the people   SI082C
    Among the hairy earthmen   AL0405
    Among the hairy earthmen   DO0165
    Among the hairy earthmen   NE0152
    And name my name   BE030C
    And name my name   KN0313
    And read the flesh between the lines   CA0371
    And walk now gently through the fire   EL050C
    Animal fair   NE02C4
    Barnaby's clock   EL106C
    Been a long time   AL0410
    Bequest of wings   HA0159
    Brain fever season   CA0374
    Bright coins in never-ending stream   KN0320
    By the seashore   ST022C
    Condillac's statue   MCC15C
    Configuration of the North Shore   KN0305
    Continued on next rock   KN010C
    Continued on next rock   KN0307
    Continued on next rock   NE0156
    Continued on next rock   SA015C
    Continued on next rock   W00411
    Days of grass, days of straw   NE0203
    Dorg   KN031C
    Entire and perfect chrysolite   KN0306
    Eurema's dam   AS0401
    Eurema's dam   BE0291
    Eurema's dam   NE02CC
    Eurema's dam   NE0202
    Fall of Pebble-Stone   KN0319
    Fire   EL050C
    Flaming ducks and giant bread   KN0315
    For all poor folks at Picketwire   SI048C
    Four sides of infinity   EL094C
    Ginny wrapped in the sun   SI07CC

Lafferty, R.A.

Lafferty, R.A.
    Snuffles   GA0250
    Splinters   GR0040
    Symposium   EL0980
    Through other eyes   SI0660
    Thus we frustrate Charlemagne   RO018C
    Thus we frustrate Charlemagne   SI0120
    Thus we frustrate Charlemagne   SU0150
    What's the name of that town?   CO049C
    When all the lands pour out again   KN0309
    World as will and wallpaper   EL072C

Laidlaw, M.
    Hiss of dragon   CA0238

Lake, David
    Creator   WO0419
    Redeem the time   HA0159

Lamont, G.
    Mirror at sunset   NE0205

Lamport, Felicia
    Sigh for cybernetics   ME0361

Landolfi, Tommaso
    [Untitled]   HA0164
    Gogol's wife   ME0367

Lang, Allan Kim
    Blind man's lantern   AN0102
    Blind man's lantern   CA0100
    Cinderella story   FR01CC
    Eel by the tail   CO025C
    Eel by the tail   SA0150
    Guest expert   AL04C5
    Romance of the first radical   ME015C
    Thaw and serve   MA02C4
    World in a bottle   CO0140

Lang, Daniel
    Man in space   ME0359

Langart, Darrel T.
    What the left hand was doing   ME036C

Langdon, George
    Of those who came   CA02CC
    Of those who came   NO0300

Langdon, John
    Hermit on Bikini   DE0500

Langelaan, George
    Fly   ME0358

Langelaan, George
    Fly   FL015C

Lanier, Sterling E.
    Jcin our gang?   AN0101
    Join our gang?   CA010C

Larionova, Olga
    Useless planet   GI0130

Lasswell, Horace D.
    Men in space   ST021C

Latham, Philip [pseud. of R.S. Richardson]
    Blindness   CL050C
    Dimple in drace   KN0302
    Rose Bowl-Pluto hypothesis   KN0305
    Xi effect   AL0400
    Xi effect   EL010C
    Xi effect   CRC100

Laumer, Keith
    Bad day for vermin   GA0147
    Body builders   CA0277
    Bclo [anthology]   LA0070
    Brass God   LA0100
    Castle of light   LA010C
    Cocoon   LA0130
    Combat unit   LA007C
    Courier   LA0070
    Courier   LA0100
    Devil you don't   MC0150
    Dincchrome   LA013C
    Doorstep   LA0130
    End as a hero   LA0130
    Field test   LA0070
    Forest in the sky   IF0102
    Frozen planet [anthology]   FRC1C0
    Galactic diplomat [anthology]   LA0100
    Hybrid   AL0402
    Hybrid   LA013C
    In the queue   KN0307
    In the queue   NE0156
    King of the city   GA0146
    Last command   AN0107
    Last command   CI011C
    Last command   HA016C
    Last command   KE010C
    Last command   KN046C
    Last command   LA007C
    Last command   CL018C
    Lawgiver   HA03C0
    Limiting velocity of orthodoxy   DA0140
    Lcng remembered thunder   LA013C
    Mind out of time   EL020C

Laumer, Keith
    Native intelligence   LA0100
    Night of the trolls   LA007C
    Nine by Laumer [anthology]   LA0130
    Of death what dreams   FI0100
    Placement test   LA013C
    Placement test   WH0175
    Plague   AN0109
    Plague   N0024C
    Prince and the pirate   LA01CC
    Protest note   LA0100
    Prototaph   AN0106
    Prototaph   AS0555
    Relic of war   LA007C
    Right to resist   OL0150
    Right to revolt   OL0150
    Saline solution   LA01CJ
    Short history of the bolo fighting   LA007C
        machines
    Street scene   EL0440
    Test to destruction   EL03CC
    Three blind mice   B00260
    Trick or treaty   IF010C
    Trip to the city   LA013C
    Trip to the city   WH013C
    Ultimatum   LA010C
    Ultimatum   N00240
    Walls   LA013C
    Wicker wonderland   LA010C
    Worlds of the imperium   KN0160

Laurance, Alice
    Call from Kerlyana   G00C3C
    Cassandra rising [anthology]   LA016C
    Schlossie   LA0160

Lawrence, D.H.
    Rocking-horse winner   WH015C

Lawrence, J.A.
    This is my beloved   NE0208
    Twinkle, twinkle, little bat   NE0207

Lawrence, Margery
    Terror of the Anerly house school   DE056C

Lawson, Jack B.
    Competitors   W00405

Leacock, Stephen
    Man in asbestos: an allegory of the   C001C0
        future

Leahy, John Martin
    Voices from the cliff   F001C0

LeGuin, Ursula K.

Leiber, Fritz, Jr.

Leiber, Fritz, Jr.

Princess in the tower 250,000 miles high	NE0207
Rite of spring	CA0237
Rite of spring	CA0374
Rump-titty-titty-tum-tah-tee	C00490
Rump-titty-titty-tum-tah-tee	KN0480
Rump-titty-titty-tum-tah-tee	LE01CC
Sanity	C00130
Sanity	KN028C
Sanity	LE0100
Sanity	SC030C
Secret songs	AM0513
Secret songs	KN045C
Ship of shadows	AS0401
Ship of shadows	FE0110
Ship of shadows	WC0410
Ship sails at midnight	DE0470
Ship sails at midnight	LE010C
Sixty-four square madhouse	IF010C
Smoke ghost	NE0310
Space-time for springers	LE01C0
Space-time for springers	ME0359
Space-time for springers	PO030C
Space-time for springers	PO0330
Space-time for springers	PC0374
Square root of brain	WO0164
Square root of brain	WO04C9
Sunken land	SI0620
Taboo	GR019C
Time in the round	GA0142
Try and change the past	DE022C
Try and change the past	LE0100
Try and change the past	SI096C
237 talking statues, etc.	FE023C
237 talking statues, etc.	ME0364
Waif	EL068C
Wanted: an enemy	DE037C
Wanted: an enemy	LE010C
What's he doing in there?	GA0143
When the change winds blow	SI0127
When the change winds blow	WC0405
When the last gods die	SI046C
When you care, when you love	FEC110
Winter flies	KN046C
Winter flies	NE0367
X marks the pedwalk	KE0100
Yesterday house	SI0124

Leibscher, Walt

Do androids dream of electric love?	SC0450

Leif, Evelyn

Bed sheets are white	EL0220

Leinster, Murray [pseud. of William F. Jenkins]

Nobody saw the ship	SI0600
Other now	GA0140
Other now	KN0280
Other world	CO0670
Pipeline to Pluto	CO0520
Plague	CO0280
Plants	GR0220
Politics	CU0070
Politics	JA013C
Power	DE047C
Power	LE016C
Power	LE0220
Propagandist	CO022C
Propagandist	CO0340
Propagandist	GA037C
Proxima Centauri	AS0170
Proxima Centauri	LE016C
Ribbon in the sky	CO019C
Runaway sky scraper	RO024C
Sentimentalists	YE0405
Sidewise in time	AS017C
Sidewise in time	SI104C
Sidewise in time [anthology]	LE0160
Skag with the queer head	CO0400
Strange case of John Kingman	BL0120
Strange case of John Kingman	LE0130
Symbiosis	GA0370
Symbiosis	LE0130
Things pass by	MA0480
This star shall be free	CO0250
This star shall be free	SA0150
Wabbler	CL0500
Wabbler	CR01C2
Wabbler	ME023C
Wabbler	PC0293

Lem, Stanislaw

Advisers of King Hydrops	LE020C
Automatthew's friend	LE0200
Computer that fought a dragon	SU018C
How Erg the self-inducting slew a paleface	LE020C
How microx and gigant made the universe expand	LE0200
How the world was saved	ST022C
Hunt	LE020C
In hot pursuit of happiness	RO0270
King Globares and the sages	LE0200
Mask	LE02C0
Mortal engines [anthology]	LE0200
Patrol	SU0180
Sanatorium of Dr. Vliperdius	LE0200
Tale of King Gnuff	LE020C

Lewis, Oscar
    Last years   BO0151

Lewis, Richard O.
    DOCS   OL0165

Lewis, Roy
    Evolution man   ST0210

Ley, Willy
    Geography for time travelers   GR0130
    Invasion   FO0240
    Letter to Martians   GR0130
    Meaning of the word "impossible"   SC030C
    Space war   GR013C
    V-2 rocket cargo ship   HE0100
    Where do we go from here?   ME0358

Leyson, Burr
    Shake hands with the man on the moon   FU010C

Lichtenberg, Jacqueline
    Vanillamint tapestry   LA0160

Liebscher, Walt
    Alien cornucopia   AS0555

Lightner, A.M.
    Best friend   BO030C
    Best friend   FU013C
    Great day for the Irish   FU0130
    Mars jar   FU0130
    New game   EC030C
    New game   FU010C
    New game   FU0100

Lindholm, M.
    Bones for Dulath   SA012C

Lindner, Robert
    Jet-propelled couch   AL036C

Locke, David M.
    Power of the sentence   BE0290

Locke, Robert Donald
    Dark nuptial   ST018C

Lockhard, Leonard
    Lagging profession   ME0361

LoMedico, B.T.
    Hole in Jennifer's room   EL0920

Loran, Martin
    Case of the perjured planet   BA0240
    Ounce of dissension   BA0235
    Ounce of dissension   WI0206

Lord, Glenn
    Wolfshead [anthology]   HO0280

Lory, Robert
    Rundown   CO0490
    Star party   WO0405

Lott, S. Makepeace
    Escape to Venus   AL0310

Louden, Leo
    Green boy   EL0880

Loughlin, Richard L.
    Journeys in science fiction   L001CO
     [anthology]

Lovecraft, Howard P.
    Cats of Ulthar   DE0190
    Color out of space   CO0280
    Color out of space   M00320
    Doom that came to Sarnath   SI0620
    From beyond   DE0590
    Horror from the middle span   DE0560
    Outsider   SA0150
    Shadow out of time   WO0330
    Whisperer in darkness   M00380
    White ape   EL0520

Lovell, Bernard
    Some mysteries of Venus resolved   AL0310

Lovin, R.
    Apostle   EL0700

Lowenkopf, Shelly
    Addict   NO0210

Lowndes, Robert W.
    Highway   LE0220

Lucian
    Interplanetary warfare   EV0100
    True history   DE0370
    True story [excerpt]   GU0130

Lucie-Smith, Edward
    Astronaut [poem] [excerpt]   BE0500
    Holding your eight hands   HA0162

Ludwig, Edward W.
  Rocket man   DE016C

Lukodyanov, Isai
  Black pillar   MO015C
  Farewell on the shore   MA0420
  Formula for the impossible   MA0390

Lunan, D.
  Comet, cairn, and capsule   AS0575

Lundwall, Sam J.
  Nobody here but us shadows   WO015C
  Utopia   AL065C

Lupoff, Richard A.
  After the dreamtime   NE0204
  Musspelsheim   EL112C
  Partridge project   CA031C
  Sail the tide of mourning   NE0205
  Sail the tide of mourning   CA0235
  With the Bentfin Boomer Boys on EL022C
    little old new Alabama

Lyle, David
  Human race has, maybe, thirty-five AL0665
    years left

Lynch, Hal
  Age of retirement   AL041C

Lynn, Elizabeth A.
  Jubilee's story   K10070
  We all have to go   ED015C
  Woman who loved the moon   SA0120

Lytle, B.J.
  Jamey's visitor   EL078C
  Old Max   EL086C
  Tunnel   EL122C

MacAnn, K.W.
  Rejection slip   AS0555

MacApp, C.C.
  And all the earth a grave   GA0147
  Flask of fine Arcturan   GA0148
  Impersonators   WI0206
  Price of islands   GA0280

MacBeth, George
  Bedtime story   MA0470
  Circe undersea   ME0366
  Crab-apple crisis   AL0665
  Crab-apple crisis   GR0250

MacBeth, George
    Crab-apple crisis   HO010C
    Crab-apple crisis   ME0367
    Crab-apple crisis   SA010C
    Fast car wash   J0015C
    Lamps [poem]   BE050C
    Silver needle   ME0290
    Soft world sequence   M00163

MacCreigh, James
    Big man with the girls   HO013C
    Let the ants try   PO019C
    Little man on the subway   F00100
    Wings of the lightning land   F0012C

MacDonald, Anson [pseud. of Robert A. Heinlein]
    By his bootstraps   AS065C
    By his bootstraps   HE010C

MacDonald, John D.
    Annex   F1009C
    Annex   HA0161
    Big contest   KN063C
    Big contest   ME0310
    Child is crying   C0046C
    Common denominator   GA014C
    Dance of a new world   GR0190
    Escape to chaos   AL0411
    Flaw   BE020C
    Flaw   BL012C
    Game for blondes   GA0141
    Games for blondes   BE0203
    Hunted   P00190
    Incubation   CR023C
    Legend of Joe Lee   ME0365
    Legend of Joe Lee   WA016C
    Mechanical answer   GR0280
    Miniature   C00130
    Ring around the redhead   C00370
    Spectator sport   AS0340
    Spectator sport   C00280
    Susceptibility   GA014C

MacDonald, John P.
    Half-past eternity   N0018C

MacDonald, Philip
    Hub   MA0191
    Private-keep out!   FR0150
    Private-keep out!   FE0230

MacFarlane, Wallace
    Changing woman   W00413
    Dead end   C00550
    Dead end   C00560

MacFarlane, Wallace
- Free vacation — AN0107
- Gardening notes from all over — KN0313
- Graduation day — SI0480
- How shall we conquer? — NE0203
- Last leaf — KN0309
- Rubaiyat of Ambrose Bagley — GE0180
- To make a new neanderthal — BE0290

Mackelworth, R.W.
- Expanding man — NE0305
- Final solution — NE0303

Mackenroth, Nancy
- Most beautiful music — EL0840
- To sleep, perchance to dream — EL0680
- To sleep, perchance to cream — EL0760

MacKenzie, Jonathan Blake
- Overproof — AN0105
- Overproof — CO0610
- Thin edge — AN0103

Macklin, Edward
- Key to chaos — NE0301
- Trouble with H.A.R.R.I. — CO0490
- Unremembered — WC0405

MacLean, Katherine
- And be merry — CO0280
- And be merry — KN0580
- And be merry — PO0295
- Be merry — KN0480
- Brain wipe — EL0940
- Contagion — EE0201
- Contagion — CO0340
- Contagion — SA0240
- Defense mechanism — CO0130
- Defense mechanism — ME0260
- Fear hound — WO0409
- Fittest — NE0230
- Gambling hell and the sinful girl — PO0430
- Games — CO0310
- Incommunicado — CO0700
- Interbalance — MA0200
- Missing man — AN0109
- Missing man — NE0157
- Night-rise — LA0160
- Origin of the species — TE0150
- Other — ME0367
- Other — SA0300
- Pictures don't lie — CO0250
- Pictures don't lie — CR0100
- Pictures don't lie — CO0100
- Pictures don't lie — SA0150

MacLean, Katherine
    Pictures don't lie   SI0600
    Second game   AS0585
    Small war   EL1020
    Snowball effect   AL0401
    Snowball effect   AL0450
    Snowball effect   GA0141
    Unhuman sacrifice   AM051C
    Unhuman sacrifice   KN0160
    Urhuman sacrifice   MAC55C

MacLennan, Phyllis
    Thus love betrays us   BE0291
    Thus love betrays us   MA021C
    Thus love betrays us   WO0413

Maddern, Philippa C.
    "They made us not to be and they are   KNC320
        not"
    Ignorant of magic   HA0159

Maddern, Pip
    Broken pit   HA0158
    Ins and outs of the Hadhya city-state   HA0158
    Single changes   HA0158

Maddux, Rachel
    Final clearance   MA0196

Madsen, Svend Age
    Good ring   RO0270

Magazine of Fantasy and Science Fiction
    Best from Fantasy and Science Fiction   MA0191
        1st series [anthology]
    Best from Fantasy and Science Fiction   MA0192
        2nd series [anthology]
    Best from Fantasy and Science Fiction   MA0193
        3rd series [anthology]
    Best from Fantasy and Science Fiction   MA0194
        4th series [anthology]
    Best from Fantasy and Science Fiction   MA0195
        5th series [anthology]
    Best from Fantasy and Science Fiction   MA0196
        6th series [anthology]
    Best from Fantasy and Science Fiction   MA0197
        7th series [anthology]
    Best from Fantasy and Science Fiction   MA0198
        8th series [anthology]
    Best from Fantasy and Science Fiction   MA0199
        9th series [anthology]
    Best from Fantasy and Science Fiction   MA0199
        10th series [anthology]
    Best from Fantasy and Science Fiction   MA02C1
        11th series [anthology]

Magazine of Fantasy and Science Fiction
    Best from Fantasy and Science Fiction   MA0202
       12th series [anthology]
    Best from Fantasy and Science Fiction   MA0203
       13th series [anthology]
    Best from Fantasy and Science Fiction   MA0204
       14th series [anthology]
    Best from Fantasy and Science Fiction   MA0205
       15th series [anthology]
    Best from Fantasy and Science Fiction   MA0206
       16th series [anthology]
    Best from Fantasy and Science Fiction   MA0210
       20th series [anthology]
    Best from Fantasy and Science Fiction,   MA0208
       18th series [anthology]

Magidoff, Robert
    Russian science fiction [anthology]   MA0360
    Russian science fiction 1968   MA0390
       [anthology]
    Russian science fiction 1969   MA0420
       [anthology]

Mailer, Norman
    Of a fire on the moon [excerpt]   AL0650

Malamud, Bernard
    Jewbird   DA0200
    Jewbird   ME0364

Malcolm, David
    Beyond the reach of storms   CA0210
    Potential   NE0305
    Twice bitten   WI0204

Malec, Alexander
    Diehl   MA0450
    Extrapolation [anthology]   MA0450
    Landmark   MA0450
    Matayama   MA0450
    Monsignor Primo Macinno   MA0450
    Once was   MA0450
    Opaxtl   MA0450
    Project inhumane   MA0450
    Project inhumane   ME0366
    Proof positive   MA0450
    Remote incident   MA0450
    10:01 A.M.   AN0106
    10:01 A.M.   MA0450
    Thing-thing   MA0450
    To relieve the sanity   MA0450

Mallette, Mose
    Seven wonders of the universe   MA0206

AUTHOR INDEX

Maloney, Russell
      Inflexible logic   BR038C

Malpass, E.L.
      Return of the Moon Man   MA047C
      Return of the Moon Man   CB0140
      When grandfather flew to the moon   ME0357

Malstrcm, Robert C.
      Great A   NE0201

Malzberg, Barry N.
      After the unfortunate accident   MA046C
      Afterthe great space war   MA0455
      Ballad of slick Sid   MA0455
      Battered-earth syndrome   EL102C
      Bearing witness   EL0700
      Before the great space-war   GE015C
      Choral   GR007C
      Chronicles of a comer   MA046C
      Closed sicilian   MA046C
      Conquest   NE0201
      Conquest and Gehenna   HA0164
      Conversations at Lothar's   EL054C
      Culture lock   EL0720
      Death to the keeper   MA0460
      Delightful comedic premise   ST0220
      Destruction and exculpation of earth   MA0455
      Down here in the dream quarter   MA0455
         [anthology]
      Down here in the dream cuarter   MA0455
      Dreaming and conversions: two rules   N00403
         by which to live
      Falcon and the falconeer   HA0233
      Falcon and the falconeer   H00120
      Final stage [anthclogy]   FE0170
      Final war   H00110
      Final war   MA046C
      Fireday, firenight   EL068C
      Fireday, firenight   EL0760
      Fireday, firenight   MA0455
      Galaxy called Rome   HA0168
      Galaxy called Rome   MA0455
      Galaxy called Rome   SI0126
      Gehenna   W00412
      Geraniums   EL098C
      Going down   EL0660
      Graven images [anthology]   GR0070
      Guidance   EL0800
      In the cup   MA0460
      In the stocks   NE0207
      Inaugural   AS0555
      Initiation   MA0460
      Institutions   EL1140
      Isaiah   MA0455

Malzberg, Barry N.

It doesn't really matter	EL078C
January 1975	AS0555
January 1975	MA0455
Leviticus: in the ark	MA0455
Leviticus: in the ark	SI0480
Making it all the way into the future on Gaxton Falls of the red planet	NO0404
Making it through	EL050C
Making it to Gaxton Falls on the Red Planet in the year of our lord	MA0455
Making the connections	MA0455
Management	MA046C
Many worlds of Barry Malzberg [anthology]	MA046C
Men inside	NE0202
Natural history	EL086C
Neglected visions [anthology]	MA0465
Notes for a novel about the first ship ever to Venus	CA0368
Notes leading down to the conquest	NE0203
Notes leading down to the events at Bedlam	MA0455
On the air	NE0200
On the campaign trail	MA0455
Opening fire	EL094C
Out from the Ganymede	NE0202
Over the line	EL074C
Prose bowl	FR0210
Reconstitution	MA046C
Redundancy	MA0455
Report to headquarters	MA0455
Report to headquarters	NE0205
Running around	EL098C
Second short shortest fantasy story ever published	MA046C
Sedan Deville	MA0455
Seeking assistance	MA0455
Several murders of Roger Ackroyd	AS044C
Shared tomorrows [anthology]	FR0210
State of the art	MA0455
State of the art	NE0204
Streaking	MA0455
Terminus est	NO0401
Thirty-seven northwest	MA0455
Those wonderful years	EL12CC
Transfer	MA0455
Trashing	MA0455
Triptych	SI0120
Try again	EL1120
Two odysseys into the center	NO0402
Uncoupling	EL066C
Union forever	EL106C
Union forever	MA046C
Ups and downs	EL018C

Malzberg, Barry N.
    Vox populi   MA0455
    Wonderful, all-purpose transmogrifer   FE0170
    Yahrzeit   EL116C

Manhattan, Avro
    Cricket ball   AS034C

Mann, T.
    Wardrobe   DI026C

Manning, Lawrence
    Gcod-bye, Ilha!   C0016C
    Good-bye, Ilha!   ME0230
    Living galaxy   C0046C
    Man who awoke   AS0170

Mansfield, Roger
    Starlit corridor [anthology]   MA047C

Margroff, Robert E.
    Book   KN0308

Margulies, Leo
    Get out of my sky [anthology]   MA0475
    Giant anthology of science fiction   MA048C
    Three times infinity [anthology]   MA0485
    Unexpected [anthology]   MA049C

Marks, Winston K.
    Call me Adam   C0031C
    Double take   AS0340
    John's other practice   EE02C5
    Mate in two moves   C0019C
    Water eater   C00490

Marlowe, Stephen
    Lion's mouth   LE022C

Marlowe, Webb
    Flight into darkness   HE01C0

Marquis, Don
    Ghosts   ME031C

Marsh, W.
    Ethicators   ME0356

Marti-Ibanez, Felix
    Nina Sol   MA0203

Martin, George R.R.
    And seven times never kill man   MA054C
    Beast for Norn   WE029C
    Bitterblooms   BE0303

Martin, George R.R.
    Fast-friend   DA0140

Martin, George R.R.	
Fast-friend	DA0140
For a single yesterday	MA054C
For a single yesterday	SI0480
FTA	AS0555
In the house of the worm	CA0275
Lonely songs of Laren Dorr	MA054C
Meathouse man	CA0236
Meathouse man	KN0318
Men of Greywater Station	MA054C
Men of GreywaterStation	MA054C
New voices in science fiction [anthology]	MA052C
New voices 2 [anthology]	MA0521
Night of the vampires	MA054C
Night shift	MA054C
Nor the many-colored fires of a star ring.	DA0140
Patrick Henry, Jupiter, and the little red brick spaceship	MA054C
Run to starlight	CA0277
Runners	MA054C
Second kind of loneliness	KA0070
Slide show	EL0980
Song for Lya	AN0140
Song for Lya	AS04C1
Song for Lya	WO0415
Songs of stars and shadows [anthology]	MA054C
Starlady	FO0290
Stone city	MA052C
Storms of Windhaven	CA0235
Storms of Windhaven	WO0416
This tower of ashes	B00240
This tower of ashes	MA054C
Weekend in a war zone	ED015C
With morning comes mistfall	BE0299
With morning comes mistfall	NE0159
Martin, M., Jr.	
Hide and seek	EL092C
Martinc, Joseph P.	
Not a prison make	AN010C
Not a prison make	GR0250
Pushbutton war	AN015C
Pushbutton war	CA010C
To change their ways	WI0206
Martinsen, M.	
Dead alien	DA0273
Martinson, Harry	
Hades and Euclid	DI023C

Masefield, John
    Sealman   MA0330

Mason, Carol
    Anthropology through science fiction   MA0550
       [anthology]

Mason, Douglas R.
    Folly to be wise   NE0309
    Man who missed the ferry   NE0307

Mason, J.K.
    Arctic rescue   EL1180

Masson, David I.
    Lost ground   HA0161
    Psychosmosis   ME0290
    Psychosmosis   SI0380
    Take it or leave it   HA0300
    Transfinite choice   HA0233
    Transfinite choice   MO0162
    Traveller's rest   ME0366
    Traveller's rest   SI1000

Mateyko, G. M.
    On handling the data   CR0104

Matheson, Richard
    Born of man and woman   BE0201
    Born of man and woman   SC0210
    Born of man and woman   TE0150
    Dance of the dead   FO0300
    Dance of the dead   FO0330
    Dance of the dead   FO0373
    Dress of white silk   MA0191
    Holiday man   FE0230
    Jazz machine   ME0364
    Last day   AL0401
    Lover when you're near me   BE0203
    Lover when you're near me   GA0141
    Mantage   KC0160
    One of the books   GA0340
    Pattern for survival   MA0195
    Shipshape home   CO0280
    SRL AD   ER0460
    Steel   NO0210
    Test   MA0194
    Third from the sun   GA0140
    Through channels   CO0520
    Waker dreams   GA0140
    Witch war   BE0202
    Witch war   KE0100

Matschat, Cecile
    Year after tomorrow [anthology]   DE0310

McCaffrey, Anne

McCardell, R.L.

McClellan, Gary D.

McClintic, Winona

McClintock, Michael W.

McCloud, Richard

McCloy, Helen

McComas, J. Francis

McComas, J. Francis
    Shock treatment   MA0330
    Special wonder [anthology]   MC018C

McConnell, James
    Learning theory   C00430
    Learning theory   KA0070
    Nor dust corrupt   EE02C8

McCormack, F.
    March hare mission   KN058C

McCullough, Ken
    Chuck Berry, won't you please come   EL022C
        home

McDaniel, D.
    Prognosis: terminal   F00450

McDowell, Emmett
    Veiled island   C004CC

McEvoy, Seth
    Which in the wood decays   KN0317

McGregor, R.J.
    Perfect gentleman   ST018C

McGuire, John J.
    Queen's messenger   EE02C8
    Return   SC040C
    To catch an alien   FC0376

McHargue, Georgess
    Hot and cold running cities; an   MC028C
        anthology of science fiction
        [anthology]

McIntosh, J.T.
    Wrong world   C00140

McIntosh, J.T. [pseud. of James McGregor]
    Bliss of solitude   CR0103
    First lady   C001CC
    First lady   CR0100
    Hallucination orbit   GAU141
    Immortality .... for some   C00760
    Machine made   CA0230
    Machine made   C0016C
    Machine made   WI0202
    Made in U.S.A.   B001CC
    Made in U.S.A.   DE025C
    Made in U.S.A.   GA022C
    Poor planet   C00610
    Stitch in time   CA017C

McIntosh, J.T. [pseud. of James McGregor]
        Venus mission   WO0300
        You were right, Joe   GA0143

McIntyre, Vonda N.
        Aztecs   CA0237
        Aztecs   MC0285
        End's beginning   MC0285
        Fireflood   MC0285
        Fireflood [anthology]   MC0285
        Genius freaks   KN0312
        Genius freaks   MC0285
        Mountains of sunset, the mountains of   EE0300
            dawn
        Mountains of sunset, the mountains of   MC0285
            dawn
        Of mist, and grass, and sand   AL0650
        Of mist, and grass, and sand   AN0140
        Of mist, and grass, and sand   MC0285
        Of mist, and grass, and sand   NE0159
        Of mist, and grass, and sand   SA0240
        Only at night   MC0285
        Recourse, Inc.   GE0150
        Recourse, Inc.   MC0285
        Screwtop   CR0250
        Screwtop   MC0285
        Screwtop   SA0230
        Spectra   KN0311
        Spectra   MC0285
        Thanatos   DA0170
        Wings   GO0030
        Wings   MC0285

McKay, Kevin
        Pie row Joe   HA0159

McKenna, Richard
        Bramble bush   KN0303
        Casey Agonistes   KN0220
        Casey Agonistes   KN0490
        Casey Agonistes   MA0199
        Casey Agonistes   MC0300
        Casey Agonistes   ME0359
        Casey Agonistes [anthology]   MC0300
        Fiddler's green   KN0302
        Fiddler's green   MC0300
        Hunter, come home   KN0130
        Hunter, come home   MA0203
        Hunter, come home   MC0300
        Mine own ways   MA0200
        Mine own ways   MC0300
        Mine own ways   ME0361
        Night of Hoggy Darn   KN0570
        Night of Hoggy Darn   SI0126
        Secret place   KN0100

Meck, S.P.
    Awlo of Ulm   AS017C
    Submicroscopic   AS0170

Melton, H.
    We hold these rights   DE0267

Melville, Herman
    Bell-tower   FR007C
    Dr. Materialismus   FR007C
    Tartarus of Maids   SA015C

Mendelson, Drew
    Blind man, singing   NE02C8
    Museum piece   NE0205
    Star train   AS0180

Menville, Douglas
    Ancestral voices [anthology]   ME0150

Meredith, Richard C.
    Earthcoming   NO0150

Merliss, R.R.
    Stutterer   ME0356

Merril, Judith
    Auction pit   NE0170
    Barrier of dread   GR019C
    Best of Judith Merril [anthology]   ME017C
    Beyond human ken [anthology]   ME023C
    Beyond the barriers of space and time ME026C
        [anthology]
    Big man with the girls   HO013C
    Daughters of earth   ME017C
    Daughters of earth   PE0150
    Dead center   BO0151
    Dead center   ME0170
    Death is the penalty   FO019C
    Deep down dragon   CO072C
    Deep down dragon   GA0146
    England swings SF [anthology]   ME029C
    Exile from space   FA0215
    Fifth annual of the year's best SF   ME036C
        [anthology]
    How near is the moon?   ME0358
    Human? [anthology]   ME0310
    In the land of unblind   ME017C
    Lady was a tramp   ME0170
    Lonely   ME017C
    Project nursemaid   CO0700
    Rain check   SA0180
    Rockets to where?   ME0359

Merril, Judith
- S-F: the year's greatest science fiction and fantasy, 1956 [anthology]   ME0356
- S-F: the year's greatest science fiction and fantasy, 1957 [anthology]   ME0357
- S-F: the year's greatest science fiction and fantasy, 1958 [anthology]   ME0358
- S-F: the year's greatest science fiction and fantasy, 1959 [anthology]   ME0359
- SF 12 [anthology]   ME0367
- SF the best of the best part 2 [anthology]   ME0201
- Shrine of temptation   ME0170
- So proudly we hail   PO0371
- Stormy weather   ME0170
- Survival ship   HE0400
- Survival ship   MA0550
- Survival ship   RO0180
- That only a mother   KA0070
- That only a mother   ME0170
- That only a mother   PO0293
- That only a mother   PR0150
- That only a mother   RO0180
- That only a mother   SA0150
- That only a mother   SA0240
- That only a mother   SC0210
- That only a mother   TE0150
- Whoever you are   ME0170
- Wish upon a star   ME0170
- Year's best S-F; the 6th annual [anthology]   ME0361
- Year's best S-F; the 7th annual [anthology]   ME0362
- Year's best S-F; the 8th annual [anthology]   ME0363
- Year's best S-F; the 8th annual [anthology]   ME0363
- Year's best S-F; the 9th annual [anthology]   ME0364
- Year's best S-F; the 10th annual [anthology]   ME0365
- Year's best S-F; the 11th annual [anthology]   ME0366

Merritt, A.
- Moon pool   MO0400
- People of the pit   MO0320

Merwin, Sam, Jr.
- Exiled from earth   CR0200
- Exit lane   CO0340

Merwin, Sam, Jr.
    Judas Ram   GAC140

Metcalfe, John
    Not there   DE0560

Michaux, Henri
    And more changes still   ME0367

Middleton, Richard
    Shepherd's boy   MA0193

Millar, Jeff
    Tcto, I have a feeling we're not in   KN0317
        Kansas anymore

Miller, Jesse
    Phoenix house   KN0316
    Pigeon city   MI0180
    Twilight lives   MA0521

Miller, Lion
    Available data on the worp reaction   AS0340
    Available data on the worp reaction   CR0102

Miller, P. Schuyler
    As never was   HE010C
    As never was   HE0170
    As never was   SI0123
    Cave   AL0425
    Chrysalis   SI0420
    Old man Mulligan   AS0451
    Sands of time   GRC140
    Sands of time   HEC1CC
    Sands of time   SI1000
    Status quondam   HE0130
    Tetrahedra of space   AS0170
    Trouble on Tantalus   AS0650
    Trouble on Tantalus   GRC31C

Miller, R. Dewitt
    Swenson, dispatcher   BE0206
    Within the pyramid   HE0100

Miller, Walter M., Jr.
    Big hunger   AL0480
    Blood bank   GR010C
    Canticle for Leibowitz   CE010C
    Canticle for Leibowitz   MA0195
    Canticle for Leibowitz   WA010C
    Canticle for Leibowitz [excerpt]   BE0206
    Canticle for Leibowitz [excerpt]   MI0180
    Command performance   AL0450
    Command performance   BE0203
    Command performance   GA0141

Miller, Walter M., Jr.

Conditionally human	CO0150
Conditionally human	YE0404
Crucifixus Etiam	AM0514
Crucifixus Etiam	FI0090
Crucifixus Etiam	ME0310
Crucifixus Etiam	SI0940
Darfsteller	AS0370
Dark benediction	FI0095
Death of a spaceman	NO0230
Dumb waiter	CO0550
Dumb waiter	CO0560
Dumb waiter	KN0190
Dumb waiter	SI0128
Envoi	AL0480
Hoofer	ME0356
I made you	AL0425
I made you	AL0450
I, dreamer	NO0200
Izzard and the membrane	YE0403
Lineman	NO0230
Little creeps	LE0220
Momento homo	BE0205
Momento homo	JA0130
Momento homo	MI0150
No moon for me	SL0180
Vengeance for Nikolai	FE0260
Will	BE0205
Wolf pack	ME0260

Mills, Robert P.

Best from fantasy and science fiction 9th series [anthology]	MA0199
Best from fantasy and science fiction 10th series [anthology]	MA0200
Best from fantasy and science fiction 11th series [anthology]	MA0201
Decade of fantasy and science fiction [anthology]	MA0330
Last shall be first	MA0330
Twenty years of the magazine of fantasy and science fiction	FE0230
Worlds of science fiction [anthology]	MI0150

Milstead, John

Sociology through science fiction [anthology]	MI0180

Miner, Horace M.

Body ritual among the Nacirema	ST0210

Mirer, Artur.

Old road	BE0020
Test	BE0020

Mitchell, Adrian
    Discovery [poem]   BE05CC

Mitchell, Edward Page
    Ablest man in the world   MI0250
    Balloon tree   MI0250
    Balloon tree   SI0620
    Both from that bourne   MI0250
    Case of the Daw twins   MI0250
    Cave of the splurgles   MI0250
    Clock that went backwards   MI0250
    Crystal man [anthology]   MI025C
    Day among the liars   MI0250
    Devil's funeral   MI0250
    Devilish rat   MI0250
    Exchanging their souls   MI0250
    Extraordinary wedding   MI0250
    Facts in the Ratcliff case   MI0250
    Flying weathercock   MI0250
    Inside of the earth   MI0250
    Last cruise of the Judas Iscariot   MI0250
    Legendary ship   MI0250
    Man without a body   MI0250
    Old squids and little speller   MI025C
    Our war with Monaco   MI0250
    Pain epicures   MI025C
    Professor's experiment   MI025C
    Senator's daughter   MI025C
    Shadow on the Fancher twins   MI0250
    Soul spectroscope   MI025C
    Story of the deluge   MI0250
    Tachypomp   MI025C
    Terrible voyage of the toad   MI025C
    Uncommon sort of spectre   MI025C
    Wonderful corot   MI0250

Mitchell, J.A.
    Last American   DE0400

Mitchison, Naomi
    After the accident   HA03CC
    Factory   NO0403
    Mary and Joe   HA0163
    Mary and Joe   NO0401
    Miss Omega Raven   NO0402
    Valley of the bushes   WE0290

Mohler, Wil
    Journey of ten thousand miles   FE0200

Mohs, Mayo
    Other worlds, other gods [anthology]   NO01C0

Monig, Christopher
    Love story   CR0230

Moore, C.L.
    Fruit of knowledge   MOO170
    Gnome there was   AS0452
    Greater than gods   AS0450
    Greater than gods   MOO170
    Home there's no returning   ME0356
    Jirel meets magic   SA0220
    No woman born   CRO100
    No woman born   KN0570
    No woman born   LE0130
    No woman born   MOO170
    Scarlet dream   CRO230
    Shambleau   CRO200
    Shambleau   MOO170
    There shall be darkness   GRO190
    Trust in time   MOO170
    Vintage season   MOO170
    Vintage season   SC0211
    Wild surmise   FOO371

Moore, Hal R.
    Sea bright   MA0205

Moore, Raylyn
    Certain slant of light   GRO040
    Different drummer   MA0210
    Different drummer   OL0165
    Fun palace   KN0317
    If something begins   CA0420
    Modular story   KN0318
    Poverello   ELO700
    Trigononomy   EL1060
    Way back   LA0160

Moore, Ward
    Adjustment   KA0070
    Adjustment   MA0197
    Dominions beyond   BE0205
    Dominions beyond   HOO120
    Durance   SI0480
    Fellow who married the Maxill girl MA0200
    Fellow who married the Maxill girl ME0361
    Flying Dutchman   CRO200
    Frank Merriwell in the White House OL0150
    It becomes necessary   ME0362
    Lot   AL0450
    Lot   MA0193
    Lot's daughter   MA0330
    No man pursueth   MA0196
    Peacebringer   COO130
    Second trip to Mars   SA0270
    We the people   CRO230

Moravec, Hans
    Cable cars in the sky   FOO430

Moudy, Walter F.
      Survivor   GR0250
      Survivor   KE0100
      Survivor   ME0366

Mrozek, Slawomir
      Ugupu bird   HA0163

Muir, Edwin
      Horses   AL0650

Mulisch, Harry
      What happened to Sergeant Masuro?   W00405

Mundie, Edward
      Gift   HA0158

Mundis, Jerrold J.
      Christmas in Watson Hollow   DI0230
      Do it for Mama!   DI0250
      Luger is a 9mm automatic handgun with   M00166
         a parabellum action

Murphy, Robert
      Fallout island   SA0270
      Phantom setter   SA0270
      Replacement   MA0200

Murphy, S.R.
      Mooncup   EN0070

Murry, Colin
      Custodians   MU0100
      Custodians and other stories   MU0100
         [anthology]
      Hertford manuscript   MU0100
      Paradise beach   MU0100
      Piper at the gates of dawn   MU0100

Myers, Howard L.
      Misinformation   MI0180
      Out, wit!   AN0109
      Out, wit!   HA0165

Nabors, William
      State of ultimate peace   HA0145

Nadler, Maggie
      Latest feature   AS0555

Nash, Ogden
      Tale of the thirteenth floor   MA0330

Nathan, Robert
      Digging the weans   ME0357

Nathan, Robert
    Pride of carrots   CO049C
    Weans   FI0095

Naylor, Charles
    New constellations [anthology]   DI023C
    Repairing the office   DI024C
    Strangeness [anthology]   DI026C

Neal, H.C.
    Who shall dwell   KE010C
    Who shall dwell   PL0150

Nearing, H., Jr.
    Cerebrative Psittacoid   CR0100
    Hyperspherical basketball   MA0192
    Maladjusted classroom   MA0193
    Mathematical voodco   MA0191

Nelson, Alan
    Narapoia   AS034C
    Narapoia   MA0191
    Shopdropper   CO019C
    Silenyia   CO0640

Nelson, Ray
    Eight o'clock in the morning   MA0203
    Eight o'clock in the morning   ME0364
    Time travel for pedestrians   EL0220

Nesvadba, Josef
    Captain Nemo's last adventure   HA0166
    Captain Nemo's last adventure   RO027C
    Last secret weapon of the third Reich   ME0365
    Lost face   HA0163
    Vampire Ltd   SU0180

Neville, Kris
    Ballenger's people   MA0465
    Bettyann   EL0760
    Bettyann   HE0130
    Bettyann   SI0820
    Bettyann   SL021C
    Cold war   AS07CC
    Dominant species   KN0309
    Experiment station   CO040C
    Forest of Zil   HA0160
    Franchise   SL021C
    From the government printing office   EL030C
    Gratitude guaranteed   DE0500
    Gratitude guaranteed   FE0230
    Gratitude guaranteed   PR021C
    Hold back tomorrow   EL0100
    New apples in the garden   KN028C
    Old man Henderson   EN0100

Niven, Larry
At the core	IF0102
Becalmed in hell	FE023C
Becalmed in hell	KN0480
Becalmed in hell	NE0151
Becalmed in hell	NIC150
Becalmed in hell	WO0406
Bigger than worlds	FO0043C
Bird in the hand	WO0411
Bordered in black	HA0233
Bordered in black	NI0120
Borderland of sol	NI015C
Cautionary tales	AS044C
Cautionary tales	NI0120
Cloak of anarchy	BE0291
Cloak of anarchy	NI015C
Cloak of anarchy	FO045C
Coldest place	NIC15C
Convergent series	NI0120
Convergent series [anthology]	NI0120
Cruel and unusual	NI0120
Deadlier weapon	NI0120
Death by ecstasy	WCC41C
Defenseless dead	EL116C
Down and out	GA010C
Dry run	NIC12C
Eye of an octopus	NIC150
Flash crowd	TH021C
Flatlander	CO061C
Fourth profession	CA0231
Fourth profession	CA0234
Fourth profession	WO0412
Grammar lesson	NI012C
Hole man	AN014C
Hole man	AS0401
Hole man	WA013C
How the heroes die	NI015C
Inconstant moon	AS0401
Intent to deceive	NI015C
Jigsaw man	EL030C
Jigsaw man	NI0150
Like Banquo's ghost	NI012C
Meddler	NI012C
Mistake	AS0555
Mistake	NIC120
Neutron star	AS040C
Neutron star	AS0645
Neutron star	SA015C
Night on Mispec Moor	NI0120
Nonesuch	NI012C
Not long before the end	NE0155
One face	NI012C
One face	SI0127
Plaything	AS0555
Plaything	NI0120

Niven, Larry
    Rammer   BE0290
    Rotating cylinders and the possibility   NI0120
       of global causality violation
    Safe at any speed   AS0555
    Safe at any speed   NI015C
    Schumann computer   NI012C
    Singularities make me nervous   DE0265
    Singularities make me nervous   NI012C
    Spirals   P00430
    Subject is closed   NI0120
    Tales of known space [anthology]   NI015C
    There is a tide   NI015C
    There is a wolf in my time machine   Y0015C
    Time travel   AL065C
    Transfer of power   NI0120
    Wait it out   AS0575
    Wait it out   NI0150
    Wait it out   SI0940
    Warriors   NI015C
    Wrong way street   NI012C
    Wrong-way street   GA0148
    Wrong-way street   SI100C
    Wrong-way street   ST0230

Noakes, Donald
    Long silence   BE0291

Nodvik, Stan.
    Postponed cure   BE030C

Nolan, William F.
    And miles to go before I sleep   H00120
    And miles to go before I sleep   N002CC
    Future is now [anthology]   N0015C
    Happily ever after   N00230
    He kilt it with a stick   N0018C
    Human equation [anthology]   N0018C
    Joy of living   N00210
    Man against tomorrow [anthology]   N0020C
    One of those days   ME0363
    Pseudo-people [anthology]   N0021C
    Toe to tip, tip to toe, pip-pop as you N0015C
       go
    Violation   EL072C
    Wilderness of stars [anthology]   N0023C
    Worlds of Monty Wilson   AS0555

Norton, Andre
    All cats are gray   B00260
    All cats are gray   N00250
    All cats are gray   Y0015C
    Bullard of the space patrol [anthology] JA010C
    Desirable lakeside residence   EL102C
    Falcon blood   SA012C

Norton, Andre
    Fur magic   WO0180
    Gates to tomorrow [anthology]   NO0240
    Gifts of Asti   EL0760
    Gifts of Asti   NO0250
    London bridge   NO0250
    Long live Lord Kor!   NO0250
    Long night of waiting   EL0860
    Long night of waiting   NO0250
    Many worlds of Andre Norton [anthology]   NO0250
    Mousetrap   BE0205
    Mousetrap   NO0250
    On writing fantasy   NO0250
    People of the crater   EL0480
    People of the crater   WO0360
    Space pioneers [anthology]   NO0270
    Space police [anthology]   NO0300
    Space service [anthology]   NO0330
    Toads of Grimmerdale   NO0250

Norton, Henry
    Man in the moon   CO0250

Norwood, Rick
    Omnia triste   CL0110

Nourse, Alan E., M.D.
    Brightside crossing   AS0575
    Brightside crossing   GA0340
    Brightside crossing   KN0120
    Brightside crossing   NO0390
    Brightside crossing   WA0130
    Canvas bag   MC0180
    Canvas bag   NO0360
    Circus   NO0360
    Coffin cure   CO0490
    Coffin cure   NO0390
    Compleat consummators   AS0555
    Compleat consummators   MA0204
    Counterfeit   AL0450
    Counterfeit man [anthology]   NO0360
    Dark door   NO0360
    Expert touch   HA0232
    Expert touch   NO0360
    Family resemblance   CO0190
    Family resemblance   CO0400
    Family resemblance   NO0390
    Hard bargain   FL0150
    High threshhold   CO0280
    Image of the gods   NO0360
    Letter of the law   NO0390
    Link   NO0360
    Love they Vimp   NO0390
    Meeting of the board   NO0360
    Miracle too many   ME0365

Nourse, Alan E., M.D.
    My friend Bobby   NO0360
    Native soil   NO0390
    Nightmare brother   CO0520
    Nightmare brother   EN0100
    Nightmare brother   NO0390
    Nightmare brother   SL0180
    Nize kitty   EL1180
    Ounce of cure   NO0360
    Problem   NO0390
    Second sight   NO0360
    Tiger by the tail   AS0340
    Tiger by the tail   CO0370
    Tiger by the tail   GA0141
    Tiger by the tail [anthology]   NO0390

Novitski, P.D.
    Nuclear fission   CA0376

Novotny, John
    On camera   CO0490
    Trick or two   MA0330

Nye, Cassandra
    Drumble   DI0240

O'Brien, Clancy
    Generation gaps   MI0180
    Matter of freedom   EL0700

O'Brien, Fitz-James
    Diamond lens   FR0070
    Diamond lens   GU0130
    What was it?   DA0230
    What was it?   KN0160
    Wondersmith   MO0320

O'Donnell, K.M.
    Chronicles of a comer   EL0300
    Chronicles of a comer   EL0500
    Chronicles of a comer   EL0560
    City lights, city nights   EL0720
    Final war   HA0161
    Final war   MA0208
    Getting around   EL1200
    In the pocket   NO0401
    It wasn't my fault   EL0900
    Oversight   EL1120
    Pacem est   HA0163
    Still-life   EL0220

O'Donnell, Kevin, Jr.
    Do not go gentle   RY0100
    Low grade ore   AS0173
    Low grade ore   AS0440

Olander, Joseph D.
   School and society through science   CLO165
      fiction [anthology]
   Science fiction of the forties   POO293
      [anthology]
   Science fiction: contemporary   WAO130
      mythology [anthology]
   Time of passage [anthology]   OLO170
   Tomorrow, inc. [anthology]   GRO3CO

Oliver, Chad
   Art and the eye   SLO210
   Any more at home like you?   POO373
   Between the thunder and the sun   MAO197
   Blood's a rover   COO310
   Blood's a rover   SIO400
   Boy next door   MEO310
   Caravans unlimited: stability   ELO581
   Didn't he ramble   BEO208
   End of the line   FEO20C
   Far from this earth   HAO300
   Far from this earth   KEO10C
   Far from this earth   MAO550
   Field expedient   WOO300
   Final exam   WHO18C
   Gift   ELO740
   King of the hill   ELO220
   Last word   ALO405
   Last word   MAO195
   Let me live in a house   COO520
   Life game   NOO210
   Middle man   ELO582
   Mother of necessity   COO430
   Mother of necessity   MCO4CO
   North wind   NCO230
   Of course   BEO2C5
   Of course   COO580
   Of course   MIO180
   Of course   STO210
   Pilgrimage   MCO180
   Rite of passage   COO580
   Second nature   ELO76C
   Shaka!   ELO580
   Stick for Harry Eddington   HAO232
   Transformer   NCO20C
   Win the world   LEO22C

Oliver, J.T.
   Peaceful Martian   FCO100

Olney, Ross R.
   Tales of time and space [anthology]   CLO180

Clsen, Bob
   Four-dimensional-roller-press   WOO240

Ozick, Cynthia
    Pagan rabbi   HAO164

Padgett, Lewis [pseud. of Henry Kuttner]
    Cure   PAO150
    Deadlock   GRO280
    Endowment policy   COO37C
    Ex machina   BLO12C
    Ex machina   PAO18O
    Exit the professor   PAO15O
    Gallegher plus   FAC18O
    Gnome there was   MEO230
    Gnome there was [anthology]   PAO150
    Iron standard   GRO22C
    Jesting pilot   FAO15C
    Line to tomorrow   DEO590
    Margin for error   COO13C
    Mimsy were the Borogoves   COO73O
    Mimsy were the Borogoves   FAC15C
    Mimsy were the Borogoves   SCO21O
    Open secret   LEO13C
    Piper's son   TEO150
    Private eye   SIO68O
    Project   COO31C
    Proud robot   HEC1CC
    Proud robot   PAO18O
    Rain check   FAC15C
    Robots have no tails [anthology] FAO18C
    See you later   PAO15O
    This is the house   FAO15O
    Time locker   HEO10C
    Time locker   HEO170
    Time locker   PAO18O
    Twonky   HEO100
    Twonky   FAO150
    Twonky   SIO64C
    We kill people   LEO220
    What you need   COO28C
    What you need   PAO15C
    When the bough breaks   ASO7CC
    When the bough breaks   DEO37C
    World is mine   PAO18C

Page, Gerald W.
    Enigma ship   DAO273
    Guardian angel   NEO309
    Happy man   MAO47C
    Happy man   WHO150
    Mercyship   DAO27C
    Spacemen live forever   NEO308
    Urhappy man   ALO425
    Waygift   EDO15C

Page, N.W.
    But without horns   GRO16C

Fage, W.A.
    Air serpent   MC0365

Faige, Leo
    How high on the ladder?   F0010C

Paine, A. Lincoln
    Dreistein case   C0C720

Palmer, C.H.
    Citizen 504   M00365

Paltock, Robert
    Human mutant   EV0100

Pangborn, Edgar
    Angel's egg   C0025C
    Angel's egg   CR01C1
    Angel's egg   KN0160
    Angel's egg   SI0123
    Children's crusade   EL058C
    Frehman angle   EL116C
    Golden horn   MA0202
    Harper Conan and Singer David ZE015C
    Legend of Hombas   EL0581
    Master of Babylon   BL021C
    Mount charity   CA0368
    Mcunt charity   NE0157
    Music master of Babylon   GA0340
    My brother Leopold   SIC5C0
    Night wind   CA0372
    Red hills of summer   C001CC
    Witches of Nupal   EL0582
    World is a sphere   CA037C

Fangborn, M.C.
    Back road   CA0376

Panshin, Alexei
    Destiny of Milton Gomrath   AS0555
    Destiny of Milton Gomrath   SI074C
    How can we sink when we can fly? CA0231
    How can we sink when we can fly? CA0234
    How can we sink when we can fly? FC0130
    Lady sunshine and the magoon of SI0480
       Beautus
    Ncw I'm watching Roger   KN0310
    One Sunday in Neptune   SI0940
    One Sunday in Neptune   W00410
    Sense of direction   SA021C
    When the vertical world becomes CA0371
       horizontal

Paredes, Horacio V.
    Population control, 1986   SA0300

Parkes, Lucas [pseud. of John Beynon Harris]
    Moon   WI0206

Parnov, Jeremy
    Everything but love   SH0150
    He who leaves no trace   GI0130
    Last door to Aiya   GI01CC
    Mystery of green crossing   MA0390
    Pale Neptune equation   NE0280

Parry, Jay A.
    Roboroots   AS0175

Paul, Barbara
    Answer "affirmative" or "negative"   AN0109
    Slow and gentle progress of trainee LA0160
        bell-ringers

Paul, Frank R.
    SF, The spirit of youth   SC0300

Paulsen, Kathryn
    Twenty-eighth day   DI0230

Paxson, D.L.
    Song of N'Sardi-El   KI007C

Payes, Rachel Cosgrove
    And the power   EL05CC
    And the power...   EL0300
    Come take a dip with me in the   EL0660
        genetic pool
    Deaf listener   G00030
    Escape to the suburbs   LA016C
    Grandma was never like this   EL0520
    Half life   EL054C
    In his own image   EL1120

Peake, Mervyn L.
    Boy in darkness   IN010C

Pearl, Clinton
    Crash alert   FU010C
    Space secret   FU010C

Pearson, Martin
    Ajax of Ajax   W00270
    Embassy   F00190

Pearson, Michael
    Out of this world 10 [anthology]   WI021C
    Strange orbits [anthology]   WI0245
    Strange universe [anthology]   WI0250

Peart, Noel
    Spud failure definite   OB0140

Peck, Richard E.
    Gantlet   CL0590
    Gantlet   HA0164
    Gantlet   KN031C

Pedersen, Con
    Pushover planet   WI0205

Peel, Jesse
    Heal the sick, raise the dead   AS0175
    Heal the sick, raise the dead   AS0440

Peirce, Hayford
    High yield bondage   BE0301
    Mail supremacy   AS0555
    Mail supremacy   BE0301
    Unlimited warfare   AN014C

Penman, Thomas
    Seafarer   NE0326

Perkins, Lawrence A.
    Hidden ears   AN01C8

Petaja, C.
    Terrible quick sword   EL1080

Pethebridge, Denis
    Space: Third millennium   MA047C

Petracca, Joseph
    Tolliver's travels   HE0130

Peyton, Green
    Ship that turned aside   CO0130

Phelan, R.C.
    Something invented me   ME0361

Phelps, Gilbert
    Winter people   WI0210

Philips, Louis
    Lop-eared cat that devoured HA0168
        Philadelphia

Phillifent, John T.
    Aim for the heel   AN0107
    Ethical quotient   AN0102
    Ethical quotient   CA0100
    Owe me   GR0300

Phillips, A.M.
    Death of the moon   WO0270
    Time-travel happens   HE0100

Phillips, Peter
    At no extra cost   BE0202
    C/O Mr. Makepeace   CO0310
    C/O Mr. Makepeace   KN0220
    Counter charm   AS0340
    Counter charm   CO0280
    Dreams are sacred   AM0512
    Dreams are sacred   AS0651
    Dreams are sacred   BL0100
    Dreams are sacred   WI0210
    Field study   GA0140
    Lost memory   CA0200
    Lost memory   CO0520
    Lost memory   GA0141
    Lost memory   KE0100
    Lost memory   MA0465
    Lost memory   MO0200
    Manna   CO0130
    Manna   KN0480
    Manna   SI0960
    Plagiarist   CR0230
    She who laughs   FO0150
    University   GA0141
    Unknown quantity   CA0230
    Warning   ME0260

Phillips, R.A.J.
    Day in the life of Kelvin Throop   AN0104

Phillips, Rog [pseud. of Roger Phillips Graham]
    Game preserve   ME0358
    Yellow pill   AS0651
    Yellow pill   CR0103
    Yellow pill   HA0260
    Yellow pill   KA0070
    Yellow pill   ME0359

Phillips, Y.
    Once around the moon   ST0230

Picard, Don
    Gato-O   GE0180

Pickens, Thomas
    Routine patrol activity   GO0030

Fierce, J.J.
    Best of Cordwainer Smith [anthology]   SM0180

Pierce, John R.
    Higher things   NO0401

Poe, Ecgar Allan
    Science fiction of Edgar Allan Poe   POO100
      [anthology]
    Some words with a mummy   POO100
    Scnnet: to science [poem]   SA0150
    System of Dr. Tarr anc Prof. Fether   POO100
    Tale of the ragged mountains   FR0070
    Tale of the ragged mountains   POO100
    Tale of the ragged mountains   SI0620
    Thousand and second tale of   FOC100
      Scheherazade
    Thousand-and-second tale of   CEO370
      Scheherazade
    Unparalleled adventure cf one Hans   POO100
      Pfall
    Von Kempelen and his discovery   POO1CO

Pohl, Carol
    Science fiction discoveries   FOO290
      [anthology]
    Science fiction: the great years   FOO120
      [anthology]
    Science fiction: the great years v.2   PCO295
      [anthology]

Pohl, Frederik
    Afterword   BE0299
    Assignment in tomorrow [anthology]   POO15C
    Best of Frederik Pohl [anthology]   POO18C
    Beyond the end of time [anthology]   FCO190
    Bitterest pill   GA0144
    Census takers   MA0196
    Census takers   FOO180
    Children of night   GA0148
    Children of night   FOO18O
    Children of night   POO21C
    Critical mass   GA0147
    Day after the day the Martians came   EL030C
    Day million   AL04C2
    Day million   AL0665
    Day million   KN048C
    Day million   NE0152
    Day million   FOO18C
    Day million   WA013C
    Day million   WOU407
    Day of the boomer dukes   FOO260
    Day the icicle works closed   FOO18C
    Day the icicle works closed   POC26C
    Day the Martians came   FOO180
    Deadly mission of Phineas Snodgrass   AS0555
    Digits and dastards [anthology]   POO21C
    Dcomship   WOO414
    Earth eighteen   POO21C
    Eighth galaxy reader [anthology]   GA0147
    Enjoy,enjoy   CA0265

Pohl, Frederik

Expert dreamers [anthology]	PO0240
Father of the stars	IF010C
Father of the stars	PO0180
Father of the stars	PO0210
Fiend	NE0303
Fiend	PL0150
Fiend	PL0155
Fiend	PO0210
Five hells of Orion	PO0210
Gentlest unpeople	GA0143
Gift of Garigolli	WO0415
Gold at the starbow's end	AN0109
Gold at the starbow's end	WO0413
Golden ages gone away	CL0110
Grandy devil	FC0180
Growing up in Edge City	SI0480
Guest editorial	IF0170
Happy birthday, dear Jesus	PO0180
Hated	PO0180
Haunted corpse	GA0142
Haunted corpse	PO0260
How to count on your fingers	GR0130
How to count on your fingers	PO0180
How to count on your fingers	PO0210
I plingot, Who you?	PO0260
I plingot, who you?	SI0580
I remember a winter	KN0311
If reader of science fiction [anthology]	IF0100
Knights of Arthur	PO0260
Legal rites	MA0490
Let the ants try	SI0700
Lovemaking	PL0155
Man who ate the world	KO0160
Man who ate the world	PO0260
Mars by moonlight	PO0260
Martian star-gazers	NE0363
Martians in the attic	PO0180
Meeting	AS0401
Meeting	BE0291
Merchants of Venus	AC0200
Merchants of Venus	HO0110
Midas plague	AM0510
Midas plague	FI0095
Midas plague	GR0100
Midas plague	PO0180
Midas plague	SC0212
Middle of nowhere	PO0260
Mute inglorious Tam	BE0300
My lady green sleeves	DE0250
Nightmare with Zeppelins	GA0144
Ninth galaxy reader [anthology]	GA0148
Omnibus	PO0260
On binary digits and human habits	PO0210

Pohl, Frederik

Punch	AS0555
Punch	C00490
Punch	PL015C
Punch	F00180
Quaker cannon	FR021C
Richest man in Levittown	P0018C
Schematic man	HA0162
Science fiction discoveries	F00290
[anthology]	
Science fiction of the forties	P00293
[anthology]	
Science fiction roll of honor	SC0300
[anthology]	
Science fiction: the great years	F00120
[anthology]	
Science fiction: the gret years v.2	PC0295
[anthology]	
Second if reader of science fiction	IF0102
[anthology]	
Seven deadly virtues	P00260
Seventh Galaxy Reader [anthology]	GA0146
Shaffery among the immortals	MA0210
Shaffery among the immortals	NE0158
Srowmen	FC0180
Srowmen	F00260
Speed trap	P00180
Star fourteen [anthology]	F00330
Star of stars [anthology]	F00300
Star science fiction stcries 1	P00371
[anthology]	
Star science fiction stories 2	F00372
[anthology]	
Star science fiction stcries 3	FC0373
[anthology]	
Star science fiction stcries no. 4	P00374
[anthology]	
Star science fiction stcries no. 6	P00376
Star short novels [anthclogy]	PC0400
Survival kit	P0026C
Tenth galaxy reader [anthology]	GA0149
Third offense	DE022C
Three portraits and a prayer	FI0090
Three portraits and a prayer	GA0146
Three portraits and a prayer	P00180
Time waits for Winthrop [anthology]	GA031C
Tunnel under the world	AL045C
Tunnel under the world	GA0149
Tunnel under the world	GR0300
Tunnel under the world	P00180
Under two moons	IF0102
Waginig of the peace	PC0260
We never mention Aunt Ncra	H00120
We never mention Aunt Ncra	PC0180
We purchased people	FEC17C

Pohl, Frederik
  What to do until the analyst comes CO0640
  What to do until the analyst comes SA0150
  Whatever counts GAC190
  With Redfern on Capella XI FO0210
  Wizards of Pung's Corners BOC10C
  Wizards of Pung's Corners FO0260
  Wizards of Pung's Corners SUC15C
  World of Myrion Flowers DE0250
  World of Myrion Flowers KEC100

Poleshchuk, Alexander
  Homer's secret GI0100
  Secret of Homer MO015C

Pollock, F.L.
  Finis MO0365

Popp, Lilian M.
  Journeys in science fiction LC0100
   [anthology]

Porges, Arthur
  Emergency operation CO0190
  Fly AS034C
  Fly BE0203
  Fly ME023C
  Guilty as charged BE0205
  Guilty as charged MI0180
  One ninety-eight ($1.98) MA0194
  Problem child ME0365
  Rats BE0202
  Rescuer AL0450
  Rescuer AS0651
  Ruum BR052C
  Ruum CR0100
  Ruum CR0170
  Ruum WI02C1

Posner, Richard
  Jacob's bug EL120C
  Running EL0520
  Running EL124C
  Vacation EL0940

Post, Melville Davisson
  Angel of the Lord WA016C

Potter, E.
  Children of Cain RY010C

Pouln, A., Jr.
  Coming [poem] SA0150

Priest, Christopher
    Anticipations [anthology]   PR016C
    Ersatz wine   MO0166
    Head and the hand   HA0165
    Infinite summer   CA0236
    Infinite summer   PR017C
    Infinite summer   SI096C
    Infinite summer   WE029C
    Infinite summer [anthology]   PR017C
    Men of good value   NE0326
    Negation   PR016C
    Negation   PR017C
    Palely loitering   PR017C
    Real-time world   NE0319
    Real-time world   WO0412
    Run   ME029C
    Watched   CA0241
    Watched   PR017C
    Whores   NE02C8
    Whores   PR017C

Priestley, Lee
    Sign among the stars   FU010C

Friestly, J. B.
    Mr. Strenberry's tale   KU010C

Proctor, Maurice
    No place for magic   WA016C

Prokofieva, R.
    More soviet science fiction   PR015C
      [anthology]

Pronzini, Bill
    Deathlove   GR0040
    Dry spell   AS0555
    Evergreen library   HO0120
    How now purple cow   AS0555
    I wish I may, I wish I might   AS0555
    Inaugural   AS0555
    Man who collected "The Shadow" WA016C
    Our times   HO011C
    Prose bowl   PR021C
    Shared tomorrows [anthology]   PR021C

Pugner, Carol
    Science fiction reader [anthology]   HA026C

Pumilia, Joe
    Hung like an elephant   GE015C
    Willowisp   GE018C

Purdom, Tom
    Holy grail   PO0376

Purdom, Tom
    Toys   CA0360
    Toys   SA0180
    War of passion   NC0150

Purdy, Ken W.
    Dannold cheque   HA0162
    In the matter of the assassin Merefirs   HA0165
    Noise   KA0070
    Noise   FL0150

Rabelais, Francois
    Phalanstery of Theleme   DE0370

Rackham, John [pseud. of J.T. Phillifent]
    Advantage   NE0306
    Computer's mate   NE0308
    Hell-planet   NE0302
    Last salamander   CA0210
    Poseidon project   NE0309
    Stoop to conquer   NE0319

Rager, Edward
    Crying Willow   AS0555

Ramsay, Kathryn
    Night at the fair   ED0150

Randall, Marta
    Captain and the kid   CA0376
    Megan's world   CR0250
    Scarab in the city of time   NE0200
    Scarab in the city of time   NE0205
    Secret rider   SI0960
    State of the art on alyssum   NE0207

Randers, Jorgen
    Limits to growth [excerpt]   AL0650

Rankine, John
    Maiden voyage   NE0302
    Six cubed plus one   NE0307
    Two's company   MI0180
    Two's company   NE0301

Ransom, James
    Fred one   MA0204

Raphael, Rick
    Filbert is a nut   AN0150
    Filbert is a nut   CA0100
    Sonny   AN0103
    Sonny   ME0365

Rees, L.
    Eye of the beholder   WI0245

Reese, John
    Rainmaker   HE0400

Reeves, Rosser
    E = MC (squared)   MA0201
    Effigy   MA0201
    Infinity   MA02CC

Reginald, R.
    Ancestral voices   ME0150

Reid, J.
    Probability storm   CA0374

Reines, Donald F.
    Interplanetary copyright   GR013C

Repp, Ed Earl
    Kleon of the Golden Sun   FO010C

Repton, Humphry
    From a private mad-house   DE04CC

Reynolds, Mack
    Adventure of the ball of Nostradamus   SC04CC
    Adventure of the extra-terrestrial   AN0105
    Acventure of the snitch in time   DE022C
    Adventure of the snitch in time   SC040C
    Albatross   EA010C
    Black sheep astray   AS075C
    Business, as usual   AS034C
    Business, as usual   CE059G
    Business, as usual   KN016C
    City's end   CL059C
    Cold war...continued   NC0403
    Compounded interest   ME0357
    Criminal in Utopia   GR030C
    Criminal in Utopia   HA0161
    D.P. from tomorrow   DE05CC
    Dark interlude   BE0202
    Dark interlude   DE025C
    Dark interlude   GA014C
    Dark interlude   FR021C
    Discord markers   CO025C
    Down the river   AL0411
    Earthlings go home   ME0363
    Fiesta brava   AN0107
    Freedom   GR025C
    Freedom   ME0362
    Generation gap   EL0740
    Genus traitor   AN0104
    Good Indian   AN0102

Reynolds, Mack
    Good Indian   CA010C
    Gun for hire   MC0180
    Isolationist   C0013C
    Man in the moon   LE0220
    Martians and the Coys   ER046C
    Mercenary   HA0145
    Pacifist   GR0250
    Pacifist   ME0365
    Pacifist   SA0100
    Prone   C0072C
    Prone   HA0260
    Prone   HA029C
    Radical center   CL0150
    Science fiction carnival [anthology]   ER0460
    Spooky   EL082C
    Subversive   AL0402
    Survival, A.D. 2000   EL1140
    Thou beside me   C0040C
    Utopian   HA03CC
    Visitor   ZE0150

Reynolds, Ted
    Boarder incident   AS0440

Rice, Jane
    Idol of the flies   TE0150
    Loolies are here   KN010C
    Loolies are here   KN0301
    Loolies are here   PR021C
    Rainbow gold   MA02CC
    Willow tree   MA0199

Richardson, Robert S. [pseud. of Philip Latham]
    Kid Anderson   C0043C
    Space fix   GR0130
    To explain Mrs. Thompson   P0C240

Richmond, L.
    Shortstack   C0014C

Richmond, Walt
    Poppa needs shorts   MC040C
    Poppa needs shorts   ME0364
    Prologue to an analogue   CA010C
    Shortstack   C0014C
    Shortstack   KE010C
    Shortstack   KE010C

Richter, Conrad
    Doctor Hanray's second chance   SA027C
    Sinister journey   SA027C

Ridenour, Louis N.
    Pilot lights of the apocalypse   C0043C

Riley, Frank
    Cyber and Justier Holmes   BE0206

Ritchie, Jack
    For all the rude people   WA0160

Robb, Stewart
    Letter from a higher critic   AN0106

Roberson, Rick
    Astoria incident   EN0070
    Beckoning trail   EN010C
    Cloudlab   EN010C
    Universe ahead [anthology]   EN010C

Roberts, Frank
    Happening   EA0240
    It could be you   BA0235
    It could be you   ME0365

Roberts, Keith
    Boulter's canaries   NE0303
    Boulter's canaries   RO0150
    Breakdown   RO0150
    Coranda   MO0163
    Deeps   KN0301
    Deeps   MC028C
    Deeps   RO0150
    Escapism   RO0150
    Inner wheel   NE0306
    Lady Margaret   DC0170
    Machine and men [anthology]   RO0150
    Manipulation   RC0150
    Manscarer   AL0402
    Manscarer   ME0290
    Manscarer   RC0150
    Pace that kills   RC0150
    Signaller   DC0165
    Sub-lim   NE0304
    Sub-lim   RO0150
    Synth   NE0308
    Synth   RO0150
    Therapy 2000   RO0150
    Therapy 2000   WO0410
    Weihnachtabend   HA0165

Roberts, Wills Davis
    Personage of royal blood   SC0460

Robertson, Morgan
    Battle of the monsters   CE0370
    Beyond the spectrum [anthology]   ME015C

Robin, Ralph
    Budding explorer   MA0192

Robin, Ralph
    Pleasant dreams   CO0280

Robinett, Stephen
    Helbent 4   EE0301
    Helbent 4   GA01CO
    Helbent 4   WO0416
    Linguist   HA0168
    Tomus   KN0319

Robinson, Frank M.
    Dream street   BE0206
    Dream street   SA0210
    East wind, west wind   CL059C
    East wind, west wind   HA025C
    East wind, west wind   NO0402
    Fire and the sword   BL01CC
    Fire and the sword   HA0234
    Girls from earth   BE02C3
    Girls from earth   SL0210
    Girls from earth   WI0210
    Hunting season   YE04C3
    Oceans are wide   YE0405
    One thousand miles up   BE02C5
    Reluctant heroes   DI0130
    Reluctant heroes   DI0220
    Reluctant heroes   GAC140
    Santa Claus Planet   EE0201
    Two weeks in August   AS0340
    Wreck of the Ship John B.   HA016C

Robinson, Jeanne
    Stardance   EE0303
    Stardance   CA0237

Robinson, Kim Stanley
    Coming back to Dixieland   KN0318
    Disguise   KN0319
    In Pierson's orchestra   KN0318

Robinson, Spider
    Half an oaf   B00240
    Overdose   GA01CC
    Satan's children   MA0521
    Stardance   BE0303
    Stardance   CA0237

Robles, Edward G, Jr.
    See?   AS0340

Rocklynne, Ross
    At the center of the gravity   MO0290
    Backfire   CO0280
    Ching witch   EL0220
    Diversifal   BR008C

Rocklynne, Ross
    Empress of Mars   AL0480
    Into the darkness   AS0451
    Into the darkness   CA0255
    Jaywalker   GA014C
    Men and the mirror   AS017C
    Pressure   BL010C
    Quietus   AS0451
    Quietus   HE0100
    Quietus   HE0170
    Randy-Tandy man   CA0370
    Time wants a skeleton   AS0452
    Time wants a skeleton   AS0650
    Winner take all   CE0530

Roddenberry, Gene
    Charlie's law   ST0161
    Menagerie   ST0164

Rodman, Howard
    Man who went to the moon--twice   EL03CC

Rogers, Joel Townsley
    Beyond space and time   B0015C
    Moment without time   ST018C
    No matter where you go   MA0199

Rogers, Kay
    Experiment   MA0193
    Flirtation walk   LA016C

Rogers, M.
    Klysterman's silent violin   SI0127

Rogoz, Adrian
    Altar of the random gods   R0027C

Roher, Robert
    Keep them happy   MA02C5
    Man who found Proteus   ME0365

Rohmer, Sax
    Tragedies in the Greek room   WA016C

Rome, David
    Parky   ME0362
    Robinson   BA024C
    There's a starman in ward 7   ME0366

Rose, Mark
    We would see a sign   AM0512

Roselle, Daniel
    Transformations [anthology]   R0018C

Rush, Norman
    Closing with nature   DI0250

Russ, Joanna
    Adventuress   KN0302
    Barbarian   D00165
    Barbarian   KN0303
    Existence   SI0480
    Few things I know about whileaway   DI0240
    Gleepsite   KN0100
    Gleepsite   KN0309
    Gleepsite   W00412
    I gave her sack and sherry   KN0100
    I gave her sack and sherry   KN0302
    Innocence   AS0555
    M is for many   CA0372
    Man who could not see devils   MC0150
    Masterpiece   MC0155
    My boat   W00417
    My dear Emily   MA0202
    Nobody's home   NE0200
    Nobody's home   NE0202
    Nobody's home   SA0240
    Nobody's home   SI0128
    Old fashioned girl   FE0170
    Poor man, beggar man   CA0368
    Poor man, beggar man   NE0157
    Reasonable people   KN0314
    Second inquisition   KN0306
    Second inquisition   NE0156
    Second inquisition   SA0220
    Soul of a servant   EL1060
    This night, at my fire   KN0460
    Useful phrases for the tourist   ED0150
    Useful phrases for the tourist   SI0580
    When it changed   EL0220
    When it changed   NE0158
    When it changed   SA0230

Russel, E.R.
    Ultimate invader   W00390

Russell, Bertrand
    Planetary effulgence   ME0363

Russell, Eric Frank
    Allamagoosa   AS0370
    Allamagoosa   CC0220
    Allamagoosa   D00130
    Allamagoosa   RL0070
    And then there were none   B00245
    And then there were none   F00120
    And then there were none   SC0211
    And then there were none   SL0210
    And then there were none   YE0403

Russell, Eric Frank

Appointment at noon	AS0340
Basic right	C00160
Best of Eric Frank Russell [anthology]	RU007C
Big shot	MA0490
Boomerang	C00550
Boomerang	C00560
Dear devil	CA026C
Dear devil	C00130
Dear devil	RU007C
Dear devil	SI0440
Dear devil	SL018C
Diabologic	B00100
Displaced person	CA042C
Exposure	C00310
Fast falls the eventide	BE02C3
Fast falls the eventide	RU007C
Glass eye	ME0230
Great radio peril	MC040C
Hobbyist	AL040C
Hobbyist	AS07CC
Hobbyist	CA0105
Hobbyist	CR0103
Hobbyist	RUC07C
Homo saps	RU007C
I am nothing	BE0203
I am nothing	RU007C
Illusionaries	N0027C
Impulse	C00250
Into your tent I'll creep	BE0208
Into your tent I'll creep	RU007C
Jay score	AS0452
Jay score	HE04CC
Jay score	RU007C
Late night final	AS070C
Late night final	CA01C5
Late night final	RU0070
Legwork	C00150
Mana	RU007C
Mechanical mice	CA0255
Metamorphosite	DE0340
Metamorphosite	GR019C
Metamorphosite	RU007C
Minor ingredient	AN015C
Minor ingredient	CA0100
Muten	ER046C
Now inhale	C00720
Panic button	C00580
Present from Joe	CR01C0
Room	PL015C
Second genesis	NE0309
Sole solution	AL0450
Still life	C00100
Study in still life	RU007C
Symbiotica	HE0100

Russell, Eric Frank
    Take a seat   ME0310
    Test piece   CO0280
    Test piece   DE0250
    This one's on me   CO040C
    Ultima thule   LE0220
    Waitabits   AS0651
    Weak spot   RU007C
    Witness   MO035C

Russell, Ray
    Better man   AS0555
    Better man   NO0230
    Better man   FL0155
    Darwin sampler   NO015C
    Long night   AS0555
    Most primitive   EL0720
    Put them all together, they spell   ME0357
        monster
    Room   AS0555
    Room   NO020C
    Xong of Xugan   EL0640
    Xong of Xuxan   HO012C

Russell, William Moy
    Three brothers   OB014C

Ryan, Charles C.
    Starry messenger   [anthology]   RY010C

Rymer, G.A.
    Atavists   CB0140
    Chain of command   CO040C

Saari, Oliver
    Sitting duck   DI0130
    Under the sand-seas   DI019C

Sabah, Victor
    Imaginary journey to the moon   HA0165

Saberhagen, Fred
    Fortress ship   ME0364
    Goodlife   SI0128
    Life hater   IF010C
    Martha   AS0555
    Masque of the red shift   IF0102
    Patron of the arts   DI011C
    Starsong   WO0409
    To mark the year on Azlaroc   FO029C
    Wings out of shadow   IF017C
    Without a thought   SI064C
    Young girl at an open half-door   KE0100

Sackett, Sam
    Hail to the chief   OL0150

Safronov, Y.
    Thread of life   MA0390

Sagan, Carl
    Intelligent life in the universe   AL0310

Saha, Arthur W.
    1972 annual world's best SF   WC0412
        [anthology]
    1974 annual world's best SF   W00414
        [anthology]
    1979 annual world's best sf [anthology] WC0419

Sail, Lawrence
    After weightless [poem]   HA0167
    Cymbal player [poem]   HA0165
    Fisherman [poem]   HA0164
    Picture by Klee [poem]   HA0167
    Report from the planet Proteus [poem] HA0165

Saint Clair, Eric
    Olsen and the gull   MA0204

Saint Clair, Margaret
    Age of prophecy   C00400
    Brightness falls from the air   MC0180
    Child of void   AS0590
    Child of void   C00250
    Counter charm   EL0520
    Gardener   DE0590
    Horrer Howce   GA0143
    Mrs. Hawk   MA0490
    Nuse man   GA0145
    Old-fashioned bird christmas   GA0146
    Pillows   C00340
    Prott   C00520
    Prott   CR010C
    Quis custodiet...?   C00460
    Sorrows of witches   SA0120

Saki
    Open window   TE0150
    Sredni Vashtar   SA0150
    Story teller   AL3060
    Tobermory   L00100

Sallis, James
    And then the dark   SA0100
    Anxiety in the eyes of the cricket J00150
    At the fitting shop   EL0220
    Binaries   KN010C
    Binaries   KN0309

Sallis, James
    Creation of Bennie Good   KN0306
    Delta flight   GE0150
    Doucement, s'il vous plait   KN0311
    Faces & hands   N00401
    Few last words   KN0304
    Few last words   KN0460
    Fifty-third American dream   EL0220
    First few kinds of truth   GE0150
    History makers   KN0305
    Jim and Mary G.   KN0100
    Jim and Mary G.   KN0307
    Kazoo   N00163
    Letter to a young poet   KN0303
    My friend Zarathustra   KN0313
    Only the words are different   KN0309
    Shores beneath [anthology]   SA0080
    Tissue [2 stories]   EL0220
    War book [anthology]   SA0100
    Writer as teacher   CL0110

Salmonson, Jessica Amanda
    Amazons!   SA0120

Salomon, Louis B.
    Univac to univac   H00100

Samachson, Joseph
    Feast of demons   P00240

Sambrot, William
    Creature of the snows   ME0361
    Island of fear   SA0270
    Leprechaun   ME0363
    Night of the leopard   WA0100
    Space secret   SA0270

Sanders, Thomas E.
    Speculation [anthology]   SA0150

Sanders, Winston P.
    Barnacle bull   AN0101
    Barnacle bull   CA0100
    Industrial revolution   AN0103
    Pact   MA0199
    Say it with flowers   AN0105
    Word to space   M00100

Sandrelli, Sandro
    Scythe   W00150

Sansom, William
    Among the dahlias   DI0260
    Witnesses   BR0380

Santesson, Hans Stefan
    Crime prevention in the 30th century   SA0180
      [anthology]
    Days after tomorrow [anthology]   SA0180
    Fantastic universe omnibus   FA0215
      [anthology]

Santos, Domingo
    Round and round and round again   WO0150

Saparin, Victor
    Magic shoes   MA0360
    Trail of Tantalus   PR018C

Sargent, Pamela
    Aunt Elvira's zoo   EL0960
    Clone sister   EL0180
    Darkness of day   EL0582
    Desert places   CA0371
    Friend from the stars   EL0900
    Gather blue roses   DA0200
    IMT   SC046C
    Irvisible girl   EL082C
    Matthew   EL116C
    More women of wonder [anthology]   SA0220
    New women of wonder [anthology]   SA023C
    Ncvella race   KN032C
    Renewal   DA018C
    Sense of difference   EL030C
    Sense of difference   EL0500
    Shadows   CA0265
    Weapons   EL0660
    Women of wonder [anthology]   SA024C

Sarowitz, Tony
    Child of penzance   AS018C
    Passionate state of mind   NE02C9

Satterfield, Charles
    With redfern on Capella XII   GA025C

Saturday Evening Post
    Post reader of fantasy and science   SA0270
      fiction [anthology]

Sauer, Rob
    Voyages   SA0300

Saunders, C.R.
    Aghewe's sword   SA012C

Saunders, Jake.
    Back to the stone age   BE0302

Savchenko, V.
    Professor Bern's awakening   DU0100
    Second oddball expedition   SH0150
    Success algorithm   NE0280

Saxton, C.
    Day   EL102C

Saxton, Josephine
    Alien sensation   LA016C
    Elouise and the doctors of the planet   EL022C
        Pergamon
    Heads Africa tails America   KN0309
    Jane Saint's travails   SA0120
    Ne deja vu pas   ME029C
    Power of time   NE02C1
    Power of time   SA022C
    Triumphant head   MC0150
    Triumphant head   SA023U
    Wall   ME0366

Saye, Lee
    Morning rush or Happy Birthday, dear   EL1200
        Leah
    No room for the wanderer   GE015C

Schachner, Nat
    Past, present, and future   AS017C
    Shining one   EL124C

Schaeffer, Robin
    Meeting the aliens on Algol VI   EL1140
    Revolution   EL072C

Schafhauser, Charles
    Gleeb for Earth   GA0141

Schaub, M.H.
    Serpentine   EL1140

Schenck, Hilbert, Jr.
    Ec Lear wasn't so crazy   ME0361
    Me   ME0360
    Morphology of the Kirkham wreck   CA0238

Schimmel, Michael
    Man who took the fifth   AS018C

Schmidt, Stanley
    Lost newton   MA055C
    Lost newton   MI0180
    May the best man win   CL0150

Schmitz, James H.
    Agent of Vega   N00300

Schmitz, James H.
    Agent of Vega [anthology]   SC0150
    Balanced ecology   AN0105
    Balanced ecology   CH010C
    Balanced ecology   MC040C
    Balanced ecology   NE0151
    Balanced ecology   SC0180
    Caretaker   GA0141
    End of the line   NC0270
    End of the line   SI09C0
    Grandpa   AL0401
    Grandpa   AL0450
    Grandpa   AM0514
    Grandpa   AS0651
    Grandpa   CL0500
    Grandpa   HA0260
    Grandpa   SI0780
    Greenface   SC019C
    Illusionists   SC0150
    Just curious   HA0232
    Lion loose   SC019C
    Machmen   SC018C
    Nice day for screaming [anthology]   SC018C
    Novice   AN01C2
    Novice   AS0590
    Novice   CA010C
    Novice   SI066C
    Other likeness   SC018C
    Planet of forgetting   WO04C6
    Pork chop tree   SC0190
    Pride of monsters [anthology]   SCC19C
    Resident witch   CA0360
    Rogue psi   WH0175
    Searcher   SC0190
    Second night of summer   C00340
    Second night of summer   SCC15C
    Spacemaster   NE0303
    Tangled web   SC0180
    Trouble tide   C0014C
    Truth about cushgar   SC015C
    We don't want any trouble   AS034C
    We don't want any trouble   P0015C
    Where the time went   EL0520
    Winds of time   SC018C
    Winds of time   SC019C
    Witches of Karres   AS070C
    Witches of Karres   KN048C
    Witches of Karres   KN0580
    Witches of Karres   SC0212

Schneider, Paul
    Balance of terror   ST0161

Schnirring, Mary-Alice
    Child's play   TE0150

Schoenfeld, Howard
    Built down logically   AS0340
    Built up logically   AL0450
    Built up logically   KN0480
    Built up logically   MC0180
    Built up logically   MA0191

Scholz, Carter
    Eve of the last Apollo   KN0318
    Ninth symphony of Ludwig Van Beethoven   CA0374
        and other lost songs

Schongut, Emanuel
    Tomorrow's children   AS0590

Schrader, Steven
    Cohen dog exclusion act   HA0164

Schramm, Wilbur
    Voice in the earphones   SA0270

Schulz, Charles M.
    Peanuts   ST0210

Schumack, S.W.
    Persephone and Hades   AN0140

Scortia, Thomas N.
    Alien night   MA0475
    Armageddon tapes-tape one   EL0580
    Armageddon tapes-tape three   EL0582
    Armageddon tapes-tape two   EL0581
    Blood brother   EL0740
    Bomb in the bathtub   GA0143
    Bomb in the bathtub   HA0130
    By the time I get to Phoenix   AC0200
    Final exam   EL1000
    Flowering narcissus   EL0130
    Icebox blonde   SC0450
    Judas fish   HA0300
    Sea change   AL0510
    Sea change   WA0130
    Shores of night   EE0206
    Strange bedfellows [anthology]   SC0450
    Tarrying   EL0700
    Thou good and faithful   BE0299
    Thou good and faithful   SC0460
    Tower   EL0540
    Two views of wonder [anthology]   SC0460
    Weariest river   EL0720
    Weariest river   EL1240
    When you hear the tone   EE0290
    Woman's rib   BE0291

Scott, Jody
    Go for Baroque   MA0201

Scott, Robin
    Big connection   NO0401
    Early warning   AN0106
    Last train to Kankakee   EL0220
    Maybe Jean-Baptiste Pierre Antoine de   KN0306
        Monet, Chevalier de Lemarck, was a
        little bit right
    Who needs insurance?   NE0152

Scott, Walter, Sir
    Secret weapon   EV0100

Seabright, Idris [pseud. of Margaret St.Clair]
    Altruists   DE0500
    Brightness falls from the air   AL0410
    Brightness falls from the air   BE0202
    Causes   MA0330
    Egg a month from all over   AS0340
    Egg a month from all over   CE0100
    Egg a month from all over   NE0310
    Hole in the moon   MA0192
    Listening child   MA0191
    Man who sold rope to the gnoles   NE0230
    New ritual   MA0193
    Short in the chest   C00310
    Short in the chest   C00640
    Short in the chest   SI0125
    Wines of earth   MA0197

Sell, William
    Other tracks   C00370

Sellers, Sally
    Perchance to dream   AS0173
    Perchance to dream   AS0440

Sellings, Arthur [pseud. of Robert A. Ley]
    Black form   GA0143
    Gifts of the gods   NE0307
    Gifts of the gods   NE0309
    Last time around   WO0411
    Mission   CB0140
    Start in life   AL0425

Senarens, Luis P.
    Frank Reade, Jr's air wonder   EL0520
    Frank Reade, Jr's air wonder   MO0380
    Frank Reade, Jr's strange adventures   MO0320
        with his new air ship
    Lost in a comet's tail   MO0320

Serling, Rod
    Avenging ghost   SE0180
    Back there   SE0180
    Curse of seven towers   SE0180
    Dead man's chest   SE0180
    Death's masquerade   SE0180
    Ghost of ticonderoga   SE0180
    Ghost town ghost   SE0180
    House on the square   SE0180
    Judgement night   SE0180
    Midnight sun   SE0150
    New stories from the twilight zone SE0150
        [anthology]
    Night of the meek   SE0150
    Return from oblivion   SE0180
    Riddle of the crypt   SE0180
    Rip Van Winkle caper   SE0150
    Rod Serling's the twilight zone   SE0180
        [anthology]
    Shelter   SE0150
    Showdown with Rance McGrew   SE0150
    Thirteenth story   SE0180
    Tiger god   SE0180
    Twilight zone   SE0180
    Whole truth   SE0150

Service, Pamela A.
    Chariot ruts   AS0175

Sexton, Anne
    Acdict   WH0150

Shaara, Michael
    All the way back   AL0410
    Book   CO0140
    Book   SI0128
    Grenville's planet   CR0102
    Man of distinction   GA0143
    Orphans of the void   SI0126
    Soldier boy   CO0550
    2066: Election day   GR0250
    2066: Election day   EE0208

Shackleton, C.C.
    Ultimate construction   HA0160

Shaeffer, R.
    Trippers   EL0860

Shamir, Moshe
    Doctor Schmidt   SA0300

Shango, J.R.
    Matter of ethics   CO0190

Shapiro, N.
    Journey of the soul   EL1180

Shapley, Harlow
    On lethal space clouds   DC0160

Sharkey, Jack
    Multum in Parvo   ME0360
    To each his own   GA0230
    To each his own   GA0280
    Trade-in   MA0204
    Twerlik   ME0365

Sharovsky-Raffe, Arthur
    Everthing but love [anthology]   SH0150

Shaw, Bob
    Altar egos   BE0500
    Amphitheatre   FR0160
    Appointment on Prila   HA0161
    Appointment on Prila   HA0290
    Burden of proof   AN0107
    Cosmic kaleidoscope [anthology]   SH0160
    Deflation 2001   SH0160
    Element of chance   SH0160
    Frost animals   CA0376
    Full member of the club   SH0160
    Full member of the club   W00415
    Giaconda caper   SH0160
    Happiest day of your life   AS0555
    Invasion of privacy   W00411
    Light of other days   AL0665
    Light of other days   AN0106
    Light of other days   HA0260
    Light of other days   KN0480
    Light of other days   MC0400
    Light of other days   ME0367
    Light of other days   NE0152
    Light of other days   SI0125
    Light of other days   W00407
    Little night flying   SH0160
    Silent partners   SH0160
    Skirmish on a summer morning   SH0160
    Uncomic book horror story   SH0160
    Unreasonable facsimile   EL0860
    Unreasonable facsimile   SH0160
    Waltz of the bodysnatchers   SH0160
    Waltz of the bodysnatchers   WE0290

Shaw, Lao
    Everybodyvskyism in Cat City   ST0210

Shaw, Larry
    Simworthy's circus   BR0460

Shcherbakov, Vladimir
    We played under your window   GI0130

Sheckley, Robert
    Accountant   AS0590
    Accountant   MA0194
    Ask a foolish question   SH0180
    Bad medicine   HA0234
    Bad medicine   SH018C
    Battle   SH018C
    Budget planet   HA0161
    Can you feel anything when I do this?   KN0480
    Can you feel anything when I do this?   PL0155
    Carrier   NC0230
    Doctor Zombie and his furry little   HA0164
        friends
    Early model   AL0401
    Feeding time   AS0555
    Fool's mate   SH0210
    Ghost V   SH0180
    Ghost V   SH021C
    Gray flannel armor   SH021C
    Gun without a bang   HC012C
    Hands off   SH018C
    Holdout   DE0250
    Holdout   KE0100
    Hour of battle   HA01CC
    Human man's burden   CO076C
    Hunting problem   SH0180
    I see a man sitting on a chair, and   EL044C
        the chair is biting his leg
    Immortality Inc.   SH0180
    In a land of clear colors   DI023U
    Is that what people do?   PR016C
    King's wishes   SI096C
    Last weapon   FO0371
    Leech   CO052C
    Love, incorporated   KA007C
    Love, incorporated   PL0150
    Love, incorporated   PL0155
    Meeting of the minds   WI0206
    Minimum man   GA0143
    Monsters   CR0104
    Monsters   MA0470
    Monsters   MA055C
    Monsters   SI0128
    Never-ending western movie   PO0290
    Odor of thought   FO0372
    Operating instructions   ME026C
    Paradise II   DE059C
    People trap   MA02C8
    People trap   SH0210
    Perfect woman   AS0340
    Perfect woman   AS0555
    Pilgrimage to earth   AM051C

Sheckley, Robert

Pilgrimage to earth	SHO180
Pilgrimage to earth	SHO210
Potential	ASO651
Potential	DEO500
Prize of peril	DOO130
Prize of peril	MEO201
Prize of peril	MEO359
Prize of peril	SHO180
Prize of peril	SHO210
Prospector's special	ASO575
Robert Sheckley omnibus [anthology]	SHO180
Seventh victim	KAOO70
Seventh victim	MCO400
Seventh victim	NOO200
Seventh victim	SHO210
Shall we have a little talk?	SHO210
Shape	NOO240
Shape	SIO126
Skulking permit	SHO210
Slaves of time	NOO404
Something for nothing	CEO100
Something for nothing	GRO300
Something for nothing	SHO180
Specialist	GAO141
Specialist	SHO180
Specialist	SHO210
Specialist	SIO680
Specialist	SUO150
Specialist	WAO130
Spy story	PLO150
Starting from scratch	ASO555
Store of the worlds	ALO450
Store of the worlds	SHO180
Store of the worlds	SHO210
Street of dreams, feet of clay	CLO590
Street of dreams, feet of clay	DAO200
Street of dreams, feet of clay	SAO150
Street of dreams, feet of clay	WOO409
Suppliant in space	WCO414
Ticket to Tranal	SHO180
Untouched by human hands	NOO240
Warm	GAO141
Warm	SIO127
We are alone	HOO100
Welcome to the standard nightmare	HAO166
Welcome to the standard nightmare	NOO403
Wind is rising	SHO210
Wonderful world of Robert Sheckley [anthology]	SHO210
Zirn left unguarded	ALO510
Zirn left unguarded,the Jenghik palace in flames,Jon Westerly dead	NOO402

Shiel, M.P.
        Place of pain   MO0320

Shiras, Wilmar H.
        Children of the atom   TE0150
        In hiding   BL0120
        In hiding   CA0340
        In hiding   KN0480
        In hiding   KN0580
        In hiding   LE0130
        In hiding   SC0212
        In hiding   SL0210
        In hiding   TE0150
        Opening doors   BE02C0
        Opening doors   BL0120

Shirley, John
        Almost empty rooms   NE0207
        Under the generator   CA0373
        Uneasy chrysalids, our memory   SI0480
        Will the chill   CA0376

Shofner, P.
        Pity the poor outcated man   NC0403

Shore, Wilma
        Bulletin from the trustees   MA0204
        Bulletin from the trustees   SI1000
        Goodbye Amanda Jean   SI0121
        Is it the end of the world?   MA0210

Sidney, Kathleen M.
        Arthropologist   KN0317
        Teacher   KN0318

Silverberg, Robert
        (Now + n) (Now - n)   NC0402
        (Now + n) (Now - n)   SI0580
        (Now + n) (Now - n)   SI0980
        Absolutely inflexible   SI0360
        Absolutely inflexible   SI1000
        After the myths went home   DO0165
        After the myths went home   SI0860
        After the myths went home   WO0410
        Alaree   SI0440
        Alaree   SI0860
        Aliens [anthology]   SI0100
        Alpha 1 [anthology]   SI0120
        Alpha 2 [anthology]   SI0121
        Alpha 4 [anthology]   SI0123
        Alpha 5 [anthology]   SI0124
        Alpha 6 [anthology]   SI0125
        Alpha 7 [anthology]   SI0126
        Alpha 8 [anthology]   SI0127
        Alpha 9 [anthology]   SI0128

Silverberg, Robert

Silverberg, Robert
Man who never forgot	SI070C
Man who never forgot	SIC76C
Many mansions	CA037C
Many mansions	SI098C
Men and machines [anthology]	SI064C
Mind for business	SI092C
Mind to mind [anthology]	SI066C
Mirror of infinity [anthology]	SI068C
Misfit	SI092C
Ms. Found in an abandoned time machine	EL116C
Ms. Found in an abandoned time machine	EL124C
Mugwump	SIC34C
Mugwump	SI074C
Mugwump 4	SI036C
Mugwump 4	SI096C
Mutant season	EL052C
Mutants [anthology]	SI070C
Neighbor	SI036C
Neighbor	SIC84C
Neutral planet	SI084C
New Atlantis [Anthology]	SI072C
New dimensions 1 [anthology]	NE0201
New dimensions 2 [anthology]	NE0202
New dimensions 3 [anthology]	NE0203
New dimensions 4 [anthology]	NE0204
New dimensions 5 [anthology]	NE0205
New dimensions 7 [anthology]	NEC2C7
New dimensions 8 [anthology]	NE0208
New dimensions 9 [anthology]	NE0209
New men for mars	SI092C
Nightwings	ASC4CC
Nightwings	SI028C
Nightwings	SI060C
Old man	SI092C
One way journey	SI076C
Other dimensions [anthology]	SI074C
Outbreeders	SI076C
Outbreeders	SI084C
Overlord's thumb	SI084C
Overlord's thumb	SIC92C
Ozymandias	SI09CC
Czymandias	SI092C
Pain peddlers	SI084C
Pain peddlers	SI102C
Parsecs and parables [anthology]	SIC76C
Passengers	KN010C
Passengers	KN0304
Passengers	NE0155
Passengers	SI028C
Passengers	SI036C
Passport to Sirius	SI084C
Point of focus	SI034C
Point of focus	WI02C6
Precedent	SI034C

Silverberg, Robert
Push no more	SC045C
Quick freeze	SI08CC
Reality trip	CA036C
Ringing the changes	MC015C
Road to nightfall	FA0215
Road to nightfall	SI028C
Road to nightfall	SI038C
Road to nightfall	SI0760
Schwartz between the galaxies	DE0265
Schwartz between the galaxies	SIC54C
Science fiction bestiary [anthology]	SI0780
Science fiction hall of fame. v.1 [anthology]	SC0210
Sea of faces	CA0371
Shadow of wings	SI036C
Ship-sister, star-sister	EL1200
Shores of tomorrow [anthology]	SI0800
Silent colony	CA026C
Silent colony	SIC8CC
Sixth palace	SI028C
Sixth palace	SIC36C
Sixth palace	SI0400
Some notes on the pre-dynastic epoch	SI0980
Something wild is loose	BO026C
Something wild is loose	SI0660
Something wild is loose	SI0840
Song the Zombie sang	EL044C
Sound decision	AN015C
Sound decision	CA01CC
Sound decision	PR021C
Sound decision	SA0210
Sound decision	SI0800
Strange gifts [anthology]	SI082C
Stress pattern	SI03CC
Sundance	CL010C
Sundance	SA015C
Sundance	SI010C
Sundance	SI0280
Sundance	SIC36C
Sundance	SI084C
Sundance [anthology]	SI0840
Sunrise on Mercury	SI0760
Sunrise on Mercury	SIC94C
Sunrise on Mercury [anthology]	SI0860
Then was an old woman	SI086C
This is the road	CA0310
This is the road	SI054C
Thomas the Proclaimer	AN019C
Thomas the Proclaimer	SI0320
Threads of time [anthology]	SI0880
To be continued	SI082C
To see the invisible man	HA0232
To see the invisible man	HO010C
To see the invisible man	SI0280

Silverberg, Robert
    To the dark star   EL0200
    To the dark star   HA0161
    To the dark star   SI0360
    To the stars [anthology]   SI0900
    To worlds beyond [anthology]   SI0920
    Tomorrow's worlds [anthology]   SI0940
    Translation error   ROC210
    Translation error   SI0360
    Translation error   SI1040
    Trips   FE0170
    Trips   SI054C
    Trips   SI062C
    Trips in time [anthology]   SI096C
    Unfamiliar territory [anthology] SI098C
    Voyagers in time [anthology]   SI100C
    Warm man   MC0180
    Warm man   SI028C
    What we learned from this morning's AC02C0
        newspaper
    When we went to see the end of the EE0291
        world
    When we went to see the end of the ED015C
        world
    When we went to see the end of the FI009C
        world
    When we went to see the end of the NE0158
        world
    When we went to see the end of the SI042C
        world
    Why?   SI034C
    Wind and the rain   EL102C
    Wind and the rain   HA0166
    Wind and the rain   HO0110
    Windows into tomorrow [anthology] SI1020
    Worlds of maybe [anthology]   SI1040

Silverstein, Shel
    Distortion   ME0361

Simak, Clifford D.
    Aesop   SI110C
    All the traps of earth   SI106C
    All the traps of earth   SI1080
    All the traps of earth   SI112C
    All the traps of earth [anthology] SI1060
    Answers   SI1160
    Answers   SL0210
    Asteriod of gold   W00240
    Auk house   CE0267
    Autumn land   HA0234
    Autumn land   SI112C
    Beachhead   CE034C
    Beachhead   SI052C
    Beachhead   SI1160

Simak, Clifford D.

Golden bugs	SI1140
Good night, Mr. James	DE0470
Good night, Mr. James	GA0140
Good night, Mr. James	SI1060
Good night, Mr. James	SI1120
Green thumb	CR0104
Green thumb	SI1180
Hobbies	SI1100
Honorable opponent	GA0142
Honorable opponent	SI1180
How-2	AS0585
How-2	DI0160
How-4	EE0205
How-4	GA0190
Huddling place	AL0400
Huddling place	MO0350
Huddling place	SC0210
Huddling place	SI1100
Huddling place	SI1120
I am crying all inside	AS0070
Idiot's crusade	SI1180
Immigrant	AL0410
Immigrant	SI1080
Immigrant	SI1160
Installment plan	SI1060
Jackpot	SI1180
Junkyard	GA0141
Kindergarten	DE0500
Kindergarten	SI1160
Leg. forst.	SI1140
Limiting factor	AM0510
Limiting factor	CO0340
Loot of time	EL0480
Lulu	SI1080
Lulu	SI1180
Marathon photograph	SI0880
Mirage	SI1160
Mr. Meek plays polo	CA0277
Nebula award stories six [anthology]	NE0156
Neighbor	DA0270
Neighbor	SI1080
Neighbor	SI1180
New folks' home	AN0103
New folks' home	SI1080
No life of their own	AS0590
No life of their own	SI1060
Operation stinky	SI1180
Over the river and through the woods	WO0406
Paradise	SI1100
Project mastodon	SI1060
Retrograde evolution	SI1160
Second childhood	GA0140
Second childhood	SL0210
Senior citizen	EE0301

Simak, Clifford D.

    Shadow show   SI1160

Simak, G.O.

Simonds, Bruce

Singer, Isaac Bashevis

Skal, Dave

Skinner, B.F.

Sky, Kathleen

Sladek, John T.

Sladek, John T.
    Elephant with wooden leg   DI026C
    Elephant with wooden leg   GA01C0
    Elephant with wooden leg   ST022C
    Happy breed   EL03CC
    Heavens below   DI0240
    Man who devoured books   KA007C
    Masterson and the clerks   MO0164
    Masterson and the clerks   SA008C
    Mystery diet of the gods: a revelation   DI023C
    1937 A.D.!   HAC160
    Poets of Millgrove, Iowa   MO0162
    Secret of the old custard   SI0125
    Steam-driver boy   NO0402

Slesar, Henry
    After   FL0150
    Before the talent dies   FE026C
    Chief   AS0555
    Chief   ME0361
    Doctor   AS0555
    Ersatz   EL03CC
    Examination day   AS0555
    Examination day   OL0165
    Examination day   FL015C
    Invisible man murder case   DA023C
    Merchant   AS0555
    My father, the cat   FA0215
    Survivor I   EL044C

Sloane, William Milligan
    Edge of running water   SL015C
    Let nothing you dismay   SL021C
    Rim of the morning   SL015C
    Rim of the morning [anthology]   SL015G
    Space, space, space [anthology]   SL018C
    Stories for tomorrow [anthology]   SL021C
    To walk the night   SL015C

Smagin, Boris
    Silent procession   BE002C

Smith, Clark Ashton
    City of the singing flame   SI0620
    Great God Awto   SM015C
    Immortals of Mercury   SM015C
    Maker of gargoyles   SM0150
    Master of the asteroid   SM015C
    Metamorphosis of earth   DE0340
    Morthylla   SM015C
    Mother of toads   SM0150
    Murder in the fourth dimension   SM015C
    Phoenix   DE0530
    Plutonian drug   DE047C
    Root of ampoi   SM015C

Smith, Clark Ashton
    Schizoid creator   SM0150
    Seed from the sepulcher   SM0150
    Seedling of mars   SM0150
    Symposium of the Gorgon   SM0150
    Tales of science and sorcery   SM0150
       [anthology]
    Theft of the thirty-nine girdles SM0150
    Tomb-spawn   SM0150
    Voyage to Sfanomoe   DE0370

Smith, Cordwainer [pseud. of Paul M.A. Linebarger]
    Alpha Ralpha Boulevard   MA0201
    Alpha Ralpha Boulevard   SI0460
    Alpha Ralpha Boulevard   SM0180
    Angerhelm   P00376
    Ballad of lost C'mell   C00760
    Ballad of lost C'mell   SC0211
    Ballad of lost C'mell   SM0180
    Burning of the brain   SI0121
    Burning of the brain   SM0180
    Crime and glory of Commander Suzdal AL0410
    Crime and glory of Commander Suzdal C00610
    Crime and glory of Commander Suzdal SM0180
    Dead lady of Clown Town   SI0560
    Dead lady of Clown Town   SM0180
    Down to the sunless sea   CA0235
    Drunkboat   ME0364
    Game of rat and dragon   BE0206
    Game of rat and dragon   CR0102
    Game of rat and dragon   GA0142
    Game of rat and dragon   KN0480
    Game of rat and dragon   SI0680
    Game of rat and dragon   SM0180
    Game of rat and dragon   SU0150
    Game of rat and dragon   WA0130
    Golden the ship was ___ oh! oh! oh! SM0180
    Lady who sailed the soul   GA0250
    Lady who sailed the soul   SM0180
    Mother Hilton's littul kittons   SM0180
    No, no, not Rogov!   ME0360
    On the Gem Planet   D00165
    On the Gem Planet   GA0146
    On the storm planet   DC0170
    Planet named Shayol   AM0513
    Planet named Shayol   SM0180
    Scanners live in vain   AL0401
    Scanners live in vain   F00100
    Scanners live in vain   P00190
    Scanners live in vain   SC0210
    Scanners live in vain   SM0180
    Think blue, count two   C00140
    Under old earth   SM0180
    When the people fell   GA0144

Smith, Edward E.
    Atlantis   GR0190
    Vortex blasters   MO0350

Smith, Evelyn E.
    Baxbr Daxbr   CR0103
    Baxbr Daxbr   DE0530
    Baxbr Daxbr   L00100
    Baxbr Daxbr   WI0203
    Day in the suburbs   MI018C
    Galactic patrol   AL048C
    Hardest bargain   GA0250
    Last of the spode   C00640
    Martian and the magician   AS0340
    Not fit for children   GA0141
    Once a Greech   GA0340
    Skylark of space [excerpt]   SC0300
    Softly while you're sleeping MA0201
    Tea tray in the sky   GA0141
    Vilkar party   DE0250
    Vilkar party   GA0142

Smith, George A.
    Lost art   B00151

Smith, George Henry
    Flame tree planet   EL070C
    In the Imagican   NE0152
    Last crusade   CA0360

Smith, George O.
    Amateur in chancery   P00240
    Cosmic jackpot   BR0460
    Counter foil   SI064C
    QRM--Interplanetary   CU007C

Smith, Lowell Kent
    Ernie   KN0315

Smith, Paula
    African blues   AS044C

Smith, Philip H.
    Miracle too many   ME0365

Smith, Ritchie
    Seafarer   NE0326

Smith, Ron
    I don't mind   MA0196
    Strong attraction   BA0235

Smitter, Wessel Hyatt
    Hand   ER0380

Snyder, G.
    Lady of ice   MA0521
    Smokey the bear sutra   EL1020

Sohl, Jerry
    I am Aleppo   EL0940

Somp
    Noneatrins   SU0180

Spark, Muriel
    Portobello Road   ME0362

Spencer, William
    Eternal machines   NE0302
    Horizontal man   NE0306
    Long memory   NE0307
    Long memory   NE0309

Spies, Adrian
    Miri   ST0161

Spillane, Mickey
    Veiled woman   WA0160

Spinrad, Norman
    Age of invention   GR0300
    Age of invention   MA0206
    Big flash   KN0100
    Big flash   KN0305
    Big flash   SA0300
    Big flash   WH0150
    Big flash   WO0410
    "It's a bird! It's a plane!"   HA0130
    Carcinoma angels   EL0300
    Carcinoma angels   MC04C0
    Carcinoma angels   SI0123
    Down the rabbit hole   SA0100
    Equalizer   KN0280
    Last hurrah of the golden horde   AL0402
    Last hurrah of the golden horde   HA0233
    Last hurrah of the golden horde   MO0165
    Last of the Romany   KE0100
    Last of the Romany   SI1020
    Lost continent   SI0125
    National pastime   EE0299
    National pastime   ED0150
    National pastime   NO0403
    Night in Elf Hill   EL0200
    No direction home   CA0231
    No direction home   CA0234
    No direction home   HA0164
    Riding the torch   SI0880
    Subjectivity   AN0104
    Thing of beauty   AC0200

Spinrad, Norman
    Thing of beauty   AN0140
    Thing of beauty   BE0299
    Thing of beauty   NE0159
    Thing of beauty   PC0450
    Weed of time   MC015C
    Weed of time   WO0414

Spofford, H.P.
    Ray of displacement   MO0365

Springer, Sherwood
    Lorelei at Storyville Wet   AS0172
    No land of Nod   ST0180

Stableford, Brian M.
    Captain Fagan died alone   WO018C
    Engineer and the executioner WO0416
    Sun's tears   WO0414

Standish, Robert
    Test-tube terror   SA027C

Stantor, Will
    As long as you're here   FE023C
    Barney   AS0340
    Barney   MA0191
    Dodger fan   MA0197
    Gumdrop king   MA0202
    Last present   MA0196
    You are with it   KN016C

Stanyukovich, Kirill
    Golub-yavan   DI028C

Stapledon, Olaf
    Flames   ST015C
    Flying men   CE037C
    Humanity on Venus   MO0320
    Last and first men   AL031C
    Last and first men   KU010C
    Last and first men   ST015C
    Last and first men   WI028C
    Last Terrestrials   KU010C
    Martians   KU010C
    Odd John   KN016C
    Odd John   ST015C
    Odd John   WO033C
    Sirius   ST015C
    Star maker   ST015C
    To the end of time [anthology] ST015C

Starr, B.
    People who could not kill   DE0267

Stine, G. Harry
    One reason why we lost   ME0358
    Test stand   F0024C

Stockham, Richard
    Valley   AL0405

Stocktcn, Frank R.
    Tale of negative gravity   DE037C
    Tale of negative gravity   LC0100

Stone, L.F.
    Human pets of Mars   AS0170
    Rape of the solar system   W0027C

Stones, Jonathan
    Alpha in Omega   CB0140

Stopa, John
    Kiddy-lib   EL018C

Stout, T.
    Christmas with Frankenstein   DA0273
    Living fossil   DA0271
    Sting from the stars   DA0273

Stover, Leon E.
    Apeman, spaceman [anthology]   ST021C
    What we have here is too much   KN03C9
        communication
    What we have here is too much   MC040C
        communication

Street, Claire Edwin
    Mysterious gem   EL104C
    To the world of Zzzd   EL122C

Strete, Craig
    Bleeding man   W00415
    Horse of a different technicolor GA010C
    Three dream woman   NE0208
    Time deer   HA0167
    Time deer   NE0161
    Who was the first Oscar to win a KN0318
        negro?

Strick, Philip
    Antigrav [anthology]   ST0220

Stringer, David
    Acclimatization   NE0305
    High eight   NE0304

Strugatsky, Arkady
    Destination: Amaltheia   DI028C

Strugatsky, Arkady
    Emergency case   PA0210
    He will wake in two hundred years   BE0020
    Second Martian invasion   BE0020
    Six matches   FR0180
    Spontaneous reflex   DU0100
    Wanderers and travellers   MO0150
    Wanderers and travellers   PA0210
    White cone of the Alaid   GI0100

Strugatsky, Boris
    Destination: Amaltheia   DI0280
    Emergency case   PA0210
    He will wake in two hundred years   BE0020
    Second Martian invasion   BE0020
    Wanderers and travellers   MO0150
    White cone of the Alaid   GI0100

Struther, Jan
    Ugly sister   MA0192

Stuart, Don A. [pseud. of John W. Campbell]
    Cloak of Aesir   AS0450
    Forgetfulness   AS0650
    Forgetfulness   HE0100
    Forgetfulness   KN0190
    Night   AS0645
    Twilight   KN0120
    Who goes there?   HE0100
    Who goes there?   KN0580

Stuart, William W.
    Husband for many wife   HE0100
    Inside John Barth   GA0144
    Star-crossed lover   CO0760

Stubbs, Harry C.
    First flights to the moon [anthology]   ST0230

Sturgeon, Theodore [pseud. of E.H. Waldo]
    Abreaction   HA0100
    Affair with a green monkey   ST0330
    And now the news   CE0100
    And now the news   DO0130
    And now the news   JA0130
    Ard now the news   KA0070
    Ard now the news   KN0540
    And now the news   MA0196
    Artnan process   ST0320
    Baby is three   SC0211
    Baby is three   ST0300
    Baby is three   TE0150
    Bianca's hands   KN0490
    Bianca's hands   ST0270
    Bulkhead   ST0360

Sturgecn, Theodore [pseud. of E.H. Waldo]

Sturgecn, Theodore [pseud. of E.H. Waldo]

Killdozer	WI0245
Love of heaven	CO0400
Make room for me	ST0325
Man who learned lcving	NE0155
Man who learned loving	WA010C
Man who lost the sea	KN058C
Man who lost the sea	MA0203
Man who lost the sea	ME036C
Man who lost the sea	SI0127
Martian and the moron	CE0590
Maturity	CO0670
Memorial	CO052C
Memorial	PO0293
Memorial	WA013C
Memory	CR020C
Mewhu's jet	CO0130
Mewhu's jet	PO0295
Mewhu's jet	ST0360
Microcosmic god	AS0452
Microcosmic god	CA0255
Microcosmic god	CO016C
Microcosmic god	MO035C
Microcosmic god	SC021C
Minority report	CE037C
Minority report	ST036C
Morality	ST03CC
More than human	KN0480
Mcre than human [anthology]	ST03CC
Mr. Costello, hero	BO01CC
Mr. Costello, hero	MC040C
Mr. Costello, hero	PO0150
Mr. Costello, hero	ST033C
Music	ST027C
My fear is great	ST036C
Nail and the oracle	PL015C
Never underestimate	CO028C
Never underestimate	CO064C
Occam's scalpel	EE029C
Occam's scalpel	CA0231
Occam's scalpel	CA0234
Occam's scalpel	WO0412
Other Celia	KN0280
Other Celia	ST033C
Other man	ME0357
Perfect host	ME023C
Pod and the barrier	ST032C
Pod in the barrier	ST0330
Professor's teddy bear	MA049C
Professor's teddy-bear	ST0270
Rule of three	GA0140
Runesmith	EL044C
Saucer of loneliness	GA0141
Saucer of loneliness	MI0150
Saucer of loneliness	ST027C

Sturgeon, Theodore [pseud. of E.H. Waldo]
    Scaro   ST027C
    Sex opposite   ST027C
    Shottle bop   AS0452
    Shottle bop   DA0230
    Silken swift   ST0270
    Skills of Xanadu   SI0124
    Slow sculpture   AS04C1
    Slow sculpture   NE0156
    Slow sculpture   SA015C
    Slow sculpture   WO0411
    Special aptitude   ST036C
    Stars are the styx   GA014C
    Starshine [anthology] ST032C
    Sturgeon in orbit [anthology] ST0325
    Talent   AS034C
    That law   KO016C
    Thunder and roses   AS0651
    Thunder and roses   AS070C
    Thunder and roses   CA0105
    Thunder and roses   STC36C
    Tiny and the monster CO0250
    Tiny and the monster ST036C
    To here and the easel PO040C
    To marry Medusa   GA031C
    Touch of strange   FE023C
    Touch of strange [anthology] ST033C
    Touch of your hand   ST033C
    Ultimate egoist   ME031C
    Unite and conquer   GR019C
    Unite and conquer   TO0360
    Wages of synergy   ST018C
    Wages of synergy   ST0325
    Way home [anthology]   ST036C
    Way of thinking   ST027C
    What dead men tell   BL01CC
    When you care, when you love FE020C
    When you care, when you love STC240
    When you're smiling   CR0101
    Widget, The [Widget], and Boff EO015C
    World well lost   SC045C
    World well lost   ST027C
    World well lost   ST032C
    Yesterday was Monday   CO0370

Styron, William
    Pie in the sky   CE01CC

Suggs, Robert C.
    Kon-tiki myth   ST021C

Sullivan, Charles William
    As tomorrow becomes today [anthology] SU0150

Sullivan, J.F.
    Impossibility, a study of reason and   ME0150
        science

Sullivan, Timothy Robert
    Rauncher goes to Tinker Town   NE0209

Sutherland, Herb
    Blond kid   CB0140

Sutherland, James
    At the second solstice   CL0110
    Swords of Ifthan   AS0555
    Swords of Ifthan   EL0980

Sutton, Jeff
    After Ixmal   AL0510
    Forerunner   EL0520

Sutton, Lee
    Soul mate   MA0199
    Soul mate   M00100

Suvin, Darko
    Other worlds, others seas [anthology]   SU0180

Swann, Thomas Burnett
    Manor of roses   FE0200

Swenson, May
    Earth will not let go [poem]   SA0150
    Southbound on the freeway   HC0100

Swift, Jonathan
    Gulliver's travels [excerpt from book   WH0150
        III]
    Laputa   CE0370
    Satirical science fiction   EV0100
    Voyage to Laputa [excerpt]   GU0130

Szilard, Leo
    Calling all stars   SZ0150
    Grand Central Terminal   CO0430
    Mark Gable foundation   HA0210
    Mark Gable foundation   F00240
    Mark Gable foundation   SZ0150
    My trial as a war criminal   ME0362
    My trial as a war criminal   SZ0150
    Nightmare for future reference   SZ0150
    Report on "Grand Central Terminal"   SZ0150
    Voice of the dolphins [anthology]   SZ0150

Taine, John [pseud. of Eric T. Bell]
    Before the dawn   W0033C
    Ultimate catalyst   AS0450

Tall, Stephen
    Bear with the knot on his tail   MA0210
    Bear with the knot on his tail   W00412

Tarkington, Booth
    Veiled feminists of Atlantis   M00410

Tate, Peter
    Beyond the weeds   NE0367
    Mainchance   MC0150
    Mars pastorale   M00165
    Post-mortem people   KE010C
    Post-mortem people   MC0163
    Same autumn in a different park   ME0290

Taylor, Bruce
    Attendant   NE0209

Taylor, J.A.
    Oak and the ash   RY0100

Taylor, Robert
    Sense of beauty   HA0234

Teich, Phillip
    Beings of game p-u   KN0319

Teichner, Albert
    Christlings   KN0310
    Fantasy's profession   KN0313
    Junkmakers   GA0280

Telfair, David
    In a quart of water   MC015C

Temple, William F.
    Date to remember   C00250
    Date to remember   SA015C
    Forget me-not   BE0201
    Four-sided triangle   AS045C
    Green car   AS0585
    Two shadows   BE0202
    Two shadows   CA0230
    Unpicker   EL0520
    Way of escape   C00370

Tenn, William [pseud. of Philip Klass]
    Alexander the Bait   C00280
    Bernie the Faust   KN0480
    Bernie the Faust   ME0364
    Bernie the Faust   NE0304

Tenn, William [pseud. of Philip Klass]
    Bernie the Faust   PL015C
    Betelgeuse bridge   GA0140
    Betelgeuse bridge   HE0400
    Brooklyn Project   CO0640
    Brooklyn Project   SI1000
    Child's play   AS0651
    Child's play   AS07C0
    Child's play   PR015C
    Child's play   SI03CC
    Children of wonder [anthology]   TE015C
    Counter-transference   BE0203
    Custodian   JA013C
    Custodian   CL017C
    Custodian   TE018C
    Deserter   CHC1CC
    Deserter   PO0371
    Down among the dead men   AL0405
    Down among the dead men   DE0250
    Down among the dead men   SI0125
    Down among the dead men   TE018C
    Eastward ho!   AL0450
    Eastward ho!   HO0120
    Eastward ho!   MA0199
    Eastward ho!   SI0123
    Errand boy   TE015C
    Everybody loves Irving Bommer   TE0180
    Firewater   SI01CC
    Firewater   YE0404
    Flirgleflip   TE018C
    Generation of Noah   BE0202
    House dutiful   ME023C
    Icnian cycle   GR0310
    Jester   CO055C
    Jester   CO056C
    Liberation of earth   AL045C
    Liberation of earth   KN0540
    Liberation of earth   MA0470
    Liberation of earth   PO012C
    Liberation of earth   SA0100
    Liberation of earth   SI0600
    Liberation of earth   TE0180
    Masculinist revolt   FE02C0
    Me, myself and I   TE0180
    Null-p   AMC51C
    Null-p   CR017C
    Null-p   DE059C
    Of all possible worlds [anthology]   TE0130
    Or Venus, have we got a Rabbi   DA02C0
    Party of the two parts   SA018C
    Project hush   AS0340
    Servant problem   CO058C
    She only goes out at night   FA0215
    Sickness   WI02C6
    Tenants   TE0180

Tenn, William [pseud. of Philip Klass]
    Time in advance   AL0425
    Time in advance   AS0585
    Time waits for Winthrop   GA0310
    "Will you walk a little faster?"   C00250
    Venus and the seven sexes   BR0460
    Venus and the seven sexes   F00293
    Venus and the seven sexes   SI058C
    Venus is a man's world   C00160
    Venus is a man's world   GA014C
    Winthrop was stubborn   WI0204

Tennenbaum, Michael
    Choice of weapons   AS0180
    Choice of weapons   AS0440

Tevis, Walter S., Jr.
    Big bounce   AS0645
    Far from home   AS0555
    Far from home   MA0199
    IFTH of OOFTH   GA0145

Tharp, Beebe
    Harp that conquered hell   DI023C

Thayer, Frank D., Jr.
    Family tree   DEC560

Thomas, Cogswell
    Paradise regained   BE0299
    Paraside regained   EL102C

Thomas, D.M.
    Head-rape   M00164
    Hospital of transplanted hearts   HA0162
    Seeking a suitable donor   J0015C
    Spectrum   MC0165
    Tithonus   AL0665

Thomas, Gilbert
    Luana   MA0206
    Luana   ME0367

Thomas, John
    Publish and perish   CL0165

Thomas, John B.
    Return to a hostile planet   EL112C

Thomas, Theodore L.
    Clone   KN0490
    Day of succession   KN016C
    December 28th   FL015C

Thomas, Theodore L.
        Doctor   GR014C
        Doctor   KN0100
        Doctor   KN0302
        Doctor   SI012C
        Early bird   AS0750
        Early bird   HA0166
        Far look   AL0650
        Far look   AM0514
        Far look   hA025C
        Far look   ME0357
        Intruder   KN0460
        Lonely man   GA0147
        Satellite passage   ME0359
        Test   MA0202
        Weather man   AN0102
        Weather man   AS0651
        Weather man   CA0100
        Weather man   CL05C0
        Weather man   SA0210
        Weather on the sun   AS0575
        Weather on the sun   KN0308

Thompson, J.C.
        Right man for the right job   KN0490

Thompson, James E.
        Amphibious cavalry gap   AS0555
        Synchronicity   AS0555

Thompson, R.W.
        Ultimate honor [excerpt]   AL065C

Thompson, Will
        No one believed   ME0260

Thorne, Roger
        Take a deep breath   ME0357

Thornley, Cam
        They'll do it every time   AS044C

Thorp, Roderick
        Sunburst   KN03C6

Thurber, James
        Friend to Alexander   KN045C
        Interview with a Lemming   HA0160
        Interview with a Lemming   Y0015C

Thurston, Robert
        Get FDR!   CL0110
        Good life   CL011C
        Goodbye, Shelley, Shirley, Charlotte,   KN0311
          Charlene

Thurston, Robert
    Jack and Betty   KN0316
    Kingmakers   MA0520
    Punchline   CL0110
    Stop me before I tell more   KN0309
    Theodore and Theodora   NE0205
    Up against the wall   CL0165

Tilley, Robert J.
    "Willie's blues"   WO0413
    Something else   FE0230
    Something else   MA0205
    Something else   ME0366

Time magazine
    No way out, no way back   AL0665

Timperley, R.
    Scrabo   DA0272

Tiptree, James, Jr.
    And I awoke and found me here on the   AL0480
        cold hill's side
    And I have come upon this place by lost NO0402
        ways
    And I have come upon this place by lost WA0100
        ways
    Beam us home   DO0165
    Filomena & Greg & Rikki-Tikki & Barlow NE0202
        & The Alien
    Girl who was plugged in   AS0401
    Girl who was plugged in   NE0203
    Her smoke rose up forever   FE0170
    Houston, Houston, do you read?   NE0162
    Houston, Houston, do you read?   WO0417
    I'll be waiting for you when the   BE0290
        swimming pool is empty
    Last flight of Dr. Ain   HA0234
    Love is the plan, the plan is death   GO0030
    Love is the plan, the plan is death   NE0159
    Man who walked home   AL0650
    Man who walked home   BE0291
    Man who walked home   WO0413
    Milk of paradise   EL0220
    Momentary taste of being   SI0720
    Momentary taste of being   WO0120
    Painwise   SI0125
    Psychologist who wouldn't do awful   CA0236
        things to rats
    Psychologist who wouldn't do awful   NE0200
        things to rats
    She waits for all men born   DA0170
    Snows are melted, the snows are gone   HA0162
    We who stole the dream   DE0268
    We who stole the dream   DE0275

Tiptree, James, Jr.
    We who stole the dream   WO0419
    Women men don't see   HA0167
    Women men don't see   SA023C
    Your haploid heart   WO0410

Tofte, Arthur
    Alone in space   EL104C
    Fateful first day on Efene   FU0130
    Speeders   EL100C
    Survival on a primitive planet   EL1140
    Terrafied   EL054C
    Thirst for blood   EL0920
    When the cold came   EL0960

Toman, Michael D.
    Shards of divinity   GE0180

Toomey, Robert E., Jr.
    Lost in the marigolds   KN03C9
    Re-creation   AS0555

Townes, Robert Sherman
    Problem of Emmy   C00550
    Problem of Emmy   C00560

Tracey, R.
    Siren singers   BA0240

Transue, Jacob
    This corruptible   KN0304

Tremaine, F. Orlin
    True confession   MC02CC

Trivers, Barry
    Conscience of the king   ST0161

Tschirgi, Robert D.
    Singular case of extreme electrolyte   ME0366
       balance associated with Folie a
       Deux

Tsiolkovsky, Konstantin
    On the moon   MA0330

Tubb, E.C.
    Enane   WO0414
    Fresh guy   ME0359
    Fresh guy   SA015C
    Home is the hero   CA020C
    J is for Jeanne   ME0366
    Last day of summer   ME0356
    Lazarus   BE050C
    Ming vase   ME0364

Tubb, E.C.
    Mistaken identity   DA0270
    Seekers   NE0306
    Unfortunate passage   CA0170

Tucker, Wilson
    Able to zebra   TU0150
    Exit   MO0260
    Exit   TU0150
    Gentlemen-the Queen   TU0150
    Home is where the wrec is   TU0150
    Job is ended   TU0150
    MCMLV   TU0150
    Mountaineer   TU0150
    My brother's wife   TU0150
    Science fiction subtreasury   TU0150
       [anthology]
    Street walker   TU0150
    Time exposures   AS0585
    Time exposures   CA0368
    Tourist trade   EE0202
    Tourist trade   HE0400
    Wayfairing strangers   TU0150

Turner, George
    In a petri dish upstairs   HA0159

Tushnet, Leonard
    Aunt Jennie's tonic   MA0550
    Aunt Jennie's tonic   WC0412
    Gifts from the universe   MA0208
    Plague of cars   NE0201

Tushnet, Lloyd
    In re Glover   EL0220
    In re Glover   CL0170

Tuttle, Lisa
    Changelings   HA0168
    Family monkey   CA0237
    Family monkey   MA0520
    Hollow man   MA0521
    I have heard the mermaids   EL1140
    Storms of Windhaven   CA0235
    Storms of Windhaven   WC0416
    Stranger in the house   CL0110

Twain, Mark [pseud. of S.L. Clemens]
    Connecticut yankee   GA0370
    From the "London Times" of 1904 FR0070
    Selection from the London Times KN0160
    Sold to satan   HA0210

Updike, John
    Chaste planet   HA0168

Updike, John
    Dance of the solids [poems]   MC0150
    During the Jurassic   ME0367

Utley, Steven
    Black as the pit, from pole to pole   BE0303
    Black as the pit, from pole to pole   NE0207
    Custer's last jump   BE0302
    Custer's last jump   CA0236
    Custer's last jump   CA0373
    Hung like an elephant   GE0150
    Local allosaurus   NE0205
    Predators   CA0275
    Sport [poem]   HA0166
    Thirteenth labor   DE0267
    Time and Hagakure   AS0173
    Upstart   AS0555
    Womb, with a view   GE0150

Vance, Jack
    Abercrombie station   VA0220
    Assault on a city   CA0371
    Augmented agent   WH0175
    Best of Jack Vance [anthology]   VA0220
    Cil   VA0250
    Coup de grace   AS0585
    Devil on Salvation Bluff   PO0373
    Dodkin's job   SI1020
    Dogtown tourist agency   SI0480
    DP!   GR0250
    Dragon masters   AS0400
    Eight fantasms and magics [anthology]   VA0250
    Gift of gab   CR0102
    Gift of gab   WI0202
    Green magic   MA0203
    Green magic   MC0180
    Guyal of Sfere   SI0460
    Guyal of Sfere   VA0250
    Hardluck diggings   CO0340
    Howling bounders   HA0290
    I'll build your dream castle   CO0220
    King of thieves   LE0220
    Last castle   AS0400
    Last castle   NE0152
    Last castle   VA0220
    Men of the ten books   EE0202
    Men of the ten books   WI0201
    Men return   AL0405
    Men return   SI0121
    Men return   VA0250
    Miracle workers   VA0250
    Mitr   AL0510
    Moon moth   SC0212
    Moon moth   SI0120
    Moon moth   VA0220

VanVogt, A.E.

Co-operate or else	AL040C
Concealment	AL0411
Confession	VA0150
Cooperate-or else	DE047C
Dear pen pal	DE040C
Dear pen pal	PO0293
Dear pen pal	VA0180
Defense	VA0180
Destination: universe [anthology]	VA0180
Don't hold your breath	EL102C
Don't hold your breath	VA014C
Dormant	CR010C
Dormant	DO010C
Dormant	ST0180
Dormant	VA0180
Enchanted village	CO034C
Enchanted village	MA055C
Enchanted village	MC028C
Enchanted village	MO035C
Enchanted village	VA0180
Ersatz eternal	AC0200
Ersatz eternal	VA0150
Far Centaurus	CL010C
Far Centaurus	CO022C
Far Centaurus	GR022C
Far Centaurus	SI040C
Far Centaurus	VA018C
Final command	GR028C
First Martians	DI019C
Fulfillment	AL045C
Fulfillment	HE0130
Future perfect	PO045C
Future perfect	VA014C
Ghost	VA0205
Great judge	AS034C
Great judge	WI021C
Heir unapparent	HA0232
Home of the gods	VA014C
Human operators	BE0290
Human operators	EL044C
Human operators	SI0127
Juggernaut	CO073C
Letter from the stars	PO019C
Lost: fifty suns	VA0150
Monster	VA0180
Not only dead men	CH010C
Not only dead men	CO025C
Process	BE0201
Proxy intelligence	VA014C
Rat and the snake	VA015C
Recruiting station	CO0280
Resurrection	AM0515
Resurrection	KN048C
Resurrection	KN0580

VanVogt, A.E.
    Resurrection   SI06C0
    Rogue ship   KN054C
    Rogue ship   MA0480
    Rulers   VA0180
    Rull   GR0310
    Rull   P00295
    Rull   VA0140
    Sea thing   VA0205
    Sea thing [anthology]   VA0205
    Search   VA0180
    Seesaw   AS0452
    Seesaw   DE037C
    Seesaw   KN012C
    Seesaw   SI0960
    Semantics of twenty-first century   VA0140
        science
    Silkie   IF01CC
    Silkie - Prologue to   VA0140
    Slan   VA0210
    Sound   VA0180
    Sound of wild laughter   VA0150
    Storm   AL0510
    Storm   AS0650
    Timed clock   VA0150
    Triad [anthology]   VA021C
    Vault of the beast   AS0451
    Vault of the beast   AS0700
    Vault of the beast   CA0255
    Violent male   VA014C
    Voyage of the space beagle   VA0210
    War of nerves   VA014C
    Weapon shop   SC0210
    Weapons shops of Isher   E00150
    Weapons shops of Isher   HE01CC
    Witch   VA0205
    World of A   VA021C

Varley, John
    Air raid   BE03C2
    Air raid   VA028C
    Barbie murders   CA0238
    Black hole passes   VA0280
    Good-bye, Robinson Crusoe   AS0173
    Good-bye, Robinson Crusoe   AS044C
    Gotta sing, gotta dance   VA0280
    In the bowl   CA0235
    In the bowl   NE0162
    In the bowl   VA028C
    In the hall of the Martian Kings BE0303
    In the hall of the Martian kings VA0280
    Lollipop and the tar baby   CA0237
    Lollipop and the tar baby   KN0319
    M and M, seen as a low-yield   KN0318
        thermonuclear device

Verne, Jules
    Round the moon   KU0100
    Twenty thousand leagues under the sea   GU0130
       [excerpt]
    Twenty thousand leagues under the sea   KN0160
    Twenty thousand leagues under the sea   VA0150

Vickory, S.
    Touch of peace   WH0150

Vidal, Gore
    Visit to a small planet [play]   LO0100

Vincent, Harl
    Prowler of the wastelands   M00380
    Rex   M00200

Vinge, Joan D.
    Crystal ship   CR0250
    Crystal ship   VI0070
    Eyes of amber   SA0230
    Eyes of amber   VI0070
    Eyes of amber [anthology]   VI0070
    Fireship   CA0241
    Media man   VI0070
    Mother and child   KN0316
    Peddler's apprentice   EE0301
    Peddler's apprentice   W00416
    Phoenix in the ashes   KI0070
    Tin soldier   KN0314
    Tin soldier   SA0220
    Tin soldier   VI0070
    To bell the cat   VI0070
    View from a height   CA0238
    View from a height   VI0070

Vinge, Vernor
    Apartness   W00406
    Bookworm, run!   AN0106
    Grimm's story   KN0304
    Long shot   EE0291
    Long shot   W00413
    Peddler's apprentice   EE0301
    Peddler's apprentice   W00416
    Science fair   KN0309
    Whirligig of time   DE0265

Vivian, T.J.
    Tilting island   M00365

Voiskunsky, Eugeny
    Black pillar   MC0150
    Farewell on the shore   MA0420
    Formula for the impossible   MA0390

Voltaire
    Visitors from outer space   EVO10C

Vonnegut, Kurt, Jr.
    Big space fuck   ELO220
    Big trip up yonder   POO15C
    Deer in the works   DIO250
    EPICAC   KEO1CC
    Harrison Bergeron   ALO4C2
    Harrison Bergeron   ALO665
    Harrison Bergeron   MAO201
    Harrison Bergeron   MAO47C
    Report on the barnhouse effect   HEO40C
    Report on the barnhouse effect   LOO1CC
    Report on the barnhouse effect   SAO15C
    Tomorrow and tomorrow and tomorrow ALO65C
    Tomorrow and tomorrow and tomorrow BOO1CC
    Unready to wear   GAO141
    Welcome to the monkey house   PLO155
    Welcome to the monkey house   WOO409

Vonwalc, E.G.
    Hemeac   SUO15C
    Hemeac   WOO409

Vucak, Stefan
    Fulfilment   HAO158

Wagner, George
    Lost and found   ASO175

Wakefield, H. Russell
    Death of a bumblebee   DEO560

Walde, A.A.
    Bircher   WOO407

Waldrop, F.N.
    Tomorrow's children   SIO7CC

Waldrop, Howard
    Black as the pit, from pole to pole BEO303
    Black as the pit, from pole to pole NEO207
    Custer's last jump   BEC302
    Custer's last jump   CAO236
    Custer's last jump   CAO373
    Mary Margaret Road-grader   BEO302
    Mary Margaret Road-grader   KNO318
    My sweet lady Jo   CAO371
    Sun up   DAO14C

Walker, M.
    Your soldier unto death   SAO1CC

Wallace, F.L.
Accidental flight   GA0310
Big ancestor   AL0411
Bolden's pets   C00190
Delay in transit   GA0190
Delay in transit   MA0465
End as a world   GA0142
Growing season   FR0100
Impossible voyage home   C00400
Mezzerow loves company   GA0340
Student body   AM0514
Student body   GA0141
Student body   SA0300
Tangle hold   GA0220

Wallace, Robert
Living doll   ME0365

Wallace, Robin E.
Canis familiaris   ED0150

Wallmar, J.
Evergreen library   H00120

Wallmar, J.M.
Chasing shadows   DE0267

Walpole, Horace
Saturnian Celia   MA0330

Walsh, Buthram
Case of Omega Smith   CB0140

Walter, W. Grey
Singers   F00240

Walton, B.
To each his star   AL0480

Walton, Harry
Episode on Dhee Minor   GR0300
Schedule   GR0220

Wandrei, Donald
Blinding shadows   DE0340
Colossus   AS0170
Colossus   DE0370
Crater   DE0560
Finality unlimited   DE0470
Infinity zero   DE0400
Scientist divides   WA0130
Strange harvest   DE0590

Ward, Charles W.
    Preliminary investigation of an early   ST0210
        man site in the Delaware River
        Valley

Warrick, Patricia
    Anthropology through science fiction   MA0550
        [anthology]
    Introductory psychology through science KA0070
        fiction [anthology]
    New awareness [anthology]   WA0100
    Political science fiction [anthology]   GR0250
    School and society through science   CL0165
        fiction [anthology]
    Science fiction: contemporary   WA0130
        mythology [anthology]

Waterloo, S.
    Love and a triangle   ME015C

Watkins, William Jon
    Butcher's thumb   GR004C
    Coming of age in Henson's tube   AS0173
    Coming of age in Henson's tube   F0043C
    Two poems   HA0166

Watson, Ian
    Event horizon   CA0140
    Programmed love story   HA0167
    Rooms of paradise   HA0159
    To the pump room with Jane   NE0326
    Very slow time machine   CA0238
    Very slow time machine   FR016C

Waugh, Charles G.
    Mysterious visions [anthology]   WA016C
    Science fictional solar system   AS0575
        [anthology]
    13 crimes of science fiction   AS0585
        [anthology]

Waugh, E.
    Love among the ruins   FI0095

Webb, Leland
    Man for the moon   FL015C

Webb, Ron
    Girl with the hundred proof eyes   MA0204

Weinbaum, Stanley G.
    Adaptive ultimate   WE0150
    Adaptive ultimate   WE0158
    Best of Stanley G. Weinbaum   WE0150
        [anthology]

Weinbaum, Stanley G.
    Brink of infinity   WE0158
    Circle of zero   WE0158
    Flight on Titan   WE0158
    Graph   WE0158
    Iceal   WE0150
    Ideal   WE0158
    Ideal [selections]   KN0160
    Last Martian   WE0158
    Lotus eaters   DE0370
    Lotus eaters   MO0320
    Lotus eaters   WE0150
    Lotus eaters   WE0158
    Lotus eaters   WO0300
    Mad moon   MO0290
    Mad moon   WE0150
    Mad moon   WE0158
    Martian odyssey   AS0645
    Martian odyssey   CE0190
    Martian odyssey   MA0550
    Martian odyssey   SC0210
    Martian odyssey   SI0780
    Martian odyssey   WE0150
    Martian odyssey   WE0158
    Martian odyssey   WE0153
    Martian odyssey [anthology]   WE0158
    Parasite planet   AS0170
    Parasite planet   WE0150
    Parasite planet   WE0158
    Parasite planet   WO0270
    Planet of doubt   SI0940
    Planet of doubt   WE0158
    Point of view   WE0158
    Proteus island   WE0158
    Proteus islands   WE0150
    Pygmalion's spectacles   WE0150
    Pygmalion's spectacles   WE0158
    Red peri   WE0158
    Redemption Cairn   WE0150
    Redemption Cairn   WE0158
    Revolution of 1980   WE0158
    Shifting seas   WE0150
    Shifting seas   WE0158
    Smothered seas   WE0158
    Valley of dreams   WE0150
    Valley of dreams   WE0158
    Worlds of If   SI0740
    Worlds of If   WE0150
    Worlds of If   WE0158

Weiner, Andrew
    Empire of the sun   EL0220

Weinstein, Richard S.
    Oceans away   DE0280

Wellen, Edward
    Androids don't cry   BE0299
    Deadly game   ME0363
    Down by the Old Maelstrom   KN0311
    Encyclopedia of galactic culture   GR010C
        [excerpts]
    IOU   GA0280
    Latest from Sigma Corvi   GO003C
    Mouthpiece   AS0585
    Sanity clause   AS0555
    Too long at the fair   N00404

Wellman, Manly Wade
    Adventure of the Martian client   HO0120
    Adventure of the Martian client   HO0120
    Desrick on Yandro   MA0192
    Island in the sky   MA048C
    Little black train   MA0194
    Men against the stars   DI013C
    Men against the stars   GR0220
    Valley was still   MA049C
    Vandy, vandy   MA0193
    Walk like a mountain   MA033C

Wells, Angus
    Best of Arthur C. Clarke [anthology] CL0200

Wells, Basil
    Quest of Thig   BR008C

Wells, H.G.
    Aepyornis Island   LO01CC
    Aepyornis Island   WE02CC
    Aepyornis Island   WE021C
    Aepyornis Island   WE0250
    Apple   WEC200
    Apple   WE0210
    Argonauts of the air   WE0210
    Argonauts of the air   WE0250
    Beautiful suit   WE0210
    Best science fiction stories   WE0200
        [anthology]
    Catastrophe   WE021C
    Change, from In the days of the comet DI0240
    Chronic argonauts   EL052C
    Chronic argonauts   EL1240
    Chronic argonauts   M00380
    Chronic argonauts   SA0150
    Complete short stories of H.G. Wells WE0210
        [anthology]
    Cone   WE021C
    Country of the blind   AL0665
    Country of the blind   M00320
    Country of the blind   SI062C
    Country of the blind   WE0210

Wells, H.G.

Country of the blind	WE025C
Crystal egg	DO01CC
Crystal egg	EL1240
Crystal egg	KN016C
Crystal egg	WE0200
Crystal egg	WE021C
Crystal egg	WE0250
Crystal egg	WE0270
Deal in ostriches	WE021C
Diamond maker	WE020C
Diamond maker	WE021C
Door in the wall	WE021C
Dream of Armageddon	WE0200
Dream of Armageddon	WE021C
Dream of Armageddon	WE025C
Empire of the ants	SI042C
Empire of the ants	WE021C
Empire of the ants	WE025C
Filmer	WE0200
Filmer	WE021C
Filmer	WE025C
First men in the moon	WE0220
First men in the moon	WO0330
Flowering of the strange orchid	WE021C
Flying man	WE021C
Food of the gods	WE0220
Food of the gods	WE026C
Grisly folk	WE0210
Hammerpond park burglary	WE0210
In the abyss	WE02CC
In the abyss	WE0210
In the abyss	WE0250
In the abyss	WE027C
In the Avu observatory	WE020C
In the Avu observatory	WE0210
In the Avu observatory	WE0250
In the Avu observatory	WE027C
In the days of the comet	WE0220
In the days of the comet	WE0260
In the modern vein: an unsympathetic love story	WE0210
Inexperienced ghost	WEC21C
Invasion from Mars [abridged]	KU010C
Invisible man	KN0130
Invisible man	WE02CC
Invisible man	WE022C
Island of Dr. Moreau	WE0220
Jilting of Jane	WE0210
Jimmy goggles the god	WE0210
Land ironclads	CU007C
Land ironclads	EL1240
Land ironclads	HO0119
Land ironclads	MO0365
Land ironclads	WE021C

Wells, H.G.
    When the sleeper wakes   WE023C

Wells, Robert
    Machine that was lovely   CB0140

Wentz, Elma
    Beyond doubt   GR0250
    Beyond doubt   PO0190

Wesley, Joseph
    Womb to tomb   AN0108
    Womb to tomb   HA0162

West, Jessamyn
    Little men   PO04CC

West, John Anthony
    Case history   KN0490
    George   MA0201
    Gladys's Gregory   FE023C

West, W.G.
    Last man   M00410

West, Wallace
    Dawningsburgh   GA0147
    Glimpses of the moon   CI022C
    Sculptors of life   C00550

Westlake, Donald E.
    Earthman's burden   C00140
    Question   AS0555
    Winner   H001CC
    Winner   NC0401
    Winner   WA016C

Weston, Peter
    Andromeda 1 [anthology]   WE029C

Whaley, Stephen V.
    Man unwept [anthology]   WH015C

Wharton, Thom Lee
    Bystander   KN01CC
    Bystander   KN03C8

White, Don
    Peggy and Peter go to the moon   MA02C3

White, E.B.
    Door   HA021C
    Hour of letdown   WI0205
    Morning of the day they did it   E00151
    Supremacy of Uruguay   BR038C

Wilhelm, Kate

How many miles to Babylon?	WI0150
Infinity box	KN0309
Infinity box	WI0165
Irfinity box [anthology]	WI0165
Ladies and gentlemen, this is your crisis	BE0302
Ladies and gentlemen, this is your crisis	KN0318
Ladies and gentlemen, this is your crisis	WI018C
Man without a planet	MA0202
Mile-long spaceship	BE0208
Mile-long spaceship	KN012C
Moongate	KN0320
Most beautiful woman in the world	WI015C
Mrs. Bagley goes to Mars	WI018C
Nebula award stories nine [anthology]	NE0159
On the road to Honeyville	KN0311
Perchance to dream	WI0150
Planet story	SI048C
Planet story	WI018C
Planners	KN0100
Planners	KN030C
Planners	NE0154
Planners	WI015C
Plastic abyss	WI0135
Plausible improbable	WI015C
Red canary	KN0312
Red canary	WI0165
Scream	HA0167
Scream	KN0313
Sirloin and white wine	WI015C
Somerset dreams	KN0305
Somerset dreams	KN048C
Somerset dreams	WI0180
Somerset dreams [anthology]	WI018C
Staras flonderans	KN03C1
State of grace	KN0319
State of grace	WI0180
Stranger in the house	WI0135
Symbiosis	WI018C
Time to keep	WI015C
Unbirthday party	WI015C
Village	WI0165
Whatever happened to the Olmecs?	BE0299
When the moon was red	WI0150
Where have you been, Billy Boy, Billy Boy?	WI0165
Where late the sweet birds sang	KN0315
Why is it so hard?	CL0110
Windsong	KN0304
Windsong	KN0460
Windsong	WI015C

William, Robert Moore
    Castaway   CO0250

Williams, Eric
    Sunout   NE0305

Williams, Jay
    Asa rule   MA0196
    Somebody to play with   MA0201

Williams, Ralph
    Business as usual, during alterations   AN0150
    Business as usual, during alterations   CA0100
    Business as usual, during alterations   GR0300
    Business as usual, during alterations   KN0280
    Emergency landing   AS0340
    Emergency landing   CO0130
    Head hunters   CO0280
    Head hunters   SL0210
    Pax galactia   NO0300

Williams, Robert Moore
    Red death of Mars   DE0310
    Red death of Mars   GR0220
    Refuge for tonight   EE0200
    Refuge for tonight   EL0120
    Robot's return   GR0280
    Robot's return   HE0100
    Robot's return   HE0170
    Robot's return   MA0550
    Seekers   WO0270
    Sound of bugles   DI0190

Williams, William Carlos
    Heel & toe to the end   [poem]   SA0150

Williams-Ellis, Amabel
    Changeling   WI0204
    Out of this world 1 [anthology]   WI0201
    Out of this world 10 [anthology]   WI0210
    Out of this world 2 [anthology]   WI0202
    Out of this world 3 [anthology]   WI0203
    Out of this world 4 [anthology]   WI0204
    Out of this world 5 [anthology]   WI0205
    Out of this world 6 [anthology]   WI0206
    Out of this world 7 [anthology]   WI0206
    Strange orbits [anthology]   WI0245
    Strange universe [anthology]   WI0250
    Worlds apart [anthology]   WI0280

Williamson, Ian
    Chemical plant   CA0230
    Chemical plant   WI0201

Wilson, F. Paul
    Lipidleggin'   AS0180

Wilson, Gahan
    [spot]   EL0220
    Cartoon illustrations   MA0205
    Cartoon illustrations   MA0206
    Cartoons   MA0210
    Gahan Wilson horror movie pocket   HA0167
       computer
    M-1   FE0230
    Science fiction horror movie pocket   HA0164
       computer

Wilson, Richard
    Back to Julie   P0015C
    Carson effect   ME0365
    Course of Empire   AS0555
    Deny the slake   MC018C
    Don't fence me in   AS0555
    Eight billion   MA0205
    Far king   AS0175
    Friend of the family   P00372
    Harry Protagonist, braindrainer   AS0555
    Honor   DE0250
    If you were the only ____   GA0149
    Kill me with kindness   GA0143
    Kin   AS0555
    Love   DE0250
    Man spekith   W00410
    Man working   P00374
    Mother to the world   KN010C
    Mother to the world   KN0303
    Mother to the world   NE0154
    Venus papers   EA010C
    Watchers in the glade   GA0148

Wilson, Robin Scott
    Clarion II [anthology]   CL011C
    Gone fishin'   HA0163
    Something new under the sun   H00119

Winn, Pip
    Right off the map   KN0308

Winter, J.A., M.D.
    Expedition polychrome   N00240
    Expedition mercy   C00190
    Expedition polychrome   N00330

Winterbotham, R.R.
    Fourth Dynasty   C00280

Wise, Dave
    Achievements   NE0205

Wolfe, Gene

Feather tigers	CA042C
Fifth after the war	KN031C
Fifth head of Cerberus	NE0158
Forlesen	KN0314
From the notebook of Doctor Stein	EL0582
Going to the beach	EL106C
Hero as werwolf	CA0235
Hero as werwolf	DI024C
Horars of war	DI011C
Horars of war	KN046C
Horars of war	NO04C1
How I lost the Second World War and helped turn back the German invasion	AN014C
How the whip came back	KN03C6
Island of Doctor Death	KN03C7
Island of Doctor Death and other stories	KN01CC
Island of Doctor Death and other stories	NE0156
LaBefana	HA0166
Loco parentis	EL0220
Many mansions	KN0319
Marvelous brass chess playing automation	CA0374
Mathoms from the time closet [3 stories]	EL022C
Melting	KN0315
Method bit in "b"	KN0308
Morning glory	MC015C
New Atlantis [anthology]	WO012C
Our neighbor by David Copperfield	HA0159
Paul's treehouse	KN03C5
Peritonitis	EL12CC
Remembrance to come	KN03C6
Robot's story	EL022C
Rubber bend	CA0372
Seven American nights	CA0241
Seven american nights	KN032C
Silhouette	SI072C
Silhouette	WC012C
Sonya, Crane Wessleman, and Kitte	KN03C8
Straw	DO0165
Three fingers	CI023C
Three million square miles	CIC25C
To the dark tower came	KN0319
Toy theater	KN0309
Trip, trap	KN0302
Westwind	IF017C
When I was Ming the merciless	CA0275

Wollheim, Donald A.

Best from the rest of the world [anthology]	WO015C

Wollheim, Donald A.
    Daw science fiction reader [anthology]   WOO18O
    Disguise   SLO210
    End of the world [anthology]   WOO210
    Every boy's book of science fiction   WOO240
        [anthology]
    Flight into space [anthology]   WOO270
    Hidden planet [anthology]   WOO30O
    Lysenko maze   KAOO70
    Mimic   CAO26O
    1972 annual world's best SF   WOO412
        [anthology]
    1973 annual world's best SF   WOO413
        [anthology]
    1974 annual world's best SF   WOO414
        [anthology]
    1975 annual world's best SF   WOO415
        [anthology]
    1976 annual world's best sf [anthology]   WOO416
    1977 annual world's best sf [anthology]   WOO417
    1979 annual world's best sf [anthology]   WOO419
    Planet passage   GAO37O
    Planet passage   WOO270
    Portable novels of science [anthology]   WOO330
    Storm warning   CAO255
    Storm warning   COO250
    Storm warning   SIO600
    Swordsmen in the sky [anthology]   WOO36O
    Ultimate invader [anthology]   WOO390
    World's best science fiction: 1965   WOO4O5
        [anthology]
    World's best science fiction: 1966   WOO406
        [anthology]
    World's best science fiction: 1967   WOO4O7
        [anthology]
    World's best science fiction: 1969   WOO409
        [anthology]
    World's best science fiction: 1970   WOO410
        [anthology]
    World's best science fiction: 1971   WOO411
        [anthology]

Wood, Edward W.
    Land of trouble   BOO30O

Wood, Margaret
    Knitting   CBO14O

Wood, W.
    Submarined   MOO365

Woods, P.F.
    Countenance   MOO162
    Integrity   MOO163

603

Woolf, V.
    Solid objects   DI026C

Woolrich, Cornell
    Music from the dark   WA016C

Worthington, Will
    Food goes in the top   AL0402
    Plenitude   MC028C
    Plenitude   ME02C1
    Plenitude   MF0360
    Plenitude   SU0150
    Who dreams of ivy   MA020O

Wright, Gary
    Mirror of ice   HA0160
    Mirror of ice   HA0260
    Mirror of ice   HA029C
    Mirror of ice   NE0153

Wright, Lan
    Operation Exolus   CA017C

Wright, Sewell Peaslee
    Infra-medians   WC0240

Wright, Sydney Fowler
    Automa I, II, and III   CO055C
    Better choice   CO0400
    Brain   HE01CC
    Obviously suicide   ASC34C
    Obviously suicide   PO0190
    Rat   KU0100

Wyal, Pg
    Castle on the crag   HA0162
    Freak   CL015C
    Hotsy-totsy machine   ED015C
    Newsocrats: confessions of a eunuch   ED015C
      dreamer

Wylie, Dirk
    When time went mad   PO0295

Wylie, Philip
    Answer   SA0270

Wyndham, John [pseud. of John Beynon Harris]
    Adaptation   MO035C
    And the walls came tumbling down   DE0340
    Chronoclasm   PO0371
    Chrysalids   WY0180
    Compassion circuit   AM0513
    Compassion circuit   WY021C
    Consider her ways   CR0104

Yarbro, Chelsea Quinn
    Cautionary tales [anthology]   YA010C
    Dead in irons   DA014C
    Dead in irons   SA023C
    Dead in irons   YA010C
    Disturb not my slumbering fair   YA0100
    Everything that begins with an "M" YA0100
    False dawn   SA024C
    False dawn   SC0450
    Fellini beggar   YA0100
    Frog pond   MA0550
    Frog pond   YA01CO
    Generalissimo's butterfly   YA0100
    Indulgence   YA0100
    Into my own   YA01CO
    Into my own   ZE0150
    Lammas night   YA01CO
    Meaning of the word   YA0100
    Space/time arabesque   LA0160
    Swan song   YA01CC
    Two views of wonder [anthology]   SC046C
    Un bel di   SC0460
    Un bel di   YA010C

Yarov, Romain
    Founding of civilization   MA0390
    Founding of civilization   SU0180

Yarov, Romen
    Goodbye, Martian!   MC015C

Yeats, William Butter
    Second coming   WH0150

Yefremov, Ivan
    Cor serpentis   MA036C
    Cor serpentis   FR0130
    Shadows of the past   NA0360

Yemtsev, Mikhail
    Everything but love   SH0150
    He who leaves no trace   GI0130
    Mystery of green crossing   MA0390

Yep, Laurence
    Looking-glass sea   SC045C
    My friend, Klatu   EL1080
    My friend, Klatu   EL1240
    Selchey Kids   WO04C9

Yolen, Jane
    Zoo 2000 [anthology]   YO0150

Yore, Mary Jane
    Teamwork   EL046C

Wyndham, John [pseud. of John Beynon Harris]
　　　　Consider her ways　　　　　　　　　　　　FI0095
　　　　Consider her ways　　　　　　　　　　　　KN0480
　　　　Consider her ways　　　　　　　　　　　　WI0280
　　　　Consider her ways　　　　　　　　　　　　WY0150
　　　　Consider her ways [anthology]　　　　　WY0150
　　　　Day of the Triffids　　　　　　　　　　　ER0520
　　　　Day of the Triffids　　　　　　　　　　　WY0180
　　　　Dumb Martian　　　　　　　　　　　　　　CA0200
　　　　Dumb Martian　　　　　　　　　　　　　　CR0100
　　　　Dumb Martian　　　　　　　　　　　　　　WI0203
　　　　Dumb Martian　　　　　　　　　　　　　　WY0210
　　　　Exiles on Asperus　　　　　　　　　　　　LE0160
　　　　Exiles on Asperus　　　　　　　　　　　　M00370
　　　　Jizzle　　　　　　　　　　　　　　　　　MA0192
　　　　Jungle journey　　　　　　　　　　　　　MC0320
　　　　Kraken wakes　　　　　　　　　　　　　　WY0180
　　　　Long spoon　　　　　　　　　　　　　　　WI0210
　　　　Long spoon　　　　　　　　　　　　　　　WY0150
　　　　Lost machine　　　　　　　　　　　　　　M00200
　　　　Meteor　　　　　　　　　　　　　　　　　WY0210
　　　　Moon　　　　　　　　　　　　　　　　　　WI0206
　　　　No place like earth　　　　　　　　　　　WI0201
　　　　Odd　　　　　　　　　　　　　　　　　　WY0150
　　　　Oh, where, now, is Peggy Macrafferty?　WY0150
　　　　Operation peep　　　　　　　　　　　　　P00190
　　　　Opposite number　　　　　　　　　　　　　WY0210
　　　　Pawley's peepholes　　　　　　　　　　　DA0272
　　　　Pawley's peepholes　　　　　　　　　　　MA0470
　　　　Pawley's peepholes　　　　　　　　　　　WY0210
　　　　Perforce to dream　　　　　　　　　　　　ME0260
　　　　Pillar to post　　　　　　　　　　　　　GA0141
　　　　Pillar to post　　　　　　　　　　　　　WY0210
　　　　Random guest　　　　　　　　　　　　　　CE0100
　　　　Random guest　　　　　　　　　　　　　　SU0150
　　　　Random guest　　　　　　　　　　　　　　WY0150
　　　　Re-birth　　　　　　　　　　　　　　　　B00150
　　　　Seeds of time [anthology]　　　　　　　WY0210
　　　　Stitch in time　　　　　　　　　　　　　WY0150
　　　　Survival　　　　　　　　　　　　　　　　EE0203
　　　　Survival　　　　　　　　　　　　　　　　WY0210
　　　　Technical slip　　　　　　　　　　　　　CA0280
　　　　Time to rest　　　　　　　　　　　　　　WY0210
　　　　Una　　　　　　　　　　　　　　　　　　CR0101
　　　　Wild flower　　　　　　　　　　　　　　　WY0210

Xlebnikov, A.
　　　　Human frailty　　　　　　　　　　　　　　MA0420

Yaco, M.
　　　　Winning of the great America greening　KN0314
　　　　　　revolution

Yarbro, Chelsea Quinn
　　　　Allies　　　　　　　　　　　　　　　　　YA0100

Youd, Christopher S.
    Christmas tree   GR031C

Young, Peter
    Man manifold   CB014C

Young, Robert F.
    Added inducement   Y0018C
    Clay suburb   CA0235
    Courts of Jamshyd   Y0018C
    Dandelion girl   ME0362
    Dandelion girl   Y0018C
    Drink of darkness   YC018C
    Emily and the bards sublime   Y00180
    Flying pan   Y00180
    Garden in the forest   C0031C
    Ghosts   EEU299
    Girl who made time stop   Y00180
    Goddess in granite   MA0197
    Goddess in granite   Y0018C
    Hcpsoil   YC0180
    Juke doll   N00210
    Jungle doctor   BE0206
    Little red school house   YC0180
    Nikita Eisenhower Jones   AS0575
    Nikita Eisenhower Jones   MA0200
    Nct to be opened   BE0201
    Ogress   N0015C
    Cne love have I   KE01CC
    Cther kids   EA010C
    Peeping Tommy   AS0555
    Production problem   Y00180
    Promised planet   Y00180
    Rcmance in a twenty-first century   WI0245
        used car lot
    Romance in a twenty-first century   Y0018C
        used car lot
    Stars are calling, Mr. Keats   Y0018C
    Starscape with frieze of dreams   KN0308
    Thirty days had September   C0076C
    Tc fell a tree   MA033C
    When time was new   IF0100
    Worlds of Robert F. Young [anthology] Y0018C
    Written in the stars   YC018C
    Years   HA0165
    Ycu ghosts will walk   Y00180

Young, Roger Flint
    Suburban frontiers   C0037C

Young, Wayland
    Choice   SA030C

Zabelir, Igor
    Valley of the four crosses   DIC280

Zelazny, Roger
    Game of blood and dust   WA0130
    Graveyard heart   SA0080
    Graveyard heart   ZE0190
    Great slow kings   ZE0180
    He who shapes   NE0151
    Home is the hangman   AN0140
    Home is the hangman   NE0161
    Keys to December   SI0900
    Keys to December   WO0407
    Keys to December   ZE0180
    Kjwalll'kje'k'Koothaill'kje'k   SI0500
    Last inn on the road   MO0165
    Love is an imaginary number   ZE0180
    Lucifer   ZE0180
    Malatesta collection   WH0180
    Man who loved the Faioli   HA0234
    Man who loved the Faioli   ZE0180
    Misfit   WH0175
    Moment of the storm   MA0206
    Monster and the maiden   GA0148
    Monster and the maiden   HO0120
    Monster and the maiden   ZE0180
    Museum piece   MC0155
    Museum piece   ZE0180
    Nebula award stories three [anthology] NE0153
    Rose for Ecclesiastes   AL0665
    Rose for Ecclesiastes   MA0204
    Rose for Ecclesiastes   MA0360
    Rose for Ecclesiastes   SC0210
    Rose for Ecclesiastes   WA0100
    Rose for Ecclesiastes   WH0150
    Rose for Ecclesiastes   ZE0180
    Rose for Ecclesiastes   ZE0190
    This moment of the storm   DO0170
    This moment of the storm   ZE0180
    This mortal mountain   CA0360
    This mortal mountain   ZE0180

Zelikovich, E.
    Dangerous invention   MA0360

Zhuraveleva, Valentina
    Astronaut   DI0280
    Astronaut   MA0360
    Astronaut   WI0204
    Hussy   SH0150
    Stone from the stars   PR0180
    Storm   MA0390

Zindel, P.
    Let me hear you whisper   EL1100

Zirul, Arthur
    Beautiful things   ME0359

Zoline, Pamela
    Heat death of the universe   AL0402
    Heat death of the universe   ME0290
    Heat death of the universe   M00163
    Heat death of the universe   SA0230
    Heat death of the universe   SA0300
    Heat death of the universe   SI0680
    Holland of the mind   DI0260
    Holland of the mind   J00150

Zoss, Joel
    Valve transcript   M00164

Zubkov, E.
    Robot humor   MA0420

Designed by Ellen Pettengell
Cover photograph by Sidney Pivecka
Composed by Kap Graphics
  on Compugraphic's 7700
  in Optima
Printed on Antique Glatfelter, a pH
  neutral stock, and bound by
  Malloy Lithographing, Inc.